MAN'S MANY WAYS

Catherine Jane Sands
306 South Ruby St.
Ellensburg, Wash. 98926

925-4241

MAN'S MANY WAYS

RICHARD A. GOULD
UNIVERSITY OF HAWAII

NATURAL HISTORY MAGAZINE
THE AMERICAN MUSEUM OF NATURAL HISTORY

HARPER & ROW, PUBLISHERS
NEW YORK, SAN FRANCISCO, EVANSTON, LONDON

Sponsoring Editor: Walter .H. Lippincott, Jr.
Project Editor: David Nickol
Designer: Gayle Jaeger
Production Supervisor: Valerie Klima

Library of Congress Cataloging in Publication Data
Gould, Richard A   comp.
    Man's many ways.

    Consists mostly of articles which have appeared in
Natural history magazine.
        1. Ethnology—Addresses, essays, lectures.
I. Natural history.   II. Title.
GN325.G67   301.2   73-2705
ISBN   0-06-042435-5

Richard A. Gould, "Chipping Stones in the Outback," February 1968. Photographs by Richard A. Gould. "Journey to Pulykara," December 1970. Photographs by Richard A. Gould.

Daniel R. Gross, "The Great Sisal Scheme," March 1971.

Michael J. Harner, "The Sound of Rushing Water," June-July 1968. Illustrations courtesy of Michael J. Harner.

Marvin Harris, "The Myth of the Sacred Cow," March 1967.

William Irons, "The Turkmen Nomads," November 1968. Photographs by William Irons.

Richard Borshay Lee, "Trance Cure of the !Kung Bushmen," November 1967. "Eating Christmas in the Kalahari," December 1969.

Paul S. Martin, "Pleistocene Overkill," December 1967.

Joan Mencher, "Namboodiri Brahmans of Kerala," May 1966. Photographs by Joan Mencher.

June Nash, "Devils, Witches, and Sudden Death," March 1972. Photographs by June Nash.

William F. Pratt, "The Anabaptist Explosion," February 1969. Photographs by Todd Webb and Jane Latta, Photo Researchers.

W. M. S. Russell, "The Slash-and-Burn Technique," March 1968. Photographs by Harold C. Conklin and Robert M. Netting.

Muriel Schein, "Only on Sundays," April 1971.

Shin'ichiro Takakura, "Vanishing Ainu of North Japan," October 1966.

Colin M. Turnbull, "A People Apart," October 1966. A full account of the Ik people can be found in Colin Turnbulls' *The Mountain People*, published in October 1972 by Simon & Schuster.

045859

CONTENTS

EDITOR'S PREFACE A former professor of mine at The University of Chicago once referred to cultural anthropology as a form of "intellectual imperialism." One aspect of imperialism as we know it is the tendency toward bigness, a tendency clearly evident in the field of anthropology today. Bigness is both a problem and a challenge for anthropology in the 1970s. First is the bigness of *size*. More and more students are taking an interest in the social sciences generally and in anthropology in particular, swelling the size of classes in universities, colleges, and even secondary schools. To meet this demand, educational institutions have expanded their programs, thus straining existing library facilities. Books and journals that a few years ago were numerous enough to meet the needs of students are now in short supply. Second is the bigness of *scope*. Anthropology encompasses a wide range of other disciplines, from nuclear physics (radiocarbon dating in archeology, for example) to child psychology (here one thinks immediately of the recent work of scholars such as Bruno Bettelheim and Erik Erikson in relating child development to the study of human cultures). The subject of anthropology also encompasses all human societies, past and present. This is perhaps its most explicitly "imperialistic" aspect. In other words, any aspect of human behavior in any human society is considered fair game for study by the anthropologist. Third is the bigness of the *unknown*. It is a truism to say that in general the social sciences are able to make predictions about human behavior which, although often fascinating and remarkably accurate, are still less exact than the types of predictions the so-called "hard sciences" such as chemistry and physics are able to make concerning the behavior of energy and matter. Social scientists strive to formulate laws of human behavior that will offer high degrees of predictability, but most of these scholars will freely admit to much room for improvement. One reason is that much basic evidence remains to be collected. There are still human societies in remote parts of the world which remain largely unstudied and unknown. We also need to know more about aspects of behavior in societies already well known to us. The whole question of poverty, both in terms of its origin and its nature, is a recent and timely example.

This book attempts to respond constructively to the problems of bigness facing anthropologists today. In considering these problems, the editors (at Harper & Row and *Natural History* Magazine as well as myself) realized that, if many articles by anthropologists that have appeared in *Natural History* were gathered and organized, the book could help to satisfy the needs of students and faculty who are trying to solve these problems.

It should be pointed out that *Natural History* Magazine covers a wide range of subjects (geology, animal behavior, and conservation among others), with anthropology as but one field among many. I do not wish to create the impression that *Natural History* is a periodical devoted exclusively to the social sciences.

To meet the problem of size, we felt that a book of this kind could make these articles widely available in a compact, well-organized format, thus helping to ease the strain that many college libraries currently feel in providing basic materials for student use. It happens, too, that many of the articles in this reader contain unusually fine photographs, which should add to its general appeal. Most of these articles have not been reprinted elsewhere, so in fact this volume constitutes a fairly fresh offering on an already much-exploited market. To meet the problem of scope, articles dealing with a wide variety of subjects and societies were selected. Boatbuilding, surfing, fighting, curing, hallucinating, weaving—these are some of the human activities covered, and the societies included range from desert Aborigines of Australia and Jívaro Indians of South America on the one hand to modern women of rural Greece and Hutterite and Amish religious sects of Canada and the United States on the other. Finally, and perhaps most difficult to achieve, the style and content of each article communicates a feeling of the intellectual excitement that derives from making fresh and important discoveries in an area of anthropological research. Many of these articles were written by scholars who had recently returned from extended periods of fieldwork, and the feelings engendered by the field experience carry over into their writing. This is particularly evident in Part I, "The Anthropologist in the Field," which contains vivid accounts of individuals or small groups that these anthropologists came to know well in the course of their field studies. Evident in these articles is a sense of work being conducted on the frontiers of a field of research. For students who might one day consider the field of anthropology as a career, it is important to know that wide areas exist where individual scholars can gather basic new evidence and make useful and important contributions. This awareness should go far in dealing with the problem of the wide area of unknowns that still face the social scientist.

Each piece of new knowledge acquired by an anthropological fieldworker represents not only an intellectual achievement and an increase in self-awareness but also a kind of triumph in performing under sometimes difficult circumstances. Most anthropologists, averse to any romanticizing of their fieldwork or the societies they study, tend to understate these difficulties and prefer, quite rightly, to emphasize the scientific significance of their work. So this preface seems a good place to point out that underlying each article in this reader is a hard core of field experience, representing the successful resolution of uncomfortable interpersonal situations and the overcoming of physical and emotional hardships. Each of these articles is a human as well as a scientific document.

Richard A. Gould

ACKNOWLEDGMENTS   In undertaking this reader, I received advice in discussions with many people, including undergraduates, graduate students, and colleagues here at the University of Hawaii and elsewhere. Among these especially were Dr. P. Bion Griffin, Dr. Aram Yengoyan, Dr. David Tuggle, Dr. Robert Tonkinson, John Pfeiffer, and Karl Hutterer. Special thanks, of course, go to the contributors and to the Social Science Research Institute of the University of Hawaii for their assistance in typing the manuscript. Finally, my wife, Betsy, deserves special praise for her editorial help and encouragement, especially in the final phase of preparation.

PART ONE

THE ANTHROPOLOGIST IN THE FIELD I was once asked the difference between an anthropologist doing fieldwork and a tourist. In trying to give an intelligent answer, I realized that this question was not so simple. My initial reaction was to describe the academic training that anthropologists normally acquire before they enter the field. But I then realized that this reply was inadequate, because it was an essentially quantitative response to a qualitative problem. My friend did not want to know how much background anthropologists have, but he did want me to tell him the essential characteristics that make anthropology a unique discipline. Not only are anthropologists almost pathologically afraid of being mistaken for tourists, but their methods differ from those of the other social sciences; the crux of this difference lies in the nature of anthropological fieldwork.

Naturally exceptions arise to any generalization about a field as diverse as anthropology, but I shall risk making a few general statements, nevertheless, and hope that my more unorthodox colleagues will not be unduly distressed. Anthropologists in the field observe human behavior of particular societies for fairly long periods of time. The time element is important, because anthropologists are (or should be) concerned with the question of sampling. I live in Hawaii, a place that sees tourists in large numbers every year. With rare exceptions, these visitors see only a small part of Hawaiian life, a part largely prepared for them in advance by people whose job it is to entertain tourists. Unlike a tourist, the anthropologist is a social scientist whose academic training and experience equip him to see beneath and beyond the superficialities of the society he visits.

The "Backstage" View of Human Behavior

According to American anthropologist Gerald D. Berreman, the anthropologist in the field must always remember that:

Impression management is a feature of all social interaction. It is apparently a necessary condition for continued social interaction. An understanding of its nature and of the resultant performances is essential to competent ethnography. Methodological procedures must be employed which will reveal not only the performance staged for the observer, but the nature of the efforts which go into producing it and the backstage situation it conceals.[1]

Berreman's views echo those of sociologist Erving Goffman, who stressed how important it is for scholars to realize that all social establishments are: ". . . surrounded by fixed barriers to perception in which a particular kind of activity regularly takes place."[2] Both Berreman and Goffman see social establishments as performances for the benefit of audiences, and in Berreman's case the audience includes the anthropologist. As Paul Bohannan ("A Man Apart") discovered, the laughter directed at the jesting by Dago'om (the Tiv man who eventually dies) was not entirely what it seemed at first. In public situations it was meant to appear as a simple response to Dago'om's clowning, but in time Bohannan realized that Dago'om's plight was far from amusing and that the people watching him were not so amused as they seemed. The "backstage" situation surrounding Dago'om was dramatically different from his public image, and an awareness of this behind-the-scenes situation was necessary before the anthropologist could correctly interpret the peculiar behavior that occurred at Dago'om's funeral.

Food Sharing and Social Interaction

In practical terms the anthropologist must spend enough time with the people he is studying to acquire an adequate sample of the behavior and attitudes that characterize that society. This can, and usually does, take years of fieldwork and involves, among other things, learning the language and basic etiquette of the society under study and making close personal contacts with people in the communities being observed. First impressions and romantic illusions that may have been present at the start tend to fall away as the process of fieldwork continues. Many experienced anthropologists feel that this process can be lengthy and attempt to revisit the communities they have studied to observe changes and to gain a more objective view of the society. The author of the second paper in this volume, Richard Borshay Lee, did not fully appreciate the significance of his Bushmen informants' efforts to belittle his gift of meat to them until his second trip to the Kalahari Desert and after several years of fieldwork. Despite appearances to the contrary, the Bushmen's belittlement was a mark of their appreciation for the gift, although it was tempered by a certain amount of social commentary on the anthropologist's behavior. But this episode was more than just a personal encounter between the anthropologist and his informants. The behavior and comments of Lee's informants during this episode revealed shared attitudes and expectations that the Bushmen have toward the distribution of meat. In a society that depends, as the Bush-men's does, entirely on the hunting and gathering of wild foods, the sharing of food is a central event in any day's activities and serves as the focus for key values in the culture. An anthropologist interested in the behavior of hunting and gathering societies must be aware of attitudes surrounding the distribution and sharing of food; Lee's description of "eating Christmas" in the Kalahari is a valuable addition to that awareness.

Cultural Relativism

The papers by Bohannan and Lee both deal with living, viable human societies in which activities are largely based on indigenous traditions that have not been profoundly altered by the influence of Western culture. Even the concept of Christmas among the Bushmen is alien, vaguely understood, and of little direct im-portance in their lives. The other two papers in this part, however, deal with societies that have been shattered or altered by the influence of Western culture. Colin M. Turnbull's description of the Ik people of Uganda goes beyond the superficial view of them by earlier visitors as ". . . a warm and friendly people, full of fun," to show how national policies (in the form of government restric-tions on their hunting activities in the Kidepo Game Park) and famine combined to force them into a kind of refugee existence. Eventually food became so scarce that Turnbull was forced to hide while he ate his own meals. Meanwhile he observed how the stronger young people took food from children and old people, sometimes leaving them to starve. Once Turnbull had penetrated the "barrage of deception" that the Ik place around their lives, he found a people who do not kill, but, in his words:

. . . they just let each other die. Meanwhile they live a life devoid of affection. A women's attitude of childbirth is that it is a nuisance, another mouth to feed for two or three years . . . The most equable kind of interpersonal relationship, regardless of kinship, is that of mutual economic reliance, but this is temporary at best and inevitably ends in cheating and mutual recrimination.

At the close of his fieldwork with the Ik, Turnbull had no more illusions about the people he was studying. It should be mentioned here that his earlier fieldwork among the Ituri Forest Pygmies[3] had presented him with an example of human affection and sharing quite different from that of the Ik.

Anthropologists have long been accustomed to dealing with people whose behavior by Western cultural standards might be considered shocking or bizarre. Yet, as the economist Stuart Chase has pointed out, there can be no taboos or restrictions on what social scientists can or should study, no matter how strongly these areas of study may· conflict with Western norms.[4] Cannibalism,

physical mutilations, infanticide, wife exchange, sorcery—these
and many more subjects that operate outside the range of Western
values—are nevertheless legitimate and necessary subjects in
the study of anthropology. When this sort of behavior is encountered in the field, it can place a strain on the anthropologist
and limits his degree of participation in the culture he is studying.

To cope with this recurring situation, anthropologists have
evolved an unformalized but useful attitude called *cultural relativism.* In this two-sided concept behavior is observed in a given
society and appraised on its own terms rather than by the yardstick of Western culture. Thus anthropologists generally refrain
from making absolute judgments about different cultures, preferring instead to see how each one adapts to its particular
ecological and social conditions. This does not mean that anthropologists refrain from comparing cultures. Indeed, comparative
studies are one of the most important approaches in anthropological research. But comparing cultures does not mean judging
cultures, that is, trying to say that certain cultures or institutions
within them are good or bad. Turnbull's description of the Ik is not
a moral judgment, although philosophers, writers, politicians, and
other individuals may, of course, choose to make such judgments
on the basis of the evidence he has presented.

If this one side of the concept of cultural relativism were left
unexplored, it could easily be a trap for the unwary. Some students and colleagues who have interpreted this attitude to mean
that "anything goes" think that viewing all cultures as equally
valid implies some sort of endorsement of them by the anthropologist. They sometimes forget that the anthropologist, too, is a
member of a human society, with its own values and expectations.
His culture is no more or less valid that the cultures he is studying
or has learned about. It is just as important for him to live according to the values of his own society as it is for the people he is
studying to pattern their lives on their own terms. An anthropologist
does not abandon his own culture merely because he is participating to some extent in an alien culture. Thus "going native"
in the sense that one abandons the values of his culture for those
of another ought to be avoided by most anthropologists. Not
only does it look strange both to Westerners and to the people
being studied, but it is also bad science; the observer loses any
chance of keeping his objectivity.

The idea of cultural relativity is much older in Western
thought than the discipline of anthropology. Earlier examples may
exist, but there are none that are both as early and at the same
time as eloquent as Michel Montaigne's famous essay, "Des

Cannibales." Written in 1579 at a time when Spanish and Portuguese explorers were bringing back accounts of the natives of the New World to the courts of Europe, this essay described the practice of cannibalism among the Indians of Brazil as reported to Montaigne by early voyagers. He concluded that cannibalism in this instance was not a sign of callousness or indifference to human life, but that the Indians saw this act as a way of venerating their ancestors; the eating of human flesh by the Indians was a symbolic act of respect for human life. Montaigne was far ahead of his time in expressing these sentiments; ideas like these form the basis for the present-day anthropological view of cultural relativism. Anthropologists should be willing to look at the Ik people in the same way. Despite the horrors of their recent existence, they must be viewed by the social scientist as an example of a human society under stress. After their behavior has been observed objectively and with as little distortion as possible (distortion that may arise from preconceived ideas about human nature) social reformers and politicians may want to use these observations as the basis for changing the conditions of Ik life.

The idea of cultural relativism is currently under attack by some scholars who argue, as does anthropologist Marvin Harris, that:

While cultural relativism is a scientifically acceptable way of relating to cultural differences, it is important to establish the fact that it is not the only scientifically admissible attitude. Nothing prevents an anthropologist from forming ethical judgments about the value of different kinds of cultural patterns. We need not regard cannibalism, warfare, human sacrifice, and poverty as worthy cultural achievements in order to carry out an objective study of these phenomena.[5]

Some anthropologists go further and actively seek ways to use their findings to reform the living conditions of the people they study. Anthropologists who do try to use their findings to change social conditions perform what is now variously called *applied* or *action anthropology*—a subarea of anthropology with special problems of its own.

Salvage Ethnology

Lola, the Selk'nam Indian interviewed by Anne M. Chapman, stands as perhaps the most tragic case presented in this volume and represents a situation all too familiar to anthropologists today. Lola was the last traditional Selk'nam Indian still living in 1966, and her death that winter represented the extinction of a culture. Chapman was faced with the problem of learning what she could about this Indian culture through the memory of a single aged informant. This approach is sometimes called *salvage ethnology*, and it is subject to serious shortcomings, having to do with problems of cultural sampling. The views of a single person, no matter how intelligent or eloquent, cannot simply be accepted as a valid picture of his culture. As long as this limitation is understood and accepted, there should be no problem, and Chapman's paper furnishes a good example of how salvage ethnology should be performed and reported. Instead of generalizing about the culture from a single informant's point of view, the anthropologist has tried to get to know her informant as well as possible. She wanted to know about Lola's personality, her special interests and skills (such as basket making and singing), and her life history. Then she allowed her questions to follow the lines of Lola's interests; the data she recovered from Lola about Selk'nam culture tended to be strongest in those areas. For example, in 1966, the year of Lola's death, Chapman recorded 92 traditional chants—the best sample of these ever obtained.[6]

The Selk'nam, like the other Indians of Tierra del Fuego (the southernmost tip of South America), were contacted early by Europeans because their land lay along the only direct sailing route between the Atlantic and Pacific oceans. Geography played a cruel trick on these people, for from the time of Magellan's arrival in 1520 onward these formerly isolated people were among those most often visited by European explorers and adventurers. One result of this contact was disease; the Indians of Tierra del Fuego were vulnerable because they lacked immunity to the white man's illnesses. Charles Darwin, traveling on the *Beagle,* visited these people in 1832, but by then their numbers were already reduced by disease, and more epidemics followed. Similar situations occurred in many other parts of the world, with massive epidemics of measles, influenza, cholera, and smallpox, and in some cases wholesale extinction of societies occurring everywhere the white man went. In some cases these contagious diseases traveled in advance of the white man from one group to the next. Many of the larger societies recovered, and the survivors maintained or reestablished viable cultural traditions which anthropologists today can treat in much the same way they study other living societies. In terms of population some of these groups are larger than they were aboriginally, and anthropologists no longer refer to such things as the "disappearing Indian." But some groups did not survive, and like the Selk'nam, many other human societies quietly vanished and would be virtually unknown today were it not for scraps of valuable information recovered from the memories of the elderly survivors by anthropologists like Anne Chapman.

Notes

1   Gerald D. Berreman, "Behind Many Masks," *Society for Applied Anthropology Monograph No. 4*, 1962, p. 24.

2   Erving Goffman, *The Presentation of Self in Everyday Life*, New York, Doubleday, 1959, p. 238.

3   Colin M. Turnbull, *The Forest People*, New York, Doubleday, 1962.

4   Stuart Chase, *The Proper Study of Mankind*, New York, Harper & Row, 1956, pp. 39–40.

5   Marvin Harris, *Culture, Man, and Nature*, New York, T. Y. Crowell, 1971, p. 139.

6   "Chants of Tierra del Fuego," issued by Folkways Inc. in April 1972, contains some of these chants.

A MAN APART Dago'om danced into the compound about noon one day in the middle of August, during the break in the rains that the administrative officers and missionaries called the "little dry." Onto his goatskin bag, colored a brilliant orange with dye from the stalks of guinea corn and then worn brown by use and dirt, Dago'om had hung tassels of raffia, bits of coconut shell, and two small calabash-gourd bottles. Dangling among these things was a small monkey skull, about the size of a lemon. It lacked the desiccated, bleached quality of bone, but shone with a brown patina, like ivory that has been in constant contact with sweat and sun. The tiny skull hanging among the tassels of raffia reminded me of a shrunken head from Ecuador that I had once seen in the Pitt-Rivers Museum.

Like all Tiv, a people of central Nigeria, Dago'om danced with his knees bent. Like all Tiv, he also invented gestures and steps. Dago'om's most successful ploy was to lean over forward, knees bent and far apart; then to flip his buttocks upward so that his large potbelly seemed to slip down between his knees. It was almost as funny as he meant it to be.

He danced forward, seeming to tack against the wind— first to one diagonal and then to the other. Each change of direction was signaled by his own special belly-slip. His heavily calloused feet stamped and shuffled in the dust of the compound —each heavy step seemed to thrust him farther into the earth. But then he raised his right hand—as thick and heavy as his feet—and turned a delicate movement with his wrist. The flick imparted grace to Dago'om's movements; the clumsiness and heaviness were those of a clown, not a dunce. The skill of the movement made the shape of his body irrelevant. He maintained one rhythm with his feet, a counterrhythm with his hands and arms, and still another with his trunk. The whole was nevertheless a unity.

His trick of keeping his eyes almost closed produced the effect of a veil drawn between himself and the world, making any contact save laughter difficult. And, after the first few times, even the laughter—mine included—had a cold touch of terror in it. Yet, we always laughed. But I looked away whenever the absurd, toothy grin spread over his face, lifted upward on his squat, sinewy neck. Dago'om was funny, but our laughter was overdetermined. Yet it was the only contact possible. He would not allow any other. If you didn't laugh, you would be engulfed in uncharted and unpredictable confusion—and, for some odd reason, hatred. I came later to understand why Dago'om's life might have been dominated by hate.

He knew only one song: "M gema hundu ve; m gema hundu ve; m ma msolom yum; m gema hundu ve." As he sang it, the song meant, "I am very drunk; I am very drunk; I drank a lot of beer and I am very drunk." He often did drink a lot of beer.

There is an irony in the song: it is in the word *hundu*. In the Tiv language, it means both drunk and mad. Tiv told me that drunkenness and madness are the same thing—but there is the difference that from too much drink you only get the "little madness" that you can sleep off. But that is getting ahead of the story.

On September 10th, Dago'om returned from a beer party in Yengev. When I heard that he was *ihundu* I was not surprised. But it took until the next day for me to realize that he was mad as well. Once the true meaning of the word sank in, I turned back in my memory (for such things seldom get into anthropologists' notes) to see whether I could remember any symptoms or clues. I recalled that one evening, he and Anwase, both a little drunk, had taken turns doing solo dances in the middle of the compound. The sun had broken through after a rain, and everyone came outside into the brilliant orange light that is never seen anywhere except at dusk in West Africa. Dago'om never let Anwase finish a dance, but kept rushing at him and playfully "killing" him with his heavy clown's hand. Anwase was a trim, light man who moved with grace; it was a pleasure to watch him even as he walked across the compound. He danced with the sad lightness of a jester, and I remembered being disappointed that, as Dago'om had demanded the center of the stage, Anwase had always easily and smilingly allowed him to have it. But this event provided no hint of madness.

I also remembered, with a stroke or or two of conscience, that Dago'om made a nuisance of himself sometimes, and that I had more than once shut the door of my hut to keep him from disturbing me. His clowning had a monotony that I found tedious or worse when I was alone with him. When all of us were together, and when my hosts and my servants were there to laugh at him, I found him funny too. Now, I realized that I, like everyone else, avoided being alone with Dago'om—nobody could bear laughing at him except with the reinforcement of crowds. Alone, Dago'om made me uncomfortable. His clowning called up my pity, unmixed with the wry absurdity that I obviously got from the others. Dago'om had always been kind and thoughtful. He often brought me eggs, which were difficult to buy here in northern Tivland. I repaid him with cigarettes. He once gave me a duck, with great mock ceremony.

The night before he went to the beer drink in Yengev, he came to our compound, bringing his wife with him. There were a couple of small pots of beer in our compound, and Dago'om came for a foretaste of what he was to drink the next day. He forced his frightened and overdressed, but rather pretty, wife to bring a calabash of beer across the compound and give it to me. She wore a bright orange piece of Manchester cloth and a man's undershirt (of the sort the British call vests) with white knee socks and tennis shoes. On her head was a stylishly tied cloth. Her face was smeared with face powder, imported (in Caucasian shades) from Britain. She seemed particularly subdued for a Tiv woman. I later learned from her friends that she became frightened when Dago'om made her dress up and go with him to beer drinks; when I talked to her in her own surroundings, and when I adjusted to her normal social situations, she was not afraid.

I accepted the beer from her with both my outstretched hands and thanked her. I tasted it and sent it into the kitchen for my servants. Dago'om stormed over, called for a chair, and insisted that his wife sit down opposite me. For a Tiv woman, this is a completely artificial situation. For her, it was terrifying, as well as strange. I thought then that she was afraid of me—but I now think that was not so. She was afraid of him. When I tried to talk to her, she remained dumb. When I tried to talk to Dago'om or to one of the other dozen people standing or sitting about, Dago'om in a loud voice repeated to her everything that I had said. I was uncomfortable enough that after about fifteen minutes I excused myself and went into my hut. I couldn't take it. I did not know why he had come or what he wanted—neither did he.

The next morning his wife went with him to the beer drink in Yengev. No one else from our compound, or from his, was present. Later I talked with her several times, but she did not disclose much about what he did there. She said, in a tight, closed voice, that he had got drunk from beer, and that after he stopped drinking he became more and more *ihundu*, and it never left him.

She brought him back, God knows how, as far as our compound. Gu, my host, helped her handle him after their arrival but he refused to go the rest of the way back to Asanyi's compound, where he lived. It was just nightfall, and he was ranting and shouting. When she tried to get him to go home, he loudly screamed threats at her—that he would beat her or kill her if she mentioned it again. She retired to a nearby hut, while Anwase and two younger men took over. With gentleness and patience they finally got Dago'om to sleep in Abum's hut. The next morning, at dawn, Dago'om was unconscious. Anwase and one of his brothers made a stretcher from an old *chado* cloth and two saplings and carried him home, but I knew little about this at the time.

I did know that Dago'om was in our compound and that he was *ihundu*, but he avoided me. I bumped into him only once. When he saw me, he fell to his knees and started to sing, "M gema hundu ve . . ." but he never finished it. With a wild shout, he bounced high and was off in the other direction. I noted to myself that the beer drink in Yengev must have been very successful indeed. Later, Anwase told me that he was asleep in Abum's hut.

When Anwase returned, he told me by direct imitation, by reference to a madman in the next lineage area to ours, and by references to the sprites of death, which sometimes bring madness, that Dago'om was mad instead of merely drunk. Dago'om had told me this himself: "M gema hundu ve," meaning not merely "I am drunk," but "I have turned mad;" the way he had jumped into the air and run away screaming was his metaphor.

The day after Dago'om was carried home, I walked the half-mile to see him. He caught sight of me as I entered Asanyi's compound and bolted in the other direction. I talked about him with Nege and Abu. Abu claimed to have the same father as Dago'om, but a different mother. I was soon to learn that Abu's father was Dago'om's maternal grandfather and that Dago'om had no father.

Nege, a sensible and patient man, was a little more distantly related to Dago'om. He told me Dago'om had attacked several people earlier that day, and had mauled one girl when he picked up a stick and started laying about him. He had then run into the bush when he saw me coming—Nege said it was unlike him, because Dago'om liked me—and this proved again that he was obviously mad. Abu opened his one eye widely and said that they would have to put him into stocks. Abu had a way of hovering rather than projecting his words as he spoke. He stood closer to my face than most Tiv. I was tempted to stand back (a feeling I associate with France, not Africa).

It was four days before I got back to see Dago'om again. I came into the compound and found him in stocks. He sat on the bare ground—a deep insult for Tiv, used in court as a symbol of a degraded and suppliant condition. One foot was stretched before him, inserted through a hole that had been gouged through one end of a heavy log of prosopis, a hardwood tree related to mesquite. A second hole had been drilled at right angles to the first. After his foot had been inserted through the large hole, wooden pegs were driven into the smaller hole so that he could move his foot comfortably, but could not remove it. The log was about eight feet long; a rope had been tied from the far end of the log to one of the overhanging branches of a venerable fig tree that grew in the middle of the compound. Dago'om could not reach the other end of the log to untie the rope; neither could he stand up to untie it from the branch, only a couple of feet above his head as he sat. The skin of his foot looked dull and dead contrasted to the brilliant orange of the newly cut prosopis wood. His other leg was doubled back under him.

Dago'om had the look of death. His smooth brown body was covered by a gray film. There is a vivid Tiv metaphor for dying: "He is sloughing his skin," using the same word as for a snake. Surprisingly, his scrotum had swollen to the size of a dinner plate. Scrotal hydroceles and scrotal elephantiasis are common among Tiv, but they do not develop suddenly. It is one of the many times that I wished anthropologists had some medical training. Dago'om's eyes were held broad open, and it was impossible, looking into them, to determine where the pupil began. Even over the whites of his eyes, there seemed to be a thin, dimming film.

He recognized me, and said my name twice. But that was all I could understand of what he tried earnestly to tell me. We were alone, and there was nobody for me to ask. In the minutes of complete concentration, I felt keenly that he was trying to get through to me, to tell me something—and that I was trying as hard and as unsuccessfully to understand him.

As I walked home along the bush path, which had been newly hoed and widened that morning, it occurred to me that Dago'om had entered the final phase of sleeping sickness. Probably he had had it all along, and if I had been trained to see it, perhaps I could have taken him to a hospital and stopped the progress of the disease. It could have been avoided or halted with pentamidine injections; although I knew that pentamidine was not a part of Tiv culture and that Dago'om lived twenty-five miles from a dispensary. I knew that I could not have convinced Dago'om to take the trip to get the injections, even if I had known what his illness was. Yet, had I been able to give them to him on the spot, he probably would have taken them. I became aware of an intense sense of guilt—a habit among those brought up as Protestants when they look on suffering.

My reaction to this situation was to do something. For me, the most exhausting part of Dago'om's illness and death was my struggle with the fact that nobody did anything. Although I had seen many mental patients, I had never before known one both before and after the onset of his madness. There was no change in Dago'om's personality—only in his behavior. The madness had been in him all along. Dago'om got worse with his disease and his terror. I became more depressed with that most despicable of situations—pity without being able to act.

I found that no one had known Dago'om well. Certainly I had not. No anthropologist ever gets to know more than half a dozen of his informants with anything that can correctly be called intimacy. Intimacy is difficult enough with people who are like you. Across cultural barriers it involves accepting even more things about the other person that are not part of all that one admires. Dago'om had amused me, and I had allowed myself to be amused so that I would not have to do anything. I was amused at his poor clowning so that I would not have to pity him—at that time, I still believed I must not pity people from other cultures because that would be ethnocentric.

During the next few days, knowing that Dago'om was going to die, I tried to get some information about him so that I could better understand what would be said when all of his kinsmen met at his funeral to discuss who had killed him, and how. I assumed that Dago'om would be given the funeral of an ordinary adult male. I had seen a number of them and thought I knew what would happen: all the disputes among his kinsmen would have to be aired. Then the "fault" would have to be determined. That is done by a post-mortem operation in which the heart is examined for a substance called *tsav*. If the dead person's heart shows the sacs of blood in the pericardium that Tiv associate with *tsav*, and all supernatural or unusual ability, then that person was guilty of his own death. If the chest is empty, as they put it, then the killer is still at large in the community. Tiv never merely die from natural causes—to natural causes must be added an evil volition to set those causes in motion. And the volition comes only from close kinsmen.

I soon discovered that Asanyi, the head of the compound in which Dago'om lived, was gone. When I tried to find out where he had gone, I was told by one person that he had had a dispute about a wife in a lineage to the northwest of us; another person told me that he had gone to Makurdi to sell some crops; still another said there was a matter of a marriage ward—one of his half-sisters—that he had to care for in the area of her husband's lineage. Obviously, Asanyi had disappeared. Nobody knew where he was, but they created plausible explanations.

I became inwardly incensed, thinking somebody ought to send for him so that the healing ritual could be carried out, for I knew that nothing ritual could be done in Asanyi's absence. It was my servant, Asema, who set me right on that. So long as Asanyi was gone, he said, the local witches could not kill Dago'om with their *tsav*. Without the compound head's concurrence, Dago'om could not die. Since everybody knew that Asanyi was a frightened man who could never hold off all the witches in the community his absence was a good thing. My own position became absurd. I had no faith in the ritual they might perform for Dago'om, but I was put off that nobody did anything. It was inconsistent, and I knew it—and still felt somebody should do something. As I examined my own reactions, I soon discovered that part of my feelings of inconsistency and guilt came from the people in the community; it wasn't all a product of my Protestant upbringing. The community felt guilty.

Discovering anything about Dago'om, even genealogical information of the sort that Tiv usually give freely, proved unexpectedly difficult. I knew where he fitted into the standard genealogies, but it soon became evident that he was there by grace and not by right. Again, it was Asema who came to my aid. He told me that gossip had it—and he thought it was probably correct—that Dago'om had been born of a "sister marriage." This is a euphemism for a recognized and approved liaison between young people within the same lineage, who nevertheless do not share a common grandparent. Sexual relations between two grandchildren of a single individual are incestuous, but beyond that they are not. The requirements for marriage, however, are more strict.

A young man, whose name Asema never learned, had come over from the MbaShija segment, and had paid a goat to the mother of Dago'om's mother. He thereby got her permission, as well as the girl's, to "untie the shell" that, like all Tiv girls, she wore around her neck as a symbol of sexual non-availability. He had a right thereafter, recognized by the entire community, to sleep with the girl in her mother's hut, although she was too closely related for him to marry.

Dago'om's mother, then probably about fifteen, had been a fool, Asema said. She had refused to go to a husband when she became pregnant. She claimed that she loved this boy from MbaShija, and she was not going to take her baby someplace else and become the third wife of a repugnant old man. Her father tried to force her into the marriage, but she ran away from her husband's compound and came back to her own. He tried to convince her to elope with a suitable young husband who came courting. She refused and bore Dago'om "in her father's house." Dago'om thus became her "brother" rather than her son, and her father became his "father." Dago'om became a member, through a female link, of his own agnatic lineage. An even greater difficulty was that he had no "mother's lineage." His nickname—with which he had been taunted as a child—meant "God sent us an orphan."

I saw Dago'om five times in the next eleven days. Only once could I make any sense of what he said, although I recognized some words and my own name. Nege said that Dago'om talked nothing but foolishness now. Yet, about five days before he died—when I was again alone with him—he managed to to break through his veil for about two minutes. He repeated to me with great urgency that since I was a guest in these parts and could not be harmed by the vicious people here, I must take all of his children and get them out of this compound, out of this lineage area, before they were all killed as he himself was being killed. The plea was interspersed with nonsense syllables, but I recognized that they were the kind of nonsense syllables that Dago'om sometimes muttered as he danced. Again I was struck with the cold fact that madness does not change us, it only makes us more so.

The only difficulty was that Dago'om had no children.

Or had he? Asema told me, when I relayed to him what Dago'om had said, that gossip told him Dago'om had had a love affair with one of Asanyi's junior wives a few years ago. Asanyi discovered it and banished Dago'om for several weeks. This woman bore a child that the entire compound thought resembled Dago'om rather than Asanyi. Asema added that the man who relayed this story had agreed that the child did indeed resemble Dago'om. Although we tried to discover which of Asanyi's children was meant, we never could. Asema did discover, however, that Asanyi had made Dago'om give him a goat in settlement of the matter and only then did he agree to help Dago'om get the money for a wife of his own. Was it that child to which Dago'om might have been referring?

Then one day the old mother of Torbum, with whom Dago'om's wife had stayed in our compound the night that he went mad, told me something else. She said that her lineage sister had borne Dago'om a child about a year before, but it had died after only a few weeks and almost surely the witches were involved because Dago'om "didn't have anybody."

Dago'om sat mad, pitiably babbling, losing weight, his potbelly almost gone, his swollen scrotum like a beach ball between his legs. Asanyi stayed away. Dago'om was an eldest child, even if he was not a legitimate child. Eldest children cannot be killed by the witches without the concurrence of the compound head. If Asanyi stayed away, Dago'om's death could not be laid to him. I understood this, but I still had pictures in my head of the fine moots, which Tiv call "asking sessions," in which the kinsmen of Dago'om would be faced with his condition and asked why they had allowed it to happen; why they had not protected him from evil. I thought perhaps they would call in MbaShija, the lineage of Dago'om's genitor. But, day after day, nothing happened.

Then one morning Asema woke me with coffee and the news that Asanyi had come back. I rushed over to see him. He was pleasant enough, but only said that he would have to rest today. Perhaps he could do something tomorrow. I said that when he went to a diviner, would he please let me know so that I could go along. Asanyi replied laconically that he would. He had nothing to hide, so he did not object if I saw what went on.

But the next day, Asanyi said that he had looked into his heart, and now thought the best thing to do was to forget the diviner and find a man who knew madness medicine and who would come to cure Dago'om.

When I talked to Dago'om that day, he had been moved into a reception hut. Nege told me that Dago'om had not eaten since the madness had descended on him. He was certainly thin and weak, but he sat up and seemed little changed.

That evening I went to Ukusu, where our base camp was located and where my wife was working. Just after dawn the next morning, I heard someone outside our hut calling my name. I answered. It was Anwase, who had come to tell me Dago'om had died in the night, and that they were going to bury him. Without shaving or even waiting for coffee, I rushed off with Anwase. The water was high and we had to wade through swamps up to our waists. When I entered our compound, Gu told me that Asanyi reported to him that Dago'om had struggled with death "on the ground," and that death had outwitted him. It was a standard Tiv metaphor of death—to struggle on the ground and lose. Yet, "on the ground" has a double meaning. When the term is used for marriage wards, it means that they have not been assigned to guardians, that they have no one in their natal lineages to protect them. Gu and Anwase assured me that it did not have this meaning here, but the image nevertheless seemed significant to me. Gu also volunteered the information that Ambu had been sent for. Ambu was the senior elder of MbaShija, the lineage of Dago'om's reputed genitor.

Anwase retired to his hut for a nap. Gu and I went to Asanyi's for the funeral preparations. The compound was almost empty when we arrived. Asanyi came out of his reception hut slowly and greeted us with the words, "Death defeated him." For almost two hours, nothing happened. Dago'om's wife was crying. She did not wail as widows are supposed to do, with ululations and long broken sobs interspersed with pentatonic phrases of funeral dirges all centering around the question, "Why have you left?" Rather she cried uncontrollably. Members of only three neighboring compounds came, nobody from farther away. When it was over, I asked Anwase why no MbaShija had come. He replied with a trite phrase that I found chilling, "He wasn't theirs."

No questions were asked. No seating arrangements formed themselves for me to note. No moot to be settled. No wailing to be talked above.

Two youngsters from the compound carried the body out-side under the direction of Nege, who had taken care of Dago'om since his return from the Yengev beer drink. A cloth had been spread on a bedframe made from the ribs of raffia palm leaves. The body, which had been covered with a thick layer of pale, imported talcum powder, lay on it. African corpses have a characteristic gray color. When the pink powder is added, they lose all human association. I had seen powdered corpses before here in the bush, and had assumed that it was done for cosmetic reasons since powder is often used that way by women. Dago'om's wife had been powdered the night before the beer drink. I nevertheless found it so repulsive that I could not believe it was true. I turned to Gu and asked him why the powder. He replied matter-of-factly that it cut down on the stink.

Without questioning or even caviling about who was to do what—an accompaniment of all other Tiv funerals I have seen—the time came to bury him. A grave had been dug along a path about a hundred yards from the compound. As they carried his body out, the women of the compound gathered around Dago'om's wife and wailed, but only for a minute or two and only out of kindness to her. The dirge was led by a leprous old woman, her hands almost gone, with a gritty but true voice, ululating, then singing in falling intervals, "Dago'om, why have you left us?"

It is a disgrace to his community if a Tiv goes to his grave without the wailing of the wives of his compound, and without the cause of his death being determined by its men—his fathers and brothers. These women—the wives of Dago'om's brothers—were keenly conscious of their own insecurity in a lineage in which such a death and such a burial could occur. In her short and raucous dirge, the old leper woman was seeing herself.

Dago'om's widow came along the path after us, approaching his grave as close as she dared—a Tiv woman who looks into a grave becomes barren. But the forces of life held her at a respec-table distance.

The black topsoil had been thrown to one side of the grave, and the rust-red laterite below it piled on the other side. The grave was about four feet deep, narrow at the top, with a shelf that made it wider below. The young men of the compound lifted Dago'om's body into the grave, while the elders looked on. They performed no ceremony. Usually Tiv sacrifice a chick at this stage of the funeral ceremony, dripping blood on the chest of the corpse, sometimes on its nipples, and then throwing the sacrificed chick into the bush as a sign that the dead person is going to join the community of the dead. That ceremony is performed, however, only for men who leave living sons. Dago'om's children were either dead or not his own, according to Tiv belief.

The two young men arranged his body—"shoved it" would be more accurate—into the shelf of the grave so that its head was to the southwest, the "top of the country." They covered the shelf with a few pieces of wood, and got back up onto the surface. The opening was covered over with three logs. With a start I saw that one of the logs was the stocks in which Dago'om had spent the last three weeks of his life. I found it fitting but melancholy. What more suitable way to get rid of it? On top of the logs they put a layer of thatching grass, then they piled on the topsoil; finally, the red subsoil was smoothed into the shape of an oval mound.

That was all. Gu put it precisely: "We have put him in the ground. That's all of that." Those who had washed him, prepared his corpse, and buried him accepted small torches of thatching grass from the oldest lineage member present. Each stood on top of the mounded grave and swung the miniature torch around his own head and feet (only some swung them around their trunks as well), changing hands with the burning grass. Each then dropped his torch onto the mound and backed off. This ritual was to "gather up the dreams" so that no one would be haunted, so that no one's luck would "close up on him."

Walking home with Atsegher and Gu, I was tense. Tiv funerals usually provide a catharsis for everybody present, including the ethnographer. But not so with Dago'om's. I felt that something should have happened, that somebody ought to have done something. I felt an intense desire to stir them up. But I, too, did nothing.

Back in the compound, Asema asked me what had happened; he had chosen not to attend. I told him, and wondered whether Dago'om had had the medicine that caused his madness administered to him at the beer drink in Yengev. Asema said he thought it unlikely, because madness medicine is a very powerful substance and is usually administered by your brothers or your wife spreading it on the thatch over the entryway to your hut. The dangling ends of the thatching grass stroke your back as you go in and out, the medicine enters your body, and you become mad. When I tried to tell Asema about my feeling of unfulfilled tension, he asked, "But did they beget him?" It was another way of saying, "He wasn't theirs."

Dago'om "had nobody." He "sat alone," and there was no one to avenge him when he was dead any more than there was anyone to protect him when he was alive. He was expendable.

Two weeks later, the rains had reached their peak. I heard that Dago'om's mother had arrived at Asanyi's, but the bridge over the Anu river was three feet under a rushing torrent of water. A few Tiv chose to cross it—I did not. I also heard that his wife's mother had come for her daughter and had taken her home to Ga'ambe where she would have a better chance of forgetting Dago'om and of going to another husband. I asked whether anyone at Asanyi's would inherit her. Anwase said that while somebody could go to try to collect the bridewealth that had been given for her, he thought it unlikely that anyone would or that they would take the woman. They would, Anwase finished, forget her. He suggested that I might want to talk to Dago'om's mother about that. A few days later, when the bridge was again passable, I went to find her. Nobody knew where she had gone.

Nothing ever happened. A man was expendable. He went mad and died. The Tiv were uncomfortable about it, ashamed of it, and quickly forgot it. It took me longer because my culture will not admit that anybody is expendable, whatever the "facts" may be and whatever our techniques for doing the same thing.

RICHARD BORSHAY LEE

EATING CHRISTMAS IN THE KALAHARI The !Kung Bushmen's knowledge of Christmas is thirdhand. The London Missionary Society brought the holiday to the southern Tswana tribes in the early nineteenth century. Later, native catechists spread the idea far and wide among the Bantu-speaking pastoralists, even in the remotest corners of the Kalahari Desert. The Bushmen's idea of the Christmas story, stripped to its essentials, is "praise the birth of white man's god-chief"; what keeps their interest in the holiday high is the Tswana-Herero custom of slaughtering an ox for his Bushmen neighbors as an annual goodwill gesture. Since the 1930s, part of the Bushmen's annual round of activities has included a December congregation at the cattle posts for trading, marriage brokering, and several days of trance-dance feasting at which the local Tswana headman is host.

As a social anthropologist working with !Kung Bushmen, I found that the Christmas ox custom suited my purposes. I had come to the Kalahari to study the hunting and gathering subsistence economy of the !Kung, and to accomplish that it was essential not to provide them with food, share my own food, or interfere in any way with their food-gathering activities. While liberal handouts of tobacco and medical supplies were appreciated, they were scarcely adequate to erase the glaring disparity in wealth between the anthropologist, who maintained a two-month inventory of canned goods, and the Bushmen, who rarely had a day's supply of food on hand. My approach, while paying off in terms of data, left me open to frequent accusations of stinginess and hard-heartedness. By their lights, I was a miser.

The Christmas ox was to be my way of saying thank you for the cooperation of the past year; and since it was to be our last Christmas in the field, I determined to slaughter the largest,

Editor's Note: The !Kung and other Bushmen speak click languages. In the story, three different clicks are used:

1. The dental click (/), as in /ai/ai, /ontah, and /gaugo. The click is sometimes written in English as tsk-tsk.

2. The alveopalatal click (!), as in Ben!a and !Kung.

3. The lateral click (//), as in //gom. Clicks function as consonants; a word may have more than one, as in /n!au.

meatiest ox that money could buy, insuring that the feast and trance dance would be a success.

Through December I kept my eyes open at the wells as the cattle were brought down for watering. Several animals were offered, but none had quite the grossness that I had in mind. Then, ten days before the holiday, a Herero friend led an ox of astonishing size and mass up to our camp. It was solid black, stood five feet high at the shoulder, had a five-foot span of horns, and must have weighed 1,200 pounds on the hoof. Food consumption calculations are my specialty, and I quickly figured that bones and viscera aside, there was enough meat—at least four pounds—for every man, woman, and child of the 150 Bushmen in the vicinity of /ai/ai who were expected at the feast.

Having found the right animal at last, I paid the Herero £20 ($56) and asked him to keep the beast with his herd until Christmas day. The next morning word spread among the people that the big solid black one was the ox chosen by /ontah (my Bushman name; it means, roughly, "whitey") for the Christmas feast. That afternoon I received the first delegation. Ben!a, an outspoken sixty-year-old mother of five, came to the point slowly.

"Where were you planning to eat Christmas?"

"Right here at /ai/ai," I replied.

"Alone or with others?"

"I expect to invite all the people to eat Christmas with me."

"Eat what?"

"I have purchased Yehave's black ox, and I am going to slaughter and cook it."

"That's what we were told at the well but refused to believe it until we heard it from yourself."

"Well, it's the black one," I replied expansively, although wondering what she was driving at.

"Oh, no!" Ben!a groaned, turning to her group. "They were right." Turning back to me she asked, "Do you expect us to eat that bag of bones?"

"Bag of bones! It's the biggest ox at /ai/ai."

"Big, yes, but old. And thin. Everybody knows there's no meat on that old ox. What did you expect us to eat off it, the horns?"

Everybody chuckled at Ben!a's one-liner as they walked away, but all I could manage was a weak grin.

That evening it was the turn of the young men. They came to sit at our evening fire. /gaugo, about my age, spoke to me man-to-man.

"/ontah, you have always been square with us," he lied.
"What has happened to change your heart? That sack of guts
and bones of Yehave's will hardly feed one camp, let alone all
the Bushmen around /ai/ai." And he proceeded to enumerate
the seven camps in the /ai/ai vicinity, family by family. "Perhaps you have forgotten that we are not few, but many. Or are
you too blind to tell the difference between a proper cow and
an old wreck? That ox is thin to the point of death."

"Look, you guys," I retorted, "that is a beautiful animal, and
I'm sure you will eat it with pleasure at Christmas."

"Of course we will eat it; it's food. But it won't fill us up to
the point where we will have enough strength to dance. We will
eat and go home to bed with stomachs rumbling."

That night as we turned in, I asked my wife, Nancy: "What
did you think of the black ox?"

"It looked enormous to me. Why?"

"Well, about eight different people have told me I got
gypped; that the ox is nothing but bones."

"What's the angle?" Nancy asked. "Did they have a better
one to sell?"

"No, they just said that it was going to be a grim Christmas
because there won't be enough meat to go around. Maybe I'll
get an independent judge to look at the beast in the morning."

Bright and early, Halingisi, a Tswana cattle owner,
appeared at our camp. But before I could ask him to give me
his opinion on Yehave's black ox, he gave me the eye signal that
indicated a confidential chat. We left the camp and sat down.

"/ontah, I'm surprised at you; you've lived here for three
years and still haven't learned anything about cattle."

"But what else can a person do but choose the biggest,
strongest animal one can find?" I retorted.

"Look, just because an animal is big doesn't mean that it has
plenty of meat on it. The black one was a beauty when it was
younger, but now it is thin to the point of death."

"Well I've already bought it. What can I do at this stage?"

"Bought it already? I thought you were just considering it.
Well, you'll have to kill it and serve it, I suppose. But don't
expect much of a dance to follow."

My spirits dropped rapidly. I could believe that Ben!a and
/gaugo just might be putting me on about the black ox, but

Halingisi seemed to be an impartial critic. I went around that day feeling as though I had bought a lemon of a used car.

In the afternoon it was Tomazo's turn. Tomazo is a fine hunter, a top trance performer (*see* "The Trance Cure of the !Kung Bushmen," page 314), and one of my most reliable informants. He approached the subject of the Christmas cow as part of my continuing Bushmen education.

"My friend, the way it is with us Bushmen," he began, "is that we love meat. And even more than that, we love fat. When we hunt we always search for the fat ones, the ones dripping with layers of white fat: fat that turns into a clear, thick oil in the cooking pot, fat that slides down your gullet, fills your stomach and gives you a roaring diarrhea," he rhapsodized.

"So, feeling as we do," he continued, "it gives us pain to be served such a scrawny thing as Yehave's black ox. It is big, yes, and no doubt its giant bones are good for soup, but fat is what we really crave and so we will eat Christmas this year with a heavy heart."

The prospect of a gloomy Christmas now had me worried, so I asked Tomazo what I could do about it.

"Look for a fat one, a young one . . . smaller, but fat. Fat enough to make us //gom ('evacuate the bowels'), then we will be happy."

My suspicions were aroused when Tomazo said that he happened to know of a young, fat, barren cow that the owner was willing to part with. Was Toma working on commission, I wondered? But I dispelled this unworthy thought when we approached the Herero owner of the cow in question and found that he had decided not to sell.

The scrawny wreck of a Christmas ox now became the talk of the /ai/ai water hole and was the first news told to the outlying groups as they began to come in from the bush for the feast. What finally convinced me that real trouble might be brewing was the visit from u!au, an old conservative with a reputation for fierceness. His nickname meant spear and referred to an incident thirty years ago in which he had speared a man to death. He had an intense manner; fixing me with his eyes, he said in clipped tones:

"I have only just heard about the black ox today, or else I would have come here earlier. /ontah, do you honestly think you can serve meat like that to people and avoid a fight?" He paused, letting the implications sink in. "I don't mean fight you, /ontah; you are a white man. I mean a fight between Bushmen.

There are many fierce ones here, and with such a small quantity of meat to distribute, how can you give everybody a fair share? Someone is sure to accuse another of taking too much or hogging all the choice pieces. Then you will see what happens when some go hungry while others eat."

The possibility of at least a serious argument struck me as all too real. I had witnessed the tension that surrounds the distribution of meat from a kudu or gemsbok kill, and had documented many arguments that sprang up from a real or imagined slight in meat distribution. The owners of a kill may spend up to two hours arranging and rearranging the piles of meat under the gaze of a circle of recipients before handing them out. And I also knew that the Christmas feast at /ai/ai would be bringing together groups that had feuded in the past.

Convinced now of the gravity of the situation, I went in earnest to search for a second cow; but all my inquiries failed to turn one up.

The Christmas feast was evidently going to be a disaster, and the incessant complaints about the meagerness of the ox had already taken the fun out of it for me. Moreover, I was getting bored with the wisecracks, and after losing my temper a few times, I resolved to serve the beast anyway. If the meat fell short, the hell with it. In the Bushmen idiom, I announced to all who would listen:

"I am a poor man and blind. If I have chosen one that is too old and too thin, we will eat it anyway and see if there is enough meat there to quiet the rumbling of our stomachs."

On hearing this speech, Ben!a offered me a rare word of comfort. "It's thin," she said philosophically, "but the bones will make a good soup."

At dawn Christmas morning, instinct told me to turn over the butchering and cooking to a friend and take off with Nancy to spend Christmas alone in the bush. But curiosity kept me from retreating. I wanted to see what such a scrawny ox looked like on butchering, and if there *was* going to be a fight, I wanted to catch every word of it. Anthropologists are incurable that way.

The great beast was driven up to our dancing ground, and a shot in the forehead dropped it in its tracks. Then, freshly cut branches were heaped around the fallen carcass to receive the meat. Ten men volunteered to help with the cutting. I asked

/gaugo to make the breast bone cut. This cut, which begins the butchering process for most large game, offers easy access for removal of the viscera. But it also allows the hunter to spot-check the amount of fat on the animal. A fat game animal carries a white layer up to an inch thick on the chest, while in a thin one, the knife will quickly cut to bone. All eyes fixed on his hand as /gaugo, dwarfed by the great carcass, knelt to the breast. The first cut opened a pool of solid white in the black skin. The second and third cut widened and deepened the creamy white. Still no bone. It was pure fat; it must have been two inches thick.

"Hey /gau," I burst out, "that ox is loaded with fat. What's this about the ox being too thin to bother eating? Are you out of your mind?"

"Fat?" /gau shot back, "You call that fat? This wreck is thin, sick, dead!" And he broke out laughing. So did everyone else. They rolled on the ground, paralyzed with laughter. Everybody laughed except me; I was thinking.

I ran back to the tent and burst in just as Nancy was getting up. "Hey, the black ox. It's fat as hell! They were kidding about it being too thin to eat. It was a joke or something. A put-on. Everyone is really delighted with it!"

"Some joke," my wife replied. "It was so funny that you were ready to pack up and leave /ai/ai."

If it had indeed been a joke, it had been an extraordinarily convincing one, and tinged, I thought, with more than a touch of malice as many jokes are. Nevertheless, that it was a joke lifted my spirits considerably, and I returned to the butchering site where the shape of the ox was rapidly disappearing under the axes and knives of the butchers. The atmosphere had become festive. Grinning broadly, their arms covered with blood well past the elbow, men packed chunks of meat into the big cast-iron cooking pots, fifty pounds to the load, and muttered and chuckled all the while about the thinness and worthlessness of the animal and /ontah's poor judgment.

We danced and ate that ox two days and two nights; we cooked and distributed fourteen potfuls of meat and no one went home hungry and no fights broke out.

But the "joke" stayed in my mind. I had a growing feeling that something important had happened in my relationship with the Bushmen and that the clue lay in the meaning of the joke. Several days later, when most of the people had dispersed back to the bush camps, I raised the question with Hakekgose, a Tswana man who had grown up among the !Kung, married a

!Kung girl, and who probably knew their culture better than any other non-Bushman.

"With us whites," I began, "Christmas is supposed to be the day of friendship and brotherly love. What I can't figure out is why the Bushmen went to such lengths to criticize and belittle the ox I had bought for the feast. The animal was perfectly good and their jokes and wisecracks practically ruined the holiday for me."

"So it really did bother you," said Hakekgose. "Well, that's the way they always talk. When I take my rifle and go hunting with them, if I miss, they laugh at me for the rest of the day. But even if I hit and bring one down, it's no better. To them, the kill is always too small or too old or too thin; and as we sit down on the kill site to cook and eat the liver, they keep grumbling, even with their mouths full of meat. They say things like, 'Oh this is awful! What a worthless animal! Whatever made me think that this Tswana rascal could hunt!' "

"Is this the way outsiders are treated?" I asked.

"No, it is their custom; they talk that way to each other too. Go and ask them."

/gaugo had been one of the most enthusiastic in making me feel bad about the merit of the Christmas ox. I sought him out first.

"Why did you tell me the black ox was worthless, when you could see that it was loaded with fat and meat?"

"It is our way," he said smiling. "We always like to fool people about that. Say there is a Bushman who has been hunting. He must not come home and announce like a braggard, 'I have killed a big one in the bush!' He must first sit down in silence until I or someone else comes up to his fire and asks, 'What did you see today?' He replies quietly, 'Ah, I'm no good for hunting. I saw nothing at all [pause] just a little tiny one.' Then I smile to myself," /gaugo continued, "because I know he has killed something big.

"In the morning we make up a party of four or five people to cut up and carry the meat back to the camp. When we arrive at the kill we examine it and cry out, 'You mean to say you have dragged us all the way out here in order to make us cart home your pile of bones? Oh, if I had known it was this thin I wouldn't have come.' Another one pipes up, 'People, to think I gave up a nice day in the shade for this. At home we may be hungry but at least we have nice cool water to drink.' If the horns are big, someone says, 'Did you think that somehow you were going to boil down the horns for soup?'

"To all this you must respond in kind. 'I agree,' you say, 'this one is not worth the effort; let's just cook the liver for strength and leave the rest for the hyenas. It is not too late to hunt today and even a duiker or a steenbok would be better than this mess.'

"Then you set to work nevertheless; butcher the animal, carry the meat back to the camp and everyone eats," /gaugo concluded.

Things were beginning to make sense. Next, I went to Tomazo. He corroborated /gaugo's story of the obligatory insults over a kill and added a few details of his own.

"But," I asked, "why insult a man after he has gone to all that trouble to track and kill an animal and when he is going to share the meat with you so that your children will have something to eat?"

"Arrogance," was his cryptic answer.

"Arrogance?"

"Yes, when a young man kills much meat he comes to think of himself as a chief or a big man, and he thinks of the rest of us as his servants or inferiors. We can't accept this. We refuse one who boasts, for someday his pride will make him kill somebody. So we always speak of his meat as worthless. This way we cool his heart and make him gentle."

COLIN M. TURNBULL

A PEOPLE APART This is written from inside a small, circular mud hut, dark—despite the brilliant sunshine outside—because the door has to be closed to ward off unwelcome visitors who are not deterred even by the eight-foot stockade around the house. There are no windows, but some light and air come in through the eaves, where the thatched roof clears the wall by four or five inches. The floor slopes at a ridiculous angle, and the furniture, a bed and two tables made of saplings lashed together with vine, only seems to add to the discomfort. Outside, however, life is even less comfortable, for there is no shelter from the blazing heat, any more than there is from the freezing rain that is likely to follow in an hour or two, blown down the valley by gale force winds. Distances between villages may not be enormous, but because of the rugged mountain terrain, with ravines a thousand feet deep to be negotiated, it may take a good eight-hour trek to cover as little as ten miles or less, as measured by a straight ruler on a flat map. And even where the land is level for a few hundred yards it is covered with sharp thorns that tear at the arms and legs and, when broken off, penetrate the stoutest soles. Yet, except in moments of temporary despair, it all seems worth while, for although it is like taking blood from the proverbial stone, there is much knowledge to be had from such conditions. The field worker unlucky or unwise enough to have made such a choice is bound to learn not only about the people he is studying but also about himself.

Perhaps even more important, when conditions are as extreme as they are here, in the very northeasternmost corner of Uganda, they make the anthropologist think very carefully about the validity of his results. Here the human environment is just as difficult to cope with as the geographical, and if it is hard for the field worker to accurately and conscientiously survey mountain farmland that frequently slopes at an angle of over seventy degrees, it is even harder for him to maintain his equilibrium while attempting to relate to a people who, while not wishing him any harm, nonetheless wish to strip him of everything he possesses, whether they can conceive of any use for it or not.

Nor is it easy to feel at home with a people who regard each other in a similarly covetous light, and who consequently surround themselves with a barrage of deception and ring their homes with tight, virtually impenetrable stockades and thorn fences, dividing brothers from each other and parents from children. While it is true that the anthropologist is no more separated from such people than they are from each other, it is questionable whether he can in a brief year or two ever truly penetrate such formidable defenses and understand just how such a society can survive. Even the hardest head, professing the greatest scientific detachment, can surely not fail to judge harshly when a plump, hearty youth is seen beating a starving, tiny, demented girl for the fun of stealing from her the only food she has seen for a day or two; or when an adult audience roars with laughter as one of their number sneaks food from the bowl of a blind elder as he is eating; or when parents abandon children (or vice versa) to die, not because they could not be fed, but because it would simply take too much trouble—any amount of trouble being too much. The field worker may eventually learn to penetrate the stockades by wriggling through the low doorway on his stomach or on his side, having first announced his intention so as to avoid being attacked, but can he ever penetrate a mentality that looks on with mild amusement as food and water that could save a life are stolen from the dying?

Anthropologists all too often claim to have understood and explained primitive societies *in toto*, as though there was no more to be said on the matter. They present a clearly defined system that would work admirably, like a mechanical model; but also like a mechanical model, it would get nowhere. Perhaps we are all too much concerned with explanation, and too little concerned with understanding. A society like this one, however, defies any explanation, at least for a very long time; none of the standard social systems, of which the theoreticians are so fond and so proud, fit even in part; the field worker is driven, rather like the people he is studying, simply to concentrate on surviving, in the hope that understanding will come, even if system does not.

Anthropology, the study of man, is divided into several different areas in these days of specialization. It is a study of man as a biological entity, as a historical entity, and as a social entity. One of the pities of such specialization is that there is an inevitable tendency to separation, as though man were capable of being rent into discrete parts and still exist. Even within a division, such as social anthropology, there are subdivisions. There are those who seek to answer very specific theoretical problems, and who select a society for study because it illustrates those problems. Others answer a call to solve more empirical problems, such as those posed by the rapid social changes taking place in formerly undeveloped areas. Others, like myself, prefer to undertake a more general quest without any specific expectation except the broadening of our knowledge of human society. We choose a society to study because, in the first place, it is unknown and promises fresh data, and perhaps also because it is generally in line with our own interests, likes, or dislikes.

I like forests, and I am interested in hunters and gatherers, so when casting about for somewhere to go for further research I first chose the Andaman Islands, where the Onge still live (on the Little Andaman) in depleted numbers, but still relatively untouched by civilization. The study would have provided invaluable data for comparison with other hunters and gatherers in similarly forested environments; it would have been of particular interest to me because of my previous work among the pygmy hunters of the Congo. But it was not to be; for various reasons the Indian government refused permission, and with little time left I had to make an alternative choice.

Just then Elizabeth Marshall, author of *The Harmless People*, returned from northern Uganda where she had been gathering material on the Dodos, one of the great Karimojong peoples. She suggested that since I was so interested in hunters, why not visit the Teuso, who allegedly lived high up in the mountains above the Uganda/Kenya escarpment, and who had first been reported in a very brief note in an academic journal in 1931. She painted a delightful picture of a warm and friendly people, full of fun, whom she had met during their occasional visits to the administrative center of Kaabong, a tiny outpost near the point where Uganda, Kenya, and Sudan all meet in an incredible conglomeration of jagged mountains, arid deserts, and lush, gemlike, and isolated valleys. I reluctantly gave up the idea of a cool forest, and prepared for the hills.

Here again anthropologists differ widely in the kinds of preparations they make. I think all of us read up on whatever literature is available, but in this case it amounted to no more than a few pages. Some then prepare as for any other kind of expedition, purchasing camping equipment and such supplies as cannot be bought locally in the field. Medical supplies have to be carefully assembled, and the necessary innoculations taken. It is all very matter of fact, and when the anthropologist arrives in the field all he has to do is to set up his tent, or tents, assemble all his camping equipment and stores, and then proceed to work much as if he were still in his office, but with an abundant supply of raw material all around. Such an anthropologist deliberately establishes himself outside the community he is studying; some even stay in nearby resthouses or hotels if a town is not too far away. They visit the "field" daily, and pursue a diligent course of study, which they carefully plot as they go along, step by step. They are free from local involvement, emotional or otherwise, and can more easily preserve the intellectual detachment we all aim for. They necessarily miss a great deal by not living in the village with the people, but they claim that their vision, if limited, is clearer by being more objective.

There is no right or wrong way; it depends a great deal on the purpose, as well as the nature, of each individual case, and on the personality of the field worker. I prefer to enter a society as completely as possible, for although it becomes impossible to maintain as high a degree of objectivity at the time, one gathers much more material and in much more intimate detail, and this can be treated as objectively as you like when, once out of the field, the material is being analyzed. Of course, it is then too late to fill in any gaps that might result from being too immersed in the subject itself, but on the whole I find the rewards are richer. My previous two major experiences of this kind, in India and in the Congo, had both been immensely fruitful and, at the same time, immensely pleasurable. Minor physical discomforts were quickly obliterated by the constant excitement of discovery and the pleasure of companionship with people who welcomed my desire to learn their ways and were anxious that I understand them well. I saw no reason to think it could be otherwise with the Teuso. That was my first mistake.

The second mistake I made was to assume that the Teuso were hunters until I saw their intensive cultivation, and then to assume that they were farmers. My third mistake, and the greatest, was to assume that these gentle, smiling, friendly looking people who extended such a warm welcome were as gentle and as amicable as they appeared. It took a long time—almost a year—to convince me otherwise.

I arrived at Kaabong at a time when drought was beginning to result in famine. The famine struck the Turkana in Kenya even more heavily, and they were beginning to intensify their raids on the Dodos in Uganda, so that for two weeks the local administration was reluctant to allow me into the danger area. During these two weeks I stayed at Kaabong and met some of the Teuso who filtered down through the mountains in search of food. Two Teuso boys had, during a previous famine, decided to go to the mission school, where they were well fed, as well as well taught. They spoke their own language and Karimojong, which is the lingua franca in this area, and they also knew some English and Swahili. From them, I was able to work up a fairly respectable vocabulary and determine the basic grammatical pattern. I found it relatively easy on paper, but enormously difficult in practice, for the sounds were utterly unlike anything I had ever attempted to make, or had even heard, in a linguistic context. In the course of learning to splutter appropriately, I learned that "Teuso" is only a name applied by the Dodos, and that the tribal name is Ik. Their language is utterly unknown to any of the neighboring tribes, with whom they communicate only in Karimojong. It was unlike any African language known to me, and did not seem to conform to the Sudanic classification it had tentatively been accorded. Perhaps it was the somewhat Bushmanoid appearance of the people that tempted me to see a possible linguistic connection in that direction, but from the outset it was quite plain that the Ik were a people apart from all others in the region, linguistically, physically, and culturally.

As soon as permission came through, I spent a month visiting all the different villages, traveling by jeep as far as practicable, then simply walking or climbing. The effects of the drought had been disastrous. The fields, which had been planted with such evident care and labor, had received just enough rain at the beginning of the season to bring out the young shoots. Then the sun had come to stay in the cloudless sky, burning everything. It burned the crops of the Ik; it also burned the grass that the Dodos needed for their cattle, and it dried up the few water sources that both needed to survive. The outlook was bad, and I was impressed by the cheerfulness with which the Ik accepted the almost certain disaster. Even after the grain that should have been reserved for next year's sowing had been consumed and when there was no longer any chance of rain coming in time to yield a harvest, the Ik, for a reason I could not then understand, remained optimistic. All, that is, except a few old people who were barely strong enough to crawl from their huts to talk. They simply said that they would die, since there was nobody to bring them food, and they were too weak to hunt or gather the wild vegetables that were still about. When I asked if they did not have children to help them, they just laughed—a laugh I quite misunderstood. It was a hollow, hopeless sort of sound that I have heard all too often since, and those who have made it have, as they predicted, mostly died. They did indeed have children, who remained obstinately optimistic and singularly well fed while the skin hung off their parents in long, wrinkled folds, leaving bones to stick out as though in angry protest.

The optimism of the youths, whose plumpness was perhaps comparative but who nonetheless could at least walk upright instead of having to drag themselves along the ground, lay in their knowledge that the drought, two thousand feet down below the escarpment, was even more disastrous for the Turkana. The Turkana, like all Karimojong, live by cattle. They drink the blood and milk of the cows and occasionally eat the flesh of their goats and sheep. The drought became so severe that raids on the Dodos were no longer sufficient remedy, for there simply was no food or water for the vast herds they possessed. Their only recourse, as the Ik well knew, was to climb up the escarpment, invade Uganda, and graze their cattle there.

By then I had decided to make my headquarters near the frontier police post of Pirre, on the side of Mount Morungole, overlooking the Kidepo National Park. There was a cluster of seven Ik villages there, and I had already seen a good deal of the remaining six villages to the east, along the top of the escarpment itself. It was, of course, into Kidepo that the greatest Turkana invasion came, with many thousands of cattle. They drove the Dodos from Pirre; this tiny police post, housed in about a dozen huts, was completely incapable of doing anything against such numbers. The track to Kaabong was barely passable even by jeep, the radio equipment broke down, and the local administration was in a quandary as to what to do, short of calling in the army and creating an international incident.

So the Turkana took possession of Pirre, and I confess that I found them a welcome change, wild and aggressive though they were. They said they had no wish to fight, but only wanted to graze their cattle. They promised they would do no harm if left alone, and although they have probably one of the most unsavory reputations in the whole of Africa, I never doubted their word for an instant, nor did they go back on it even under provocation.

The Ik now displayed their talent for survival. They busied

themselves making spears for the Turkana, who had recently been persuaded to surrender theirs as a peace gesture toward the Dodos. For this service they bled the Turkana much as the Turkana bleed their cattle, but with rather less consideration. The Ik began to grow fat again. They then persuaded the Turkana that the Dodos were a menace and began instigating raids between the two, acting first as spies for one side, then for the other, drawing pay in the edible form of cattle from both sides. Ik villages that had never possessed a single goat began to build *bomas* and to fill them with literally hundreds of cattle. They ate these as rapidly as possible, for they knew very well that any attempt to keep them would only result in their being stolen back. The youths continued to put on weight, but the old people remained as thin and emaciated as ever.

The Turkana were eventually forced out by the army, which left the Ik with only the Dodos to prey on, and the Dodos themselves were near starvation. The old people among the Ik began to die, and children, and even some of the youths. The selfishness shown over food was terrible to see, but seemed almost excusable under the circumstances. I myself was driven into hiding every time I wanted to eat, although I had barely enough for myself, since fresh supplies were unobtainable and I had given what I could to the old. Yet I was wary of even biting into a dry biscuit in case someone should hear the crunching and come and demand a share. When people knew anyone was eating, myself included, they came and sat around in a silent, hungry circle, knowing that nothing would be left for them, but hoping. I would have excused them anything during those days, just as I hoped they would excuse me.

The new year came, and with it the first rains in over twelve months. Work in the fields was slow to begin with, for few people had the strength. But the rains brought up edible grasses, wild berries and fruits appeared, and gradually the danger of full-scale starvation receded. Now the crops are well on the way to bringing in a fine harvest, and the wild foods grow in abundance all around. What has not grown, however, is any evidence that the Ik—even in such relatively good times—have any consideration for one another. Food is still the dominant thought, food getting the dominant activity. And, still, it is each individual for himself. At dawn, children flock out in a large, single, unruly band and scavenge the surrounding countryside for anything that might have come up during the night. The three- to seven- or eight-year olds are too young to risk going any great distance, where they would stand a better chance. Their older brothers and sisters, having beaten the younger ones to get what they had not yet eaten, go farther out on hunting parties of their own. If caught by their parents, they, in turn, will be beaten and robbed. The adults steal from each other and angrily denounce each other, kinship affording not the slightest bond of mutual respect. A mother will leave her children, even one barely weaned, in care of a father while she goes off to gather for herself, sometimes staying away for a week. Meanwhile the father will go off and leave the children in care of grandparents too old to fend for themselves. To get water, for instance, may well involve a walk of three miles and a descent (and climb, in the reverse direction) of a thousand almost sheer feet. When someone dies, there is no wailing or mourning, merely a great deal of grumbling by the next of kin because of the obligation it places on them to provide ritual purification involving a feast for relatives.

I saw one father hurriedly bury his ten-year-old son by the door of his hut, so as to avoid the expense. The night before, he had beaten his wife to stop her crying when the child died, for by so doing she announced the fact he wished to conceal. All day he sat on a rock and grumbled at his son for dying, at his wife for crying, and at his relatives for demanding a proper burial, including the appropriate feast, to which they would have to be invited. It is, perhaps, at least comforting that the mother cried, but it is the only time I have heard it.

The old people tell stories of better times when, not so long ago, Kidepo Park was theirs to hunt in as they pleased; when the boundaries of the three countries were not subject to armed patrols; and when they could roam at will in search of food and game, instead of being restricted and compressed as they are now. They wonder why the animals in the Park are protected and allowed to live and flourish while they must die. They wonder why their children have abandoned them, for they remember how brothers would all join together, in the old days, to look after their parents. But even the old people, now, have only one concept of good. It is nothing that can be applied to an action, or to a relationship between one human and another; it is only a condition, clearly defined as "having a full stomach." This is the basis of their life, of their law, of their morality. It is a goal that justifies any action except killing, for the Ik never kill. Their legend of origin tells how God gave spears to the Karimojong, together with cattle, so that they have wealth but also the means to bring death. God gave the Ik the digging stick, and told them not to kill. They don't, they just let each other die. Meanwhile they live a life devoid of affection. A woman's attitude to childbirth is that it is a nuisance, another mouth to feed for two or three years. A mother may be amused by her baby, but that is about as close as she seems to get to affection for it. When it is sick or hungry it is simply slapped and cursed as an annoyance. The most equable kind of interpersonal relationship, regardless of kinship, is that of mutual economic reliance, but this is temporary at best and inevitably ends in cheating and mutual recrimination.

The tightly stockaded internal divisions, which turn every village into a series of independent fortresses—each occupied by a nuclear family, each with its own single, sometimes booby-trapped private entrance—is sufficient evidence of the state of degeneration into which this society has been thrown by events it cannot understand. Youths have no concept of what their grandparents are talking about when the old folk grumble about the young deserting the old. One, wanting some food I was about to give to an old, old woman, said "Why give it to her? She is going to die anyway." When I said it might make her a little happier meanwhile, he became angry at the waste, for such he considered it.

The economic noose that has been drawn around its neck may be enough to explain the condition into which Ik society has fallen, although even of that I am not yet convinced. It is difficult to understand how, even under such circumstances, a human society can exist and survive as successfully as this one does, devoid of nearly all those qualities that we consider raise us above the level of animals. And however well one may be able to explain the society as it functions at present, is that explanation valid without any understanding of the people themselves? For even simply as people, I still cannot understand the Ik. I cannot bring myself to accept that a loveless society can exist, and constantly look for something I must have missed, fearing all the while that it is not there. The Ik are not a people one can dislike, as much as one dislikes almost everything they do, feeling that even animals would behave with more consideration for each other. One cannot dislike them because they themselves are without the ability to like or dislike, except with regard to the fullness of their bellies: in personal relationships there is a total hiatus.

At the moment it is impossible for me not to be largely subjective. There is always the hope that once I am out of the field, back in familiar and comfortable surroundings, with the leisure and strength to go over every detail in search of the truth, a different truth will emerge. Yet with all this in mind I fear that the truth has already been found. It makes me both angry and sad.

LOLA At the end of the winter of 1966 in Tierra del Fuego, an Indian woman named Kiepja died in a government hospital, not far from where she had been born 90 years earlier in a tent made of guanaco skin. Of the then ten surviving Selk'nam (Onas), she was the only one who had actually lived as an Indian. She had witnessed the end of a culture that had existed "since the beginning of time," that of a prehistoric people who lived solely by hunting, gathering, and fishing.

When Isla Grande (the largest in the Tierra del Fuego archipelago, just south of the Strait of Magellan) was first settled by Europeans in about 1870, the Indians, mainly Selk'nam, were still independent and only slightly affected by the sporadic contacts they had had with Europeans since the sixteenth century. Their population was then about 3,500, certainly no more than 4,000. During the following decades most of the Selk'nam were slaughtered or died from diseases and other results of the usurpation of their land. In 1919 Father Martin Gusinde counted 279 Selk'nam. Ten years later fewer than 100 remained. By 1966, there were only eight, including four whose fathers were of European descent. All were over the age of 50 and had been born shortly before or after the aboriginal culture had been shattered. All but one, Kiepja, spoke Spanish fluently; several also spoke some Selk'nam. But Kiepja, who was also called Lola, spoke her own language fluently and only some Spanish. She had remained psychologically and emotionally identified with her culture; moreover, she was a shaman and thus possessed a profound knowledge of its mystical traditions. She was happy recalling the ancient way of life, but it saddened her all the more when she realized that nearly everyone had died, that her world had disappeared forever.

Despite her tragic life, she laughed easily and joked about herself and others. Sometimes she would call me her daughter; other times, when I would tie her apron for her, she would look over her shoulder at me and laugh while rocking from one foot to the other, saying *ala ala,* meaning that I was treating her like a baby.

I first met Lola during my Christmas vacation in 1964. At

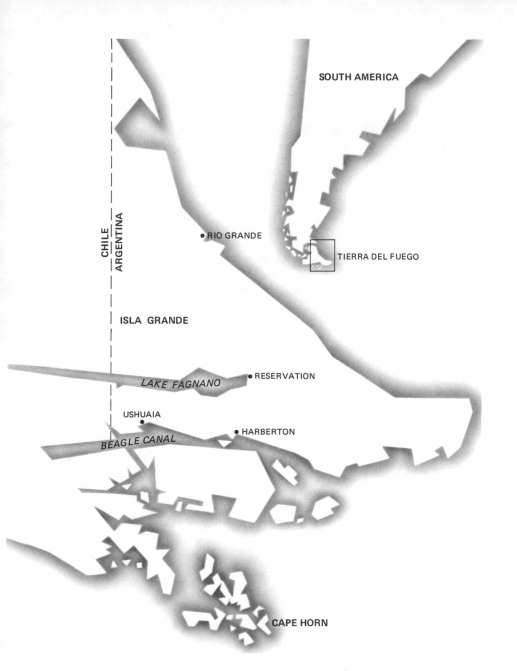

the time, I was working with a French archeological mission on the Chilean side of the island, and Lola was living on the reservation located near Lake Fagnano on the Argentinian side. As an ethnologist, I hoped to be able to work with her, and was relieved to discover that contact was easy. On my first visit, she sang a chant mourning the death of her mother. I returned the following day with a tape recorder and spent the next three weeks with Lola and her friend Angela Louij, also a Selk'nam.

With Angela's help as an interpreter, I found that Lola had a great fund of knowledge concerning her culture. I checked her memory by asking her the names of Indians mentioned by Lucas Bridges in *Uttermost Part of the Earth*, some of whom had died shortly after the turn of the century. Sometimes she replied that she did not know, but when she did give names, they were correct. During those weeks we recorded 38 chants. The recordings were technically deficient for a number of reasons, but as I was committed that year to other field work, I was obliged to leave.

I came back to Paris at the end of 1965 and played the tapes for Gilbert Rouget, the head of the ethnomusicology department at the Musée de l'Homme. He suggested that I return to Tierra del Fuego to rerecord what I had brought and if possible, to record other chants. Also Claude Lévi-Strauss believed that this might be the last opportunity to obtain new data concerning a group that, for decades, had been considered extinct.

Only two collections of recordings of this group existed, and both had been made on cylinders. The first dated from 1907–08; the other was made in 1923–24. In January, 1966, we felt that this might be the last chance to accurately record authentic chants of this culture.

In March, 1966, I returned to Tierra del Fuego for a three-month stay. This time the main problem was the language barrier. Although adequate for her everyday needs, Lola's Spanish was rudimentary. While speaking it, she gave the impression of an almost childlike mentality, thus concealing her passionate temperament and complex nature, her bewilderment and profound sorrow. Her world had slowly sunk into nonexistence as those around her had died strange deaths, and gradually she interiorized all the realities of her existence, while to strangers she became *la reliquia* ("the relic").

The only place I could work with Lola was on the reservation and given the situation there, it was not possible to bring another Indian who might have acted as an interpreter. It was difficult for me to learn Selk'nam, partly because Lola could only translate isolated words. Moreover, Selk'nam is a tonal and glottal-stop language. Often when I was endeavoring to pronounce a word, Lola would frown, looking intently at my mouth, her lips moving soundlessly, and when my version finally came out, she would sigh in relief and laugh, saying *eso es* ("that's it"), as if we had won a battle against great odds.

From March to June I lived mostly on the reservation, on a sheep ranch a few steps from Lola's hut where Luis Garibaldi Honte, a relatively well-to-do and acculturated Indian, kindly let me stay. He had instructed his employee to supply Lola with lamb meat and other necessities. Don Luis had taken care of her on several occasions when she had been ill. He and his family were not there much of the time during winter, however, as they preferred to remain in Río Grande, so the only other person on the ranch, besides Lola and myself, was a *puestero* ("mounted shepherd"). Every week or two, I would go to Río Grande for several days to study my material and to purchase supplies. I did not want Lola to become too accustomed to my company lest she feel all the more lonely after my departure.

She had had twelve children, seven with her Indian husband, and after his death, five more from her union with a Chilean. They had all died, most of them as adults. Her grandchildren, excepting one who lived on the continent, had also died. She had one living descendant, a great-grandson, who had been adopted by the Garibaldis.

Until she was about twenty-five years old, Lola had had little contact with Europeans. Then, in about 1900, her husband went to work at Harberton, a sheep farm on the south coast of the island. Harberton was founded by an English missionary, Thomas Bridges, one of the first white settlers in Tierra del Fuego and virtually the only one who consistently befriended the Selk'nam. But even then, at the beginning of this century, and for several decades afterward, Lola and her family, like the other Indians, would revert to their nomadic life in the winter, principally to hunt guanaco. The great ceremony called *hain* (which included rites of initiation for the boys, the *kloketen*) continued to be held sporadically and Lola often participated.

During these years her mother and her maternal uncles trained her to become a shaman, a *xoon*. One night, sometime during the year 1926, she dreamed that the spirit of one of her deceased shaman uncles visited her and transmitted his power to her by means of his chant. His spirit had flown over Lake Fagnano (called Kami by the Indians) seeking her. This uncle had died on the opposite side of the lake from where she was then living. In her dream she heard his spirit singing: "Where are you, my daughter?" When she heard his call, she repeated it, thus awakening herself. At that precise moment, she said, his power penetrated her "like the cutting edge of a knife." It was then that, in the traditional manner, she became a shaman.

When I met Lola she had been living alone on the reservation for many years, most of the time in a wooden hut. She cooked her meals, gathered firewood, fetched water, and did other chores. She also wove baskets, which she sometimes sold. She had owned some sheep and a few horses, inherited from some of her children and from other Indians. But she told me that all of her animals had been stolen, some by two of the Indians and the rest by other neighbors. But what she missed most of all was a favorite horse. Until about 1961, when she was already well over 80, she would take long rides to visit someone or to buy *maté* ("herb tea") or food. But after she fell off the horse several times, Don Luis thought it wise not to allow her to ride. She never got over what seemed to her a gross affront.

Lola was aware that she was much more Indian than the other surviving Selk'nam. The difference between her and the others was accentuated because she was a shaman and was therefore deeply influenced by the mystical and mythological traditions of her culture. Although some of the other Indians secretly admired her for her shamanistic power, they had no lingering fear of her since she was not a full-fledged shaman. As was usually the case with a woman shaman, she did not have the power to kill. Over the years she had treated a few of the Indians and even some whites in shamanistic seances. But she did not always use her "power" when curing. Once when I was frying potatoes the grease splattered, burning my hand. Taking my hand in hers, she rubbed cold water on the burn with the palm of her hand. Then she blew on it for several minutes until the pain disappeared entirely. And when I complained of a backache she told me to lie face down on her bed. Then she pressed hard with the palms of her hands and blew with quick puffs on the aching part.

She had several friends among her people but did not see them too often. She knew that most of the non-Indians on the island had little or no respect for her. But she was very responsive to the few who liked her and joked with them in her broken Spanish. Occasionally tourists would come to the reservation where she lived, and invariably, they wanted to photograph her. Flanked by several strangers she would stand rigid, scowling into the camera. If not given anything for being thus bothered, she would become indignant. But she never showed her indignation to the tourists.

Twice in the last few years her huts had burned down. The memory of these fires terrified her, although she had not been burned. Her last hut had been built on the Garibaldi farm, close to the main house so that she would not be as isolated as she previously had been.

I was worried myself about Lola's hut burning down. As winter set in, in the last year of her life, we spent more and more time huddled over the stove. Often she would overload it and burning split logs would fall out. Exclaiming excitedly she would try to shove them back into the stove. Every night before I left I would say *hauk* ("fire") *chon* ("water"), reminding her to pour water over the stove before she went to bed.

Behind her hut there was a tepee-shaped, open-fronted structure made of logs over which rags were thrown. Here, weather permitting, she would build a fire and sit weaving a basket. She told me that when alone she would go there sometimes, just to sit by the fire. Perhaps she felt closer to her old way of life there.

She frequently proposed that we go to certain places many kilometers away. She was convinced she could walk greater distances than she actually could. But together we walked short distances to gather firewood or to visit places she had lived before or campsites of Indians she had known.

When rain threatened, she often went outside "to cut the sky," as she would say in Selk'nam, so that we might have good weather. One day when I called her attention to the cloudy sky, instead of taking her usual broomstick or walking stock to clear the sky, she took her meat knife, saying a knife was better. To insult the clouds, she sputtered, chanted, and shouted at them, while making large sweeping movements, usually with a stick. Her purpose was to push the clouds away toward the west, the sky of the rain. On a cloudy or rainy day she would clear the sky several times if necessary, until finally that day or the next, the sun would reappear. When the effect was not immediate she would sometimes laugh, saying that the clouds *no quieren*, meaning that they did not want to leave. Of course, when she insisted upon "cutting the sky" long enough, the clouds would leave. Clearing up the weather was one of the attributes of the shamans.

She was not very neat and would spit almost anyplace. She knew how to use a fork, but preferred to eat with her fingers. Although she detested the idea of taking a bath, upon arising she would wash her hands and face. She swept her hut when she knew I was coming, but I have the impression that, when alone, she would not bother to do so very often. Without thinking, she would drop refuse on the floor or throw it out the door for the dogs. She had the habit of piling things pell-mell in the corners of her hut and on her bed. It followed that she spent a great deal of time searching for lost articles, particularly her meat knife. These habits were largely culturally determined. She had been brought up to live as a nomad, to change campsites every few days, to dress in guanaco skins, to clean herself with dry clay or moss, and to possess only the necessities for existence, no more.

In her later years she was given many useless things, particularly an excess of old clothing. She had a favorite man's suit jacket, a hand-me-down from years before. As she had other, less ragged jackets, I asked her why she was fond of it. "For the pockets," she replied. It had ten pockets, inside and out. This pleased her a great deal as she liked to carry the little money she had with her. She was wary of being robbed, and although at times money had been taken from her, more often she simply forgot where she had hidden the missing money. This suspicion of being robbed was, I believe, more a symptom of senility or insecurity than a cultural trait.

While Lola was not concerned about the appearance of what she wore, she was sensitive to the beauty of her face. Sometimes when I would comb her hair, she would look in the mirror laughing, saying *yo olichen* ("I pretty") or frown and say *yippen, yo vieja* ("ugly, I old").

Although she ate lamb three or four times a day with remarkable appetite, Lola would often ask if I could bring her fish and guanaco meat. I was never able to get either. There were two other items she always asked me to buy when I went to Río Grande—butter and sweet vermouth. She ate butter as if it were candy, and would have consumed half a pound a day if I had not discouraged her. And each day we invariably had an aperitif before lunch. Several times she insisted that I bring her two or three bottles together. Finally I complied. When I next left for Río Grande she still had two bottles. I began to worry, imagining she might drink too much, although so far as I knew, she never had. When upon returning I inquired, she replied that she had not touched either of them, that she was waiting for me. A few times while I was away, she walked out to the side of the road to wait for me, even though she knew I was not due that day. When I asked her why, she said that she simply wanted to wait for me there.

She delighted to sing for the tape recorder, *la máquina*, "the machine," as she called it. One of the chants we especially liked concerned an old guanaco and was a chant of mourning as well as one of the hain.

"Ra ra ra ra ra," Lola would sing, imitating the old guanaco.

The text of this chant is a myth, an allegory of the prohibition of incest. The story belongs to *lyluka*, the mythological past, and is about a man who schemed to make love to his daughters. As he was about to succeed, however, he and his daughters were transformed into guanacos. Lola once sang it with these words in Selk'nam:

"The old guanaco (when he was still a man) said to his daughters: 'I am about to die. Bury me in the white earth but do not bury me deep in the earth, leave my head and shoulders free. After I die you will perform *tachira* [mourning rites] and as you are going away singing of your grief, a man will approach you. He will look exactly like me but he will not be me. He will ask to make love to you. Do as he says.'

"And when he died the daughters did just as their father had ordered. As they walked away, while they were still singing the chant of death, the old guanaco [now metamorphosed] jumped out of his grave, hot with desire to make love to his daughters. He sniffed their tracks and chased wildly after them, urinating as he ran. When he caught up to them he said: 'I am the one your father told you about. Come let us make love.' One of his daughters ran on. When he made love to the other she, too, became a guanaco."

Lola would invariably insist that I immediately play back the tape when she had stopped singing. While listening she would most often laugh, appear very pleased, and comment *olichen* ("lovely"). But sometimes she would say *yippen* ("ugly"), scowl, and, looking worried, say that she wanted to record the same chant again, right away. Often she asked that the tapes be replayed for the pure pleasure of hearing herself again. She sang some of the chants again and again, particularly two of the mourning chants. One of these she had sung upon the death of her mother and the other when her last two sons had died. She sang these so frequently that sometimes I would not record them, especially during the last few weeks when I was low on tapes and when it was so cold that the batteries had to be taken out of the recorder every minute or so to be heated on the stove. But she wanted to be recorded each time she sang, and when I did not do so she was displeased. I tried to explain that I could not record the same chant indefinitely. She did understand, however, that I wanted to record the greatest variety of songs possible.

Quite often when I greeted her in the morning, she would smile widely, saying, "I found another," meaning that during the night she had recalled the chant of a certain person, which she had heard perhaps 50 years earlier. She would ask me excitedly to hurry, as if she were holding a hot potato, and get the machine ready lest the chant disappear from her memory before we could record it. Once recorded, I often played it back to her, then asked her to sing the same chant again, to get the best possible rendition. She did not always comply with my request. There were times she preferred to sing another chant, and some chants she did not like at all. Once in a while she became irritated at my insistence, but in the end, she would usually laugh and ask me why I wanted to record it in view of the fact that it was so ugly. At other times, however, she seemed to understand that her voice was being recorded to preserve the chants. Of the 92 chants we recorded in 1966, 38 had been recorded the year before. The rest she recalled gradually as we worked together in the last few months of her life.

She made me promise never to play the tapes for anyone on the island except Angela and one other friend. In 1965, during the three weeks we recorded, whenever anyone approached the house she became nervous and asked me to hide the recorder. The following year we had very few visitors and she seemed less timid. She explained to me that the "others" (the whites as well as some of the other Indians) would laugh if they heard her singing, that they did not understand. Once in a while she said that she was recording for the Indians to the north.

In addition to recording chants, we recorded some basic vocabulary (which bored her), proper names, place names, and kin terms. At times she seemed to be secretly amused at me, as when, for instance, I recorded her imitations of birds. These interested me because many of the names of birds are onomatopoetic. What she really enjoyed, however, were the chants. When singing those of the *hain* she would pantomine the dance steps and gestures of the spirit (always a man disguised with a mask and body paint) to whom the chant was being sung and especially of a spirit called Shorti, who during the ceremony frightened the women by chasing them and throwing things at them. Sometimes, while imitating his short, rhythmic step, she would stab me gently in the ribs with her cane, saying in a half-joking, half-serious tone:

"Shorti was very mean to the women."

When telling me about certain of these spirits and the pranks the Indians played on one another during the ceremony, she would laugh until tears came to her eyes and then look at me still laughing and say *que salvajes* ("what savages").

A favorite account was one her maternal grandfather had told her mother. It concerned two *xoon* ("shamans") who were great liars. It all happened on the east coast of the island, near Cabo de Penas. It was a very cold winter and everyone was hungry. The two impostors, Koin-xoon and Hewiu-xoon, pretended they were *ochen-maten* (a *xoon* alleged to have sufficient shamanistic power to kill a whale and bring it ashore). That day no one went out to hunt, as everyone expected a whale to arrive any minute. They all stood along the beach shivering. The two impostors pointed to the sea, saying they saw a flock of gulls, a sure sign that a whale was nearing. They then sang the chant of the whale while jumping all about, making believe they were tugging a cord, dragging the tremendous whale ashore. All the others were anxiously waiting to eat the fat of the whale. But it was all a great lie. There was no whale at all. The *xoon* were making fools of everyone. The brother of Koin-xoon finally became angry and said:

"Here I am wasting my time. I am hungry but instead of hunting with my *teix* [a snare used to trap certain birds], here I am hanging around the beach all because of these liars."

During my stay the first year, Angela sometimes pretended she was tugging the invisible cord and Lola would become nearly helpless with laughter.

Speaking her own language, Lola would repeat conversations heard more than half a century before. Toward the end of my stay she thought I understood a great deal more of her language than was the case. I endeavored to grasp at least enough to make a few short comments so that she would continue talking. One of the words she repeated most often was *koliot*, "red cape," the name given to the first intruding whites, apparently after the flannel capes worn by the first policemen to arrive. This was a warning of attack. An Indian would shout it when he sighted an armed rider on the horizon; then the entire camp would scatter as well as it could. She remembered the victims of the professional killers, several of whom had been hired by one of the first European sheepmen, José Menéndez. "Bad Christians—to kill the Indians," she would say.

She spoke time and again of her maternal grandfather, Alakin, who was renowned on the island as a great prophet. Other Indians confirmed that Alakin was not feared as were most of the shamans; rather, he was most highly esteemed because of his knowledge of the legendary past and what was considered to be his ability to predict the future by means of visions. He had been killed when quite an old man, along with two of his brothers, in retaliation for having stolen metal tools from the shack of some newcomers.

Referring to an epidemic of the later decades, she said:

"Dead—dead—dead. How many dead? Look at the cemetery—it is full. So many died, every day. Trucks would go by full of the dead. They all died of *koliot* sickness—babies with their mothers, young girls not yet married."

As if it had happened the day before, she described how certain men had been wounded or killed during the last wars (really skirmishes lasting a few hours) between the Indians.

She spoke often of a war in which she had participated and which provoked the very last war among the Selk'nam a few years after the turn of the century.

She was a short distance from the camp when the enemy attacked. As the dogs with her began to bark, she ran back to the camp and there she saw her husband, Anik, wounded in the temple by an arrow. *Pobrecito* ("the poor fellow"), she would comment, "his face got all swollen." Then a certain Asherton tried to abduct her. She resisted and tried to escape. He became furious and ran after her, arrow in hand, shouting: "I'll kill you if you don't come with me!" Anik was about to be finished off when his cousin Pachek, on the enemy side, intervened, shouting: "Don't kill him! He's my cousin." Pachek also saved her from being abducted.

This battle took place on the east coast, near the Irigoyen River. Kinsmen and others, about 26 adults, were celebrating a *hain,* during which two youths were being initiated. The party was attacked by some 30 men from five different territories who were determined to revenge the death of a certain Unen-xoon, shaman and champion hunter. He had been killed by an arrow from one of Lola's party, her uncle Tael. He and his son and one of Lola's brothers were among the six killed during this battle. Eight women were abducted by the enemy, but five escaped afterward and returned to their group.

The brutality of certain Indians had impressed Lola greatly, especially the action of one who, in a rage, had dragged his wife over the fire, severely burning her sexual organs.

She had great admiration for certain shamans, particularly for Maiich, who several times had performed the most difficult of all *xoon* ordeals, or "tests," as a demonstration of his power. He would insert a wooden-tipped arrow under the skin just below the collarbone and somehow pull it diagonally across his chest, withdrawing it at his waist. She would make grimaces of terrible pain while telling about it. She often sang the chant he had sung while performing, and once she repeated some of his words:

"My body is in darkness. I am, myself, to pierce it with an arrow."

This was the time when he had not sufficiently "prepared" the "channel" through which the arrow was to pass. He bled afterward, which he would not have, had he been in complete control.

Once she became annoyed with me. I was showing her copies of the photographs that accompany Martin Gusinde's volume. Included among them are several of the "spirits" of the *hain*, actually men disguised by paint and masks. When she saw the first of these she pushed it aside, refused to look at the others, and scowling at me, said that *no es para los civilizados*, meaning whites should not have seen them.

The last weeks before I was to leave I wanted to take her out for a ride. The administrator of a large hotel recently built on the edge of Lake Fagnano had shown sympathy for Lola so I told him of my wish. One day he came for us in his station wagon as he had promised. Lola dressed up in her new clothes and took all of her money with her for fear that her hut might be robbed during her absence, which was very unlikely. We spent two days and a night in the luxurious hotel where, as winter was nearing, we were the only guests. Before each meal the administrator asked Lola what she would most like to eat. She invariably replied—fish. She sat for hours in front of the large fireplace chatting with us, with the men who were working in the hotel, and with occasional neighbors who passed by. From the immense dining room, which overlooked the lake, she pointed out the hunting grounds of her grandfather, Alakin.

As the date of my departure drew near, she began asking me when I was to return. I told her I would come the following year if I could manage it. From what I tried to explain to her she surmised that I lived on a big sheep farm near Buenos Aires and that my *patrón* had sent me to record her voice because he knew a great deal about the Indians and liked them. She had never left the island and only knew that beyond there was a "big town" called Buenos Aires. She inquired time and again about my *patrón*, asking if I were sure that he would send me back again. The more she inquired, the more I reassured her that I would return. My *patrón* became "our" *patrón*. On the day of my departure she gave me a basket she had recently finished. Previously I had offered to buy it from her, but she had always refused to sell it, saying she had promised it to someone else long before I came. Now she put the basket in my hands, saying that I was to give it to our *patrón*.

When I returned to Paris I gave it to Lévi-Strauss, telling him it was from Lola. He put it carefully under a glass in his office.

Lola refused to leave the reservation that winter. Because of her age and failing health she had been taken to Río Grande the year before. But there she had passed the days sitting near a stove, drowsing when she was not being scolded by the mistress of the house for being sullen, lazy, and dirty. This winter she was determined to stay in the country, on the land she knew, and never again to leave. I tried to persuade her to spend the winter with a part-Indian woman, Enriqueta de Santin, who was very fond of her and who lived nearby. Lola refused. The last time I went to see her I took Angela Louij with me and she remained some ten days after my departure. Then Lola was alone except for the daily visits of the *puestero* who brought her firewood, water, and meat. The winter of that year, 1966, was unusually severe with temperatures of 30 degrees below zero, and Lola was virtually snowed in from July until several days before her death in October. When she became ill, the *puestero* went on horseback to notify the Rural Police Officer at Lake Kami. Using a tractor, they transported her to the main road, and from there she was taken by car to Río Grande where she died in the government hospital a few days later. It was the end of the winter in Tierra del Fuego, October 9, 1966.

PART TWO

ADAPTATION AND TECHNOLOGY   In 1952 two well-known anthropologists, A. L. Kroeber and Clyde Kluckhohn, compiled a list of 160 separate definitions of culture, each by a different anthropologist, along with an additional 100 discussions or partial definitions.[1] Although each definition has a degree of usefulness, one can perhaps be excused if he sees in all this a certain tendency toward academic hair splitting. Despite the fact that anthropologists use the word "culture" constantly, in recent years many have tended to concentrate on studying adaptive behavior. The word "culture" hardly appears at all in the four papers in this part, for what is being discussed here is not a thing but a process—the process of human adaptation. Here an analogy with the biological sciences may be appropriate. One scholar has observed that: "When the ecologist enters a forest or a meadow he sees not merely what is there, but what is happening there."[2] The anthropologist who is concerned with questions of human adaptation and is willing to adopt an ecological approach is likely to see human behavior in the same way. He will look for processes of interaction between parts of the physical environment and particular human societies.

The Ecology of Ancient Hunters

As Paul S. Martin shows in his discussion of "Pleistocene Overkill," these processes of interaction imply a two-sided situation. To acquire the full impact of Martin's paper we should try to imagine the situation from the point of view of the mammoth, trying to cope with the new conditions of the Late Pleistocene epoch in North America and in the Old World. The climate was changing, but more important, a new predator had appeared on the scene—man. Martin calls these men "superpredators," because archeological evidence shows these people to have been exceptionally well equipped and skilled for big-game hunting on a large scale. Mammoths and other large game of this epoch were extremely vulnerable to these hunters; from the human point of view these animals must have appeared as a vast, untapped resource, ripe for the taking. By looking at the late Pleistocene from the point of view of man on the one hand and the mammoth on the other, it is easy to appreciate Martin's hypothesis that mainly man, rather than changes in climate, led to the extinction of many species of the Pleistocene megafauna.

Martin's idea is a good example of a *testable hypothesis* in science. He asks: "Can the overkill hypothesis be disproved by future experiments or discoveries? To discount the hypothesis one need simply identify a major wave of extinction anywhere in the world in the Late Pleistocene prior to man's arrival." Such a test lies well within the capabilities of archeology today, and Martin's challenge will no doubt be examined by archeologists in different parts of the world. Whether or not Martin's hypothesis is correct is less important than the fact that he has asked the right questions of his data and has thus stimulated research in a worthwhile direction. As testing proceeds, Martin may need to abandon or modify his hypothesis, but at this time it stands as the most economical explanation for the evidence presently available on this question.

If, for the time being, we accept Martin's view, then it seems obvious that the big-game hunters of the Late Pleistocene achieved an adaptation that was unstable and ultimately unsuccessful both for themselves and for the animals they hunted. When the great herds of Pleistocene game disappeared, so did the intensive hunting way of life that was based upon them. Martin concludes from this that "the subtle lesson of sustained yields, of not killing the goose that lays the golden eggs, may have been learned the hard way, and forgotten, many times before the twentieth century." In an industrial age where overexploitation of the physical environment is commonplace, this seems to be a timely comment.

Primitive Technology

The Australian Aborigines in "Chipping Stones in the Outback" represent quite a different adaptation from the superpredators described by Martin. These hunters and gatherers live in an extremely impoverished environment and depend heavily on plant foods for their diet. Because of the relative scarcity and unreliability of food and water resources, they must move frequently and over long distances. Their kind of nomadism puts a premium on portability in their material culture. The Aborigines, who lack any kind of horse or dog traction to assist them, cannot carry a large array of tools with them in their travels, particularly if these tools are bulky or heavy. They solve this problem in three ways: (1) They use multipurpose tools that are lightweight and easy to carry; (2) they use tools (mainly of stone) that can be left where they are needed and reused whenever that particular place is visited; and (3) they take the knowledge of tool making with them and use this knowledge when the need arises to make necessary tools from raw materials immediately at hand. Unlike people such as the Eskimo, who manufacture complex and specialized tool kits in advance of the varied tasks before them, the Aborigines depend more on a simple but flexible set of stoneworking techniques that can be applied on the spot almost anywhere they happen to be. Perhaps, as students raised in Western society, where an advanced and specialized technology is taken for granted, we might be tempted to rate the Eskimo type of adaptation more highly, because it corresponds more to our own cultural expectations. But, as the "instant tools" employed by the Aborigines demonstrate, we must also be prepared to appreciate the flexibility and resourceful opportunism that characterize the Aborigines' stone technology.

Slash-and-Burn Agriculture

Slash-and-burn agriculture (called *swidden* in Europe, *milpa* in Central America, and *shifting cultivation* in Southeast Asia) has characteristically been viewed by Western-trained agronomists and other agricultural experts as a primitive and inefficient type of economy, despite the fact that millions of people in the world today depend entirely on it for their livelihood. As anthropologist Harold Conklin has pointed out, descriptions of slash-and-burn agriculture are often phrased in negative terms,[3] stressing the lack of draft animals and manure fertilization, low input of human labor, use of poor soils, low population densities, and lack of special tools for this type of farming (aside from an axe or machete). Another anthropologist, Clifford Geertz, has further emphasized: "Aside from the fact that most of these depreciatory statements are dubious as unqualified generalizations (and a few are simply incorrect), they are not of much help in understanding how swidden farming systems work."[4] The paper by W. M. S. Russell attempts to show how slash-and-burn agriculture succeeds in several different parts of the world and to point out the nature of the adaptation it represents.

Given the generally negative view that has prevailed concerning slash-and-burn agriculture, what can be said positively for it? Geertz and other anthropologists who have closely observed this agricultural system emphasize the fact that it tends to maintain the natural forest ecosystem that was already present.[5] This is accomplished through the practice of generalized or mixed cropping; that is, by raising a wide variety of plants in a single garden plot or field rather than depending on a single or limited number of plant species in the way that modern, fallow agriculture tends to do. This also involves frequent use of food plants that are native to the forest where the farming is carried out and relatively long periods of what Russell calls "forest fallow" or regrowth of forest plants to allow nutrients to build up within the soil. By approximating the variety and pattern of native forest growth in their gardens, slash-and-burn farmers minimize the risk of soil exhaustion and consequent deforestation and erosion. On the grounds that it conserves rather than depletes the natural resources of the environment, slash-and-burn agriculture may be said to be highly adaptive.

But what about productivity? It is true, as Russell and others point out, that slash-and-burn agriculture gives lower absolute yields than do more specialized systems of fallow cultivation. But figures on absolute yields can be misleading, especially if one adopts only the short-term view. There is also the element of risk to consider. Anthropologist Roy A. Rappaport has shown that complex ecosystems involving interdependencies between large numbers of species are more stable than simpler ecosystems where fewer species are involved. He notes that, "Therefore, if one or another species is decimated, the entire system is not necessarily endangered."[6] In short, monoculture (agricultural systems that depend upon a single or very limited number of crops) is risky. A plague or a drought can have devastating effects on a society that depends for its livelihood on a narrow spectrum of plant crops. In the case of slash-and-burn agriculture, the old axiom about safety in numbers could be rephrased to denote safety in variety. An appreciation of the factors that make slash-and-burn agriculture a successful human adaptation to the natural environment helps us to understand the long persistence of this farming technique and its continuing popularity in the face of introduced methods of Western agriculture, just as an awareness of the maladaptive factors of Late Pleistocene big-game hunting helps us to understand why both the hunting cultures and the animal species being hunted disappeared from the face of the earth.

Ecological Adaptation in Culture

In the field of human behavior, things are not always what they seem. Earlier I stressed how anthropologists try to penetrate the façade or "performance" staged for their benefit by the members of the society they are studying. In considering the broader question of human adaptations, we are faced with a similar problem. Russell's discussion of slash-and-burn systems of agriculture shows that this technique is more positively adapted to a forest habitat than many Western-trained agricultural experts and advisors had been willing to recognize. Similarly the widely accepted notion that the sacred cattle of India (which are protected from slaughter by sacred Hindu tradition) are an economic drag on the society turns out, under closer examination by Marvin Harris in "The Myth of the Sacred Cow," to be false. Harris's examination is a good example of the kind of skepticism revealed in this vignette by Stuart Chase:

A scientist and his friend were driving through Wyoming and saw a flock of sheep up on a mesa.
"They've just been sheared," said the friend.
"They seem to be, on this side," replied the scientist.[7]

Harris notes how easy it is to form the impression that the maintenance of large numbers of largely unproductive cattle in India is maladaptive. Measured by the yardstick of Western-style dairy and ranch productivity, Indian cattle do poorly. But, without invoking the explanation of *ahimsa* (the Hindu concept of the sanctity of life), Harris demonstrates that there are compelling economic reasons for understanding why cattle are positively adaptive in Indian culture and hence why their use and veneration persist in the face of strong government-sponsored efforts to do away with them. By focusing attention on the traction, dung-fuel, and dung-manuring roles of Indian cattle instead of on meat and milk, the anthropologist leads us to appreciate the significance of cattle in terms of the needs and expectations of an Indian farmer rather than those of an American rancher or a European dairyman.

Notes

1   A. L. Kroeber and Clyde Kluckhohn, *Culture: A Critical Review of Concepts and Definitions*, New York, Random House, 1963.
2   P. B. Sears, *Life and Environment*, New York, Columbia University Teachers College, 1939.
3   H. Conklin, *Hanunóo Agriculture in the Philippines*, Rome, Food and Agricultural Organization of the United Nations, 1957, p. 149.
4   Clifford Geertz, *Agricultural Involution*, Berkeley, University of California Press, 1971, p. 16.
5   Ibid., pp. 16–17.
6   Roy A. Rappaport, "The Flow of Energy in an Agricultural Society," *Scientific American*, vol. 224, no. 3, 1971, p. 130.
7   Chase, op. cit., p. 11.

PAUL S. MARTIN

PLEISTOCENE OVERKILL About ten thousand years ago, as glaciers retreated into Canada and as man moved southward at the end of the last Ice Age, North America suddenly and strangely lost most of its large animals. Native North American mammals exceeding 100 pounds in adult body weight were reduced by roughly 70 per cent. The casualty list includes mammoths, mastodon, many species of horses and camels, four genera of ground sloths, two of peccary, shrub oxen, antelope, two genera of saber-toothed cats, the dire wolf, the giant beaver, tapirs, and others totaling over 100 species. Despite this fantastic loss of large animals during the Pleistocene, the most recent geologic epoch, the fossil record shows no loss of small vertebrates, plants, aquatic organisms, or marine life.

One need not be a Pleistocene geologist to ask the obvious question: What happened? To date there is no obvious answer, certainly not one acceptable to any consensus of scientists interested in the mystery. The question of just what occurred to bring about this unprecedented extinction continues to provoke a storm of controversy.

Extinction, we know, is not an abnormal fate in the life of a species. When all the niches, or "jobs," in a biotic community are filled, extinction must occur as rapidly as the evolution of new species. The fossil record of the last ten million years bears witness to this fact, for it is replete with extinct animals that were sacrificed to make room for new and presumably superior species. But this is a normal state of affairs from a paleontologist's point of view.

However, the extinction that took place at the end of the Pleistocene did not comply with biological rules of survival. Unlike former extinctions, such as occurred in the Miocene, Pliocene, and Early Pleistocene, Late Pleistocene extinction of large mammals far exceeded replacement by new species that could easily have been accommodated by the prevailing habitat. The complete removal of North American horses, for example, represents the loss of a lineage of grass-eaters, without the loss of the grass! It left the horse niche empty for at least eight thousand years, until the Spaniards introduced Old World horses and bur-ros. Some of these then escaped to reoccupy part of their pre-historic range. Today, tens of thousands of wild horses and bur-ros still live along remote parts of the Colorado River and in the wild lands of the West. Certainly nothing happened at the end of the Pleistocene to destroy horse habitat. What, then, caused these animals, not to mention mammoths, camels, sloths, and others, to become extinct?

Like the horses, camels first evolved in North America many millions of years ago. They then spread into South America and crossed to the Old World by means of the Bering bridge. Cross-ing in the opposite direction were elephants, which soon pros-pered in the New World, judging by the abundance of mam-moth and mastodon teeth in Pleistocene outcrops. From their evolutionary center in South America came a variety of eden-tates, including ground sloths and glyptodonts, the former spreading north to Alaska. But by the end of the Pleistocene, the majority of these herbivorous species had completely disap-peared. Only relatively small species within these groups sur-vived—the alpaca and llama among the camels of South America, and the relatively small edentates such as anteaters, armadillos, and tree sloths.

There was no obvious ecological substitution by other large herbivores competing for the same resources. Too many large mammals were lost, too few were replaced, and there was too little change among smaller plants and animals to accept this extinction as a normal event in the process of North American mammalian evolution.

One hypothesis commonly proposed for the abrupt and almost simultaneous extinction of large mammals is that of sud-den climatic change. We know that climates did change many times in the Pleistocene—a three-million-year period of repeated glacial advance and retreat—so perhaps the great herds were decimated in this way. A sizable group of vertebrate paleontolo-gists believe that that is indeed what happened. They maintain that with the retreat of the glaciers the early post-glacial climate grew more continental—summers became hotter, and winters colder and supposedly more severe than they had been during the time of the ice advance. The result was an upset in the breeding season, a lethal cold sterility imposed on species of large mammals adapted for reproduction at what came to be the wrong season. Perhaps also the large Ice Age mammals were confronted for the first time with excessive snow cover and blue northers, which even today can kill thousands of cattle and sheep in the High Plains. Paleozoologist John Guilday at the Carnegie Museum believes that accelerated competition occurred among the large mammals before they could readjust to the change in vegetation and climate. They proceeded to exterminate their food supply and themselves in a morbid togetherness. Then, according to Guilday, the early North American hunters who arrived over the Bering bridge delivered the coup de grâce to the few remaining large mammals after the great herds were already sadly depleted.

But we have no evidence that the large mammals were under competitive stress, then or at any other time in the Pleistocene. We know that they had witnessed, and certainly survived, the advance and retreat of earlier glacial ice sheets. And among today's large mammals most are remarkably tolerant of different types of environments. Some large desert mammals can endure months without drinking; others, such as musk ox, live the year round in the high Arctic. Reindeer and wildebeest migrate hundreds of miles to pick their pasture. Why should we believe that the great mammals of the Pleistocene were less adaptable?

Furthermore, while climatic changes had some effect upon existing fauna and its habitat, extinction apparently occurred when range conditions were actually improving for many species. From the fossil pollen record we know that mastodon and woodland musk ox of eastern North America occupied spruce forests ten to twelve thousand years ago, a habitat then rapidly expanding northward from its constricted position bordering the Wisconsin ice sheet. And the western plains grassland was extensive and spreading at the time of the extinction of grazing horses, mammoths, and antelopes.

Another objection to cold winter climates as an explanation for extinction arises when one looks to the American Tropics. There, far more species became extinct during this period than in the temperate regions. More extinct Pleistocene genera were found in a single fauna in Bolivia than are known in the richest of the fossil faunas of the United States. However, the Tropics never experienced the zero temperatures of North America. This being the case, the climatic change hypothesis cannot account for the large-scale extinction in that part of the world.

Nor can it account for the extinction that occurred on the large islands of the world, such as on Madagascar and New Zealand, which did not take place until less than a thousand years ago. In the case of the giant bird, *Aepyornis*, of Madagas-

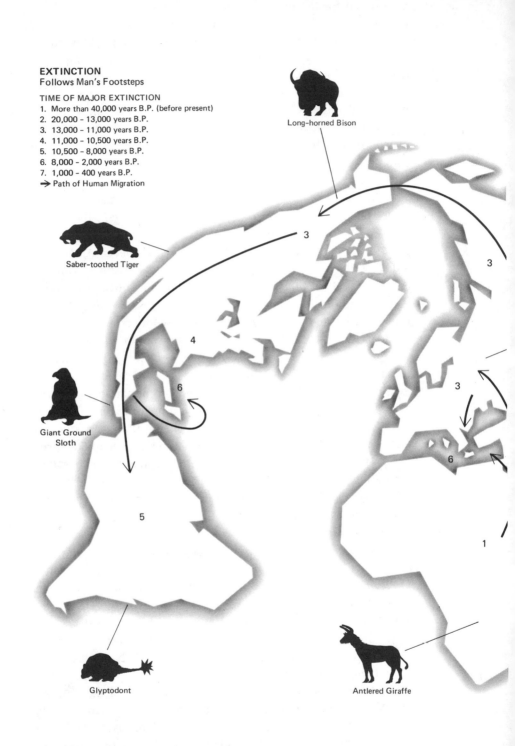

EXTINCTION
Follows Man's Footsteps

TIME OF MAJOR EXTINCTION
1. More than 40,000 years B.P. (before present)
2. 20,000 – 13,000 years B.P.
3. 13,000 – 11,000 years B.P.
4. 11,000 – 10,500 years B.P.
5. 10,500 – 8,000 years B.P.
6. 8,000 – 2,000 years B.P.
7. 1,000 – 400 years B.P.
→ Path of Human Migration

Long-horned Bison

Saber-toothed Tiger

Giant Ground
Sloth

Glyptodont

Antlered Giraffe

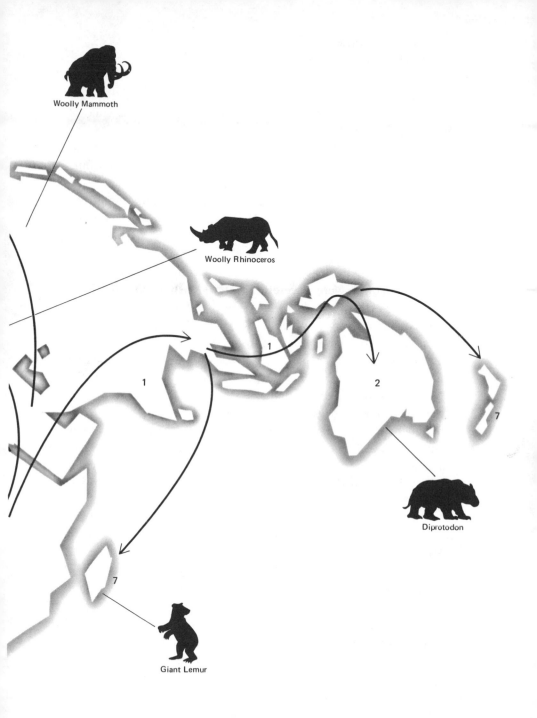

Woolly Mammoth

Woolly Rhinoceros

1

1

2

7

Diprotodon

7

Giant Lemur

car, and the giant moa from New Zealand, carbon 14 dates indicate that these birds did not perish until long after the time of major worldwide climatic upset.

Without doubt, the climatic disturbances that affected North America during the Pleistocene proved equally disturbing in New Zealand. During the last glaciation one-third of the South Island was ice covered and the remainder of the island was much colder than today. The subsequent melting of the glaciers brought a worldwide rise in sea level and divided the country in two. During the post-glacial period intense volcanic eruptions blanketed the North Island, so that by 2,000 years ago large parts of it were covered by sterile ash supporting only dwarfed vegetation. In fact, sheep raising failed in these areas until cobalt and other trace elements were added to the pastures. Yet, some 27 species of moas apparently survived the natural climatic catastrophes of the Pleistocene and disappeared only after East Polynesian invaders, the predecessors of the Maori, arrived sometime about or before A.D. 900. Thus, any credibility the climatic change hypothesis may have when applied to a single region vanishes when the global pattern is considered. Pleistocene experts generally believe that, whatever their magnitude, major climatic changes of the last 50,000 years occurred at approximately the same time throughout the world—the extinctions did not.

My own hypothesis is that man, and man alone, was responsible for the unique wave of Late Pleistocene extinction—a case of overkill rather than "overchill" as implied by the climatic change theory. This view is neither new nor widely held, but when examined on a global basis, in which Africa, North America, Australia, Eurasia, and the islands of the world are considered, the pattern and timing of large-scale extinction corresponds to only one event—the arrival of prehistoric hunters.

Some anthropologists, such as Loren Eiseley of the University of Pennsylvania, have challenged the man-caused extinction theory on the grounds that African megafauna did not suffer the same fate as the large mammals of North America. At first, this appears to be a sound argument since that continent now contains some 40 genera of large mammals that were around during the Pleistocene. Africa's fabulous plains fauna has long been regarded as a picture of what the American Pleistocene was like prior to extinction, at least in terms of size and diversity of the big mammals. During the million years of hominid evolution in Africa, it seems as if man and his predecessors would have had ample time to exterminate its fauna. And if, as I believe, Late Paleolithic hunters in the New World could have succeeded in destroying more than 100 species of large mammals in a period of only 1,000 years, then African hunters, it seems, should at least have made a dent on that continent's mammals.

It turns out that they did, for today's living megafauna in Africa represents only about 70 per cent of the species that were present during the Late Pleistocene. Thus, while the proportion of African mammals that perished during the Pleistocene was less than that in North America, the loss in number of species was still considerable. In addition to the large mammals that now inhabit the African continent, an imaginary Pleistocene game park would have been stocked with such species as the antlered giraffe, a number of giant pigs, the stylohipparion horse, a great long-horned buffalo, a giant sheep, and an ostrich of larger size than is known at present. In Africa, as in America, the wave of Pleistocene extinction took only the large animals.

The African extinction has also been attributed to climatic and climate-related change. L. S. B. Leakey would explain extinction of the giant African fauna as the result of drought. If so, the drought strangely did not affect nearby Madagascar. On that island, barely 250 miles from the African shore, extinction of giant lemurs, pygmy hippopotamuses, giant birds, and tortoises did not occur until a much later date, in fact not until within the last 1,000 years.

African big game extinction appears to coincide in time with the first record of fire, or at least of charcoal, in archeological sites. In addition, most extinct fauna is last found in many locations associated with the distinctive stone tools of Early Stone Age (Acheulean) hunters. If fire was used in hunting, man-caused extinction becomes easier to understand, because fire drives necessarily involve large amounts of waste—whole herds must be decimated in order to kill the few animals sought for food. Perhaps fire became a major weapon in the hands of the Acheulean big game hunters enabling them to encircle whole herds of animals.

In any event, African extinction ended during the period of the Early Stone Age hunters. This fact raises the possibility that the cultures that succeeded the Acheulean developed more selective methods of hunting and may even have learned to harvest the surviving large mammals on a sustained yield basis.

Even during the last 100 years, when modern weapons have reduced the ranges of many species, there has been no loss of whole genera of terrestrial mammals, as occurred during the time of the early hunters.

The case of Australia also supports the hypothesis of man-caused extinction. On that continent, no evidence of extinction, without replacement by other species, can be found until after men had inhabited the island, at least 14,000 years ago. About this time, various species of large marsupials perished, including the rhino-sized *Diprotodon* and the giant kangaroo.

About 12,000 years ago, when the Paleo-Indians swept into North America across the Bering bridge, through unglaciated Alaska, and down the melting ice corridor east of the Cordilleras, we can be confident that they were old hands at hunting woolly mammoths and other large Eurasian mammals. In contrast, the New World mammoth and other species of big game had never encountered man, and were unprepared for escaping the strange two-legged creature who used fire and stone-tipped spears to hunt them in communal bands. Probably the New World fauna of the time was no more suspicious of man than are the fearless animals that now live in the Galápagos and other regions uninhabited by men. In any case, radiocarbon dates indicate that North American extinction followed very closely on the heels of the big game hunters. The Paleo-Indians easily found and hunted the gregarious species that ranged over the grasslands, deserts, or other exposed habitat. As the hunters increased in number and spread throughout the continent, large animals whose low rate of reproduction was insufficient to offset the sudden burden of supporting a "superpredator" soon perished.

Early man may not have been able to avoid killing the herd animals in excess. To capture *any* members of a bison or elephant herd, it was necessary to kill them all, for instance, by driving them over a cliff. Even when big game became scarce and small animals became more important in the human diet, the pride and prestige associated with killing an elephant may have continued. This, in fact, seems likely, judging from the prestige

Although the musk ox disappeared along the migratory path taken by Stone Age man, glacial ice sheets effectively sealed off portions of the animal's range and protected it from the nomadic hunters. With the retreat of the glaciers, the species spread westward through northern Canada and into Alaska.

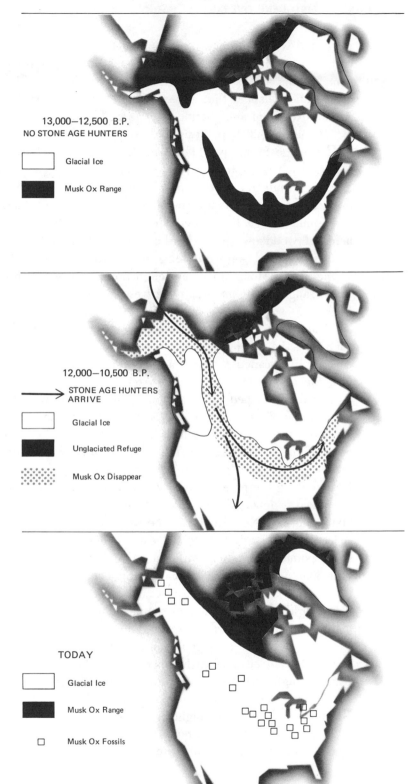

13,000—12,500 B.P.
NO STONE AGE HUNTERS

☐ Glacial Ice

■ Musk Ox Range

12,000—10,500 B.P.

→ STONE AGE HUNTERS ARRIVE

☐ Glacial Ice

■ Unglaciated Refuge

▨ Musk Ox Disappear

TODAY

☐ Glacial Ice

■ Musk Ox Range

☐ Musk Ox Fossils

associated with the unnecessary killing that persists even today within our own society. By virtue of his cultural development, man became a superpredator, less susceptible to the biological checks and balances that apparently prevent such predators as Arctic foxes from annihilating their prey, the Arctic hare.

If the overkill hypothesis is valid, how did *any* large mammals manage to survive? There are several explanations. Some species, such as tapirs, capybaras, deer, white-lipped peccaries, anteaters, and tree sloths, took refuge in the vast forests of tropical America. In temperate regions, solitary moose and bear also found refuge in wooded areas, perhaps with a few small herds of woodland bison, at the time when soon-to-be-extinct species of giant bison were being annihilated by Folsom hunters on the plains. Mountain sheep found protection on the roughest desert ranges while mountain goats escaped only in the northern Rockies.

The musk ox, that conspicuous and easily hunted game animal of the open tundra, was wiped out in Eurasia, but in America it escaped through a piece of paleogeographic good luck. Since parts of the Canadian Arctic Archipelago and Greenland were untouched by glaciation, tundra habitat was available through the Pleistocene for this species and for barren ground caribou. Some of these animals remained in the "safe region" north of the continental ice sheet, a zone unknown to the early hunters. They thus escaped the fate suffered by most species located along the path taken by nomadic hunters as they pushed into Alaska, down western Canada, across the northern United States, and into New England. The Keewatin and Laurentian ice sheets provided a barrier to the early hunters whose distinctive spear points and other artifacts are unknown in the eastern Canadian Arctic. With the final melting of ice, less than 6,000 years ago, the Greenland musk oxen were at last exposed to the New World Indians and Eskimos. But the wandering superpredators—the Paleo-Indians—were no longer present. The Eskimo had the good fortune, or good sense, to harvest musk oxen on a sustained yield basis, and the species was able to spread westward through northern Canada, ultimately recovering part of its Alaskan range. If the woolly mammoth had also occupied the Greenland refuge, it too might have survived the Pleistocene.

Can the overkill hypothesis be disproved by future experiments or discoveries? To discount the hypothesis one need simply identify a major wave of extinction anywhere in the world in the Late Pleistocene prior to man's arrival. To date, such evidence has not been found. Quite the opposite, in fact, since the chronological sequence of extinction follows closely upon man's footsteps—occurring first in Africa and southern Asia, next in Australia, then through northern Eurasia and into North and South America, much later in the West Indies, and finally, during the last 1,000 years, in Madagascar and New Zealand. The pattern shows that Late Pleistocene extinction did not occur in all locations at the same time, as it would have if there had been a sudden climatic change or perhaps a cataclysmic destruction of the earth's atmosphere with lethal radiation caused by cosmic ray bombardment, another common hypothesis. Since no synchronous destruction of plants or of plant communities is known, the long-held belief that climatic change caused extinction lacks credibility.

I do not pretend that the overkill hypothesis explains how, why, or even how many early hunters were involved. It seems reasonable to assume that fire and fire drives were a major weapon; possibly plant poisons were used in the Tropics. To the objection that too few spear points or other Stone Age artifacts have been found in the Americas to prove there was a sizable prehistoric human population, one may assert, tongue in cheek, that too few fossils of Pleistocene ground sloths, mammoths, camels, and saber-toothed cats have been found to prove there was a sizable prehistoric population of them either. The obvious difficulty with the "spear point" argument is that even the best fossil localities, with or without artifacts, do not yield data that can be reliably converted into population estimates. The case for overkill is best presented as a "least improbable hypothesis," and is not based on extensive knowledge of how prehistoric hunters may have carried out their hunting. Nor is there much hope that we will ever learn more of their techniques than the little we now know. The essence of the argument is based upon the simple matter of Late Pleistocene chronology. In no part of the world does massive unbalanced faunal extinction occur without man the hunter on the scene.

To certain comfortable concepts about pristine wilderness and ancient man, the implications of this hypothesis are startling, even revolutionary. For example, that business of the noble savage, a child of nature, living in an unspoiled Garden of Eden until the "discovery" of the New World by Europeans is apparently untrue, since the destruction of fauna, if not of habitat, was far greater before Columbus than at any time since. The subtle lesson of sustained yields, of not killing the goose that lays the golden eggs, may have been learned the hard way, and forgotten, many times before the twentieth century.

A related conceptual mistake, if the hypothesis holds, may be the long-held opposition of range ecologists to the introduction of exotic large mammals in America. Part of the opposition to the introduction of alien species is based on the idea that native North American mammals are already using all the available browsing and grazing space that could or should be occupied in this country. But remembering the numerous species of the Pleistocene, it is difficult to imagine that native mountain sheep, bison, antelope, deer, and elk occupy all available niches in the American ecosystem. The concept of game ranching, of keeping both cattle and native game species on the same range in order to make maximum use of pastures, is catching on in Africa. Since our own ranch industry is essentially a monoculture of either cattle or sheep, perhaps it's time to take a fresh look at the unfilled niches on the American ranges. Domestic livestock, wild game, and the range itself may well benefit from a greater diversity of fauna and a partial restoration of the complex ecosystem that was America for millions of years, until man arrived.

RICHARD A. GOULD

CHIPPING STONES IN THE OUTBACK   Click! Click! The thin
sound of stones being struck together reached me through the hot
summer air as I walked along the bottom of the dry creek bed
toward camp in the Clutterbuck Hills of the desert area of
Western Australia. Rounding the last bend I found an aboriginal
man, sitting cross-legged, striking flakes from a water-worn
pebble. I realized as I watched him that I was witnessing a scene
that has taken place repeatedly throughout the whole of human
history, from the time of earliest man to the present. Stone
chippings like these, mundane artifacts to be sure, have been one
of the most important sources of evidence for archeologists
studying the cultures of ancient man. Indeed in some places they
are the only evidence. Because of their importance, archeologists
constantly have sought ways to interpret how these ancient tools
were made, their functions, and their role in prehistoric cultures.
Furthermore, the archeologist has often used these same tools to
distinguish one group of prehistoric people from another.

Most archeologists begin their interpretations along strictly
archeological lines. By this I mean they examine the artifact
itself in an attempt to determine its method of manufacture and
its use.

A stone arrowhead, for example, is usually easy to identify
by inspection. Other kinds of stone tools may be harder to
interpret, requiring close and at times microscopic analysis of
such things as breakage and wear patterns, weight, size, raw
material, and different kinds of chipping.

Archeologists also check their excavation notes to see if
the artifact might be associated with something else that will
provide clues. If, for instance, a certain style of projectile point
is characteristically found associated with the remains of a certain species of game, the archeologist may infer not only the
basic function of the artifact but also its role in a special pattern
of hunting.

Inevitably, archeologists must turn to historical or ethnographic sources for ideas on which to base any but the most
superficial of interpretations. How much harder it is to under-

stand the ancient arrowheads you have uncovered if you do not know about the bow and arrow!

The reports left by early explorers and chroniclers as well as by trained ethnographers do not always supply the needed background information. These explorers and chroniclers may have been more interested in finding gold, looking for good pasture and farming land, or other practical matters than in collecting facts about the industries of the aboriginals they encountered. Ethnologists, while they are interested in the native peoples of an area, tend to be more concerned about ceremonies, kinship systems, language, and other matters than with the parts of the culture that are likely to leave behind tangible remains— such as stone tools, pottery, and other material "hardware"—for archeologists to excavate and study.

Today there is a growing interest in the lives and behavior of ancient people who lived by hunting and gathering wild foods. Most of human prehistory is the story of hunter-gatherers, and it is therefore no surprise to find that many archeologists have directed their efforts entirely toward recovering the cultures of ancient hunter-gatherers. But these archeologists, like myself, have discovered gaps in our knowledge of living, present-day hunter-gatherers. The Congo Pygmies, the Bushmen of the Kalahari Desert, and the aborigines of the Australian desert are about the only people left in the world today who still live entirely this way, and in all three cases rapid changes in their cultures are coming about through contact with Europeans. The time is fast drawing to a close when people like these can still be found living in their normal habitat, depending on their traditional foraging economy.

Although archeologists spend much of their time classifying the stone tools they uncover, hardly anyone has ever attempted to learn how the native peoples themselves classify their stone tools. It has been argued that archeologists should try to make their systems of classification conform to those of the people who originally made and used the artifacts. Thus the archeological ordering of the materials would be more realistic, for it would reflect what went on in the mind of the native user rather than simply what went on in the mind of the archeologist, and would thereby increase the prospect for meaningful interpretation. This is a good argument, but it presupposes that there is a body of evidence on how native people do, in fact, classify their artifacts. Such evidence is generally lacking, especially for hunter-gatherers.

Of the three societies available for study, only the aborigines of the Gibson Desert of Western Australia were known to make and use stone tools as a regular part of their behavior. My wife and I went there in 1966 and lived with aboriginal families both in the desert and on Aboriginal Reserves for about fifteen months.

Owing to their isolation in this arid country, direct contact with Europeans came only in the last two or three years for some of these aborigines, with at least one family being contacted by government patrols as late as July, 1967. These are mainly Ngatatjara and Pintupi people, all of whom speak various dialects of Pitjantjatjara, a language in use over wide areas of the western desert of Australia. In the desert, these people live entirely by hunting and collecting wild foods, moving on foot over long distances from one water source to another. The nomadic nature of their existence puts a premium on portability in their material culture.

The desert aborigines classify their flaked stone tools into two categories, basing this distinction on the cross-sectional shape of the working edge (*yiri*) of the stone flake from which the tool is fashioned. A fairly thick flake with a steep working edge suitable for adzing or scraping in making wooden objects is called *purpunpa*. A knifelike flake with a thin, sharp edge suited for slicing or cutting is termed *tjimari*. In nearly every case, adze flakes (the term "adze" used here is not to be confused with the much larger adze more commonly thought of as used by ship-wrights or by native woodworkers in some parts of New Guinea) are retouched along an edge to provide a sharp scraping surface. They are almost always hafted to the base of a wooden club or spear-thrower. In appearance, they resemble prehistoric stone tools (called scrapers by archeologists) from other parts of the world. Perhaps some of these were also hafted for use as woodworking tools.

Knives are retouched only if the cutting edge needs it, and this retouching is always done on one side of the edge only. In most cases, however, the extremely sharp edge of the freshly struck flake is regarded as sufficient. Flakes used as knives are sometimes given a "handle" by attaching a lump of gum, made either from spinifex (*Triodia* sp.) or blackboy (*Xanthorrhoea thorntonii*) resin, to the blunt edge of the flake.

Sometimes, if the worker is in a hurry, a sharp flake is selected, used for the immediate task, and discarded afterward.

This often occurs during the butchering of kangaroos and emus, when the man doing the butchering grasps the flake between his thumb and forefinger while slitting the animal's belly, cutting leg tendons, and removing the feet and tail.

Adze flakes are the most distinctive and widespread class of stone artifacts made by the desert aborigines. Among the Pintupi and Ngatatjara people these tools are made in three different ways. First, there is the technique of direct percussion by means of a small hammerstone. The flake is held horizontally, bulbar face upward, in one hand (before being hafted) while sharp blows are directed downward along the edge with a small stone, usually a smooth, rounded pebble. While doing this the worker generally steadies himself by propping the elbow of the arm holding the adze flake against his knee while seated in a cross-legged position. In a matter of from ten to twenty seconds, a row of tiny flakes is removed from the underside of the edge, and the flake is then ready to be hafted to a club or spear-thrower.

Often, however, the flake is first hafted and then trimmed by means of gentle blows struck with a wooden stick. In this case the hafted flake is cradled, bulbar face upward, in the hollow of one hand with the working edge cushioned against the fleshy part of the thumb. The other hand taps a stick along the edge of the flake, detaching a row of small flakes in about twenty seconds.

Finally, there is the most remarkable technique of all—that of biting the flake in order to trim the edge. This practice, which apparently does not damage the teeth, has been observed before among the desert aborigines by Professor Donald Thomson, but it has not been studied in detail. The only other mention of this technique I know of comes from Coronado's chronicler, Casteñada, who observed this method of stone flaking on the Great Plains of North America in 1541. To accomplish this technique successfully the worker must have "flat teeth," that is, teeth with the crowns worn down to a flat, rather than a serrated, surface. This is a common physiological feature among people who normally eat foods containing large amounts of grit.

Another prerequisite for this technique is exceptionally strong jaw muscles. In this respect, too, the desert aborigines are

An aborigine sharpens the edge of a stone adze by biting off small flakes with his teeth.

well endowed, for their diet contains many tough foods, particularly meat that would be regarded as grossly undercooked by European standards.

As a woodworking tool the hafted stone adze is surprisingly efficient. It takes a desert aborigine only about twice as long to complete a woodworking task with a stone adze as with metal chisels and axes. Using metal tools he can produce an undecorated wooden spear-thrower in about four to five hours of continuous work; with a hafted stone adze the same task can take about eight and a half to nine hours.

Perhaps the supreme test of the stone adze comes in making a transverse cut across the grain of a mulga (*Acacia aneura*) stave to form the tip of a digging stock. It is fairly easy to shave away the wood surface if one is working with the grain of the wood, but working across the grain of this hard wood is difficult and requires a special technique. The tip of the digging stick is placed in a small fire and allowed to char. The char is scraped away with the stone adze until the surface is clean, then it is charred and scraped again, and the process is repeated until the point on the tip of the digging stick is completed.

Some archeologists have speculated on the possible advantages of "fire hardening" of spear tips and digging sticks recovered from ancient sites in Europe and elsewhere, but the behavior of the desert aborigines indicates that, far from hardening the wooden tip, this technique of charring serves to soften the outer surface of the wood and makes it easier to scrape away with a stone adze or abrading stone.

During use there is a tendency for the center of an adze flake to wear faster than the outer edges, resulting in a slightly concave edge. Retouching is aimed at straightening and sharpening and may occur as many as twenty times during the course of making one undecorated spear-thrower. Usually the flake is reversed in the haft during the job, and the flake is finally worn down to an absolutely characteristic slug. Under magnification these worn slugs have minute "ridges" running across the steep face of the flake. They are among the most common artifacts in aboriginal campsites.

There is one type of adzing tool used by these aborigines that has never been reported before from the Australian desert. This is a small engraving tool that is included within the range of artifacts called *purpunpa*, but which is also given a special term, *pitjuru-pitjuru.* It consists of a small flake with a fairly thick but narrow tip. In about half the cases I observed, this flake was given some secondary trimming after being hafted, but otherwise it was not retouched until it grew dull from use. It is set into a gum haft at the end of a short handle, 10 to 16 inches long. Unlike ordinary adzes, this tool is regarded as a sacred object and is never shown to women, children, or uncircumcised men. It is the most specialized stone tool made by the desert aborigines and is used exclusively for making the incised decorations on sacred boards and decorated spear-throwers.

All flake knives are called *tjimari*, regardless of their size (which ranges from ¾ to 4 inches in length and ½ to 2½ inches in width) or the degree to which they are treated as sacred. The larger flake knives (generally without a handle) may serve more mundane functions, such as cutting up small game, sinews, and a variety of other domestic purposes. Unlike smaller knives that are used mainly for circumcising male novices, these large knives have no sacred connotations and can appear openly in camp with no restrictions on who can see or use them.

In most cases these knives are discarded after only a few uses, and no effort is made to resharpen them. Thus they rarely show much in the way of secondary trimming and could be extremely difficult for an archeologist to recognize once the gum handle has decomposed. At times the hafted adze may be used as a cutting tool in butchering game, but this is unusual and happens only when no flake knives are readily available.

A *yalkara*, or hand ax, generally consists of nothing more than a hand-held rock with a sharp edge, picked up off the ground when needed and thrown away after use. On every occasion when I have been present, these have been used only for woodworking tasks, such as cutting spear shafts or detaching wooden slabs for shaping into spear-throwers or sacred boards. This latter task is accomplished with wooden wedges and either a large rock or a piece of wood used as a hammer. My informants say that sometimes they trimmed the working edge of the hand ax with rough percussion flaking, but this has been less frequent since steel axes have become available.

One of the usual explanations for the use of Paleolithic hand axes in Africa and Europe has been the suggestion by many archeologists that they were used in butchering large game. In most cases, there is no reason to doubt this interpretation, but it is interesting to point out that the desert aborigines butcher all their large game (kangaroos, euros, emus) by means of wooden wedges, using untrimmed rocks or logs for pounding and small

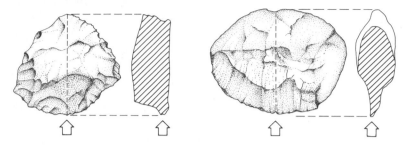

The two basic categories of flaked stone tools are the broad-edged adzing tool (*purpunpa*), top, and the narrow-edged knife (*tjimari*), bottom, shown both in full view and cross section. The knife is set in a gum "handle." Arrows indicate the cutting edges.

An adze flake is hafted to the base of a spear-thrower with the resin of native plants, usually spinifex.

(Opposite) To resharpen an adze, gentle taps of a stick remove a row of small flakes in about 20 seconds.

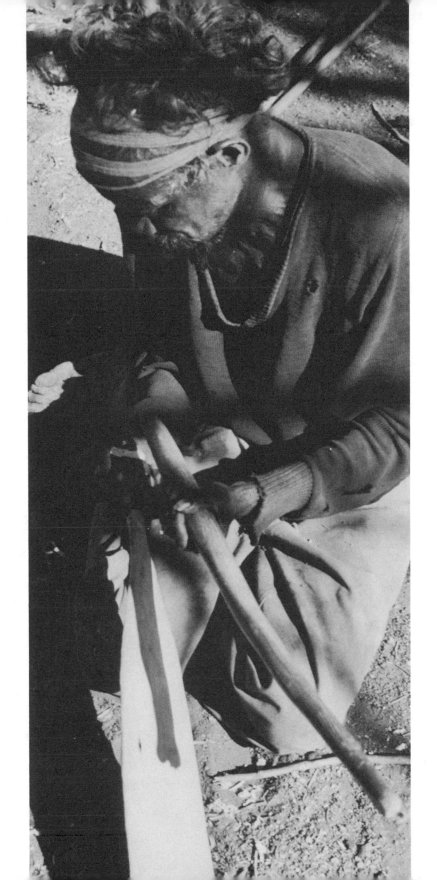

stone flakes or flake knives for cutting the skin and tendons. Among these people stone hand axes are used almost entirely for woodworking. Perhaps wooden-wedge butchering was a more widespread or even typical technique in the past.

Although the aborigines do not attempt to enhance the appearance of stone tools by careful trimming, they do tend to place an esthetic value on cherty materials of different color and texture. All agree that rough, grainy white quartzite is poor material, and they will use it only when absolutely nothing else is available. Natives from the Warburton Range area prefer the white chert found in quarries near there. The Pintupi and northern Ngatatjara men prefer the yellowish quartzites and creamy yellow cherts found in their region. These preferences have little to do with the actual working qualities of the different materials, for all are satisfactory materials for stone chipping. Rather, they reflect the close totemic ties each man has to the particular region from which he comes. The localities of these quarries often figure as places where "dreamtime" heroes, or *wati tjukurpa*, performed creative acts, and are venerated by men who believe themselves to be patrilineally descended from these ancestral beings. Thus a man may have a sense of kinship with some of these chert quarries, and he will value the stone material from them as a part of his own being.

In March, 1967, I met an extended family of twelve Pintupi people near Tjalpu-tjalpu waterhole. One of the men in the party carried a small bag containing yellow quartzite flakes from Partjar, some fifty miles to the northwest. Another man in the party had left a pile of sixteen small, round pebbles in front of his shelter at Tika-tika, the previous campsite. He had transported these from Partjar and intended to use them as hammerstones.

Here again, the aborigines have provided the archeologist with an interesting explanation for a problem he has most often explained by trade. Perhaps much of the occurrence of materials from distant areas was a matter of personal preference on the part of the individual who collected the material.

Formal instruction in the art of stone chipping and related techniques is at a minimum. Little conversation occurs at these times, but the children watch closely and sometimes try later on to imitate their parents' actions, using scraps of stone or wood lying about the campsite.

Since the making of stone tools does not apparently depend on conversation, those archeologists who have from time to time inferred the beginnings of speech from the complexity of the artifacts found at early sites might well profit from this observation. It might be added, however, that conversation does play an important part in the selection of raw material for tools. At such times the conversation is highly animated, as the virtues of this and that chert are hotly debated.

When contrasted with sacred activities, the chipping of stone tools is regarded by these aborigines as an art of little importance, the way Americans might, for instance, treat the matter of tying one's shoelaces. This casual attitude can raise certain problems for the archeologist. For one thing, there is a tendency for these people to pick up ancient stone tools from the surface of sites where they are camped and reuse these implements. Small, finely made, crescent-shaped tools of chert, along with other small, rather elegantly made stone tools (loosely classed as "microliths"), occur on the surface of many old campsites, and recent stratigraphic work near Warburton has shown that these tools predate the present culture of this region.

On one occasion I saw a Pintupi man at Partjar pick up an unusually thick lunate and haft it to his spear-thrower. He called this *yiraputja*, and I learned that any obviously worked but unidentified stone item like this, as well as any substance foreign to the area such as pearl shell, is classed by this term. It includes any substance these people think was left behind by the totemic beings in their dreamtime travels. This category is distinctly different from *kanti*, a word used to define any unworked, chert-like material suitable for making stone tools.

Reutilization of already ancient materials may have been fairly common behavior among prehistoric peoples in many parts of the world. It can result in the discovery of early tools in much later levels in an ancient site and is another possibility the archeologist must consider if he is to interpret his finds correctly.

Once my wife went out to collect honey ants with some Ngatatjara women from the Laverton Reserve. While they were out, one of the women's dogs chased and killed a kangaroo. One woman picked up a natural flake of rough quartzite from the ground and used it to slit the animal's belly and cut the intestines. Then the stone was thrown away (and later collected by my wife). On another occasion, I was traveling near Mount Buttfield, about two hundred miles northeast of Warburton, in the company of two Ngatatjara men from that region. These

Smoothing a spear shaft, this man uses an adze attached to a spear-thrower.

This close-up shows the adzing process applied.

(Opposite) Contact with advanced technology has caused rapid changes in aborigines' choice of tool materials. In this picture, a piece of broken glass is used to sharpen the spear.

men had caught several goannas early in the day. In camp late that afternoon they roasted these lizards and ate the fleshy parts. Then they placed the backbone, head, shoulders, and tail on top of a small rock, which they used as a kind of anvil. With hand-held stones, they pounded the cartilaginous bone and scraps of meat together into a pulpy mass, which they then ate.

At times I have seen men pick up an untrimmed flake of chert and use it as a kind of spokeshave by gripping it between thumb and forefinger and scraping wood from the shaft or point of a spear. This usually happens when a man, for one reason or another, does not have a hafted adze with him. Generally the flake is tossed away when the task is finished.

In all of these cases, completely untrimmed rocks were used as tools. Also, with the possible exception of the spokeshave, they were not used long enough to cause any appreciable wear. Unless such items were found in clear association with other cultural materials, it might be impossible for an archeologist to recognize them as tools. In their simplicity these instant tools are on a par with the controversial eoliths debated by archeologists for many years, and they are a persistent feature of the stone technology of the desert aborigines.

At every turn, the desert aborigines present us with the unexpected. Archeologists do not ordinarily classify stone tools on the basis of the working edge (shape and size are usually thought to be more important), but the aborigines do. Archeologists do not ordinarily consider wooden wedges as possible butchering tools, but the aborigines do. Although there is nothing else in the world today quite like the aborigines' hafted stone adze, this kind of woodworking tool may have been more widespread in the ancient past. It has become an established archeological convention to speak of fire hardening of ancient wooden spear tips and digging sticks, yet the aborigines fire soften theirs! Evidence of transport of lithic materials is common in ancient sites throughout the world. Trade is often invoked to account for it, along with simple carrying of the stone from one place to another. But why do people do this? The aborigines' unique reason is that they are motivated by sentiments of kinship toward particular totemic beings close to the source of the stone. The desert aborigines chip stone with their teeth. Perhaps this technique, too, was more widespread in ancient times, as suggested by Casteñada's account.

In short, the desert aborigines present archeologists with a set of new possibilities to use in interpreting the lithic remains of prehistoric hunting-and-gathering people. The opening up of these new possiblities is the chief value of continued ethnographic studies by archeologists. In four or five years the opportunity for studies of this kind will probably vanish as the aborigines adjust to life on reserves and in nearby towns.

THE SLASH-AND-BURN TECHNIQUE From the layers of plant pollen found buried in Danish and Irish bogs we know the kinds of vegetation that grew there during successive periods of time. An examination of the deposits also tells the story of a simple farming method that reached Europe about 5000 B.C., and that still persists in various parts of the world.

Before the Europeans could begin raising crops, something had to be done about the great forests. They did it by slashing and burning the trees. Evidence of the burning shows in the pollen record as a layer of oak charcoal. On the cleared plot the ancient agriculturists then grew wheat and barley for anywhere from ten to twenty-five years, until the declining yield showed that the soil was exhausted. Whereupon they moved on to open up a new area in similar fashion, leaving the old clearing to become overgrown by brush, and then trees. Years later, others might again clear the same plot by the slash-and-burn method, thus beginning a new cycle.

This kind of shifting cultivation was a natural one for simple farmers in their first encounter with tree-covered land. A similarly mobile type of agriculture appeared nearly 7,000 years later when the first European corn-growing pioneers plunged into the temperate-zone forests of North America. Eventually, of course, the growth of settlements and increase of population made it necessary to clear the forest permanently for the continuous use of the same patches of land. In Europe the requirements of this settled type of agriculture were gradually met by an increasingly elaborate balance of mixed farming, with crop rotations and animal manure serving to keep the soil fertile. In North America's forest belt, such permanent settlement developed much faster, and not without disastrous impoverishment of some of the land. At any rate, on both continents today a choice is made: The old temperate-zone woodlands are either conserved, for their timber-growing potential or for recreation, or else they are permanently cleared, for a settled agriculture equipped with all the resources of modern technology.

Only in the cold far north of Europe did temporary clearing

linger on to any marked extent. One reason was that the oak forests there gave way to damp spruce and pine woods growing on poor, sandy soils. The trees were cut, the litter was burned to make a thick layer of mineral-rich ash, the ground was hoed (in later periods, plowed) between the tree stumps, and oats or rye (which tolerate the cold) were grown for a while; then the farmers moved elsewhere, leaving the deserted plot to birch and alder, and at last to the returning pines. This was the same method that had been used in the oak forests. It lasted into the late nineteenth century in northern Russia, until 1918 in northern Sweden, and persists today in parts of Finland.

For the Finns, the farm in the clearing must long have been a familiar sight; in their ancient national epic, *Kalevala*, the voice of the old hero Väinämöinen is said to stumble like the hoe among the pine roots. But certainly by A.D. 1781, and probably much earlier, some Finns had transformed the old, casually shifting cultivation into a regular rotation of forest farming. In the first year, they felled the trees. In the second, they burned them. For the next four to six years they grew crops among the stumps. For twenty to thirty years after that they allowed the clearing to revert to forest, then they returned to the same plot and same cycle. Such systematic rotation appeared in Sweden, too, probably brought by Finnish immigrants.

But this way of farming eventually declined, along with the older, casual procedure, as the demand for northern timber increased among peoples farther south and as modern methods made settled agriculture more productive even in the north.

Although forest farming is dying in temperate lands, it remains much alive in the rain forests and savanna woodlands that exist on either side of the Equator, covering vast areas in Central and South America, Africa, Asia, and the islands of the Pacific. Such farming is not a curiosity for anthropologists, a quaint survival among a few backward tribes; it is the way of life for a substantial fraction of the human race. Figures for 1957 estimate that farming on temporary clearings was practiced by over 200 million people (nearly 1 in 12 of the world population), on 14 million square miles (about 30 per cent of the world's cultivable land).

A few isolated tribes with rather simple cultures, for instance in the Amazon Basin and on the uplands of Burma and Thailand, practice the haphazard shifting cultivation of the pioneers. But most forest farmers long ago adopted systematic land use. The area under crops shifts its position, but any given plot

Smoke rises as Hanunóo's newly set fire begins converting woodland slash to soil-enriching ashes.

is regularly rotated between cropping and fallow. In the fallow period the forest returns, hence this system is sometimes called forest fallow rotation.

Systematic slash-and-burn agriculture has evolved independently in all tropic regions. The farming system and the cleared plot are usually known by the same name, but this varies with locality, so the same practice is called by many names. From Central and South America we have milpa, coamile, ichali, conuco, roça; from Africa, masole, chitemene, tavy; and from the Far East, chena, djum, bewar, dippa, erka, jara, kumari, podu, prenda, dahi, parka, taungya, tamrai, rây, hwajon, djuma, humah, tagal, ladang, kaingin. English-speaking scientists have coined several additional terms, including slash-and-burn, fire agriculture, and forest fallow rotation; they now generally call the typical plots in all these places swiddens (from an

Bamboo torch fires a swidden in the Philippines. The Hanunóo farmer moves along a protective path.

old English country word for burned clearings), and the system is swidden farming.

The basic practice is similar all over the tropics. A swidden site is carefully selected. Trees are either felled, usually leaving the stumps, or completely stripped of their branches; creepers and underbrush are slashed away; and the resulting litter, or slash, is spread over the swidden. This is done in the dry season, so the debris soon dries out. It is then set on fire (sometimes with precautions to prevent the fire spreading). This leaves the swidden covered with a layer of ash, ready for planting crops in time to take advantage of the coming rains.

In Europe, and even more so in North America, a farm field conveys the idea of rows and rows of crop plants all of the same kind. By contrast, a swidden is generally like a North American vegetable garden run wild, covered with all sorts of crop plants that will be harvested at different times. In a typical Central American swidden, for instance, squash vines spread over the ground surface, cornstalks rise into the air, beans climb up the cornstalks. The most sophisticated swidden farmers known are the Hanunóo on Mindoro Island in the Philippines, who are impressive botanists. About 1,200 plant species are known in their region, but the Hanunóo themselves distinguish 1,600 different kinds—evidently their classification goes down to plant varieties. Of this number, they actually breed more than 400 kinds in their swiddens. Various other species reproduce themselves. To protect these when the swidden is burned, the farmers wrap them in green plant material.

Generally, among such peoples the swidden is cultivated intensively for a year or so, then gradually less intensively, and finally abandoned. For instance, in Ondo Province, Nigeria, one practice is to clear the swidden in February and burn soon after. Yams and corn are planted with the first rains, together with pumpkins, melons, and calabashes. When the farmers harvest the first corn, in June, they plant beans, manioc, okra, and cocoyams. In September–October they harvest the yams; in October–November they harvest a second crop of corn, which was planted in August. A third corn crop may be planted in the next rainy season, and the farmers may return for a year or two

Polite detour-marker warns traveler to avoid foot-tangling slash in a freshly cut Hanunóo swidden.

thereafter to dig the manioc and cocoyams, but they generally do not immediately plant this plot again. Fruit trees are often included among swidden crops, and their fruit may be harvested for several years after the swidden is abandoned. Meanwhile, through regeneration from stumps (which are left three feet high in Nigeria for this purpose) and by growth of seeds from the surrounding bush, the swidden gradually reverts to forest. It will not be cleared again for some time. In the interval, other swidden sites are cleared and go through the same cycle.

The periods under intensive cropping and under fallow vary in different places, but when the system is working effectively the cropping period is always relatively short, and the fallow period relatively long, as seen in the chart below.

Region	Years under intensive cropping	Years under fallow
Philippines (Hanunóo)	2–4	8–10
New Guinea	1	15–20
Ceylon	1–3	8–20
Sierra Leone	2	12–15
Ghana	1–3	10–15
Nigeria (rain forest)	1–2	8–14
Nigeria (savanna woodland)	4	Up to 30

The method of selecting new swidden sites has been studied in detail among the Hanunóo. These people choose sites where the composition of the fallow vegetation has reached the stage ready for slash-and-burn. This may be from eight to ten years after the previous cropping period. The expert Hanunóo do not work with map and calendar. They are guided by botanical criteria that are flexible and highly relevant for their purpose. This method allows for local differences (between soils for instance) and ensures that the fallow period has lasted long enough.

In some parts of the tropics, specially modified forms of swidden farming are practiced, such as the system characteristic of Zambia but found in many other woodland areas of East Africa. In this chitemene system, the farmers slash and burn not only the trees and underbrush of the swidden; they add branches brought in from the surrounding woods. In Sudan, sev-

With his bolo this Hanunóo weeds a combination crop: maize, rice, cassava, pigeon peas, banana plants.

eral tribes omit burning the swidden, and instead take advantage of the fact that termites quickly reduce the woody litter to powder. Also in this region are the Dinka, who practice a kind of termite-chitemene system—they collect wood from some distance and pile it in the swidden for the termites.

Not all swidden farmers are people with extremely simple cultures. The Hanunóo, for instance, can write, so they post notices warning neighbors to avoid walking into a clearing that has been slashed but not yet burned. However, the actual farming method is basic to the way of life of all these peoples. It is also encumbered with considerable ritual. To early European observers, the whole procedure seemed senseless, primitive, and a gross waste of land.

Yet there is often method, even in the rituals. The Hanunóo drive a hollow bamboo stick into the ground at a possible swidden site. If the soil does not rise high enough inside the stick, they discard the site and clear elsewhere. Although they regard this as a purely magical test, it can be a crude agronomic way of appraising the soil's structural readiness for tillage. And on many points, these and other swidden farmers can often give excellent scientific reasons for their practices.

Many Europeans must have had the experience that Bishop Mackenzie described to fellow missionary and explorer Dr. David Livingstone in the mid-nineteenth century. "When telling the people in England what were my objects in going out to Africa," said the Bishop, "I stated that, among other things, I meant to teach these people agriculture; but I now see that they know far more about it than I do."

Furthermore, the swidden system is extraordinarily suitable for the tropical environment. Considerable experimental work in Africa, for example, indicates how the system conserves soil fertility. To begin with, the heavy rains keep many tropical forest and woodland soils poor in nitrogen, phosphorus, and other mineral elements that plants need. Nitrogen is normally present in soils either in an insoluble form unusable to plants, in organic matter, or in soluble forms (chiefly nitrates) that plants can take up. Every year, in the tropical rainy season, much of the nitrogen in organic matter is converted by soil bacteria into nitrate. Some of this is used by the plants, but much, being soluble in the rain water, is washed out of the topsoil. This means the stock of available nitrogen is steadily diminished. Phosphorus and other mineral nutrients are also leached down beyond reach of the plant roots.

This leaching problem often also affects the damp, sandy pinewoods of northern Europe, and the benefits of forest fallow have been experimentally demonstrated in Finland as well as in Africa. When leached soils are continuously cropped without manuring, the available nutrient elements are soon used up; crop yields fall and eventually fail. This had begun to happen by 1933, for instance, in parts of Zambia where continuous cash crops of corn had replaced the chitemene system.

Forest fallow restores fertility in at least two ways. First, it constantly returns plant material to the soil as litter (leaves, dead branches, and so forth); then soil bacteria, stimulated by the tropical warmth, quickly convert the litter to organic matter, where the nitrogen content is safe from leaching. Thus the reserves of soil nitrogen gradually increase. Secondly, deep tree roots bring back phosphorus and other mineral nutrients that were leached down to lower depths, and concentrate them at the soil surface or in plant growth—"living fallow." If the fallow is allowed to remain long enough, the topsoil is much enriched in organic matter and mineral nutrients by the next time the plot is cleared.

Early European visitors supposed that burning the slash must be harmful. But agronomists have shown the reverse to be true. The phosphorus and other minerals stored in growing trees are all deposited in the ash, which makes an excellent fertilizer (especially when the forest outside the swidden is also exploited, as in the chitemene system). Although nitrogen in the growing trees is lost to the atmosphere when they are burned, very little of the new store of organic matter in the soil is destroyed by the fire. Experiments in Malawi, Sierra Leone, and Zambia have shown that the burning is in itself beneficial, for burning slash on the swidden gives a higher crop yield than burning it elsewhere and bringing the ash to the swidden. Experiments in Brazil suggest that burning affects soil bacteria (by killing some and stimulating others) in just the right way to improve the soil nitrogen cycle. It is because of this that the crops on a swidden grow and yield well for a few years—until the rebuilt stores of nutrients are exhausted.

Swidden farming can offer other benefits in the tropics. A frequent problem, for example, is actual destruction of the soil by erosion resulting from heavy tropical rains. Where soil is unprotected by fallow, the raindrops may break up part of the surface, and batter the rest to form a waterproof cap. Then the

Sowing acha seed. This crop grows where others do not; it can be stored for long periods.

rain water, instead of soaking into the soil, runs down slopes. This runoff may finally tear away the soil in sheets or gouge it into deep gullies.

On steep slopes, one elaborate answer to this problem is building terraces to check the force of the runoff and allow time for water and silt to accumulate on the terrace steps where the crops are grown. Terrace building is laborious, however, and not usually done on a plot used for only a few years at a time.

Nigerian volunteers racing to hoe new furrows for a peanut crop.

The swidden system is easier and has many built-in safe-guards against soil erosion. When choosing a site for clearing, the Hanunóo carefully avoid uneven ground and unstable soils vulnerable to erosion; for this they use their elaborate classification of soils, which agrees well with results of scientific soil analysis. Then, during the critical period when the newly cleared swidden is exposed to the danger of wind erosion, the drying slash is spread over every square foot of soil as a dead cover, or mulch. (Hanunóo teen-agers who find this chore a nuisance are lectured by their elders about soil erosion.) Creeping, erect, and climbing plants protect the soil during cropping. Afterward the new covering of forest fallow takes over: the foliage and litter break the rain's force, so that it sinks gradually into the soil.

But there is another tropical hazard—the rank growth of weeds, including grasses. Within a year or two after it is cleared, the swidden may become choked by these light-loving plants. Indeed, this often is why the swidden is abandoned so soon. If the forest fallow is able to regenerate, the shade of the trees will eventually suppress the weeds. A way to aid this process is to leave tree stumps and protect some trees during the fire, so they can provide shade for the tree seeds coming from outside the clearing. The stumps serve another purpose: new growth often sprouts directly from them.

By this method the swidden farmers give the forest a chance to return and compete successfully with the weeds. But if cropping goes on too long, the soil may become too poor for trees to get started, and grass weeds may get too much of a grip. The balance now tips in favor of grass against trees, and the plot becomes grassland.

In parts of Africa, swidden farming has become adapted for grassland fallow. But in tropical rotations the grasses are less satisfactory than trees. Their roots are too shallow to reach mineral nutrients leached into the lower soil. Furthermore, the grass supplies little litter for making organic matter. Grass fallow rotation generally supports only low-yielding, small-grained cereals like the millets, and only on the least-leached soils. Finally, tough, tall grasses like *Imperata cylindrica*, called cogon in the Far East, are liable to take over, turning the plot into a cogonal —an intractable sod that cannot be farmed (at least by ancient methods).

Proper swidden techniques, on the other hand, are admirably adapted to the tropical environment. But they accomplish their purpose only when the ratio of fallow period to cropping period remains high. This requires a great deal of land for each family. For example, if the cropping period is two years and the fallow period is eighteen years, then only 10 per cent of the land is under crops at one time. Hence the system will only support a very low population density—generally about 130 people per square mile, according to an estimate made in Java and widely accepted for the tropics as a whole. The system worked, therefore, during the thousands of years when tropical populations were kept low by parasites and infectious diseases.

But in the twentieth century, modern medicine caused a dramatic increase in populations all over the tropics. Inevitably, a greater proportion of the land was used to meet the need for more food. Also inevitably, the cropping period grew longer and the fallow period shorter. By 1964, for instance, the forest fallow period in parts of Sierra Leone had shortened drastically. It had lasted from twelve to fifteen years; it became three or four years. By 1955, it had shortened in Iboland (Nigeria, rain forest zone) from between eight and fourteen years to three or four years. On parts of the Jos Plateau (Nigeria, savanna woodland

A Nigerian swidden after first crop. The shelter and shade trees are for resting migrant workers.

zone), a sequence of four years under crops and up to thirty years of woodland fallow became four to six years under crops and one to two years under grass fallow—the woodlands had disappeared.

With this changing ratio of cropping to woodland fallow, the fallow often ceased to fulfill its functions, and eventually was unable to regenerate at all. Crop yields steadily declined as the fallow period shortened. In Benue Province (Nigeria), this deterioration was already noticeable by 1927. Today, over large areas of land, forest has been replaced by cogon grass and has become useless for food production; such cogonals cover 18 per cent of all land in the Philippines. Over other large areas, especially in Africa, India, and Burma, soil has been altogether lost by erosion.

Thus, throughout the tropics, the swidden system is tending to break down under the weight of rising populations. This, of course, is only one aspect of the growing population crisis throughout the world. Between 1958 and 1964, world agricultural production was spectacularly increased by prodigies of techno-logical effort; but production per head remained constant because of the swelling population. Even assuming that the population problem will be solved, however, the swidden method faces reappraisal.

One answer may be to replace it with new farming meth-ods. Although many swidden families have settled homes (how-ever much they shift their plots in the surrounding forest), their way of life is difficult to integrate with that of modern civilization. And it will certainly be desirable to make vast areas of land more productive, capable of contributing more to mush-rooming urban societies. To this end, intensive efforts are being made to find better forms of tropical farming. But even with all the resources of modern technology, the task is difficult and the problem far from solved (a tribute to the limited but real achievements of swidden farming, which were made without any of these resources).

In the drier parts of tropical regions, continuous cropping may well prove possible on a large scale. Experiments in savanna areas of Africa have shown that continuous cropping with com-post, animal manure, or chemical fertilizers is far more produc-tive than rotation with the grass fallows to which many such areas have been reduced. In surviving savanna woodlands, too, such methods may be better than swidden farming, although it is likely that the chemical fertilizers would have to include more nutrients than the conventional nitrogen, phosphorus, and potas-sium, which generally suffice for soils of temperate zone lands. The development of mixed farming (providing abundant animal manure) is perhaps the most hopeful solution. This would require introducing improved breeds of animals and (in Africa) eliminating the tsetse flies, harbingers of human and animal disease.

But in the heart of the rain forest there can be another answer. Much research is now directed toward developing a modernized swidden system. It would rely on a fallow made by deliberate planting of selected trees (or sometimes creeping plants), which will either restore soil fertility better and faster than natural fallows, or make possible a new combination of farming with forestry. So far, the attempts have shown little improvement over natural fallow, but research continues. It may well be that, in some such modernized form, man's oldest way of forest farming will continue to prove its worth.

NEW DELHI, DEC. 1—Prime Minister Indira Gandhi appealed today to India's holy men to stop fasting and agitating against cow slaughter.

In an effort to halt the spreading wave of fasts by the saffron-clad Hindu Sadhus, Mrs. Gandhi wrote directly to Muni Shushil Kumar, president of the All-Party Cow Protection Campaign Committee.

The Muni has announced his intention of starting a fast tomorrow to demand a nationwide ban on the slaughter of cows, which are revered by Hindus as symbols of abundance but whose meat is often eaten by India's Moslem minority.

On Nov. 7 thousands of demonstrators, led by a group of holy men smeared with white ash and draped with garlands of marigolds, rioted in front of Parliament. Eight persons were killed and 47 injured.

The New York Times
December 2, 1966

THE MYTH OF THE SACRED COW Among the popular myths of cultural anarchy, none is more widely accepted than that of the Indian sacred cow. Protected by Hindu taboo from being slaughtered and eaten, these supposedly useless animals wander about at will, impeding traffic and, it is reported, damaging crops. Indeed, in some parts of India, aged cattle are even housed in *gosadans*—bovine old-age homes.

But the myth of the sacred cow is part of a widespread overemphasis on the mismanagement of food production by primitive and peasant peoples. One often hears, especially in these times of vast aid programs for the underdeveloped countries of the world, that irrational ideologies and customs prevent the effective use of available food resources.

In the case of the sacred cow, it must be admitted that the Indian dairy industry is among the least efficient in the world. In India, the average annual yield of whole milk per cow has been reported at 413 pounds, as compared with an average of over 5,000 pounds in Europe and the United States. Furthermore, of the 79.4 million cows maintained in 1961, only 20.1 million were milk producers. Among the 47.2 million cows over three years old, 27.2 million were dry and/or not calved. If we go on to accept the proposition that India can make no profit from the negligible slaughter of its enormous cattle supply, we have completed the case for the great cattle bungle. Hence the conclusion of a 1959 Ford Foundation report on India's food problem:

"There is widespread recognition, not only among animal husbandry officials, but among citizens generally, that India's cattle population is far in excess of the available supplies of fodder and feed. . . . At least one third, and possibly as many as one half, of the Indian cattle population may be regarded as surplus in relation to feed supply."

This view is endorsed by government agronomists, and the Indian Ministry of Information insists that "the large animal population is more a liability than an asset in view of our limited land resource." Because of the perpetual food shortage for humans in India, refusal to slaughter cattle seems to prove that the mysterious has triumphed over the practical. Some would even have us believe that in order to preserve his cow the individual farmer is prepared to sacrifice his own life. Such is the myth of the sacred cow.

A better understanding of the cow complex in India involves the answers to the following two questions: (1) Is it true that the rate of reproduction and survival of the Indian population is lowered as a result of the competition between man and cattle for scarce resources? (2) Would the removal of the Hindu taboo on slaughter substantially modify the ecology of Indian food production?

The answer to the first question is that the relation between man and cattle—both cows and bullocks—is not competitive, but symbiotic. The most obvious part of this symbiosis is the role played by male cattle in cultivation. Indian farming is based on plow agriculture, to which cattle contribute up to 46 per cent of the labor cost, exclusive of transport and other activities. Obviously, tractors are not a realistic alternative.

Despite the existence of 96.3 million bullocks, of which 68.6 million are working animals, India suffers from a shortage of such animals. It is generally agreed that a pair of bullocks is the minimum unit for cultivation. But a conservatively estimated 60 million rural households dispose of only 80 million working cattle and buffaloes. This would mean that as many as two-thirds of India's farmers may be short of the technical minimum. Moreover, under existing property relations the bullocks cannot be shared among several households without further lowering the productivity of marginal farms. M. B. Desai, an Indian economist, explains why: ". . . over vast areas, sowing and harvesting operations, by the very nature of things, begin simultaneously with the outbreak of the first showers and the maturing of crops respectively and especially the former has got to be put through quickly during the first phase of the monsoon. Under these circumstances, reliance by a farmer on another for bullocks is highly risky and he has got, therefore, to maintain his own pair."

We see, then, that the draft animals, which appear to be superfluous from the point of view of what would be needed in a perfectly engineered society, turn out to be considerably less than sufficient in the actual context of Indian agriculture.

But what of the cows? The first thing to note is again obvious. No cows, no bullocks. Of course, the issue is not so easily settled. Although the need for bullocks establishes the need for cows, it does not establish the need for 80 million of them. We are, however, coming closer to the answer, because we now know that to the value of the milk and milk products produced by the cows, we must add the value of the 69 million male traction animals also produced.

Among the other immediate and important contributions of the cow is the dung. In addition to the relatively minor value of dung as plaster in house construction, this material is India's main cooking fuel. India's grain crops cannot be metabolized by human beings without cooking. Coal and oil are, of course, prohibitively expensive for the peasant family. Thus, dung alone provides the needed energy, and cattle provide the dung on a lavish scale. Of the 800 million tons annually bequeathed the Indian countryside, 300 million are consumed in cookery. This amount is the Btu equivalent of 35 million tons of coal or 68 million tons of wood, an impressive amount of Btu's to be plugged into an energy system.

Of the remaining 500 million tons of dung, the largest part is used for manuring. It has been claimed that 160 million tons of this manure is "wasted on hillsides and roads," but it must be noted that some of this probably re-enters the ecological system, since, as we shall see in a moment, the cattle depend upon hillsides and roads for much of their sustenance. (Needless to say, the intensive rainfall agriculture characteristic of large parts of the subcontinent is dependent upon manuring. So vital is this contribution that one scholar argues that substitutes for the manure consumed as fuel "must be supplied, and lavishly, even at a financial loss to government.")

In the present context, the most important point to note about the fuel and manure functions of India's cattle is that old, dry, barren animals do not cease to provide dung. On this score alone, one might expect more caution before the conclusion is reached that the sacred cow is a useless luxury.

Two additional contributions by cattle, including cows, remain to be mentioned. In 1962 India produced 16 million cattle hides. Much of this output is consumed in the manufacture of leather products vital to the traditional farming technology. In addition, despite the Hindu proscription, a considerable amount of beef *is* eaten. Those who stress the quaintness of the beef-eating taboo fail to give proper emphasis to the millions of people in India who have no caste to lose. Not only are there some 55 million members of exterior or untouchable groups, many of whom will consume beef if given the opportunity, but there are also several millions more who are pagan, Christian, or Moslem. It seems likely that a high proportion of the 20 million bovines that die each year get eaten. Moreover, it is quite clear that not all these cattle die a natural death. On the contrary, the very extent of the agitation for antislaughter bills reveals how widespread the slaughter actually is.

We see that to the contribution of the cow as a producer of milk, we must add the production of meat, bullocks, manure, fuel, and hides. The extent of the symbiosis between man and cow, however, is not thereby demonstrated. There still remains the possibility that all these needs could be met at a lower energy or monetary cost per peasant household by reducing the number of aged cows that the peasant tolerates in his ménage. To prove that the ecosystem under discussion is essentially adaptive for human life it must be shown that resources consumed by the cows, old and young, do not, from the point of view of the peasant's balance sheet, outweigh the enumerated contributions. This proof is fairly easy to establish.

Note, first of all, that one of the most persistent professional complaints against the sacred cow is that the beasts wander all over the place, cluttering up the markets, railroad stations, and roadsides. Many authorities seem not to inquire why all this wandering takes place from the point of view of the cow, since presumably she has remained uninformed of her sacred privileges. The cow is wandering about because she is hungry and is looking for food—in the ditches, around the base of telegraph poles, between the railroad ties, along the hillsides, in every nook and cranny where something edible has reared its head. The sacred cow is an exploited scavenger, a mere walking skeleton for most of the year, precisely because her ecological niche is removed from that of human food crops.

An ecological explanation of why so many cows are kept is now possible: Each farmer needs his own pair of bullocks. Lacking cash, he cannot afford to buy these animals. Rather than risk going into debt at usurious rates, he prefers to try to breed bulls (which he will exchange later for bullocks). Since all the available land is given over to human food crops, the breeding cows must scavenge for their food. Being undernourished, they breed irregularly. The farmer refrains from culling uncalved animals since they convert grain by-products and scrub vegetation into useful dung. Meanwhile, there is always a chance that the cow will eventually conceive. If a female calf is born, the scrub and chaff are converted into milk, while the calf is gradually starved to death. In the long run, the more cows an individual farmer owns, the greater the likelihood that he can replace his bullocks without going into debt.

This explanation does not involve references to ahimsa, the Hindu doctrine of the sanctity of life. Instead, the large number of cows and bullocks is seen as the result of ecological pressures generated by the human population's struggle to maintain itself. Ahimsa may thus be regarded as an ideological expression of these pressures; in other words, ahimsa itself derives power and sustenance from the material rewards it confers upon both men and animals.

In answer to the second question under consideration, it would thus seem that the basic ecology of Indian cattle production is not a mere reflex of the Hindu taboo on slaughter. Removing that taboo might temporarily alter the ecosystem. In the long run, however, the rate at which cattle are presently slaughtered in India is governed by the ability of the peasantry to slaughter them without impairing the production of traction animals, fuel, fertilizer, and milk. It is a well-known fact that the least efficient way to convert solar energy into comestibles is to impose an animal converter between plant and man. Hence, it is wrong to suppose that India could, without major technoenvironmental innovations, support any large number of animals whose principal function was to supply animal protein. It has already been shown that the supply of beef is now one of the functions of the cattle complex, but this must necessarily remain a marginal or tertiary attribute of the ecosystem. As a matter of fact, it is obvious that any large-scale drift toward animal slaughter before the traction, fuel, and manure needs of the productive cycle were met would immediately jeopardize the lives of tens of millions of Indians.

PART THREE

PATTERN AND STYLE

Systemic Archeology

At first glance, engraved designs on early colonial New England gravestones seem improbable subjects for anthropological study. Although I now live in Hawaii, I grew up in New England, where gravestones of the kinds described by archeologists James Deetz and Edwin S. Dethlefsen in "Death's Head, Cherub, Urn and Willow" are commonplace on the landscape. For many people, attuned to the notion that anthropologists study only exotic and remote societies, this subject might appear to be so familiar and close to our own culture that it cannot tell us anything new about human behavior. Yet Deetz and Dethlefsen demonstrate that these rather neglected pieces of mortuary art are in fact sensitive indicators of cultural processes that affect the acquisition and transmission of human knowledge in both time and space.

Archeologists are well known for their preoccupation with the study of stone tools, pottery, and other artifacts that might provide evidence of cultural patterning in prehistoric times. Naturally these artifacts are only those made of substances that have withstood the ravages of decay, erosion, and other natural processes through time. In some cases archeologists are lucky and find ancient articles of wood, cloth, and other organic materials that have survived because of exceptional dryness, cold, or water saturation, but such occurrences are relatively rare. Thus archeologists are usually forced to make inferences about ancient human behavior on the bases of limited and incomplete samples of the whole culture. It is not easy to understand a society's system of values or beliefs, for example, on the basis of a study of a limited part of their technology and material culture. Archeologists constantly look for methods to improve the accuracy of their inferences about past societies; Deetz and Dethlefsen have set out to provide a kind of test case of how such inferences can be developed under controlled archeological conditions. Gravestones tended to resist the forces of decay and were generally left wherever they were first placed. They contain well-defined art styles as well as inscriptions and dates, giving both historical and chronological control. Careful study of archival sources in New England history provided detailed background on the lives and travels of the stone-carvers who made the gravestones as well as on the changing religious attitudes toward death during the period covered by the dates on the gravestones. Using several techniques well known to archeologists, the authors show how new design styles replaced others in popularity as they were introduced in certain centers and later spread into the more rural parts of New England. The rates of these changes varied in different areas, and some of the changes were correlated with basic changes in religious attitudes. A shift in emphasis from mortality to immortality was marked by changes in inscriptions as well as by a shift in popularity away from the death's head motif and toward the cherub motif. Change in the style of mortuary art was thus seen partially as a function of change in religious belief.

For the archeologist this important demonstration provides a basis for inferring intangible (but no less real) aspects of human behavior such as religious attitudes from tangible remains. Perhaps even more important, though, is that the techniques used in this study, such as the battleship-shaped curve for describing the popularity of cultural traits, can give anthropologists precise ways of studying processes of cultural change. New religious ideas that entered colonial New England society at particular points (the liberal and relatively cosmopolitan centers of Cambridge and Boston) began to influence mortuary art styles. The story of the acceptance and spread of these religious ideas is traced in the designs and inscriptions on gravestones throughout New England. And one cannot help but suppose that the application of similar, concrete "archeological" methods to the study of living ethnographic societies would help us to understand better the processes of change in those cultures. This study demonstrates well what many archeologists[1] and ethnographers now call the *systemic approach* to the study of culture, in which each part of the culture is viewed as a subsystem that interacts with the other subsystems that make up the culture itself as well as its physical environment. That is, anthropologists have been made increasingly aware that one cannot treat a culture as if it were a laundry list of traits or elements that can be added up to characterize that culture. In the systemic view, cultures are seen as more than the sum of their parts, and each trait is viewed as dependent (in the statistical sense) on other traits. It then becomes the task of the anthropologist to discover these interdependencies and to understand their significance in terms of changes in cultures through time.

This approach to the study of human behavior received its first formal expression from archeologist Walter Taylor, who advocated that archeologists stop using the trait-list approach that had characterized so much of their work and use instead what he called the "conjunctive approach," by which he meant the study of processes of interaction between different cultural subsystems of which these traits were a part.[2] This approach has been much expanded and refined and currently stands as a major theme of much archeological and anthropological work currently being undertaken. Deetz and Dethlefsen apply this approach effectively. Instead of viewing the stylistic features of colonial New England gravestone art and religious beliefs as discrete traits to be added up as "typical" of that society, these scholars have looked for correlations through time which would point to the interaction of these two cultural subsystems: mortuary art and religious beliefs.

Ethnoscience

The movement of people into the island groups of the Pacific was one of the greatest human cultural achievements of all times. Anthropologists and historians have argued about how this movement actually occurred. Some scholars, such as anthropologist Peter H. Buck, favored traditional accounts indicating planned, purposeful voyages to settle new islands[3] (an example, if one wishes to accept it, of true migration), whereas others, such as historian Andrew Sharp, have argued that vessels accidentally blown off course during storms or missing their intended landfalls for other reasons accounted for most of the first arrivals on previously uninhabited islands[4] I shall not attempt to resolve this debate here—perhaps it can never be fully resolved. But it should be noted that once the islands of Micronesia and Polynesia were settled, long-distance voyages between islands became commonplace. In some areas, most notably a number of islands in the Central Caroline Islands of Micronesia, traditional practices of boatbuilding, sailing, and navigation have continued to hold an important place in the culture and can be studied by the anthropologists.

Thomas Gladwin's paper, "East Is a Big Bird," represents part of probably the most comprehensive study of traditional sailing so far attempted for any Pacific Island society. The people of Puluwat (the atoll that he studied), although they sometimes try to justify their trips on economic grounds, do not sail primarily for these reasons. Rather sailing offers even more compelling social incentives, and at the pinnacle of social esteem based on sailing rests the successful navigator. As Gladwin points out, the logical system that encloses Puluwat boatbuilding, sailing, and navigation is not based on any appreciation of abstract intellect as such any more than weaving skill among the Quechua was valued as art for art's sake. Puluwat seafaring traditions are, above all, practical. The boat must be soundly built, the sailing techniques must be appropriate to the condition of the sea and weather, and the navigation must be accurate. A failure in any of these conditions could result in disaster for the crew. Because every voyage is an ultimate test, no one in Puluwat society would question the importance of mastering these skills.

More important for Gladwin than any considerations of cultural integration, however, is the nature of the logical system itself. In approaching this question, he uses a method known to anthropologists under various guises as cognitive anthropology or *ethnoscience.* Anthropologists are understandably reluctant to draw conclusions about what people they study are thinking. They have no "mental stethoscope" for determining what motivates people to behave the way they do. But from controlled observations of patterned behavior, together with interviews, it may be possible to understand what might be called the grammatical systems that underlie the behavior being observed and to distinguish the categories that the native users see as ordered by such grammatical systems. This approach partakes heavily of linguistic theory, because anthropological linguists were among the first to try to ascertain how native categories of thought were expressed in their languages. Anthropologist Franz Boas first applied this systematic approach to anthropology in his pioneer work among the Kwakiutl Indians of British Columbia in the late nineteenth and early twentieth centuries.[5] Boas made every effort in his work to avoid imposing his own categories of experience and thought on the data he collected, even to the extent of enlisting the aid and collaboration of a literate Kwakiutl Indian named George Hunt.

Gladwin describes Puluwat sailing and navigation in much the same way as Boas looked at Kwakiutl Indian culture; that is, in terms of native categories of thought and experience. Nothing in Puluwat seafaring tradition illustrates this better than the differences between the directions of the Puluwat star compass and the magnetic compass. The intervals into which the arc of the Puluwat star compass is divided are not equal but show a bunching of star positions to the east and west, which, as Gladwin points out, ". . . reflects the greater demands for accuracy which are placed on the navigation system as a whole by longer east–west passages."[6] The islands of the Central Carolines are, in fact, situated generally in an east–west direction; as a result, the Puluwat need not contend with long north-south routes. "Thus," as Gladwin notes, "the sectors wherein the star compass is least accurate are also those where the least accuracy is needed." The Puluwat star compass is not equally accurate in all directions, but it is accurate enough for all voyaging carried out in this region. The difficulties of equating the magnetic compass, with its equally spaced points, with the Puluwat star compass are so great that Puluwat navigators who have acquired magnetic compasses use them only for holding a straight course while sailing rather than for setting a course at the start of a voyage. The message of all this is clear; in order to understand how the Puluwat star compass works, the anthropologist must first see it as the Puluwat navigators see it and especially in terms of the actual problems they must solve with it, rather than by trying to understand Puluwat navigation in terms of the magnetic compass.

Compared with the fore-and-aft rig of European-style sailing vessels, the rigging of a Puluwat canoe at first seems awkward and inefficient. For example, it requires more labor than do most European-style boats of comparable size. (However, finding a suitable crew on Puluwat is easy, so this is no problem.) Puluwat canoes sail best on a beam wind, because the narrow, shallow hull creates little resistance in the water. They are least efficient when sailing close-hauled into the wind, and tacking requires a complete reversal of the standing rigging, a big job for all hands. Running before the wind is fairly efficient until the wind velocity increases to the point where the bow is in danger of being driven under the water (caused by the high forward position of the sail). But, as Gladwin notes, rigging adjustments can be made to counter any problem that may arise in the course of a voyage, including even typhoons. When these adjustments are made, a Puluwat canoe is at least as seaworthy as any fore-and-aft–rigged European sailboat. The implication is that Puluwat sailors and navigators are well trained and prepared to make all adjustments for any contingencies; their ability to cope must be understood in terms of the way in which they rig and sail their own canoes.

Systemic Ethnography

A variation of the systemic approach to human behavior could be applied to the institution of surfing among the ancient Hawaiians. Simple forms of surfing (mainly belly boarding) were practiced by indigenous peoples over wide areas of Oceania and on the coast of West Africa, but only in eastern Polynesia did this sport receive major elaboration. In this region it became more than just a children's game; it developed into a major adult activity. Ben R. Finney and James D. Houston in "Polynesian Surfing" review the cultural background of this activity, particularly in the Hawaiian Islands, as it was seen by Europeans like Captain James Cook and others in the eighteenth and nineteenth centuries. The most important single idea to emerge from this study is the close correlation between the sport of surfing and the class structure of ancient Hawaii. The authors note that two distinct types of surfboards were used: a short type that could be used by both commoners and royalty and an elongated type that was reserved exclusively for use by royalty. Chiefs could prohibit commoners from using good surfing beaches and could claim particular waves for their own use. Ability at surfing was at least as important an accomplishment for a member of the chiefly class as were other skills like canoe paddling and spear throwing. Members of the royalty sometimes challenged each other to surfing matches that involved heavy wagers. And two large stone enclosures with raised platforms, called *heiau*, were constructed on the island of Hawaii in close proximity to outstanding surfing beaches (where it is presumed they were shrines that had some close association with this particular activity).

With the drastic decline of population generally and the decline of the royal classes particularly throughout eastern Polynesia, the sport of surfing became moribund and was almost extinct by the end of the nineteenth century. Surfing was divorced by then from its social context, and it almost died. The royal classes no longer existed to encourage the sport. The revival of surfing in the early 1900s depended at least as much on the attentions of non-Polynesians like Alexander Hume Ford and writer Jack London as it did on the Hawaiians or other native Polynesians. A great irony in the history of this sport was that it had to be reintroduced to New Zealand (culturally a part of eastern Polynesia) by Europeans after it had long been extinct there. Today the sport of surfing is more popular than it ever was before, but it is totally detached from its former associations with Polynesian social classes.

The history of surfing as presented by Finney and Houston also well illustrates the process of *diffusion* in the spread of styles from one region and culture to others. Anthropologists have long been aware that styles, techniques, and ideas can often move from one culture to another without the populations themselves moving; that is, without having to resort to the idea of migration to account for such movement. The process of diffusion seems to have occurred in varying degrees wherever different cultures were in contact with one another. In this case the idea of techniques of surfing spread beyond Polynesia as more and more Europeans observed the sport and told others about it or practiced it themselves. The idea of its associations with Polynesian social classes, however, did not spread with it. Instead it became another in a long list of outdoor sports practiced for fun within the context of Western culture.

The Integration of Art and Culture

Archeologists excavating in areas of Peru and Bolivia have been fortunate in finding ancient textiles that have been preserved from decay by the unusually dry climate. From the technological and craft point of view, some of these pre-Columbian textiles are among the finest pieces of weaving ever seen. Dr. Junius Bird, who has done extensive research on Peruvian tapestries, has commented:

The Peruvian products . . . were technically far superior in every detail [to European tapestries] . . . they frequently have over two hundred weft per inch and some exceed two hundred and fifty. . . . It would be impossible to create such a fabric without having perfect yarn for the warp. . . . Roughly, contemporary European tapestry, by contrast, seldom exceeds eighty-five weft per inch, and modern examples much fewer. . . . The extreme fineness of weave, however, is only one aspect of the Peruvian product. Every conceivable device applicable to tapestry construction was employed with care and skill.[7]

As Grace Goodell demonstrates in "The Cloth of the Quechuas," the creativity and skill in weaving that characterized pre-Columbian Peru and Bolivia are by no means extinct in these regions today, although the threat exists that these skills may soon die out. As was true in the case of traditional Polynesian surfing, this artistic and craft tradition is closely linked with social values. Goodell points out that in the area east of Oruro in the Bolivian Andes:

. . . weaving is still the critical measure of material worth: a boy weaves a belt for a girl before proposing to her; she weaves a coca bag for him in consent. . . . At regional celebrations there is rivalry among communities to establish or preserve a collective reputation for weaving excellence.

Here is no "art for art's sake" but an aspect of material culture that is linked to aspects of social life. Anthropologists dealing with traditional societies often have recourse to the concept of *cultural integration* in dealing with cases like those involving surfing among the Polynesians or weaving among the Quechua Indians of Bolivia. Today a glance at familiar and widely read magazines such as *Time* and *Newsweek* reveals the separate categories into which modern Western culture is compartmentalized (music, religion, sports, art, medicine, and so forth). Yet anthropologist Franz Boas has pointed out that in the study of primitive art, one outstanding characteristic is the way it is integrated with other elements of culture to provide an organic whole.[8] This integrated wholeness of art and social life emerges into plain view particularly in situations where either the traditional art or social life is under stress from outside modernizing influences. Goodell shows how the canons of artistic style have been challenged directly in many areas of Peru and Bolivia where the tourist demand for hastily and sloppily made textiles has been felt. In the southern Andes she found that where the quality of weaving declined, so did the related crafts of spinning and dyeing, the latter requiring a subtle knowledge of local botany and geography. As commercial, tourist-based incentives toward mass production replaced the traditional desires for each woven piece as a unique example of artistic expression, the Indians were less and less willing to take the time or effort to find and prepare native dyes or to spin fibers with the customary care, or to pass these skills on to successive generations of weavers. Then, too, new social values have challenged the art. The man from Sucre who went to work for Spaniards on a road crew wanted a plain poncho in keeping with the ponchos worn by higher-class Spaniards. His beautifully decorated poncho marked him as a hillbilly and made him ashamed. When he ordered his wife to make a plain poncho for him, she wept. She was true to the traditional canons of style and could not conceive of weaving an undecorated poncho; it violated every rule of the art that she knew. In this case a change in social value (a desire for increased status in the eyes of the Spaniards) led to a contradiction in the art.

Notes

1   Kent V. Flannery, "Culture History vs. Cultural Process: A Debate in American Archaeology," *Scientific American*, vol. 217, no. 2, 1967, pp. 119–122.
2   Walter W. Taylor, "A Study of Archaeology," *American Anthropologist Memoir* no. 69, 1948, pp. 152–202.
3   Peter H. Buck, *Vikings of the Pacific*, Chicago, The University of Chicago Press, 1959.
4   Andrew Sharp, *Ancient Voyagers in the Pacific*, London, Penguin Books, 1957.
5   Helen Codere, *Kwakiutl Ethnography*, Franz Boas, Chicago, The University of Chicago Press, 1966, p. xviii.
6   Thomas Gladwin, *East Is a Big Bird: Navigation and Logic on Puluwat Atoll*, Cambridge, Harvard University Press, 1970, p. 154.
7   Wendell C. Bennett and Junius C. Bird, *Andean Culture History*, New York, The American Museum of Natural History, 1960, p. 277.
8   Franz Boas, *Primitive Art*, New York, Dover, 1955, p. 7.

JAMES DEETZ
EDWIN S. DETHLEFSEN

DEATH'S HEAD, CHERUB, URN AND WILLOW   Enter almost any cemetery in eastern Massachusetts that was in use during the seventeenth and eighteenth centuries. Inspect the stones and the designs carved at their tops, and you will discover that three motifs are present. These motifs have distinctive periods of popularity, each replacing the other in a sequence that is repeated time and time again in all cemeteries between Worcester and the Atlantic, and from New Hampshire to Cape Cod.

DEATH'S HEAD   CHERUB   URN AND WILLOW

The earliest of the three is a winged death's head, with blank eyes and a grinning visage. Earlier versions are quite ornate, but as time passes, they become less elaborate. Sometime during the eighteenth century—the time varies according to location—the grim death's head designs are replaced, more or less quickly, by winged cherubs. This design also goes through a gradual simplification of form with time. By the late 1700's or early 1800's, again depending on where you are observing, the cherubs are replaced by stones decorated with a willow tree overhanging a pedestaled urn. If the cemetery you are visiting is in a rural area, the chances are quite good that you will also find other designs, which may even completely replace one or more of the three primary designs at certain periods. If you were to search cemeteries in the same area, you would find that these other designs have a much more local distribution. In and around Boston, however, only the three primary designs would be present.

If you were to prepare a graph showing how the designs change in popularity through time, the finished product might look something like three battleships viewed from above, the

DEATH'S HEAD, CHERUB, URN AND WILLOW

	Death's Head	Cherub	Urn and Willow
1820			▓
1810			▓
1800		▓	▓
1790		▓	▓
1780	▓	▓	
1770	▓	▓	▓
1760	▓	▓	
1750	▓		
1740	▓		
1730	▓		
1720	▓		

Stylistic sequence from a cemetery in Stoneham, Massachusetts.

lower one with the bow showing, the center one in full view, and the third visible only in the stern. This shape, frequently called a "battleship-shaped" curve, is thought by archeologists to typify the popularity career of any cultural trait across time. Prepared from controlled data taken from the Stoneham cemetery, north of Boston, where the style sequence is typical of the area around this eighteenth-century urban center of eastern Massachusetts, the graph above shows such a curve.

It is appropriate here to interrupt and pose the question: why would an archeologist study gravestones from a historic period?

Whether archeology can be considered a science in the strict sense of the word is much debated. One of the hallmarks of scientific method is the use of controls in experimentation that enable the investigator to calibrate his results. Since archeology deals largely with the unrecorded past, the problem of rigorous control is a difficult one. Much of modern archeological method and theory has been developed in contexts that lack the necessary controls for precise checking of accuracy and predictive value. For this reason, any set of archeological data in which such controls are available is potentially of great importance to the development and testing of explanatory models, which can then be used in uncontrolled contexts.

For a number of reasons, colonial New England grave markers may be unique in providing the archeologist with a laboratory situation in which to measure cultural change in time and space and relate such measurements to the main body of archeological method. All archeological data—artifacts, structures, sites —can be said to possess three inherent dimensions. A clay pot, for example, has a location in *space*. Its date of manufacture and use is fixed in *time*, and it has certain physical attributes of *form*. In a sense, much of archeological method is concerned with the nature and causes of variation along these dimensions, as shown by excavated remains of past cultures.

The spatial aspect of gravestones is constant. We know from historical sources that nearly all of the stones in New England cemeteries of this period were produced locally, probably no more than fifteen or twenty miles away; an insignificant number of them came from long distances. This pattern is so reliable that it is possible to detect those few stones in every cemetery that were made at a more remote town. Once placed over the dead, the stones were unlikely to have been moved, except perhaps within the cemetery limits.

Needless to say, the dimension of time is neatly and tightly controlled. Every stone bears the date of death of the individual whose grave it marks, and most stones were erected shortly after death. Like the spatial regularity, this temporal precision makes it possible to single out most of the stones that were erected at some later date.

Control over the formal dimension of gravestone data derives from our knowledge of the carvers, who, in many instances, are known by name and period of production, and who, even if anonymous, can be identified by their product with the help of spatial and temporal control. Thus, in most cases stones of similar type can be seen to be the product of a single person, and they reflect his ideas regarding their proper form.

Furthermore, it is known that the carvers of the stones were not full-time specialists, but rather workers at other trades who made stones for the immediate population as they were needed. We are dealing, then, with "folk" products, as is often the case in prehistoric archeology.

Other cultural dimensions can also be controlled in the gravestone data with equal precision, and with the addition of these, the full power of these artifacts as controls becomes apparent: probate research often tells the price of individual stones; status indication occurs frequently on the stones, as well as the age of each individual. Since death is related to religion, formal variations in the written material can be analyzed to see how they reflect religious variations. Epitaphs provide a unique literary and psychological dimension. Spatial distributions can be measured against political divisions. In short, the full historical background of the seventeenth, eighteenth, and nineteenth centuries permits both primary and secondary control of the material, and with the resulting precision, explanations become quite reliable.

With such controls available to the archeologist, the pattern of change in colonial gravestone design and style can be used with great effect to sharpen our understanding of cultural process in general.

To return to the battleship-shaped curves on page 118, what does this mean in terms of culture change? Why should death's heads be popular at all, and what cultural factors were responsible for their disappearance and the subsequent rise of the cherub design? The most obvious answer is found in the ecclesiastical history of New England. The period of decline of death's heads coincides with the decline of orthodox Puritanism. In the late seventeenth century, Puritanism was universal in the area, and so were death's head gravestones. The early part of the eighteenth century saw the beginnings of change in orthodoxy, culminating in the great awakenings of the mid-century. In his recent, excellent book on the symbolism of New England gravestones, *Graven Images*, Allan Ludwig points out that the "iconophobic" Puritans found the carving of gravestones a compromise. While the use of cherubs might have verged on heresy, since they are heavenly beings whose portrayal might lead to idolatry, the use of a more mortal and neutral symbol—a death's head— would have served as a graphic reminder of death and resurrection.

Given the more liberal views concerning symbolism and personal involvement preached by Jonathan Edwards and others later in the eighteenth century, the idolatrous and heretical aspects of cherubs would have been more fitting to express the sentiment of the period.

It is at this point that available literary controls become valuable. Each stone begins by describing the state of the deceased: "Here lies" or "Here lies buried" being typical early examples. Slowly these are replaced by "Here lies [buried] the body [corruptible, what was mortal] of." This slightly, but significantly, different statement might well reflect a more

Some gravestone locations and movements of carvers.

explicit tendency to stress that only a part of the deceased remains, while the soul, the incorruptible or immortal portion, has gone to its eternal reward. Cherubs reflect a stress on resurrection, while death's heads emphasize the mortality of man. The epitaphs that appear on the bottoms of many stones also add credence to this explanation of change in form over time. Early epitaphs, with death's head designs, stress either decay and life's brevity:

My Youthful mates both small
  and great
Come here and you may see
An awful sight, which is a type
  of which you soon must be

or a Calvinistic emphasis on hard work and exemplary behavior on the part of the predestined:

He was a useful man in his generation, a lover of learning, a faithful servant of Harvard College above forty years.

On the other hand, epitaphs with cherub stones tend to stress resurrection and later heavenly reward:

Here cease thy tears, suppress thy
  fruitless mourn
his soul—the immortal part—has
  upward flown
On wings he soars his rapid way
To yon bright regions of eternal
  day.

The final change seen in gravestone style is the radical shift to the urn and willow design. It is usually accompanied by a change in stone shape; while earlier stones have a round-shouldered outline, the later stones have square shoulders. "Here lies the body of" is replaced by "In memory of" or "Sacred to the memory of," quite different from all earlier forms. The earlier stones are markers, designating the location of the deceased or at least a portion of him. In contrast, "In memory of" is simply a memorial statement, and stones of this later type could logically be erected elsewhere and still make sense. In fact, many of the late urn and willow stones are cenotaphs, erected to commemorate those actually buried elsewhere, as far away as Africa, Batavia, and in one case—in the Kingston, Massachusetts, cemetery—"drowned at sea, lat. 39 degrees N., long. 70 degrees W." The cultural changes that accompany the shift to urn and willow designs are seen in the rise of less emotional, more intellectual religions, such as Unitarianism and Methodism. Epitaphs change with design and in the early nineteenth century tend more to sentiment combined with eulogy.

This sequence of change did not occur in a vacuum, unrelated to any cultural change elsewhere; indeed, the sequence of three major types also takes place in England, the cultural parent of the Massachusetts colony, but about a half century earlier. Thus cherubs have become modal by the beginning of the Georgian period (1715), and urns and willows make their appearance, as a part of the neoclassical tradition, in the 1760's. In fact, the entire urn and willow pattern is a part of the larger Greek Revival, which might explain the squared shoulders on the stones—a severer classical outline.

Thus far we have been discussing formal change through time, and some of the fundamental causes. We have seen that New England is changing in harmony with England, with an expectable time interval separating the sequences. But we have not identified the relationship of all of this to archeological method.

The battleship-shaped curve assumption is basic to many considerations of culture process in general and to such dating methods as seriation. Seriation is a method whereby archeological sites are arranged in relative chronological order based on the popularity of the different types of artifacts found in them. The approach assumes that any cultural item, be it a style of pottery or a way of making an arrowhead, has a particular popularity period, and as it grows and wanes in popularity, its prevalence as time passes can be represented graphically by a single peaked curve. Small beginnings grow to a high frequency of occurrence, followed in turn by a gradual disappearance. If such an assumption is true, it follows that a series of sites can be arranged so that all artifact types within them form single peaked curves of popularity over time. Such an arrangement is chronological, and tells the archeologist how his sites relate to one another in time.

By plotting style sequences in this manner in a number of cemeteries, we find that the assumption, not previously measured with such a degree of precision, is a sound one: styles do form single peaked popularity curves through time. By adding the control of the spatial to the form—time pattern explained above, we gain a number of understandings regarding diffusion —the spread of ideas through time and space and how this, in turn, affects internal change in style. In looking now at the three dimensions we will see that all of the secondary cultural controls become even more important.

The style sequence of death's head, cherub, and urn and willow design is to be found in almost every cemetery in eastern Massachusetts. However, when we inspect the time at which each change takes place, and the degree of overlap between styles from cemetery to cemetery, it becomes apparent that this sequence was occurring at a widely varying rate from place to place. The earliest occurrence of cherubs is in the Boston–Cambridge area, where they begin to appear as early as the end of the seventeenth century. Occasional early cherubs might be found in more distant rural cemeteries, but in every case we find them to have been carved in the Boston area and to be rare imports from there. The farther we move away from the Boston center, the later locally manufactured cherubs make their appearance in numbers. The rate at which the cherub style spread outward has even been approximately measured, and shown to be about a mile per year. It is not common in archeology to make such precise measurements of diffusion rate—the usual measurements are cruder, such as hundreds of miles in millenniums.

We can view Boston and, more significantly, nearby Cambridge as the focus of emphasis of Puritan religion with its accompanying values, and inquire what factors might contribute to the initial appearance of cherubs and the change in religious values in this central area. We have noted that the change had already been accomplished in England by the early eighteenth century, so that when the first cherubs begin to appear in numbers in Cambridge, they were already the standard modal style in England. While cherubs occur in Boston, they never make a major impression, and as many death's heads as cherubs are replaced by the urn and willow influx.

On the other hand, in Cambridge cherubs make an early start and attain a respectable frequency by the late eighteenth century. Although they never attain a full 100 per cent level there, as they do in most rural areas, they do at least enjoy a simple majority. When the cherub stones in Cambridge are inspected more closely, we find that roughly 70 per cent of them mark the graves of high status individuals: college presidents, graduates of Harvard, governors and their families, high church officials, and in one case, even a "Gentleman from London." From what we know of innovation in culture, it is often the more cosmopolitan, urban stratum of society that brings in new ideas, to be followed later by the folk stratum. If this is true, then the differences between Boston and Cambridge indicate a more liberal element within the population of Cambridge, reflected in the greater frequency of cherub stones there. This is probably the case, with the influence of the Harvard intellectual community being reflected in the cemetery. It would appear that even in the early eighteenth century, the university was a place for innovation and liberal thinking. Cambridge intellectuals were more likely to be responsive to English styles, feelings, and tastes, and this could well be what we are seeing in the high number of cherub stones marking high status graves.

Introduced into Cambridge and Boston by a distinct social class, the cherub design slowly begins its diffusion into the surrounding countryside. Carvers in towns farther removed from Cambridge and Boston—as far as fourteen miles west in Concord—begin to change their gravestone styles away from the popular death's head as early as the 1730's, but fifty miles to the south, in Plymouth, styles do not change until the fifties and sixties and then in a somewhat different cultural context. We find, however, that the farther the cemetery is from Boston, and the later the cherubs begin to be locally manufactured, the more rapidly they reach a high level of popularity. The pattern is one of a long period of coexistence between cherubs and death's heads in the Boston center, and an increasingly more rapid eclipsing of death's heads by cherubs in direct proportion to distance, with a much shorter period of overlap. One explanation is that in towns farther removed from the diffusion center, enforcement of Puritan ethics and values would lessen, and resistance to change would not be so strong. Furthermore, revivalism and the modification of orthodox Puritanism was widespread from the late thirties through the sixties in rural New England, although this movement never penetrated Boston. Such activity certainly must have conditioned the rural populace for a change to new designs.

We have, then, a picture of the introduction of a change in the highly specific aspect of mortuary art, an aspect reflecting much of the culture producing it. We see the subsequent spread of this idea, through space and time, as a function of social class and religious values. Now we are in a position to examine internal change in form through time, while maintaining relatively tight control on the spatial dimension.

One significant result of the use of gravestone data with its accompanying controls is the insight it provides in matters of stylistic evolution. The product of a single carver can be studied over a long period of time, and the change in his patterns considered as they reflect both ongoing culture change and his particular manner of handling design elements. The spatial axis extending outward from Boston shows not only systematic change in major style replacement rates but also a striking pattern of difference in style change. We find that in many cases, the farther removed we become from Boston, the more rapid and radical is change within a given single design. This has been observed in at least five separate cases, involving a number of the styles of more local distribution; we can inspect one of these cases closely, and attempt to determine some of the processes and causes of stylistic evolution.

The design in question is found in Plymouth County, centering on the town of Plympton. Its development spans a period of some seventy years, and the changes effected from beginning to end are truly profound. Death's heads occur in rural Plymouth

County, as they do elsewhere in the late seventeenth century. However, in the opening decade of the eighteenth century the carver(s) in Plympton made certain basic changes in the general death's head motif. The first step in this modification involved the reduction of the lower portion of the face, and the addition of a heart-shaped element between nose and teeth. The resulting pattern was one with a heartlike mouth, with the teeth shrunken to a simple band along the bottom. The teeth soon disappear entirely, leaving the heart as the sole mouth element. This change is rapidly followed by a curious change in the feathering of the wings.

While early examples show all feather ends as regular scallops crossing the lines separating individual feathers, shortly after the first changes in the face were made, every other row of feather ends had their direction of curvature reversed. The resulting design produces the effect of undulating lines radiating from the head, almost suggesting hair, at right angles to curved lines that still mark the feather separation. These two changes, in face and wing form, occupy a period of 35 years from 1710 through 1745. During the later forties this development, which has so far been a single sequence, splits into two branches, each the result of further modification of wings. In the first case, the arcs marking feather separations are omitted, leaving only the undulating radial lines. Rapid change then takes place, and soon we are confronted with a face surmounted by wavy and, later, quite curly hair. The heart mouth has been omitted. We have dubbed this style "Medusa." In the second case, the separating lines are retained, and the undulating lines removed; the result in this case is a face with multiple halos. At times, space between these halos is filled with spiral elements, giving the appearance of hair, or the halos are omitted entirely. The heart-shaped mouth is retained in this case and modified into a T-shaped element.

Both of these styles enjoy great popularity in the fifties and sixties, and have slightly different spatial distributions, suggesting that they might be the work of two carvers, both modifying the earlier heart-mouthed design in different ways. Yet a third related design also appears in the forties, this time with tightly curled hair, conventional wings, and a face similar to the other two. Although this third design seems to be a more direct derivative of the earlier death's head motif, it is clearly inspired in part by the Medusa and multiple halo designs. This tight-haired style has a markedly different spatial distribution, occurring to the west of the other two, but overlapping them in a part of its range. Of the three, only the Medusa lasts into the seventies, and in doing so presents us with something of an enigma. The final form, clearly evolved from the earlier types, is quite simple. It has a specific association with small children, and has never been found marking the grave of an adult, and rarely of a child over age five.

The carver of the fully developed Medusa was probably Ebenezer Soule of Plympton; a definitive sample of his style is found in the Plympton cemetery. Normal Medusas, except for the late, simple ones marking children's graves, disappear abruptly in the late sixties. In 1769, and lasting until the eighties, stones identical to Soule's Medusas, including the simple, late ones, appear in granite around Hinsdale, New Hampshire. Fortunately, a local history has identified the carver of some of these stones as "Ebenezer Soule, late of Plympton." This alone is of great interest, but if Soule did move to Hinsdale in 1769, who carved the later children's stones in Plymouth County? As yet, no answer is known.

This development raises two interesting considerations. First, we see that a style, the Medusa, which had been used for the general populace, ends its existence restricted to small children. This pattern has been observed elsewhere, with children's burials being marked by designs that were somewhat more popular earlier in time. In other words, children are a stylistically conservative element in the population of a cemetery. While no clear answer can be given to this problem, it may well be that small children, not having developed a strong, personal impact on the society, would not be thought of in quite the same way as adults, and would have their graves marked with more conservative, less explicitly descriptive stones.

The second problem raised by the Medusas is their reappearance in Hinsdale. If, as archeologists, we were confronted with the degree of style similarity seen between Hinsdale and Plympton in mortuary art, might we not infer a much greater influence than a single individual arriving in the community? After all, mortuary art would be about the only distinctively variable element in material culture over eighteenth-century New England, and such a close parallel could well be said to represent a migration from Plympton to Hinsdale. One man moved.

Placing this striking case of stylistic evolution in the broader context of culture change and style change in eastern Massachusetts, we find that it is paralleled by other internal modifications of death's head designs in other remote rural areas. The closer we move toward Boston, the less change takes place within the death's head design, and in Boston proper, death's heads from 1810 are not that different from those from 1710. Yet 1710 death's heads in Plympton and elsewhere had changed so radically by 1750 that it is doubtful that we could supply the derivation of one from the other in the absence of such an excellently dated set of intermediate forms. This difference in rate of change can be explained by referring back to the long, parallel courses of development of both death's head and cherub in the diffusion area's Boston center. However, culture change in the area of religion, marked by a shift of emphasis from mortality to immortality, probably generated a desire for less realistic and less grim designs on stones. Given this basic change in religious attitudes, what were the alternatives facing carvers in Boston as opposed to the Ebenezer Soules of rural New England? In Boston it was simply a matter of carving more cherub stones and fewer death's head stones; neither had to be altered to suit the new tastes. The choice between cherub and death's head in Boston has been seen as ultimately a social one, and if there was a folk culture component within Boston, there was nothing but folk culture in the more democratic, less-stratified rural areas. With no one to introduce cherubs and to call for them with regularity in the country, carvers set to work modifying the only thing they had—the death's head. The more remote the community, the later the local cherubs appear, diffusing from Boston, and the more likely the tendency to rework the common folk symbol of skull and wings. Thus we get Medusas and haloed T-mouthed faces populating the cemeteries of Plymouth County until cherubs finally appear. Even then, the waning popularity of the death's head in this area might be more the result of Soule's exit than their unsatisfactory appearance compared to the new cherubs.

Only a few applications of gravestone design analysis have been detailed here. A three-year program is presently under way, through which we hope to pursue numerous other aspects of this fascinating study. There is a large and important demographic dimension to these data; since precise date of death is given, as well as age at death, patterns of mortality and life expectance through time and space can be detailed. The results of this work, in turn, will add a biological dimension of style to the cultural one described above. Studies of diffusion rate, and its relationship to dating by seriation will be continued. Relationships between political units—counties, townships, and colonies —and style spheres will be investigated to determine how such units affect the distribution of a carver's products. Finally, a happy by-product will be the preservation on film of over 25,000 gravestones, a vital consideration in view of the slow but steady deterioration these informative artifacts are undergoing.

Aside from the value of this work to archeology and anthropology in general, one final comment must be made. Compared to the usual field work experienced by the archeologist, with all of its dust and heavy shoveling under a hot sun, this type of archeology certainly is most attractive. All of the artifacts are on top of the ground, the sites are close to civilization, and almost all cemeteries have lovely, shady trees.

THOMAS GLADWIN

EAST IS A BIG BIRD Puluwat is an island of green, edged in
white and set in a tropic sea. Already distant, a canoe is sailing
away. Its sail accents the scene, a white cockade bobbing over
the waves, impudent and alone.

Then the canoe and its crew are gone. In the days or weeks
thereafter no one on Puluwat can know where they are. Finally
someone, perhaps high in a tree picking breadfruit, sees a tiny
white triangle on the horizon and emits a whoop. The cry is
carried from voice to voice, and within a minute everyone on
Puluwat knows a canoe is coming. More men climb trees, and
soon eyes practiced in the scrutiny of sea and sails distinguish
a familiar mark or shape. The canoe is identified. The studied
indifference of those left behind gives way to excitement. If the
journey has been long and the day is pleasant, the lagoon will
fill with canoes paddled out to greet the travelers as they enter
the pass in the reef. The voyage is over. All of Puluwat shares
in the reaffirmation of a proud heritage.

From the canoe, the perspective is quite different. Anyone
who has sailed a small boat in the open sea need not be told
that the image of a little sail bobbing over the water would
scarcely come to the minds of those on board. The sail dominates
them not only by its size, but by its tense struggle to contain
the wind it has deflected to its own use. Vibrating, it strains at
its lashings. Alternately the sail shades the crew or blinds them
with its whiteness. The spars sway and shudder as the boat lifts
and plunges through the steep waves of the open Pacific. The
canoe itself, a narrow V-shaped hull about 26 feet long, with
platforms extending out both sides, lurches with a violence that
requires constant holding on. If the crew is lucky and the wind
holds steady, this pitching and twisting will go on, without rest,
day and night for the day or two or three it takes to reach their
destination. But the wind may drop and leave the crew drifting
under an equatorial sun. Or it may rise to a storm with gusts
wracking the canoe and driving chilling rain into the skin and
eyes of the crew. Through all of this the navigator, in sole command, keeps track of course, drift, and position, guided only by
stars and waves and other signs of the sea, and in recent years

by a large but unlighted compass. Even at night he stays awake and vigilant, trusting only himself. They say you can tell the experienced navigators by their bloodshot eyes.

There is a heroic quality to this kind of sailing. Happily, everyone on Puluwat and the other islands of their seafaring world agrees as to its heroism. Even more happily, virtually every man, every child, and any woman who cares to can experi-

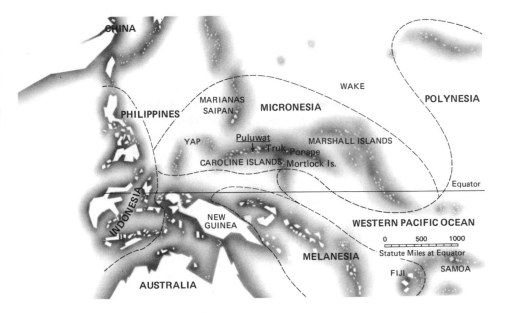

ence again and again the life of a hero. It is thus a hospitable sort of heroism despite its frequent hardships. Sailing canoes are complex and temperamental craft, but manageable enough for anyone brought up on them to qualify as crew. One is therefore not faced with a fear of failure. True, only a few achieve the skills of the navigator, but you do not have to be a navigator to be a hero.

Voyaging is hospitable, too, because, unless there is some occasion for worry, or bad weather is making everyone miserable, the prevailing mood at sea is one of good fellowship. Jokes find an audience eager for amusement, tales can be embellished endlessly without fear of losing listeners, and on most trips there is food to eat any time one becomes even a little hungry. There are discomforts, of course, and also risks. Without them there would be no zest, and no occasion for heroes. But the discomforts are transitory and, when you are used to them, quite tolerable. The risks are real, but not nearly as great as one would expect contemplating the vast stretches of ocean, the tiny

slivers of wood and cord that are a canoe, and the little dots
of land that are the islands to which Puluwatans sail. The reason
the risks are not greater lies in the realm of technology. It lies in
canoes, which may look complicated and sometimes crude, but
that are extraordinarily tough and versatile in the responses they
can make to all manner of conditions and crises. It lies in a system of navigation that, in the hands and eyes of a gifted and
vigilant navigator, covers just about every contingency. But
above all it lies in the skill and resourcefulness of a people born
to the sea and proud of its mastery.

Puluwat is one of a long chain of low coral islands that lie
between volcanic Truk on the east and Palau and Yap on the
west. Taken all together, these islands comprise the Western and
Central Carolines; they cover more than a thousand miles of the
Pacific Ocean north of New Guinea. The low islands, from Puluwat and its neighbors westward to Sonsorol, southwest of Palau,
share a similar culture and languages. They are closely related
to Truk, but differ sharply from Yap and Palau.

In recent centuries the Carolines have been controlled suc-
cessively by Spain, Germany, Japan, and the United States.
Through most of this time, however, Puluwat was little influenced. Explorers, traders, missionaries, and administrators
remained on the island only occasionally and temporarily. During World War II the Puluwatans were evacuated by the Japanese to nearby Pulusuk for military reasons, but after the war
they returned to take up a life little different from before. Only
the Americans have tried to bring about radical change, principally through education, Christian missions, and indoctrination
of leaders. Although these have had some impact, thus far one is
struck more by how little has changed than by how much.

Beyond Puluwat lies a world of little islands, some inhabited
and some not, but each with its own special shape and nature,
and each in its own assigned place upon the vast surface of the
sea. As one thinks of these islands, one over there, another there
to the north, a third over here closer, the sea itself is transformed. No longer is it simply a great body of water that,
encountering Puluwat, shoves around it and re-forms on the
other side to flow on to an empty eternity. Instead the ocean
becomes a thoroughfare over which one can think of oneself
moving toward a particular island of destination, which as one
comes upon it will be waiting, as it always waits, right where it

is supposed to be. When a Puluwatan speaks of the ocean the words he uses refer, not to an amorphous expanse of water, but rather to the assemblage of seaways that lie between the various islands. Together these seaways constitute the ocean he knows and understands. Seen in this way Puluwat ceases to be a solitary spot of dry land; it takes its place in a familiar constellation of islands linked together by pathways on the ocean.

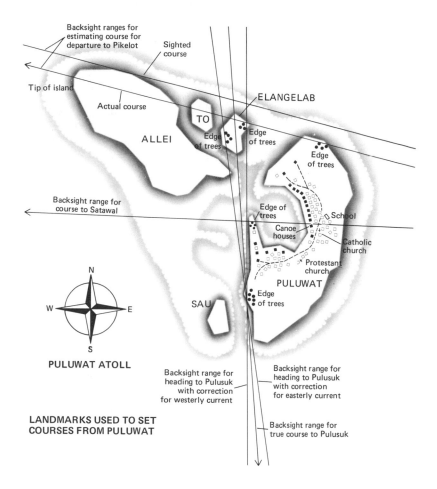

LANDMARKS USED TO SET
COURSES FROM PULUWAT

The Puluwatan pictures himself and his island in his part of the ocean much as we might locate ourselves upon a road map. On a road map, places—mostly communities—appear as locations with names, linked by lines of travel. Those we know from having visited them spring to mind: the buildings, the people, the spirit of the place. Those we know only at secondhand have a less clear image, and some are nothing but names. But each has its place, and there is a way to get to each one. Each has its part to play in the totality, which is a state or region or country.

So it is with the island world of the Puluwatan. He knows of many islands and can visualize where they are and how to get to them. Some he has visited; he knows people and places on them that set them apart. Others he has heard about because people from them have visited Puluwat, and Puluwatans have traveled the seaway there on their canoes. Still other, more distant islands are spoken of only by their names and legends. While the navigators know the star courses to them, they have never traveled these courses—but they know that if they did, the islands would be there.

Historically it was essential that Puluwat be a part of this larger island world. It would never have developed as it has if it stood alone. Dozens of islands stretched over a thousand miles of ocean from Yap on the west to Truk and the islands beyond on the east have been linked by their seafaring men and their sailing canoes into a network of social, economic, and often political ties without which they probably could not have survived, much less evolved the complex and secure way of life they now enjoy. The opportunity to exchange people, goods, and information permits these tiny communities to survive disasters—notably typhoons—to draw from a pool of ideas and innovations larger than just their own, to integrate when useful into larger political groupings, and to extend the range of choice in marriage beyond the limited number of unrelated partners available on one's own island.

These are all highly practical, indeed essential, considerations. Yet beyond its practical value, the seafaring life, the constant voyaging of sailing canoes back and forth between islands, has acquired a psychological worth of its own. It adds a measure of meaning and value to every other act, on land as well as at sea. Nothing could attest to this more eloquently than a paradox: as the seafaring culture on Puluwat renews itself with undiminished vitality—building new canoes, training young navigators, experimenting with novel techniques—the practical necessity for it has all but disappeared. Virtually all of the exchanges of people and things and ideas outlined above could be achieved reasonably well through travel on small passenger-

Small sailing canoe returns after a day of fishing along the reefs in the open ocean.

carrying ships, which have been making regular administrative and trading trips through these islands for the past twenty years.

The Puluwatans approach fishing in much the same way. Seine nets, handlines, and spearfishing are often more productive, but Puluwatans prefer trolling over the outer reefs at high speed, chasing the wheeling seabirds that signal schooling fish below. The canoes take a beating—roughter treatment and more risks than would be acceptable on a long ocean voyage. But fishing is part of what the canoes are built for, and as all the canoes strain toward a school of fish, you know at once which sails the best and which captain is most skilled and daring. This is the good way, the proud way to catch fish.

The truth of the matter is that the Puluwatans are not objective about their canoes, even less objective perhaps than we in the United States are about our automobiles. Especially for those of us who live in cities, the minor inconvenience of public transportation should weigh far less in the balance than the cost and trouble of keeping a car, yet most of us not only keep our cars but at intervals buy new ones. We say the automobile has become part of our way of life and we do not want to give it up. On Puluwat the sailing canoe is not merely a part of their way of life, it is the very heart of it. To suggest that the Puluwatans should beach their canoes and retire their navigators would be to foretell disaster. To imagine Puluwat without the élan of its seafaring life one must think of a dispirited people. While the exhilaration of trolling over the reefs can remind men they are men, the canoes that Puluwatans build, and the voyages that they undertake to distant islands, suffuse the entire island, not just its men, with a sense of purpose and fulfillment. In the last analysis everything on Puluwat is justified by the contribution it makes to the capability of boats and people to travel well and safely at sea.

There is no sign that this enthusiasm is waning. If anything, it is growing stronger. The rest of the world may see virtue in mechanization, in power and efficiency, but on Puluwat almost every young man still aspires to become a navigator. Only a handful make it, but those who fall by the wayside are willing to settle for the lesser glory of being a crew member on a Puluwat canoe. Thus far very few young people appear inclined to leave Puluwat to seek their futures in the district center on Truk or elsewhere. Rather, the young men are learning to build, to sail, and hopefully even to navigate canoes, and young women are readying themselves to be wives of seafarers.

In the Carolines there are good seasons for sailing, and bad. The Puluwatan navigator knows these times by the rising and setting of certain stars just before dawn or at dusk through the cycle of each year. He knows the weather and winds associated with each of these star months and can thus forecast the seasonal changes.

In April atmospheric pressure from the north weakens, the doldrum belt begins to move north toward the equator, and the trade winds, although still blowing fairly steadily from the northeast, drop in strength to comfortable levels. The sailing canoes have been overhauled, and one after another, or in convoys of two or three, they set off on their various journeys.

During July and August the doldrum belt has moved so far north that Puluwat lies south of it. Now the trade winds are coming from the south. Although below the equator the trades typically blow from the southeast, when they cross the equator the same winds turn and come from the southwest. This more westerly wind is fine for voyages to the east. With a southwesterly breeze one can go to Pisaras, East Fayu, or the Halls with the wind astern, and thereafter run down to Truk itself with the same wind comfortably on the beam. Then wait a week or two and the wind will often shift around to blow you home again.

Linger too long, however, and the doldrum belt will have passed again to the south. This usually happens toward the end of September. Cooler air from the north comes upon water heated by the summer sun and doldrum winds, and the mix becomes unstable. This is the season of typhoons, identical to the hurricanes that are spawning at the same time and for the same reasons in the Caribbean and adjacent Atlantic waters. These storms come up so fast and with such fury that only the most daring, or perhaps foolhardy, of navigators will venture on a long trip during late September or October. After this the weather stabilizes again, the northeast trades (which actually vary between northeast and east) dominate, and canoes that were caught on Truk can return home to Puluwat with a good wind behind them. Gradually the winds grow in strength, with an occasional letup near the end of December, until the steady, discouraging blow of the drab winter months sets in and everyone stays home to await liberation by the gentler weather of spring.

The intention to make a long trip, such as one to Truk or

Satawal, usually develops over a period of several weeks or more. This is not always true, however. If, for example, a canoe is long overdue, worried relatives on Puluwat may decide overnight to set off on a search for them and leave within a few hours. Stops are then made at all the islands, however distant, which the missing craft had planned to visit, plus any others along the way, to learn whether the canoe was sighted and when.

The actual decision on when to leave, however, is usually reached only two or three days, never more than a week, in advance. If the question is pressed, one is told this short lead time is necessary in order to be able to forecast favorable weather during the first leg of the trip. However, the weather forecasting system operates essentially as an almanac dependent upon the rising and setting of stars and the phases of the moon. The Puluwatans know quite enough about these matters to be able to forecast the positions of the heavenly bodies weeks ahead, but the final decision of whether to leave on the appointed day is determined by the look of sky and sea at the time.

Preparation for a voyage begins with rounding up a crew. Four to six men comprise a full complement. Most of them are likely to be members of the navigator-captain's canoe house or co-owners of the boat or both. Although a core group of men seems to travel regularly on each canoe, there is nothing rigid about this. The canoes are sufficiently alike that no technical problems arise from riding on an unfamiliar craft, and there are no special loyalties associated with individual canoes. The word soon gets around that so-and-so is making a trip to Truk or Ulul or Satawal. Anyone who is waiting for a chance to go there can be fairly sure of finding a place on the canoe just by asking. The navigator presumably intends to round out his crew with some of his younger relatives whose services he can virtually command, so he easily makes a place for the petitioner by dropping one of these. He must also, if possible, include in his crew at least one other man with navigational skills in case he is himself incapacitated.

If women or children are coming along, it is necessary to install a small, domed cover of plaited pandanus leaves over the lee platform. This little cabin is usually carried on any long voyage since under these circumstances there will probably be a

Extremely narrow hull of an oceangoing canoe is balanced by outrigger, extending out to the left, and lee platform, right.

good number of trade goods, gifts, and personal effects, which should be kept dry, and the shelter is welcome too for sleeping if the weather turns wet and cold. Women and children require more, however, than food and shelter. There must also be a man in the crew who is responsible at all times for each passenger. For women this is almost invariably their husbands. Particularly in the old days when it was believed that women posed a supernatural threat to the rest of the voyagers, it was essential that someone be available to assist them with any of the bodily needs that emphasized their femaleness. One could scarcely ask anyone but a husband to scoop up seawater time after time for a bath, so that as the woman poured the water over herself the sound of it striking the sea below would mask the noise of her urination. Even today, although the threat is gone, embarrassment is still possible when one or two women live with a group of men for several days on a very small boat. In these circumstances the only really appropriate intermediary is a woman's husband.

Children require even more attention. Despite the objections of their worried mothers, boys and girls are often taken on their first canoe trip to another island when they are only five, or sometimes even four years old, so that, early in their lives, they will get to know and to enjoy life at sea. To this end they are allowed the run of the boat, not cooped up in the little cabin except in bad weather. Thus, in addition to seeing that they are fed and that their other physical needs are cared for, someone must watch little children all the time. They can swim —Puluwat children swim almost as soon as they can toddle to the water—but falling overboard can still be very dangerous, especially at night. Therefore, for any child aboard there must also be two men, relatives of the child, who will be responsible for him. If there were only one he would spend all his time watching his charge and fail to do his share of the rigging, bailing, fishing, and other seagoing chores. Nor would he be able to take a nap, even when the child slept, lest the latter wake up and fall overboard. These and other considerations frequently require a little juggling of the roster before the list of crew and passengers is firmly established, but it is usually possible to please everyone—and those who might be unhappy because they have been unceremoniously pushed aside are likely to be young relatives of the navigator who made the decision, and therefore may not appropriately voice any public complaint.

As the morning wears on, the boat is gradually loaded with equipment and supplies. With everything carefully stowed the outline of the canoe does not change markedly, but the boat settles in the shallow water and is moved out a little way. Finally, all is ready and the sail, wrapped in loose folds over its spars, is carried out. When folded together, the boom and yard to which the sail is secured do not match in their respective curves, giving a clumsy appearance to the long bundle of wood

A canoe sets out on a journey.

and cloth. This clumsiness will vanish once the sail is raised. Then these same curves create the graceful, piquant sail profile that is the hallmark of canoes in the Central Carolines.

With the sail aboard there is a pause. The crew comes ashore and may share a cigarette or two, passed from hand to hand among themselves and the well-wishers who will remain behind. Often before a longer trip everyone goes to church for a prayer and a blessing. In a touching gesture, the navigator may go to ask his old navigation instructor's last-minute advice if the mentor cannot physically lend his presence to the departure. Then, without any formal farewells, the men wade out through the shallow water to the canoe. If women are going along, they board first, settling themselves as best they can in the cramped space under the cover of the lee platform. The line or lines that hold the boat are untied and someone shoves it away from shore. As one or two men start paddling, the others get ready to hoist the sail. Those on shore watch as the canoe moves away and then drift off in twos and threes about their various affairs. By the time it is out of sight no one is left in front of the canoe house to watch, except perhaps some old people who have neither an excuse nor the energy to move elsewhere for a while.

Coming up to the wide pass, bounded on one side by the southern tip of Puluwat and on the other by a tiny islet that is the roosting place of at least a thousand seabirds, the canoe quickens to the motion of the sea. Inside the lagoon it has been gliding along unperturbed by the rippling water. Now after scarcely a moment of transition it is plunging and rearing through waves flung high as they breast the current, which most of the time swirls powerfully outward over the reef. Outside, the canoes settles down a little, but a narrow 26-foot hull, even though balanced by an outrigger, has no chance to stay still while moving through the labyrinth of massive waves that march and countermarch across the western Pacific.

Once in the open the navigator establishes his strategy for the first leg of his trip. He sets his course, tests the wind, and often calls for further adjustments of mast or sail. Perhaps he tells someone to move aft so his weight will sink that end of the canoe deeper in the water and thus improve its trim when the wind is on the beam. Only after he is at sea does the navigator determine his sailing plan and make his final adjustments. Before they left he doubtless noted the general weather' and wind so that he had some idea how rough it would be and whether they would tack or run before the wind, but if the weather were not such as to create undue risks, he paid it little further heed. The sailing directions learned during the years of his apprenticeship are sufficiently complete to guide him in executing the voyage under almost all possible conditions. Beyond these general directions individual judgments must be attuned to the conditions actually observed at sea—seen with the eye, felt with the motion of the boat, and heard in the sound of the wind—conditions that cannot be inferred while standing on unyielding land with the wind blowing at full force only in the treetops.

Soon the canoe is well out at sea, settled on its initial course. The crew can relax. A line or two may be rigged for trolling,

Hipour tends the sail from the navigator's platform, where he will sit for most of the voyage.

Changing the sail.

but only if there are reefs below teeming with fish or if the trip is short. A trolling line creates drag, which on a longer trip can slow a canoe enough that it may not make its landing at a distant island before dark. Like all good sailors, Puluwatans are constantly concerned with getting the last ounce of performance from any boat they are on. The rigging and trim are continually readjusted, and even the sand is omitted from the iron cooking box to save weight on a long voyage. Every extra pound makes the canoe ride lower and thus slower in the water.

As the journey goes forward anyone is free to make a suggestion about the course the canoe is on, the set of the mast, the look of the weather, or perhaps a detour over a reef to catch some fish. The navigator is in command, with all the authority and responsibility we are accustomed to associate with the role, but this does not set him apart, aloof from the rest of the crew. He joins in the jokes and gossip and talks about his navigation quite freely, especially if he has a son or other student navigator aboard who can learn from his example. If there is some cause for anxiety or question, the responsible navigator feels obligated to pay particular attention to the suggestions or doubts of his crew members. They in turn will not speak up unless they have some seniority and competence to back up their views. Examples of these interchanges appear frequently in accounts of voyages told by navigators; it appears they are proud of their willingness to attend to these queries, rather than resenting those who question their judgment.

The routine at sea, unless there are storms, is relatively undemanding. At times everyone is talking; at other times, most are asleep—either stretched out, curled up, or propped against almost anything that offers support. No matter how crowded the canoe, people seem to find places to sleep without falling overboard. Occasionally, more often if the weather is rough, the canoe needs bailing. Someone sits on the little bench or thwart installed for this purpose down in the hull and throws the water over the lee side with a bailer, a scoop carved—like everything else—from breadfruit wood. All except the navigator take turns at this wearisome task without prodding or complaint. The crew members similarly relieve each other steering with the big steering paddle astern when this is made necessary by a following wind. Everyone is assumed to have the skill necessary to be a steersman, although it is soon obvious that some can hold a course better than others. Manning the sheet, which trims the sail and thereby trims the canoe, is more exacting. Sloppy work on the sheet can affect all aspects of the canoe's performance, as well as its safety. Most of the time the navigator tends it himself. When he wants relief he designates who shall take over. For a young man this can be an exciting responsibility, a rewarding gesture of confidence by the older navigator.

As with sleeping, so with eating. People eat when they feel like it. Usually one man gets out some food and the others join in. If fish have been caught, either they are eaten raw (especially tuna and bonito) or someone kindles a fire in the iron cooking box. It is set well aft on the outrigger platform so that sparks flying from the little, glowing heap of coconut husks will stream over the side. The fish are roasted whole on top of the fire and when they are done the fire is doused so that the husks can be used again, and also so that no more sparks will blow about.

Nowadays it is unusual for a canoe, if it does not run into some sort of trouble, to be at sea for more than four or five days, at most a week, at one stretch. In the past, trips were often longer, primarily because the canoes were slower and it took longer to get from one island to another. More distant journeys than are now customary were also made, but most of these were accomplished, as they still are, in stages, stopping at one island after another. A few, really long, unbroken voyages were made to more distant islands, islands large enough to minimize navigation problems in reaching them. They could be sighted over long distances and made large targets. These were islands such as Guam, Saipan, and Ponape. The men who made these heroic voyages were probably no better navigators than their modern counterparts, possibly even a little less accurate, but they were rugged and determined. They arrived at their destination half starved, dehydrated, and so burned by the sun they were black and almost poisoned by its effects. The return would not be made for months, and such trips were undertaken only rarely. Those recent enough to be remembered were made primarily to Saipan to trade with the Spaniards there for iron tools and knives, which could not be obtained in any other way. (In 1969, Hipour, a Puluwat navigator, using only his traditional knowledge, guided a modern ketch across 600 miles of open water to Saipan and then back again, making his return landfall unerringly on tiny Pikelot.)

Once the canoe has arrived, especially at an island where the crew have many friends and relatives, the welcome is warm and life is easy. No one need work. Their hosts feed them and entertain them with drink, good talk, and often at night a companion for their bed. If a man has not brought his wife along he can expect someone on the island who is his "brother," a relationship no less binding if it is artificial, to offer his own wife for the visitor's pleasure. Apparently not only do the visiting men appreciate this custom, but also the women. The wife who is offered in hospitality appreciates the novelty of a new sexual partner, and even the traveler's wife left at home understands and expects this sort of thing—as long as he does not try it once he is back on Puluwat! When such a warm welcome ashore is added to good fellowship and pride in their skill at sea, it is small wonder that men in return take lightly the risks and hardships of their long travels.

Finally the canoe comes home. In the past the men of the crew spent the first few days following their return living together without women in their canoe house. This ended with a small feast and ceremony in which they put behind them the world of the sea and formally returned to the island and to their families. Now, however, when the canoe has been unloaded and secured, or perhaps carried up into its place in the canoe house, the men disperse to their own houses to take up once again the lives of husbands and fathers.

Yet before long they will leave again on another trip, and another and another. Puluwat is a good island. It is a good place to be born, to grow strong, and even to die. Yet to discover its essence one cannot look only to the land. The land is only the backdrop and the place of preparation. Without its sailing canoes and seafaring men, Puluwat would have no past and no future. So with every voyage, and only through each voyage, its worth is renewed and its destiny fulfilled.

BEN R. FINNEY
JAMES D. HOUSTON

POLYNESIAN SURFING   Riding the breaking face of an ocean wave has become an international sport enjoyed along surfable shores throughout the world. Surfers number in the hundreds of thousands and crowd the beaches from San Francisco to Biarritz, from Capetown to the North Atlantic coasts of Cornwall and Devon. Two hundred years ago this was almost exclusively a Polynesian sport, and among Polynesians the surfers of early Hawaii were clearly its masters. Today's worldwide surfing movement stems from the ancient Hawaiian sport, which in turn developed from a more rudimentary wave-riding tradition brought to Hawaii by the first Polynesian settlers of a thousand or more years ago.

All surfers, ancient and modern, have had at least one thing in common: the waves they ride. And whether or not a wave is ridable depends on the right combination of ocean swell and shoreline configuration. A gradually sloping beach, an underwater reef close to shore, and the interference of a jutting headland usually produce the best waves—those that rise steeply, but break with a regular curl and leave an open shoulder in front of the moving break so a surfer can ride free of white water.

Three main ways have been developed to ride such waves: by swimming to catch it, then body-surfing down the slope; by paddling a canoe so that it slides in front of the breaking wave; and by using a surfboard. Surfboarding is the most popular, spectacular, and exhilarating, and is the form we're most concerned with here. Kneeling or lying prone, the surfer uses his hands to paddle into position. Just before it breaks, he paddles with the moving wave until he has enough speed and the wave's slope is critical enough for him to slide free. The surfer then stands and maneuvers his board with body weight and footwork, holding to the wave's breaking edge or darting in and out of its foamy shoulder as he rides toward shore.

The first step in the development of this form of surfing was probably the discovery that a stray plank and an ocean wave made a handy way for a swimmer to get back to shore. This in turn may have led to the simplest form of surfing—belly boarding—using a short board held against the belly or chest to ride a wave prone. This form was well known on many Pacific Islands, from New Guinea to Easter. It was also developed by water-loving people along the coast of West Africa, from Senegal to Nigeria, in the only example we have of wave riding as a popular recreation anywhere beyond Oceania before the nineteenth century.

In most of Oceania it remained a simple sport. In Micronesia and Melanesia, for example, it has been mainly a children's pastime. It was among the major islands of East Polynesia—New Zealand, Tahiti, the Marquesas, and Hawaii—that surfing became something more than a casual recreation. Among these islands longer boards were developed and adults did much of the surfing. And among the surfers of eastern Polynesia, the Hawaiians led the way. There the finest boards were built, the riding of waves was a highly respected skill, and the sport itself was a vital element in Hawaiian culture—which helps to explain why the sport survived there, though barely, while it died out in other Pacific island groups during the nineteenth century.

Why surfing blossomed in Hawaii is open to conjecture. The islands have some of the finest surfing conditions in the world. Many surfers would say *the* finest. They are directly in the path of strong ocean swells from both the north and south Pacific, so that good waves break there year-round, fanning south from northern storm centers during winter months, rolling up from southern storms from June to October. The coastlines, moreover, are dotted with beaches, coral reefs, and headlands that focus these swells into ideally surfable waves of every shape and size. Perhaps this in itself explains why the early Hawaiians channeled so much of their energy into wave riding.

In any event, having arrived in these islands from the Marquesas about A.D. 750, they had developed a sport that was in full flower when Captain Cook first sailed up the Kona coast in 1778. Hawaiians were then using surfboards of several kinds. They rode them prone, kneeling, or standing up, and moved with ease across the slopes of waves, turning and twisting to get the best possible ride. Their skill moved Lt. James King, of Cook's expedition, to exclaim in the first published account of Hawaiian surfing, "The boldness and address with which I saw them perform these difficult and dangerous maneuvers was altogether astonishing and is scarcely to be believed."

Other early observers were equally impressed by what they

called the Hawaiians' "favorite amusement," "national pastime," and "national sport." According to one missionary, their love of it was such that when the ocean offered a sudden run of good surf, "daily tasks such as farming, fishing, and tapa making were left undone while an entire community—men, women, and children—enjoyed themselves in the rising surf and rushing white water."

A mid-nineteenth-century artist's impression shows a Hawaiian riding the surf to shore.

The finely made Hawaiian boards, a few of which survive in museums, were shaped from the trunks of local trees with stone adzes, coral scrapers, and other pre-Iron Age tools. Koa wood, from which canoe hulls also were made, and the lighter wiliwili wood, used in making canoe outriggers, were favored for surfboard construction.

The boards were divided into two main types: the *alaia* and the *olo*. *Olo* boards were long, thick, and buoyant, while *alaia* boards were shorter, much thinner, and probably could not fully support a rider until the board was planing on a wave. An average *alaia* board would have been about eight feet long, eighteen inches wide, and an inch or so thick. The nose was wide and rounded, and the side rails tapered to a squared-off tail. Although some observers reported *olo* boards twenty-four feet long, most were probably in the fourteen- to eighteen-foot range. The board surfed during the 1830's at Waikiki by the Hawaiian chief Paki, and now on display at the Bishop Museum in Honolulu, is probably a representative *olo* type. It is nearly sixteen feet long, over eighteen inches wide, six inches thick, and weighs about one hundred sixty pounds. Like the *alaia*, both decks are convex, but its thickness and length give the *olo* a long cigar shape, compared to the planklike *alaia*.

Before the puritanical influence of missionaries took hold, "surf playing" was a Hawaiian national pastime, enjoyed by men, women, and children. Often whole villages would spend all day in the surf.

Highly maneuverable, *alaia* boards were good for catching steep, fast-breaking waves. Even though they lacked the tail fin considered essential on modern boards, the *alaia* boards could be easily turned and ridden at an angle across the wave. An eyewitness to a Hawaiian surfing a seven-foot board at Hilo in 1878 describes a typical *alaia* ride: "One instantly dashed in, in front of and at the lowest declivity of the advancing wave, and with a few strokes of the hands and feet established his position; then without further effort shot along the base of the wave eastward with incredible velocity . . . his course was along the foot of the wave, and parallel to it . . . so as soon as the bather had secured his position he gave a spring and stood on his knees upon the board, and just as he was passing us . . . he gave another spring and stood upon his feet, now folding his arms on his breast, and now swinging them about in wild ecstasy in his exhilarating ride."

Olo boards were designed for massive but slower-breaking surf and for getting long rides. Their length, narrowness, and buoyancy enabled a rider to paddle fast and catch a wave well before it became critical enough to break, and to ride it all the way to shore even though it may have crested and lost most of its force. *Olo* boards were thus ideal for the long-breaking surf at Waikiki Beach. But their bulk made quick turns and maneuvers difficult, so they were not suited to rocky beaches and fast-breaking waves. Since most of the Hawaiian surfing areas were of this latter type, it is not surprising that *alaia* surfing dominates early accounts of the sport, and that most of the ancient boards remaining—ten of thirteen in the Bishop Museum collection—are of the *alaia* type.

This distinction between *olo* and *alaia* also figures in Hawaiian social structure. Commoners (*maka' ainana*) and chiefs (*ali'i*) were rigidly divided, and it appears that the *olo* boards were exclusively reserved for the chiefly class. In addition, there is evidence that chiefs could reserve waves for their own pleasure and taboo a surfing beach to commoners. *Alaia* boards, on the other hand, were used by chiefs and commoners.

Chiefly privileges in surfing were accompanied by expertise, for chiefs were known for their surfing prowess. King Kamehameha, the high chief who conquered all of Hawaii and founded a dynasty in the early years of European contact, was particularly famed for his ability as a surfer. Instruction in surfing was part of a young chief's upbringing, and the strength and stamina derived from this and other aristocratic sports, such as canoe racing and spear handling, was undoubtedly one of the objects of the training. In addition to their own type of board, their own surfing instructors and expert board makers, Hawaiian chiefs also had special chants in which their surfing exploits were celebrated. Even King Kalakaua, the last king of Hawaii, had his own surf chant, one he appropriated from the chants of an earlier high chief who had surfed Hawaii's waves long before Captain Cook arrived.

Another measure of surfing's role in the life of these islands is its frequent mention in the legends that make up Hawaii's rich heritage of oral literature. These provide one more source of information to supplement the reports by early visitors and mission-trained Hawaiian scholars who wrote about their culture. That Hawaiian women were active surfers is confirmed by the many legends mentioning female exploits in the surf. The role of surfing in courtship also stands out in these tales. The legends tell of many a chief who is first attracted to his wife through watching her perform in the surf, and frequently a young surfer shows off in front of his favorite, hoping to win her hand.

Legends reveal the importance of competition among Hawaii's surfing chiefs. Contests, in fact, were a large part of the game. And the wagering on such matches, by contestants as well as spectators, was a favorite and often fanatic pastime that could overshadow the sport itself. Hawaiians were inveterate gamblers, known to bet everything, down to the last article they possessed. Overcome by the excitement of a surfing contest, a chief might wager canoes, fishing nets and lines, tapa cloth, and sometimes his own life or personal freedom on the outcome of the match.

The seriousness of this kind of competition is illustrated by the legendary match between Umi-laliloa, a chief of ancient Hawaii, and Paiea, a lesser chief. As a young man Umi attended a surfing match where Paiea challenged him. The wager was so small that Umi refused, so Paiea raised the bet to four double-hulled canoes. Umi accepted, handily defeated Paiea, and won the canoes. But during the match Paiea's board clipped Umi's shoulder, scratching off some skin. At the time Umi did nothing about it. Later, though, when he came to power as high chief, he had Paiea sacrificed to his god.

Like just about everything else in ancient Hawaii, surfing also had its sacred aspect. The making of a board, from the felling of the tree to the initial launching, required appropriate rituals to placate or invoke certain spirits and deities. Among the roots of a felled tree, for instance, a board builder would place a red fish, with a prayer, as an offering to the gods in return for the tree he was about to shape into a surfboard.

There is even evidence that surfing had its own *heiaus*, or stone temples. Two of these were still standing in the early 1960's, the *Kuemanu* and *Keolonahihi heiaus* on the south Kona coast of the island of Hawaii. Although how these temples were associated with surfing is not entirely clear, it is notable that both structures stand opposite well-known surfing breaks and were probably fine sites for observing the surf, for resting after surfing, or even for invoking the waves. *Kuemanu heiau* consists mainly of an upper stone terrace on a larger foundation. A deep, stone-lined water pool is sunk into one side of the foundation terrace, ideal for bathing or for rinsing off salt water. The terraces themselves are so aligned that from the upper level, which is like a bleacher, spectators might easily watch surfers riding waves less than a hundred yards away.

This surfing beauty was sketched by Jacques Arago in Hawaii about 1819. After the arrival of the missionaries and the ensuing increase in modesty, scenes like this were seldom seen again.

Although it is not specifically associated with these *heiaus*, one Hawaiian surf invocation has survived in the literature. When the ocean was flat, surfers waded in carrying strands of the *pohuehue* vine (beach morning glory), and striking the water with them, they would try to call up some ridable waves by delivering this chant:

Arise! Arise! Great surfs from Kahiki,
Powerful curling waves, arise with the Pohuehue,
Well up, long-raging surf.

Such was surfing's position in Hawaii when the first explorers came, but by the end of the nineteenth century, the sport had almost completely disappeared. The reasons for this are of a piece with the decline of Hawaiian culture as a whole: the general impact of Western civilization, which seduced the islanders away from traditional habits; the drastic drop in

Hawaiian population—from 300,000 to 40,000 in one hundred years—due to disease and social disruption; the arrival of Christianity to replace the old religion; and the repressive dictates of missionaries who discouraged gambling, men and women swim-

The first-known drawing of a man riding a surfboard. It was published in 1831 in William Ellis's *Polynesian Researches.*

ming together, exposing one's body in public, and the general frivolity and time wasting that went along with popular pleasures like surfing.

By the 1890's observers were mourning the sport's decline. "There are those living," said one, "who remember the time when almost the entire population of a village would at certain hours resort to the seaside to indulge in, or to witness, this magnificent accomplishment. . . . But this too has felt the touch of civilization, and today it is hard to find a surfboard outside of our museums and private collections."

Surfboards did take their place in museum collections, alongside other Hawaiian artifacts of activities now forgotten. But surfing didn't die. Of all the traditional sports and pastimes, it fared best. Most of the others quickly disappeared early in the period of foreign contact. As the twentieth century began, surfers could still be found in the Waikiki area of Oahu. But almost none of the former style and plumage remained. Gone were the chants, the contests, the wagering, and the chiefly privileges. The regal *olos* were no longer being constructed. The boards in use were crude copies, about six feet long, of the old *alaia* boards; many were hardly more than roughhewn planks. And only a handful of surfers remained to ride them.

During the nineteenth century few outsiders had learned how to handle a surfboard. Mark Twain, while visiting Hawaii in the 1860's, remarked, "None but the natives ever master the art of surfing thoroughly." A popular myth held that only a Hawaiian could ever stand and balance successfully on a moving board. The first sign of surfing's revival came when, soon after 1900, a group of Honolulu residents, including several eager schoolboys, challenged this myth. They rediscovered the waves at Waikiki, generating new interest in the ancient sport.

Among these new surfers was George Freeth, the Irish-Hawaiian who later brought surfing to America. Also prominent was Alexander Hume Ford, a mainlander so taken with the sport he became its key promoter. Ford conducted surfing classes at Waikiki, where his most famous pupil was Jack London. In 1907, during his cruise on *The Snark*, London spent several weeks in Hawaii and camped for a while in a tent on Waikiki Beach. He became one of surfing's most outspoken boosters.

Just as this revival was getting under way, it was threatened by hotels and new private residences along Waikiki Beach, which began to close off the beach front to surfers. Under Ford's leadership several enthusiasts formed a group to protect surfers and to promote the sport as a pastime and as a tourist attraction. About this time, Jack London's impassioned article, "The Royal Sport," in a national American magazine, heightened interest in surfing, not only in Hawaii but on the mainland as well. Aided by this and other publicity, Ford's group acquired an acre of beach-front property in 1908 and founded the Outrigger Canoe Club, for the purpose of "preserving surfing on boards and in outrigger canoes." It was an unprecedented move. The club became the world's first organization whose stated mission was the perpetuation of wave riding. A Hawaiian surfing club, the *Hui Nalu* (literally Surf Club) was founded soon thereafter, and rivalry between the two helped foster the revival. By 1911 as many as a hundred surfboards could be seen at Waikiki on a weekend.

Once revived at Waikiki, surfing thrived not only in Hawaii

but along other Pacific coastlines visited by Hawaiian surfers. In 1907 George Freeth came to southern California as part of a promotion venture sponsored by a railroad company to introduce water sports to a public whose interest in ocean recreation was just starting to grow. Freeth gave wave-riding demonstrations, offered classes, and began the exchange between Hawaii and California that has in recent years become the greatest source of energy in the sport's rapid postwar expansion.

Five years after Freeth, Duke Kahanamoku passed through California on his way to the 1912 Olympics. At the time Duke was one of the world's fastest swimmers and, like Freeth, a leading Waikiki surfer. His performances at such now familiar surfing spots as Santa Monica and Corona del Mar greatly encouraged the growing body of surfers there. With ridable waves coming from the north and south Pacific, numerous beaches and headlands to shape inviting surf, and a blossoming interest in outdoor living, California provided the ideal environment for the first successful transplant of Hawaiian surfing.

Meanwhile, down below the equator another world of surfing was coming to life. In the late 1800's a South Sea islander had taught some Australians how to body-surf waves without a board. Soon after the turn of the century tales of Hawaiian surfboarding trickled south to Australian shores. Stimulated by this notion, several body-surfers around Sydney tried to make their own boards, but with little success. Their crude planks were failures. Even a surfboard imported from Hawaii in 1912 proved impossible to ride. Australian surfers needed an example. They soon found one in Duke Kahanamoku, who arrived in 1915 to give swimming exhibitions. While there he built a board from local wood and gave Australians their first look at Hawaiian surfing. And from there the sport soon began to spread in Australia, much as it did in California. But with a major difference. It quickly became integrated with a lively organization later to be called The Surf Life Saving Association of Australia. And during the past fifty years, as the SLSA spread to other countries in the British Commonwealth, surfing has gone with it— to South Africa, to England, and, ironically, back to New Zealand, to revive a long-dead pastime there.

The subsequent spread of surfing around the world has generated from these three areas—Hawaii, California, and Australia—most of it during the past ten years. Improved world travel and communication, increased leisure time, and a growing worldwide interest in water sports all help to account for this growth. But perhaps the most important factor has been the development of the light, mass-produced surfboard made of plastic foam and covered with fiber glass.

Prior to the 1950's surfboards were heavy, cumbersome "planks." They were made of redwood or redwood and balsa strips, or they were "hollow boards" made with water-tight compartments of plywood. Both these types derived from ancient Hawaiian boards, but differed in design features as well as in performance. The plank was descended from the crude *alaia* copies being used at Waikiki at the beginning of surfing's revival. By the 1940's, after several design changes, the plank had lost most of the fine features that distinguished the *alaia*. Measuring eleven to twelve feet in length, some two feet wide, and three to four inches thick, the plank had become a massive board, resembling the *alaia* only in its basic outline.

In an attempt to re-create the fast paddling and long-wave riding features of the ancient *olo*, hollow boards were developed during the 1930's. These boards survive today as lifesaving aids at lakes and ocean beaches. They were usually fourteen to sixteen feet long, at least four inches thick, and close to two feet wide. They differed from the planks most radically in their tail design, which tapered to a point, making them fast paddlers. Both boards were heavy, weighing from sixty to one hundred twenty pounds or more, and hard to handle. Learning to surf with one of these boards usually took months or even years, which discouraged many prospective surfers.

In the late 1940's Californians began experimenting with surfboards made of light balsa wood covered with a protective layer of fiber glass and resin, and they added a tail fin to improve stability and turning. The result was a board about ten feet long, weighing only twenty to thirty pounds. It revolutionized surfing. It was light, buoyant, easy to learn on, and allowed surfers to perform maneuvers never imagined with the ponderous planks and hollow boards. California surfers introduced these new boards to Hawaii, Australia, and New Zealand, where they were labeled "Malibu boards," after the famous southern California surfing beach. The balsa board soon became readily available from surfboard shops that sprang up around the major surfing areas, and it greatly popularized the sport. Within a few years old-time surfers were complaining of the "log jams" at their favorite breaks. They had more to complain about when, after surfing was featured in several Hollywood films, it became a fad sport for teen-agers, and beaches from Malibu to Sydney were invaded by thousands of young, rambunctious surfers and surf-followers.

In the late 1950's, as the rising demand for boards made balsa more and more scarce, builders began fashioning boards from ultralight, solidified plastic foam, called polyurethane. Easy to obtain and easy to mold, this material brought mass production to surfing. New, larger firms entered the field. National advertising and installment and mail-order buying became regular features of a business once dominated by a few garage shops where boards were handcrafted for each customer. The resultant flood of foam boards were eagerly bought by veteran and novice surfers alike.

In the early 1960's these easily exportable foam boards, and the surfing techniques developed by a new generation of surfers, spread from California and Hawaii to overseas surfing centers, and then to areas where surfing had previously been unknown. Within a few years the coast of France around Biarritz had become a major new surfing area, together with hundreds of other spots scattered along both coasts of North and South America, Europe's Atlantic and Mediterranean shores, parts of Africa's coastlines, and new island surfing meccas like Mauritius and Puerto Rico. Even frigid waters have not completely limited surfing's spread to temperate latitudes. With the assistance of neoprene diving shirts and suits, surfers ride waves year-round off the coasts of Japan, Oregon and Washington, and the British Isles.

The sport has not stopped growing. New surfing areas are discovered every season. Builders continue to experiment with board shapes and surfers with riding techniques. Yet for all its expansion surfing remains inseparably linked to the islands where it first thrived. Hawaiian surfers themselves still hold an important place in their ancestral sport, and many have international standing. The Kahanamokus and Freeths of sixty years ago have their modern counterparts in such skilled instructors as Rabbit Kekai, and in overseas experts like David Nuuhiwa, who makes his home in California where he is a reigning champion.

Geographically, no one has yet found a coastline to match Hawaii's blend of balmy climate, comfortable water, exotic beauty, and year-round selection of favorable waves. Surfers everywhere look to Hawaii and save their money to travel there, arriving each year by the thousands—from places like Los Angeles, Melbourne, Lima. Some try the gentlest rollers at Waikiki, others test themselves against the raging winter storm surf on Oahu's north shore—awesome twenty-five footers that present the ultimate challenge in wave riding.

With its deep ties to the island's early culture, surfing was one of the few elements of Hawaiian life to survive into modern times. From Hawaii the sport has spread, in this century, around the globe. Today Hawaii continues to be not only the historical source but the vital center of an international surfing world.

THE CLOTH OF THE QUECHUAS When Manco Capac, the legendary founder of the Inca Empire, and his sister-wife, Mama Ocllo, emerged from the ground near Cuzco and crossed the Andean highland with their entourage, the poets tell us that it was their resplendent garments, above all else, that measured their nobility. "They went forth clothed in dresses of fine wool delicately worked with fine gold thread, and from these they took out purses, also of wool and gold, skillfully woven. . . ."

To understand the significance of textiles to the Incas, the ancient craft of weaving has to be seen as a major art medium, for long before the Spanish conquest textiles had become a measure of national wealth. As techniques were perfected through time, remarkable artistry developed. Textiles were collected as taxes, used in ceremonial rituals, and distributed to officials and to armies. The peasant valued the works of the loom for himself as well because then, as often now, he depended on weaving for all his clothing, his containers for transportation and storage, his furnishings. Thus the importance of textile production pervaded the culture at every level and is naturally expressed in its myths.

It is no wonder then that the high quality of weaving should have been the prime indicator of personal excellence in the Andes. In some areas even today the Quechuas, direct descendants of the Incas, still consider the skills of hand spinning, dyeing, and weaving to be the essential criteria of human dignity.

In remote areas, usually in an isolated valley, the geography itself has helped to preserve with little change the subtleties of the art as they were developed by pre-Columbian cultures. The land is rugged, men are isolated, and ancient techniques have not been compromised by proximity to large towns.

In the Bolivian highlands, three major areas of special weaving interest are apparent. The greatest variety of weaving techniques is found in the area east of Oruro. Here it is not uncommon to see five or more distinct means of textile production being employed by different members of one family, all in one court-yard on the same afternoon. Their looms range from the indigenous and most ancient to a later type introduced by the Spaniards and often constructed with a twentieth-century touch—an axle from an old Ford, for example, or bolts from a Toyota truck.

Nowhere else in the southern Andes have I seen a region so vitally concerned with weaving. The variety of weaving techniques and looms in this area reflects the extent and diversity of the Indians' weaving needs, and the significance of weaving to their daily lives. Furthermore, while in many parts of Bolivia (and southern Peru) only women spin yarn outside of the home, here it is commonplace for men and boys to spin outdoors as they gossip or tell stories in the winter sun. Even the more sophisticated Indian boys, who have just returned to their small hamlets from army service or cutting cane in the jungle, take up the spindle readily. And it is in this region that weaving is still the critical measure of material worth: a boy weaves a belt for a girl before proposing to her; she weaves a coca bag for him in consent. Farmers barter textiles for coffee, buttons, tin cups. At regional celebrations there is rivalry among communities to establish or preserve a collective reputation for weaving excellence.

Of all the area's assortment of looms, the principal one is the backstrap, typical of primitive craftsmen throughout the Andes and elsewhere in the New World and parts of Asia. It consists essentially of two horizontal loom bars supported a foot or more above the ground, with the warp (lengthwise yarns) extended between them. One end of this loom is fastened around the waist of the weaver, who sits cross-legged on the ground; the other end is tied to a tree or post, which he faces. In Andean prisons where Indians weave all day, having nothing else to do but cook their own meals, one can see six or more such looms spread out like a Maypole from the jail yard's central loom post.

Sometimes weavers tie what would otherwise be a backstrap loom to four pegs in the ground, rather than tire their backs with its constant support. Or they fasten the loom to two long vertical poles that lean against the wall of the house. However, neither of these adaptations allows for the same subtleties as the backstrap: with one end of the loom tied around the weaver's back, she has more control over the tension of the warps. She is able to slacken it merely by leaning forward, tightening it again by leaning back, a delicate nuance of control that cannot be achieved if both ends of the loom are fixed.

The size of these looms can be modified in many ways, depending upon the product desired. The textile on a larger loom might become a poncho, a *lliclla*, or a *costal*. For a poncho, two woven pieces, usually two to three feet wide, are sewn together with part of the seam left open for the wearer's neck and head. A *lliclla* is similar but has no opening—a strong square cloth to be tied around the shoulders for carrying bundles on the back. A *costal* is a long sack used for storage or for transporting heavy burdens by llama. *Costales* around the house tend to look lean and hungry toward summertime, but they are filled to bulging after harvest.

A smaller backstrap loom produces belts, straps, and coca bags, as well as small *costales*, in which a family keeps household luxuries and necessities—thread, a spoon, sugar, a spare candle. Village medicine men display their remedies in these *costales* on market day—bits of yellow pods, dried starfish, crushed sulfur, cactus thorns, or withered herbs, each sold from its own little sack. Headbands, saddlebags, capes, and purses are other common products of the backstrap loom.

In addition to the backstrap, the Indians of the Oruro region use a crudely made lap loom, on which they create belts using a Soumak-type technique, in which the wefts encircle the warps instead of interweaving with them. Often patterned with a bold, zigzag design of striking colors, such belts are only made by men and boys for their wives and girl friends. Making them is indeed a man's task, for they are exceedingly thick and must be firmly bound and interlaced. This type of loom was also used by pre-Spanish weavers in Peru. Today it has a specialized and highly appreciated place in the weaving repertoire of this area.

Farther southeast from Oruro, Indians weave rugs and blankets, mainly for commercial use, on upright frame looms. This enormous loom fills the weaver's hut from the rafters to the floor. Beautiful Spanish designs in a tapestry weave have characterized these rugs, but more recently, contemporary patterns have been suggested by Peace Corps volunteers. Also ubiquitous in the Oruro region is the treadle loom introduced by the Spaniards. Most remote communities here possess several treadle looms; it is on these looms that the men weave *bayeta* (a coarse

Whimsical animals parade on an *aksu*, or cape, from an isolated area near Sucre. The pictorial fantasies of this region require particular artistry because several figures evolve simultaneously across the loom.

woolen cloth for pants, vests, shirts, and women's skirts), as well as gay plaid sashes. Young boys in particular sport these sashes tied low below the waist with studied casualness. And because they are also used for weaving blankets, three or four treadle looms—one for each member of the family—may be going at one time in an Indian home.

In addition to these, there are smaller looms and methods of off-the-loom weaving and braiding that these Indians have at their disposal. The younger children sit on the ground, legs outstretched, working on a toe loom that may have as many as five or six heddles. They make straps and hat bands, often with elaborate designs. Using still other techniques they make *ribete*, the narrow edging along a poncho that protects it from fraying. Boys braid numerous strands into complex "snakeback" slingshots, which broaden out into a short woven strap where the stone will be held; they also produce splendid llama-hair rope. Finally there are the soft alpaca *tulas* with their colorful pompoms—a kind of ribbon specially made to hold a woman's long braids together behind her back while she stirs the soup or bends over the baby.

In this area of Bolivia, where textiles are so important in daily life, even the spirits of the mountains value the yarn and the loom. In communities like Ayrampampa, Saint Isidore, the patron of farmers and a peasant himself, must also have a poncho; so a local weaver is commissioned to keep his statue well attired with a bright new garment on his feast day every year. Furthermore, at planting and harvesttime the earth goddess may demand her annual tribute wrapped in a specially woven cloth. To ward off evil spirits, magical *lloq'e*, a yarn spun in the reverse direction from the normal spinner's twist, is tied around the ankle or wrist. This is worn by travelers, pregnant women, the ill—by anyone hoping for good luck. Even the statues of saints in the churches sometimes find it advisable to wear *lloq'e* on their wrists. No one can survive without the loom.

In northern Bolivia beyond La Paz, weaving takes on a different mood. This region is a series of deep valleys set among magnificent, soaring mountains; the communities own fewer

Decorative small bags for coca leaves are worn proudly by Quechua men. This one was used on Sundays and special occasions.

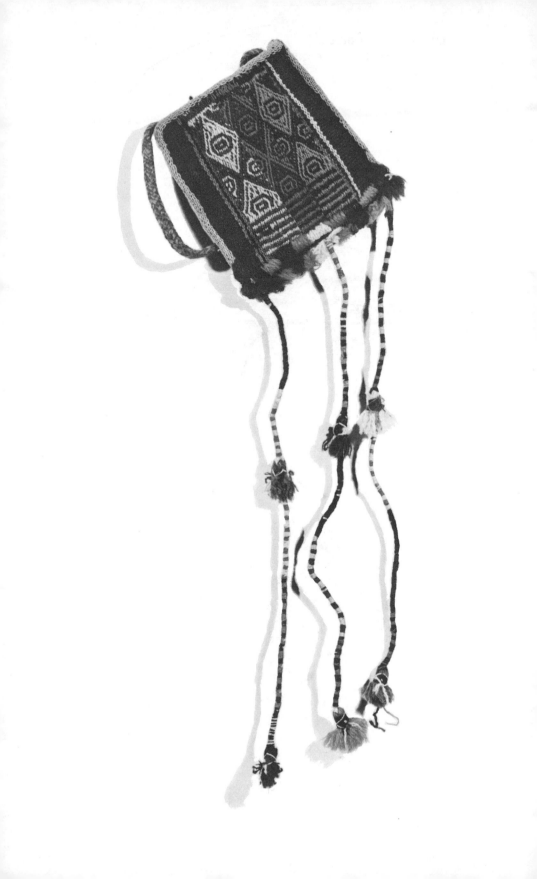

THE CLOTH OF THE QUECHUAS

Using a technique that requires strength, men from the Oruro area make thick belts on lap looms.

Although the toe loom is simply constructed, children can weave elaborately designed straps and hatbands on it.

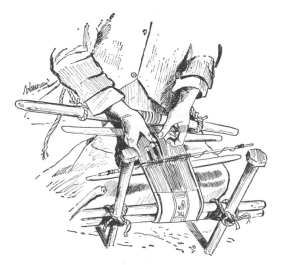

With one bar of the small backstrap loom tied around her body, the weaver controls the warp tension by leaning forward or back.

A boy weaves a sash on a Spanish treadle loom, which is also used to produce the coarse woolen homespun for his clothing.

llamas and alpaca, so most of the weaving is done with sheep's wool. Because of its nature, that is, its scale structure and kinkiness, sheep's wool is usually easier to spin than alpaca or llama hair. With it the spinners produce some of the finest of present-day highland yarns.

With all fibers like wool or hair, spinning is indispensable for weaving, and a high level of weaving can hardly flourish without good spinning. Throughout Bolivia the Indians spin with a drop spindle similar to that used elsewhere in the world: a slender stick nine or ten inches long with a round whorl toward the bottom for balance. Because it can be used even while the spinner walks or runs, it is not unusual to see heavily loaded Indian porters from the mountains industriously working the spindle, which dangles and swings by their legs as new yarn is formed.

Children learn to spin at an early age. Lying on the ground near many an Indian hut are toy spindles with bits of wool; some of the finest yarn is spun by young girls under ten.

A good spinner controls the diameter of his yarn by a sensitive fiber-selecting process, which he performs almost unconsciously with his fingers, thinning out the fiber bundles as he feeds them into the yarn he is twisting. All careful spinners aim for an even yarn without noticeable variation in its diameter. Only in areas where craftsmanship has declined and the spinners have become indifferent—often they are embarrassed by this when questioned—does one find yarn spun with considerable irregularity. In a few regions, spinners may deliberately produce such crude yarn to suit the tourist market. Tourists often cannot believe that the skillfully spun yarn is indeed hand-spun, and will pay more for proof in irregularities. Generally these "lumpy" yarns are more frequently found in knitted wear, especially sweaters, as it would be difficult to use them extensively on a native loom.

After the wool is spun into yarn, it is plied; that is, two or more yarns are twisted together to make a stronger yarn. This is usually a man's work, although I have never known an idle woman who would not pick up the plying when the need arose. The men ply the yarn at home or while working, using a larger and heavier spindle than that used in the original spinning of wool. When all the wool has been spun and plied, it is ready for dyeing.

In a few areas of the southern Andes, and especially in the

isolated north of Bolivia, vegetable, animal, or mineral dyes are still used, but in very little time the recipes and processes will be forgotten, replaced by commercial dyes. And sooner still, no one will any longer know on which hill to pick the brightest *cher'chi*, or exactly on which day its dye will be the subtle shade desired. Dyeing is a lore and a science unto itself, and requires a thorough knowledge of local geography, botany, and geology, as well as expertise in mixing mordants (which fix the dye to assure permanence); in timing the boiling, steeping, and cooling; and in anticipating color modifications that may take place with temperature change or variations in wool composition.

Three natural dyes most popular today in Bolivia and southern Peru are nogal, or walnut tree leaf, for browns and yellows; dried and powdered cochineal insects for rich red shades; and plain house soot from the cooking area of the hut for black and brown. Common mordants are lemon juice, urine, or fermented corn beer, although it may be that these are widely employed without any tested evidence of their value. Probably the deep blue of the northern headbands and coca bags dates only to the importation of indigo during this past century.

An interesting feature of weaving in some of these northern valleys is its extremely local character. In this region—perhaps here alone of all the regions in Bolivia—each community has its own distinctive motif variation or color rendering. Thus a person familiar with these local characteristics can stand in the Ayata market on Sunday and identify the exact valley of each visiting Indian, even his particular hamlet in that valley. This is done by closely examining his *capacho*, a foot-long, flat bag carried by men.

Many of the marks of differentiation are obvious; they are simply distinct patterns. However, there are others that may appear identical to the unpracticed observer. Nevertheless, the indications are consistent and are never omitted: a geometric form may be elongated, instead of rounded out; birds other than ducks may decorate a narrow band; a "rainbow" warp may be used in place of a solid shade. To the weavers these are as much a part of the design as are the major motifs.

Despite such a seemingly compulsory code, the creativity of the craftsman is never inhibited. This artistic use of a local pattern can be compared to the development of a theme in a fugue: the theme clearly distinguishes one fugue from others but in no way limits the freedom of the composer. Rather, it provides him with challenge and form. The Ayata *capachos* from a single hamlet are never the same, but each manifests the local "theme" in a slightly new way, within its implicit local restrictions.

Elsewhere in Bolivia weaving designs tend to characterize much larger geographic areas, a single theme extending at least across a wide pampa or a valley. That many of these tiny communities near Ayata, perhaps only half an hour apart on foot, can preserve such individuality in their textiles is indicative of the Indians' attitudes toward weaving. Their handmade garments are part of their identity, sometimes even more so than their names, many of which are common throughout the entire region. This localization of weaving designs is also found in parts of Central America and in the Cuzco area of Peru. What will be the reaction of these people as the commercial clothing industry drives the hand loom from their valley in the near future, and they have to wear shirts identical to those worn over a vast geographical area by total strangers?

There are many other distinct regional motifs and color characteristics in Bolivia. We have not discussed the lowland and the jungle craftsmen and their work, the special weaving of the Indians in the mines, or the less imaginative weaving of the Aymara tribe. These groups present interesting problems in themselves, but they too will soon lose the craft.

In some respects the most exciting textile region in Bolivia is around Sucre, the original capital of the country. It is in this area that the anthropologist is most strongly challenged by questions of artistic creativity: How does a primitive artist conceive the idea of his work and then enter into its elaboration? Does a craftsman deep in a weaving tradition in any sense enjoy a spontaneity comparable to that of, say, a potter or water-colorist? Why make weaving difficult with designs? The region around Sucre lends itself well to the study of influences that foreign cultures, penetrating farther into the backlands, may bring to bear upon the primitive artist.

Although it has been reported that weaving samplers are used in the central Andes, I have never seen anything that might serve as a sampler, and in fact the creative tradition communicated to me by weavers would have no room for such an aid. Most weavers of several years' experience are so thoroughly acquainted with the motifs used in their village or region, and with the manipulations possible on their looms, that weaving these motifs or transmitting them to a beginner needs no record or reminder. It is true that young weavers may often be seen using a finished product as a model, especially while warping the loom. But as soon as the first few rows of weft (the horizontal yarn) have been finished, they usually find picking out the design of one row to be a logical sequence based on what has been done in the row immediately preceding it.

However, except in pieces requiring continual repetition of a single motif, there is considerable opportunity for creativity. Most weavers invent as they go along, sometimes carrying and developing in their minds numerous different design sequences across the width of the loom at one time.

If the design sequences consist of geometric patterns, complex mathematical calculations are frequently required to work them out, especially on the backstrap loom. And if the designs are representations of men, plants, or animals, as many as five or six distinct figures in different stages may be emerging simultaneously across the loom. Yet no weaver has ever reported sketching out the over-all pattern beforehand, most do not even have the finished design firmly in mind from the start. This process does of course depend upon the creativity of the weaver, his experiences, perhaps his daring—and his humor.

On several occasions I have been able to compare eight or ten weavings by the same craftsman, gathering them from neighbors and family in his village. Never did I find two pieces alike, although the diversity represented in the "portfolio" of any one craftsman depended upon his own creative energies, as is to be expected.

The area around Sucre includes great extremes in style of weaving designs. One may walk three days or more hardly seeing a person; then, after a casual inquiry in a hut, suddenly find it to be a region of the most imaginative, bizarre weaving motifs. Here, with finely spun yarn, hand-dyed in basic color combinations, weavers have set forth a fabulous parade. Red condor birds dive through purple backgrounds, scarlet bulls graze on a green field, cows have foxes inside their bellies. If you should laugh, the Indians will usually laugh with you at a comical spotted toad or a Wizard-of-Oz lion. After the bands of repeated geometric designs characteristic of weaving in much of the southern Andes, this burst of representational fantasy is startling.

On the other hand, the weaving can be a complete contrast in color and spirit. There the designs are almost sinuous, highly baroque. In color harmonies that could never be achieved by natural dyes (and thus are subject to outside influence), intricate forms interlock abstractly. If any representational figures appear, they are likely to be stern horses and stiff riders, motifs derived from the Spanish tradition. Much of the yarn itself is commercially spun, which probably reflects the region's outside contacts as a tourist community.

In many other areas of the southern Andes I have observed a correlation between quality of hand-spinning and dyeing on the one hand and preservation of pre-Spanish designs on the other. This is not to say that such factors need always accompany one another. In Mexico, Indians who weave designs of motorcycles and political posters into their textiles maintain a very high spinning standard. However, it may be true that in Bolivia and southern Peru, a community that readily accepts the innovation of commercial yarn or dye may also be a community with a more flexible attitude toward new, even foreign designs.

But wherever one searches in such a study, one thing is constant: it is not difficult to distinguish the craftsman who weaves with an artist's love of expression and a passion for the mastery of his material from the craftsman who works merely out of need. One woman I met near Sucre was typical of the former. Her husband, who shortly before our meeting had joined the work crew of a road being built near the community, was ashamed of his peasant clothes in his new job. Because a plain poncho devoid of all design indicates higher class among mestizos (the Spaniards never liked patterned ponchos, but instead considered solid black or gray to distinguish the true "caballero"), the Indian on a road crew is marked as a hillbilly by the brilliance and intricacy of his poncho. This man therefore demanded that his wife weave a solid gray poncho for him. He would no longer be seen in the garment it had taken her half a year to create. As she explained this, she wept. He had asked her to betray the very essence of her craftsmanship: for her, weaving without design was a contradiction.

She, like many a weaver in Bolivia, is among the last to serve a historic tradition preserved from one generation to the next for more than two thousand years: the skills and craft of textile production recorded only in the minds and hands, yet for ages so critical for survival in the Andes.

PART FOUR

BEHAVIOR AND SOCIAL LIFE IN TRADITIONAL SOCIETIES

Warfare and Aggression

Napoleon A. Chagnon ("Yanomamö—The Fierce People") focuses on patterned aggression and the institution of warfare in a South American tribe. Many so-called primitive societies lack any recognizable warfare, although conflict occurs within all societies in varying degrees. Groups such as the Eskimo, Australian Desert Aborigines, and the Selk'nam have never been observed to fight in organized groups above the level of a kin-based feud. Anthropologist Alexander Lesser has observed that

. . . what is found characteristic of primitive, stateless societies are forms of armed aggression—fighting, homicide, feud—in which involvement and motivation is deeply personal, and what is not found in such societies is organized offensive warfare to conquer people or territory, with its essentially impersonal involvement and lack of personal motivation.[1]

The question then comes to mind, why do the Yanomamö fight? They do not fight for territorial gain, nor do they fight because fighting is genetically determined behavior. If the latter were the case, we would expect all other human societies to fight with equal ferocity, which clearly they do not.

What Chagnon describes is a graded series of patterned encounters involving aggressive behavior, ranging from chest-pounding duels between individuals to raiding between villages. Each encounter provides opportunities for individuals and villages to demonstrate their ferocity to their neighbors, and this indeed seems to be the ultimate motivation for all Yanomamö warfare. It is called *waiteri* ("fierceness"). It is exemplified in a wide variety of situations, such as when a man discovers his wife in adultery or accuses someone of gluttony at a feast, or when one needs to avenge the death of a relative. Even though they may fear being injured in fights, young boys are pressed by their elders to enter into fights and are encouraged to display ferocity at every opportunity. Members of small villages—rendered more vulnerable by their size—tend to be more aggressive than people in larger villages, mainly because they feel a need to show their more powerful neighbors that they are ready for violence at any time.

Yanomamö aggression is characterized by bullying, out of a need to intimidate others, and it is largely personal or family based. As Elman R. Service has aptly phrased it: "When our teen-age kids get in a fight for reasons like these we do not confuse it with organized warfare, nor do we counter it with the same means."[2] The idea that the Yanomamö are innately depraved is as misleading as the notion (attacked by Chagnon in his paper) that they are innately noble. Other cultures pattern their aggressive behavior in different ways, but wherever "warfare" is found, it is taught as part of the traditional and expected behavior of that society. The Yanomamö fight because they have learned to fight, not because it is instinctive.

The Incest Taboo

After providing a general account of the culture of the Mnong Gar of Vietnam, Georges Condominas proceeds to describe a ceremony of expiation for incest. The parties involved in this case of incest, a man named Tieng and a woman named Aang, had a common ancestor fifteen generations before. In many societies sexual relations between people as distantly related as Tieng and Aang would not be regarded as incestuous at all, but, as Condominas's account shows, among the Mnong Gar this was a serious matter. Every human society has rules regarding incest, but these rules vary from one group to the next, particularly with regard to the boundaries of kin relationship within which incest is said to occur.

The *incest taboo* has been the focus of considerable discussion by anthropologists who have sought to explain its existence in human society in both historical and functional terms. Historical discussions concerning the origins of the incest taboo have, on the whole, been rather unsatisfactory, because no empirical way exists for testing hypotheses of this kind. But explanations based on the adaptive role of the incest taboo in human societies have fared somewhat better; one can observe the operation of these taboos today and can compare it with the behavior of nonhuman societies.

Most discussion of the incest taboo centers on its universal existence within the nuclear family unit rather than on its extension to other classes of kin. Is the incest taboo an instinctive device? Or is it a cultural mechanism that must be learned and transmitted to succeeding generations? On this point there is little disagreement: most anthropologists maintain that the human incest taboo is a cultural mechanism. Indeed the fact that incest taboos are sometimes violated strongly suggests a lack of instinctive basis for it. But it is worthwhile considering whether the incest taboo is positively adaptive in human societies and, if so, in what ways. One of the earliest and most commonly voiced theories about the incest taboo is that it acts to limit inbreeding in human populations.[3] From a genetic point of view, close inbreeding among animals that mature slowly, bear few offspring at a time, and live in families is generally deleterious, but it is hard to imagine that people, no matter how intelligent, have the ability to perceive, anticipate, and prevent these biological consequences of incest. Another venerable and much-cited theory suggests that the advantages of establishing social relations between families are so great to human societies that the incest taboo was instituted to force people to seek marriage partners outside their own families.[4] This interpretation has appealed to many anthropologists, because the benefits to society accruing from the institution of the incest taboo, such as mutual defense, cooperation, food sharing, and other forms of communal behavior, would have been made possible by networks of kin ties established when people had to marry outside the family unit. Moreover, this argument can be extended to explain why in all human societies the incest taboo extends beyond the nuclear family to wider groups of kin, because such a widening of this rule could expand the network of cooperation still further. Many social anthropologists see the incest taboo as a cornerstone of human society, because it compels people to practice *exogamy*; that is, marrying outside the group within which marriage would be regarded as incestuous. Such marrying-out is essential if interfamilial alliances and networks are to be established, but, of course, this argument says little about sexual liaisons that do not involve marriage. Also, it does not adequately explain why strict incest taboos continue to be important even in complex, modern societies where kin ties are of less social importance than other factors. Sigmund Freud presented a kind of mirror image to this sociological theory regarding the incest taboo when he proposed that unregulated sexual competition within the family would be disruptive.[5] He argued that the incest taboo was necessary to keep the nuclear family intact, and this argument has been echoed by several anthropologists.[6] These three theories, which for simplicity's sake we might call the "genetic," "sociological," and "family" theories, have been discussed most often by anthropologists in dealing with this question.

The Mnong Gar amply demonstrate the essentially cultural nature of the incest taboo. Marriage or sexual relations within the same clan are thought to be incestuous. Mnong Gar clans are matrilineal; that is, membership and property are passed down from mothers to their children. Therefore any who claim a common maternal ancestor, no matter how many generations back, belong to the same clan and call each other "brother" and "sister," even if their actual kin ties are not so close as cousins. Tieng and Aang, though not at all closely related in terms of actual kinship, were members of the same matrilineal clan and therefore committed incest by having sexual relations. Other couples in Mnong Gar society may be much more closely related but may engage in sexual activity as long as they do not share a common maternal ancestor. Thus the incest taboo here helps to define the clan as a cooperative social unit. The case of the Mnong Gar lends more support to the "sociological" theory of the incest taboo than it does to the "genetic" theory, because the rules of incest in this case, aside from clanmates, do not restrict breeding between fairly close kin.

Cultural Survivals

In the paper "Journey to Pulykara" we come face to face with a society that has often been regarded by anthropologists and laymen alike as the last living survival of the Stone Age. At first glance many behavioral characteristics of the Aborigines of Australia's Western Desert could lead to such a view. As seen earlier, these people continue to make and use stone tools and live entirely by hunting and gathering wild foods. They do not wear clothes, nor do they build substantial structures of any kind. Indeed there is now archeological evidence to support the idea that this same basic aboriginal population has been living in this region under virtually unvarying environmental conditions and with the same technology and economy for at least 10,000 years.[7]

    The question of cultural survivals haunted early anthropologists and led to an intense interest in conjectural history based on the recognition of "relic" beliefs and practices among living and historic peoples which were thought to have survived from earlier stages of their history. In the absence of written documents this seemed at the time to be a worthwhile way to study culture history. An early view was expressed in 1873 by English anthropologist E. B. Tyler:

Now there are thousands of cases . . . which have become, so to speak, landmarks in the course of culture. When in the process of time there has come general change in the condition of a people, it is usual, notwithstanding, to find much that manifestly had not its origin in the new state of things, but has simply lasted on into it. On the strength of these survivals, it becomes possible to declare that the civilization of the people they are observed among must have been derived from an earlier state, in which the proper home and meaning of these things are to be found; and thus collections of such facts are to be worked as mines of historic knowledge.[8]

Detailed anthropological studies of the desert Aborigines of Australia were first published around the turn of the century, the best-known by Baldwin Spencer and F. J. Gillen. When these studies were read in Europe, they were sometimes interpreted in the light of conjectural history, thus encouraging the view that the Australian Aborigines were surviving examples of Neanderthal man or another early stage of human evolution.[9] This view is not held by anthropologists today, who now recognize living Aborigines to be fully representative of modern man (*Homo sapiens*), but it still prevails in some quarters.

The search for cultural survivals no longer preoccupies the field of anthropology, primarily because of two important developments in the history of the discipline. First, a major shift in emphasis within anthropology during the 1920s led away from an interest in the origins of social institutions and instead toward the study of social institutions in terms of their present-day operation within particular societies. And second was the rise in stratigraphic archeology.

This first shift was associated principally with the independent work of two anthropologists, A. R. Radcliffe-Brown and Bronislaw Malinowski. Both scholars stressed the use of the concept of *function* in the study of traditional societies. For Radcliffe-Brown function meant: ". . . the contribution which a partial activity makes to the total activity of which it is a part."[10] This view urges that cultures should be viewed as whole social systems rather than as mere aggregates of traits. Malinowski urged a similar view, but, especially in his famous studies of the Kula trading network of the Trobriand Islanders of Melanesia,[11] he went further and proposed that institutions may exist in a society which are larger and more complicated than any individuals operating within the institution may realize. Malinowski showed how the Trobrianders constantly engaged in exchanges of special kinds of valuables, with the overall result not a random distribution of these items but a continuous flow of one class of valuables in one direction and the other in the opposite direction throughout the archipelago. No single participant in the Kula observed the operation of the entire system, but the anthropologist, who was in a position to analyze his observations, could integrate the functions of each subsidiary activity and actor within the totality of the "big, complicated institution" that was the Kula. With the advent of functionalism, the high-water mark of conjectural history in anthropology had been passed.

Stratigraphic archeology, on the other hand, offered a new set of approaches to the study of culture history, involving the use of empirical rather than conjectural evidence. The earliest systematic excavations in archeology were conducted by General Lane-Fox Pitt-Rivers on his huge private estate at Cranbourne

Chase, England, between 1880 and 1890.[12] Pitt-Rivers was ahead of his time, but his approach to archeology was gradually adopted in other parts of Europe and was widely in use there by the 1920s. In the United States, stratigraphic archeology started late but established itself firmly when it did. The first systematic effort in this direction was made by N. C. Nelson in his excavations at the Tano ruin in New Mexico in 1914.[13] His approach was quickly and widely applied in the New World. As a result of these pioneering efforts and those that followed, archeological sequences were developed for different parts of the world; these soon replaced the conjectural sequences of culture history based on the study of survivals in living societies.

Therefore if the Australian Aborigines are not to be considered as survivals of an earlier stage of human physical and cultural evolution, how are they to be viewed? Perhaps the best approach lies in trying to appreciate the fact that their culture history reflects a successful adaptation to some of the most marginal and difficult environmental surroundings anywhere. Despite the meager resources at their disposal, they manage to live satisfying and reasonably secure lives, a fact that surely must stand as a great human achievement. Although it shows strong elements of continuity with the past, the history of the Aborigines' adaptation, as shown by archeology, is unique and must be understood in terms of the difficult problems they had to solve in surviving in this impoverished arid environment.

Pastoral Nomadism

As with slash-and-burn agriculture, pastoral nomadism presents the anthropologist with a variety of adaptations, but in this case it is based on animal rather than plant domestication. The Turkmen nomads in William Irons' paper live in Central Asia, a region with many other nomadic herding groups. One should realize, however, that nomadic herding societies live—or did live until recently—in many other parts of the world, such as the high interior plateau of Tibet, the savannah lands of Africa, the tundra and forests of Siberia, the great plains of North America, and the pampas grasslands of South America (these last two contained hunters who kept horses acquired in historic times). Although all these groups are nomadic because they need to move periodically with their herds, they are not all nomadic in the same ways.

Frederik Barth, an anthropologist who has conducted extensive work among Middle Eastern nomadic societies, suggests that pastoral nomadism should be considered in terms of a continuum between two extremes: "True nomads move to a similar ecologic niche in another area. People practicing transhumance generally utilize a different niche by reliance on alternative techniques. . . ."[14] People who practice *transhumance* move into different ecological niches during different seasons. Barth found that the Pathans of Swat, a small state lying near the headwaters of the Indus River, themselves differentiate between two patterns of herding livestock, calling persons who live by true nomadism *Ajer* and those who live by transhumance *Gujar.* The Gujars depend heavily on herds of water buffalo, which they move each summer into high pastures in the mountains and bring down in the winter to areas near Pathan villages. While in these villages, the Gujars feed their livestock on stored fodder and assist the villagers in their farming tasks. As Barth has pointed out, the region of Swat where these people live is noted for its lush summer meadows, but these meadows cannot be exploited during the whole year. The transhumant adaptation of the Gujars is therefore based partly on grazing and partly on farming at different times of the year. In the same region, however, are true pastoral nomads who depend more heavily on sheep and goats. These herdsmen move over much greater distances that the Gujars, but they do not move into different environmental niches. They pasture their herds in high mountain meadows during summer and in the low plains during winter, but in each case they depend on the same resource in the same way, namely by letting the herds graze freely.

The Turkmen nomads resemble the true nomads described by Barth more than they resemble transhumant nomads. These people move their herds of sheep and goats each year in response to the alternating wet and dry seasons of the Gorgan Plain of northeastern Iran. Although their migrations are shorter than those of the true nomads of Swat, they employ the same subsistence approach of free grazing throughout the year. The Turkmen settlement pattern, however, is unusual. During the wet season camps are situated close to the herds, so that lambs can be cared for and ewes milked. In the dry season, though, the sheep are sent south to the banks of the Gorgan River to graze, with only the young men to shepherd them while the rest of the people establish camps near permanent wells elsewhere.

The Turkmen nomads also illustrate another characteristic that is generally widespread among pastoral nomads: a strong emphasis on raiding. Irons points out that the nomadic way of life of the Turkmen has always made it difficult for centralized governments to gain political control over these people or to restrain them in any other way. This seems to be true of most, if not all, pastoral nomads. One of the best accounts of the relationship between warfare and pastoral nomadism derives from studies by anthropologist Robert B. Ekvall among the nomadic tribes of Tibet.

Raiding and fear of revenge leads to a constant state of alertness among the Tibetan nomads. They are prepared to move their entire herds and families on a moment's notice to escape pursuing raiders, as Communist Chinese troops discovered to their regret in 1935–1936 when they tried to capture some of the Tibetans' herds.[15] Knowledge of weaponry and horsemanship is cultivated among the men, who view themselves as much as warriors as they do as herders. As Ekvall describes it:

The Tibetan nomad is extremely conscious of the problem of security. The problem varies somewhat area by area, and according to the strength, status, and power of the tribal unit to which he belongs, but it is always present in some degree. In some respects, the nomad appears to be peculiarly vulnerable. . . . His livestock can never be securely barred in at night, he himself has no walls and he has few, if any, fences, which at best are flimsy or temporary. . . . Instead, in his seeming lack of defenses, he relies on constant human and animal vigilance and a being-on-guard attitude that may be, in some respects, better than a wall and, though sorely stretched and tested, is very efficient and effective.[16]

So not only the absence of government control encourages the warlike attitude of pastoral nomads such as the Tibetans; more important, this encouragement stems from the constant awareness of how vulnerable one's herd is to a raid, and, conversely, how easy and profitable it might be to raid someone else's herd.

Caste

As Joan Mencher stresses in her article, the Namboodiri Brahmans of Kerala, in southwestern India, are perhaps the most extreme example of caste organization in that country. The Brahmans head the ranked system of four *endogamous* groups; that is, groups in which marriage must take place within the group. These four groups, called *varna*, are ranked from top to bottom as follows: Brahman, Kshatriya, Vaisya, and Sudra. The first three are often referred to as the "twice-born," because their initiation ceremonies involve a symbolic rebirth. The Sudra are regarded as commoners, but a very real gulf exists between them and the Harijan or "untouchables" who stand at the very bottom of the hierarchy, even below the castes themselves. One is born into a particular caste and maintains his position by marrying within it and by avoiding pollution through certain kinds of external contacts, such as touching food or water that has been handled by a person of lower caste. Untouchables perform occupations and display habits that are considered so polluting that they are placed completely outside the caste structure of Hindu society.

Although this basic caste structure is present throughout India, anthropologists have debated the operation of numerous subcastes within the major castes, particularly as regards endogamy and occupations. How does the caste system work? The key to the system seems to lie in the arrangement known as *jajmani*, whereby goods and services are exchanged. Put simply, this arrangement allows high-caste families (the clients or *jajman*) to receive the products and services of various lower-caste specialists such as leathercrafters, carpenters, carters, sweepers, and barbers. They may also receive the ritual services of high-caste individuals (especially Brahmans) at important events, for example, marriages and funerals. In return, land-owning clients pay later for these services with produce from their farms and sometimes even with land. This economic system operates with no currency, and several anthropologists have noted that the *jajmani* system is absent in those areas of India where a cash crop economy prevails.[17] This system occurs over most of India; as anthropologist Harold Gould has put it, castes in Indian villages are: ". . . ritually subdivided into endogamous clusters in accordance with the moral valuation which the Hindu religion places upon their occupational activities"[18] and he sees *jajmani* as a system of relationships between families of these different occupational castes. Although Gould and others have emphasized the mutuality, indeed, almost symbiosis, of these relationships, other anthropologists such as T. O. Beidelman have stressed the idea of the caste as a kind of economic monopoly. To them this is not a symbiotic arrangement based on mutual benefits to all parties but rather is a competitive relationship between castes with monopolies over essential services. Although this is a marketless society, Beidelman argues, the same economic law of supply and demand, with its constant jockeying for positions of economic advantage, operates in Hindu society as it does in market economies.[19]

Whatever point of view one adopts toward castes and the operation of the *jajmani* system, it should be clear that there is more to this issue than merely the economic distribution of goods and services. The system rests on roles that are sanctioned by sacred Hindu traditions and involve ritual as well as simple economic functions. This ritual and sacred aspect of caste emerges clearly in Mencher's paper, as do some threats to the caste system that have arisen from modernization and government reform. The Namboodiri Brahmans in particular tended to maintain their positions of religious orthodoxy (especially with regard to the concept of ritual purity vis-à-vis other castes) in the face of social changes and reform, but modern education and increasing involvement with a market economy are gradually undermining their positions as the highest and most orthodox caste in Kerala.

Population and Human Affairs

"The Anabaptist Explosion" by Wiliam F. Pratt demonstrates the feedback relationship that exists between social institutions and population. By feedback here is meant a continuous two-way dependence through time, as changing demographic conditions act to change social organization and behavior and vice versa. Or, as anthropologist Charles Wagley has phrased it: "Each culture has a population policy—an implicit or explicit set of cultural values relating to population size. The social structure of each society is closely inter-related with a specific population level."[20] Wagley demonstrated this proposition by comparing the post-European contact histories of two tribes of Brazilian Indians living in similar environments with similar subsistence practices. One group, the Tenetehara, maintained its numbers at around 2000 after 300 years of European contact, while the other group, the Tapirape, declined during the same period (and after only about 40 years of contact) to less than 100. How are we to account for the extraordinary difference? Wagley notes that the Tapirape value small families, believing that a woman should not have more than three living children. Moreover, these three children should not be of the same sex. So if a woman has two sons and bears a third, this last one will be killed. This practice of killing unwanted children, *infanticide,* also occurs when three daughters have been born to a woman. Moreover, among the Tapirape, any man who has had sexual relations with a woman during her pregnancy is regarded as a father of the child, and all such men must, as cofathers, observe strict food taboos and restrictions on sexual relations while the woman is pregnant. In situations where there are three or four cofathers, the chances are that one of them will violate a taboo, in which case the infant is killed after it is born. The Tenetehara, on the other hand, show little interest in limiting the size of their families and practice infanticide only in cases when twins or deformed children are born.

Wagley also points out that differences in social organization also help to explain the differential survival of these two groups. The Tenetehara carried out cooperative economic and ceremonial activities in extended family and kin groups that could easily secede from one village to form another. The Tapirape, by contrast, had several distinct social groupings that performed different economic and ritual functions. The Tapirape had to reside in villages of at least 200, because smaller villages could not assemble enough males belonging to these different kinds of groupings to allow them to undertake their cooperative tasks. A small group of Tenetehara could always break away from the parent village and establish a new village elsewhere, making it possible for them to expand in population without disrupting their social system. Whereas the Tapirape lacked such flexibility and could not expand, the Tenetehara appear to have been expanding at the time of European contact and were thus better able to maintain their numbers in the face of European-introduced diseases and other destructive factors than were the Tapirape. Wagley concluded from these observations that "differences in social structure and of value systems between societies must be taken into account in studies of population size and of population trends in any natural area. . . ."[21]

Pratt's paper on the Hutterites and Amish, however, presents us with an even better demonstration of this principle, thanks mainly to the availability of accurate vital statistics coupled with the documented history of these sects. Here, too, we can see the value systems operating to encourage women to produce more and more children. Not only do they discourage any kind of birth control, but they also readily accept modern medical facilities and drugs, which reduce mortality. By examining the household arrangement and the positive values placed on large families, Pratt helps to explain the cultural incentives behind the phenomenal growth rate of the Hutterite population. Moreover, by considering the residential and economic arrangements of Hutterite communities he is able to explain, just as Wagley was with the Tenetehara, how easy it is for Hutterite colonies to split off from their parent communities and settle in a new part of the country. By comparison, the Amish have not grown so rapidly, but their rate of population growth is still far above the American average. Part of this relative failure can be attributed to the doctrinal views of the Amish, which forbid use of modern technology in many spheres of life, including medicine and agriculture. Also, their economy is less communally organized than that of the Hutterites; in order to expand in population, they must also expand geographically, making it more difficult for families to keep in close contact with each other and thus increasing the chances for schism.

Whereas Wagley compared two societies to show how one declined less rapidly than the other in population, Pratt compares two societies to explain how one has increased in population more rapidly than the other. Both studies demonstrate the value of trying to understand how changes in population are affected by and influence social organization and attitudes.

The Status of Women

Muriel Schein, the author of "Only on Sundays," states that her interest in the women's liberation movement was one factor that led her to study the lives of women in the traditional Greek village of Kriovrisi. Are the women of Kriovrisi downtrodden and exploited? To an ardent women's libber in New York City they would seem to be the ultimate example of women kept in bondage to male chauvinism. Most of their time is spent performing household tasks—cleaning, cooking, laundry, carrying water, sewing and knitting, and, most important, tending the children. It is unremitting work, with little time off. And it is work with a high degree of repetitiousness, unlike that of the men, which often involves travel and varied social contacts. Girls are not encouraged to go beyond six grades of education, although men may go considerably further. Publicly, women's status is low, reflected by the fact that a woman's prestige derives mainly from her husband's accomplishments as well as those of others in her family and also that a woman takes not only her husband's last name but his first name as well. In Kriovrisi, moreover, women have no choices. They must accept the idea that a woman's place is in the home or else leave the village altogether and seek education and employment in a city.

Yet even if a women's liberation movement were introduced in rural Greece now, it is unlikely that it would have much effect on Kriovrisi and other similar communities. Why not? What keeps this state of affairs so firmly entrenched, not only in Kriovrisi but also in many other parts of the world? One anthropological approach to this question studies the sexual *division of labor* in human societies. In a cross-cultural survey of 224 different human societies, anthropologist George P. Murdock discovered the following:

Such tasks as metal-working, weapon-making, pursuit of sea-mammals, hunting, manufacture of musical instruments, trapping or catching of small animals, work in bone, horn, and shell, are almost exclusively allocated to males. Water-carrying, grain-carrying, cooking, gathering of herbs, and manufacture and repair of clothing, for example, are overwhelmingly feminine. This distribution of tasks is in itself interesting, as is the suggestion that everywhere some distinction is forcefully made between women's work and men's work.[22]

Furthermore, these same cross-cultural studies indicate that although males can and sometimes will do all jobs, there are some jobs that females cannot or may not do. Anthropologist Lionel Tiger asks, "Why cannot females become fighter pilots, tank commanders, or police chiefs?"[23] Even in countries such as the Soviet Union, where equality of sex in occupations is social dogma, true equality in all occupations is still far from accomplished. The idea of a division of labor appears to be deep-rooted and of long standing in human culture. Schein points out that this is the case in Kriovrisi, where the sexual division of labor and the role of women have hardly changed since the nineteenth century.

One of the most interesting anthropological views on the origin and pervasiveness of this sexual division of labor in human society is that of Lionel Tiger. He argues that, as early men evolved a way of life based on hunting wild animals, the sexual division of labor became more regular and rigid.[24] Males formed cooperative groups in order to hunt more efficiently, leaving the women to look after the children. Thus in the course of human history both men's and women's groups, each oriented around different tasks, tended to draw apart and solidify as separate entities. Tiger further argues that males have continued to form cooperative groups, even in agricultural and herding societies, wherever there was a need for hard and concentrated physical labor. This is a kind of economic or ecological explanation for the origin and persistence of the sexual division of labor, but it is by no means the only explanation that has been proposed. Anthropologist Robert F. Murphy, for example, advocates a more psychological explanation in which sex-antagonism is seen as the basis for this separation of the sexes into different groups.[25]

Schein, however, limits her explanation of the division of labor and the current role of women in Kriovrisi to Kriovrisi itself. She points out that the women there appear to be fairly satisfied with their situation. For one thing, they form groups of their own and enjoy the social satisfaction of these groups. In Kriovrisi there is none of the stultifying loneliness that so often occurs among housewives in urban and suburban situations. Still, the women rarely question the purpose of this kind of a life, because it seems adequate and meaningful to most of them. And, of course, negative views persist toward any mother who works, both because her husband feels dishonored and because the other women could accuse such a woman of neglecting her children. It remains to be seen, however, whether the traditional sexual division of labor and women's roles will remain adaptive in nontraditional urban societies. That a women's liberation movement exists and that it is spreading suggest to some at least that these traditional views on the roles and status of women may not be adaptive in such cases and will have to change.

Notes

1   Alexander Lesser, "War and the State," in *War, the Anthropology of Armed Conflict and Aggression*, M. Fried, M. Harris,

and R. Murphy, eds., New York, Natural History Press, 1968, p. 95.

2 Elman R. Service, "War and Our Contemporary Ancestors," ibid., p. 160.

3 David F. Aberle, Urie Bronfenbrenner, Eckhard H. Hess, Daniel R. Miller, David M. Schneider, and James N. Spuhler, "The Incest Taboo and the Mating Patterns of Animals," *American Anthropologist*, vol. 65, 1963, p. 254.

4 Ibid., p. 255.

5 Sigmund Freud, *Totem and Taboo*, London, Routledge & Kegan Paul, 1950, pp. 1–17.

6 Aberle, et al., op. cit., p. 255.

7 R. A. Gould, "The Archaeologist as Ethnographer: A Case from the Western Desert of Australia," *World Archaeology*, vol. 3, no. 2, 1971, pp. 143–177.

8 E. B. Tyler, *Primitive Culture*, vol. I, London, John Murray, 1873, p. 71.

9 Freud, op. cit., p. 1.

10 A. R. Radcliffe-Brown, "On the Concept of Function in Social Science," in *Structure and Function in Primitive Societies* by A. R. Radcliffe-Brown, Glencoe, Ill., Free Press, 1959, p. 181.

11 Bronislaw Malinowski, *Argonauts of the Western Pacific*, New York, Dutton, 1961, pp. 81–104.

12 Glyn E. Daniel, *A Hundred Years of Archaeology*, London, Gerald Duckworth, 1952, pp. 169–174.

13 N. C. Nelson, "Chronology of the Tano Ruins, New Mexico," *American Anthropologist*, vol. 18, 1916, pp. 159–180.

14 Frederik Barth, "Ecologic Relationships of Ethnic Groups in Swat, North Pakistan," *American Anthropologist*, vol. 58, 1956, p. 1089.

15 Robert B. Ekvall, "The Nomadic Pattern of Living Among the Tibetans as Preparation for War," *American Anthropologist*, vol. 63, 1961, p. 1259.

16 Ibid., p. 1257.

17 Pauline Mahar Kolenda, "Toward a Model of the Hindu *Jajmani* System," *Human Organization*, vol. 22, No. 1, 1963, p. 12.

18 H. Gould, "The Hindu Jajmani System: A Case of Economic Particularism," *Southwestern Journal of Anthropology*, vol. 14, 1958, p. 428.

19 T. O. Beidelman, "A Comparative Analysis of the Jajmani System," *Monograph of the Association for Asian Studies No. 7*, Locust Valley, N.Y., J. J. Augustin, 1959.

20 Charles Wagley, "Cultural Influences on Population: A Comparison of Two Tupi Tribes," *Revista do Museu Paulista*, new series, vol. 5, 1951, p. 95.

21 Ibid., p. 104.

22 George P. Murdock, "Comparative Data on the Division of Labor by Sex," *Social Forces*, vol. 15, no. 4, 1937.
23 Lionel Tiger, *Men in Groups*, New York, Random House, 1969, p. 83.
24 Ibid., pp. 93–125.
25 Robert F. Murphy, "Social Structure and Sex Antagonism," *Southwestern Journal of Anthropology*, vol. 15, 1959, pp. 89–98.

NAPOLEON A. CHAGNON

YANOMAMÖ—THE FIERCE PEOPLE The Yanomamö Indians are a tribe in Venezuela and Brazil who practice a slash-and-burn way of horticultural life. Traditionally, they have been an inland "foot" tribe, avoiding larger rivers and settling deep in the tropical jungle. Until about 1950 they had no sustained contact with other peoples except, to a minor extent, with another tribe, the Carib-speaking Makiritaris to the northeast.

I recently lived with the Yanomamö for more than a year, doing research sponsored by the U.S. Public Health Service, with the co-operation of the Venezuela Institute for Scientific Research. My purpose was to study Yanomamö social organization, language, sex practices, and forms of violence, ranging from treacherous raids to chest-pounding duels.

Those Yanomamö who have been encouraged to live on the larger rivers (Orinoco, Mavaca, Ocamo, and Padamo) are slowly beginning to realize that they are not the only people in the world; there is also a place called Caraca-tedi (Caracas), from whence come foreigners of an entirely new order. These foreigners speak an incomprehensible language, probably a degenerate form of Yanomamö. They bring malaria pills, machetes, axes, cooking pots, and *copetas* ("guns"), have curious ideas about indecency, and speak of a new "spirit."

However, the Yanomamö remain a people relatively unadulterated by outside contacts. They are also fairly numerous. Their population is roughly 10,000, the larger portion of them distributed throughout southern Venezuela. Here, in basins of the upper Orinoco and all its tributaries, they dwell in some 75 scattered villages, each of which contains from 40 to 300 individuals.

The largest, most all-embracing human reality to these people is humanity itself; Yanomamö means true human beings. Their conception of themselves as the only true "domestic" beings (those that dwell in houses) is demonstrated by the contempt with which they treat non-Yanomamö, who, in their language, are "wild." For instance, when referring to themselves, they use an honorific pronoun otherwise reserved for important spirits and headmen; when discussing *nabäs* ("non-Yanomamö"), an ordinary pronoun is enough. Again, in one of the myths about their origin, the first people to be created were the Yanomamö. All others developed by a process of degeneration and are, therefore, not quite on a par with the Yanomamö.

In addition to meaning "people," Yanomamö also refers to the language. Their tribal name does not designate a politically organized entity but is more or less equivalent to our concept of humanity. (This, of course, makes their most outstanding characteristic—chronic warfare, of which I shall speak in detail— seem rather an anomaly.) Sub-Yanomamö groupings are based on language differences, historical separation, and geographical location.

For instance, two distinguishable groups, Waika (from *waikaö*—"to kill off") and Shamatari, speak nearly identical dialects; they are differentiated mostly on the basis of a specific event that led to their separation. The Shamatari, the group I know best, occupy the area south of the Orinoco to, and including portions of, northern Brazil. Their differentiation from the Waika probably occurred in the past 75 years.

According to the Indians, there was a large village on a northern tributary of the upper Orinoco River, close to its headwaters. The village had several factions, one of which was led by a man called Kayabawä (big tree). A notably corpulent man, he also had the name Shamatari, derived from *shama*, the "tapir," a robust ungulate found throughout tropical South America. As the story goes, Shamatari's faction got into a fight with the rest of the village over the possession of a woman, and the community split into two warring halves. Gradually the fighting involved more villages, and Shamatari led his faction south, crossed the Orinoco, and settled there. He was followed by members of other villages that had taken his part in the fight.

Those who moved to the south side of the Orinoco came to be called Shamataris by those living on the north side, and the term is now applied to any village in this area, whether or not it can trace its origin to the first supporters of Shamatari.

For the Yanomamö, the village is the maximum political unit and the maximum sovereign body, and it is linked to other villages by ephemeral alliances, visiting and trade relationships, and intermarriages. In essence, the village is a building—a continuous, open-roofed lean-to built on a circular plan and surrounded by a protective palisade of split palm logs. The roof starts at or near ground level, ascends at an angle of about 45 degrees, and reaches a height of some 20 to 25 feet. Individual segments under the continuous roof are not partitioned; from a hammock hung anywhere beneath it one can see (and hear, thanks to the band shell nature of the structure) all that goes on within the village.

The palisade, about three to six feet behind the base of the roof, is some ten feet high and is usually in various stages of disrepair, depending on the current warfare situation. The limited number of entrances are covered with dry palm leaves in the evening; if these are moved even slightly, the sound precipitates the barking of a horde of ill-tempered, underfed dogs, whose bad manners preadapt the stranger to what lies beyond the entrance.

A typical "house" (a segment under the continuous roof) shelters a man, his wife or wives, their children, perhaps one or both of the man's parents, and, farther down, the man's brothers and their families. The roof is alive with cockroaches, scorpions, and spiders, and the ground is littered with the debris of numerous repasts—bird, fish, and animal bones; bits of fur; skulls of monkeys and other animals; banana and plantain peelings; feathers; and the seeds of palm fruits. Bows and arrows stand against housepoles all over the village, baskets hang from roof rafters, and firewood is stacked under the lower part of the roof where it slopes to the ground. Some men will be whittling arrow points with agouti-tooth knives or tying feathers to arrow shafts. Some women will be spinning cotton, weaving baskets, or making hammocks or cotton waistbands. The children, gathered in the center of the village clearing, frequently tie a string to a lizard and entertain themselves by shooting the animal full of tiny arrows. And, of course, many people will be outside the compound, working in their gardens, fishing, or collecting palm fruits in the jungle.

If it is a typical late afternoon, most of the older men are gathered in one part of the village, blowing one of their hallucinatory drugs (ebene) up each other's nostrils by means of a hollow tube and chanting to the forest demons (hekuras) as the drug takes effect. Other men may be curing a sick person by sucking, massaging, and exhorting the evil spirit from him. Everybody in the village is swatting vigorously at the voracious biting gnats, and here and there groups of people delouse each other's heads and eat the vermin.

In composition, the village consists of one or more groups of patrilineally related kinsmen (mashis), but it also contains other categories, including people who have come from other villages seeking spouses. All villages try to increase their size and consider it desirable for both the young men and young women to remain at home after marriage. Since one must marry out of his *mashi*, villages with only one patrilineage frequently lose their young men to other villages; they must go to another village to *siohamou* (to "son-in-law") if they want wives. The parents of the bride-to-be, of course, want the young man to remain in their village to help support them in their old age, particularly if they have few or no sons. They will frequently promise a young man one or more of the sisters of his wife in order to make his stay more attractive.

He, on the other hand, would rather return to his home village to be with his own kinsmen, and the tendency is for postmarital residence to be patrilocal (with the father of the groom). If a village is rich in axes and machetes, it can and does coerce its poorer trading partners into permitting their young women to live permanently with the richer village. The latter thus obtains more women, while the poorer village gains some security in the trading network. The poor village then coerces other villages even poorer, or they raid them and steal their women.

The patrilineages that maintain the composition of the villages, rich or poor, include a man and his brothers and sisters, his children and his brothers' children, and the children of his sons and brothers' sons. The ideal marriage pattern is for a group of brothers to exchange sisters with another group of brothers. Furthermore, it is both permissible and desirable for a man to marry his mother's brother's daughter (his matrilateral cross-cousin) and/or his father's sister's daughter (his patrilateral cross-cousin) and, as we have seen earlier, to remain in his parents' village. Hence, the "ideal" village would have at least two patrilineages that exchanged marriageable people.

There is a considerable amount of adherence to these rules, and both brother-sister exchange and cross-cousin marriage are common. However, there are also a substantial number of people in each village who are not related in these ways. For the most part they are women and their children who have been stolen from other villages, segments of lineages that have fled from their own village because of fights, and individuals—mostly young men—who have moved in and attached themselves to the household of one of the lineage (*mashi*) leaders.

Even if the sex ratio is balanced, there is a chronic shortage of women. A pregnant woman or one who is still nursing her children must not have sexual relationships. This means that for as many as three years, even allowing for violations of the taboos, a woman is asexual as far as the men are concerned. Hence, men with pregnant wives, and bachelors too, are potentially disruptive in every village because they constantly seek liaisons with the wives of other men. Eventually such relationships are discovered and violence ensues.

The woman, even if merely suspected of having affairs with other men, is beaten with a club; burned with a glowing brand; shot with a barbed arrow in a non-vital area, such as the buttocks, so that removal of the barb is both difficult and painful; or chopped on the arms or legs with a machete or ax. Most women over thirty carry numerous scars inflicted on them by their enraged husbands. My study of genealogies also indicates that not a few women have been killed outright by their husbands. The woman's punishment for infidelity depends on the number of brothers she has in the village, for if her husband is too brutal, her brothers may club him or take her away and give her to someone else.

The guilty man, on the other hand, is challenged to a fight with clubs. This duel is rarely confined to the two parties involved, for their brothers and supporters join the battle. If nobody is seriously injured, the matter may be forgotten. But if the incidents are frequent, the two patrilineages may decide to split while they are still on relatively "peaceable" terms with each other and form two independent villages. They will still be able to reunite when threatened by raid from a larger village.

This is only one aspect of the chronic warfare of the Yanomamö—warfare that has a basic effect on settlement pattern and demography, intervillage political relationships, leadership, and social organization. The collective aggressive behavior is caused by the desire to accent "sovereignty"—the capacity to initiate fighting and to demonstrate this capacity to others.

Although the Yanomamö are habitually armed with lethal bows and arrows, they have a graded system of violence within which they can express their *waiteri*, or "fierceness." The form of violence is determined by the nature of the affront or wrong to be challenged. The most benign form is a duel between two groups, in which an individual from each group stands (or kneels) with his chest stuck out, head up in the air, and arms held back and receives a hard blow to the chest. His opponent literally winds up and delivers a closed-fist blow from the ground, striking the man on the left pectoral muscle just above the heart. The impact frequently drops the man to his knees, and participants may cough up blood for several days after such a contest. After receiving several such blows, the man then has his turn to strike his opponent, while the respective supporters of each antagonist gather around and frenziedly urge their champion on.

All men in the two villages are obliged to participate as village representatives, and on one occasion I saw some individuals take as many as three or four turns of four blows each. Duels of this type usually result from minor wrongs, such as a village being guilty of spreading bad rumors about another village, questioning its generosity or fierceness, or accusing it of gluttony at a feast. A variant of this form of duel is side slapping, in which an open-handed blow is delivered across the flank just above the pelvis.

More serious are the club fights. Although these almost invariably result from cases in which a wife has been caught in an affair with another man, some fights follow the theft of food within the village. The usual procedure calls for a representative from each belligerent group. One man holds a ten-foot club upright, braces himself by leaning on the club and spreading his feet, then holds his head out for his opponent to strike. Following this comes his turn to do likewise to his adversary. These duels, more often than not, end in a free-for-all in which everybody clubs everybody else on whatever spot he can hit. Such brawls occasionally result in fatalities. However, since headmen of the respective groups stand by with bows drawn, no one dares deliver an intentionally killing blow, for if he does, he will be shot. The scalps of the older men are almost incredible to behold, covered as they are by as many as a dozen ugly welts. Yet, most of them proudly shave the top of their heads to display their scars.

Also precipitated by feuds over women are spear fights, which are even more serious than club fights. Members of a village will warn those of the offending village that they are coming to fight with spears. They specify that they are not planning to shoot arrows unless the others shoot first. On the day of the fight, the attackers enter the other village, armed with five or six sharpened clubs or slender shafts some eight feet long and attempt to drive the defenders out. If successful, the invaders steal all the valuable possessions—hammocks, cooking pots, and machetes—and retreat. In the spear fight that occurred while I was studying the tribe, the attackers were successful, but they wounded several individuals so badly that one of them died. The fighting then escalated to a raid, the penultimate form of violence.

Such raids may be precipitated by woman stealing or the killing of a visitor (visitors are sometimes slain because they are suspected of having practiced harmful magic that has led to a death in the host's village). Raids also occur if a man kills his wife in a fit of anger; her natal village is then obliged to avenge the death. Most raids, however, are in revenge for deaths that occurred in previous raids, and once the vendetta gets started, it is not likely to end for a long time. Something else may trigger a raid. Occasionally an ambitious headman wearies of peaceful times—a rarity, certainly—and deliberately creates a situation that will demonstrate his leadership.

A revenge raid is preceded by a feast in which the ground bones of the person to be avenged are mixed in a soup of boiled, ripe plantains (the mainstay of Yanomamö diet) and swallowed. Yanomamö are endocannibals, which means they consume the remains of members of their own group. This ceremony puts the raiders in the appropriate state of frenzy for the business of warfare. A mock raid—rather like a dress rehearsal—is conducted in their own village on the afternoon before the day of the raid, and a life-size effigy of an enemy, constructed of leaves or a log, is slain. That evening all the participants march, one at a time, to the center of the village clearing, while clacking their bows and arrows and screaming their versions of the calls of carnivorous birds, mammals, and even insects.

When all have lined up facing the direction of the enemy village, they sing their war song, "I am a meat-hungry buzzard," and shout several times in unison until they hear the echo return from the jungle. They then disperse to their individual sections of the village to vomit the symbolic rotten flesh of the enemy that they, as symbolic carnivorous vultures and wasps, partook of in the lineup. The same thing, with the exception of the song, is repeated at dawn the following morning. Then the raiders, covered with black paint made of chewed charcoal, march out of the village in single file and collect the hammocks and plantains that their women have previously set outside the village for them. On each night they spend en route to the enemy they fire arrows at a dummy in a mock raid. They approach the enemy village itself under cover of darkness, ambush the first person they catch, and retreat as rapidly as possible. If they catch a man and his family, they will shoot the man and steal the woman and her children. At a safe distance from her village, each of the raiders rapes the woman, and when they reach their own village, every man in the village may, if he wishes, do likewise before she is given to one of the men as a wife. Ordinarily she attempts to escape, but if caught, she may be killed. So constant is the threat of raids that every woman leaves her village in the knowledge that she may be stolen. As a result, she always takes her smaller children with her, preferring that they be abducted, too, rather than remain to die from starvation.

The supreme form of violence is the *nomohoni*—the "trick." During the dry season, the Yanomamö do a great deal of visiting. An entire village will go to another village for a ceremony that involves feasting, dancing, chanting, curing, trading, and just plain gossiping. Shortly after arrival, the visitors are invited to recline in the hammocks of the hosts. By custom they lie motionless to display their fine decorations while the hosts prepare food for them. But now suppose that a village has a grudge to settle with another, such as deaths to avenge. It enlists the support of a third village to act as accomplice. This third village, which must be on friendly terms with the intended victims, will invite them to a feast. While the guests recline defenseless in the hammocks, the hosts descend on them with axes and sharpened poles, treacherously killing as many as they can. Those that manage to escape the slaughter inside the village are shot outside the palisade by the village that instigated the *nomohoni*. The women and children will be shared between the two accomplices.

Throughout all this ferocity there are two organizational aspects of violence. One concerns leadership: A man must be able to demonstrate his fierceness if he is to be a true leader. It is equally important, however, that he have a large natural following—that is, he must have many male kinsmen to support his position and a quantity of daughters and sisters to distribute to other men. Lineage leaders cannot accurately be described as unilateral initiators of activities; rather, they are the vehicles through which the group's will is expressed. For example, when a certain palm fruit is ripe and is particularly abundant in an area some distance from the village, everybody knows that the whole village will pack its belongings and erect a temporary camp at that spot to collect the fruit. The headman does little more than set the date. When his kinsmen see him packing, they know that the time has come to leave for the collecting trip. True, the headman does have some initiative in raiding, but not even this is completely independent of the attitudes of his followers, which dictate that a death must be avenged. However, when the purpose of a raid is to steal women, the headman does have some freedom to act on his own initiative.

As a general rule, the smaller his natural following, the more he is obliged to demonstrate his personal qualities of fierceness and leadership. Padudiwä, the headman of one of the lineages in Bisaasi-tedi, took pains to demonstrate his personal qualities whenever he could; he had only two living brothers and four living sisters in his group. Most of his demonstrations of ferocity were the cruel beatings he administered to his four wives, none of whom had brothers in the village to take their part. Several young men who attached themselves to his household admired him for this.

Padudiwä was also responsible for organizing several raids while I lived with the villagers of Bisaasi-tedi. Every one of them was against Patanowä-tedi, a village that was being raided regularly by some seven or eight other villages, so that the danger of being raided in return was correspondingly reduced. On one occasion, when three young men from Patonowä-tedi arrived as emissaries of peace, Padudiwä wanted to kill them, although he had lived with them at one time and they were fairly close relatives. The murder was prevented by the headman of the other—and larger—lineage in the village, who warned that if an attempt were made on the lives of the visitors he himself would kill Padudiwä.

Obviously then, Padudiwä's reputation was built largely on calculated acts of fierceness, which carefully reduced the possibility of personal danger to himself and his followers, and on cunning and cruelty. To some extent he was obliged by the smallness of his gathering to behave in such a way, but he was certainly a man to treat with caution.

Despite their extreme aggressiveness, the Yanomamö have at least two qualities I admired. They are kind and indulgent with children and can quickly forget personal angers. (A few even treated me almost as an equal—in their culture this was a considerable concession.) But to portray them as "noble savages" would be misleading. Many of them are delightful and charming people when confronted alone and on a personal basis, but the greater number of them are much like Padudiwä —or strive to be that way. As they frequently told me, *Yanomamö täbä waiteri!*—"Yanomamö are fierce!"

GEORGES CONDOMINAS

THE PRIMITIVE LIFE OF VIETNAM'S MOUNTAIN PEOPLE

The Montagnards of Vietnam are a so-called primitive people: that is, they follow an ancient way of life in the mountainous jungle regions that rise above the coastal plains. Technically speaking, the inhabitants of the coastal plains are the Vietnamese proper.

Ethnic groups similar to the Montagnards are found throughout Southeast Asia. All the plains people of these countries have given derogatory names—"savage"; an equivalent of the American "hillbilly"; "slaves"; and others—to their indigenous mountain tribesmen.

The adoption of local names for the Montagnards has been a source of confusion, so A. G. Haudricourt and I coined the word "Proto-Indochinese" to designate this whole group of tribes that had found refuge in the mountains of the Indochinese peninsula, from the Bay of Bengal to the Gulf of Tonkin, and along the Chinese frontier to Singapore.

But, except to ethnologists, these tribesmen are still known by the name given to them by the French—Montagnards.

The Mnong Gar, who are the subject of this article, are one of the most primitive tribes of the Proto-Indochinese group. The other mountain tribes call them the Phii Brêe, which means "men of the forest." They occupy both banks of the mid-Krong Knô, "The Male River" (in Rhadé language followed by the geographers), southern branch of the upper Srépok River, a tributary of the Mekong. Their habitat is a country of hills and mountainous foothills, covered by jungle, bamboo groves, and, in places, dense forests. This terrain, which harbors big game— elephants, tigers, gaur (wild cattle), deer of all kinds—is situated about 200 miles north of Saigon, just south of the magnificent Daak Laak (Darlac) Lake Basin, where a relatively good road leads to the city of Ban Mé Thuot.

How they dress

The Mnong Gar dress essentially the same as the other Proto-Indochinese of Vietnam. For this entire group, the most typical part of the men's costume is the *suu troany*, which is a type of loincloth. It is made of a long, narrow strip of cloth that is passed between the thighs before being wrapped around the waist and knotted at the loins. The most richly decorated end of the *suu troany* falls from the waist in front, much like a narrow apron. The *suu troany* leaves the legs and buttocks completely bare, and is often the only thing worn by the men during the day, although they may sometimes add a short, sleeveless tunic to the costume. When cold comes in the evening, they wrap themselves in large blankets and gossip in the courtyard with their neighbors. The same blanket is used during the day to carry young children on the back, and at night as a cover during sleep.

The women wrap a skirt made of a rectangle of indigo-dyed cloth around their waists. The two ends overlap in front and are held in place by a narrow belt. They may go about naked to the waist or wear a tunic, usually long-sleeved. Imported, ready-made clothing is becoming popular today, and the women often buy black calico skirts and white cotton blouses. But it is the men who are most eager for European clothes—jackets, shirts, overcoats, and capes. They are not interested in shorts, and still less in trousers.

Both men and women wear their hair in a chignon, but today most of the young men, and especially those of enlistment age, cut their hair short, "European style."

Both sexes adorn themselves with many bracelets and necklaces. The women decorate their hair with strings of tiny beads arranged like a diadem, and stick large hairpins of various shapes in their chignons. Men more commonly wear wooden combs covered with tin, and on feast days they add two red pompons.

The Mnong Gar multilate their teeth, for purely "esthetic" reasons. They break the upper incisors and file them to the gumline; the lower teeth are filed to a point. All the teeth are painted with black lacquer.

The picture of the man of the forest would be incomplete without a basket, a bush knife, and a bamboo pipe. (The women also smoke pipes; in addition, they chew on a sort of "pipe cleaner" made of a long sliver of bamboo, one end of which has been frayed into a little brush. When the pipe cleaner is drawn

This handsome young warrior, named Khuung, is one of the Montagnards, who live in the mountains of Vietnam. The hairdo and necklace he is wearing are frequently the adornments of men. The decorations he has stuck into his chignon are a small knife, a wooden comb covered with tin, various feathers, red pompons, and beaded pendants. The ear disk is of ivory. Over his shoulder is a *wiah*, an efficient bush knife; the bamboo handle is tin-sheathed.

through the bowl and pipe stem, the brush end collects all of the tobacco juice.) The basket (*sah*) is carried on the back and held in place by two braided rattan straps, which pass over the shoulders. The bush knife—the inseparable companion of all Montagnards—has a short, wide blade and a bamboo handle more than a yard long. The knife blade is fixed in the bulbous root of the bamboo, which has been prepared by bending the root at right angles to the bamboo shaft. Thus the bush knife can be balanced on the shoulder, with the blade turned upward; the handle is usually gripped while walking.

Grain is harvested by Montagnard tribesman.

The dwellings

What is most striking about the Mnong Gar dwellings is their length (at the village of Sar Luk, where I lived, two of the houses measured more than forty yards) and their massive thatched roofs. In fact, the roof is almost all that one sees. The thatch slopes from either side of the ridgepole, which is three or four yards high, to about two feet from the ground. Thus, the low, woven-bamboo wall of the house is almost completely hidden by the thatch. The roofing is rounded at either end of the house. The doors are hardly more than low, narrowing openings

Members of the Mnong Gar tribe of Montagnards take part in a ceremony in a bamboo grove in interior Vietnam.

Typical longhouse of the Mnong Gar tribe in Vietnam has immense thatched roof that nearly obscures the walls of woven bamboo.

in the front wall, and above them are arches of rattan that serve to raise the edge of the roof so the people can pass through the doors. Just under the eaves, near the doors, are long, narrow chicken coops.

The area that surrounds each house separates it from the one it faces, and this area is generally kept rather clean and neat. It is weeded from time to time, and some people even sweep the area daily. But, inevitably, it becomes a quagmire during the rainy season.

Very close to certain of the dwellings—those of the *kuang*, the "men of power"—tower tall, straight, thorny trunks of false kapok trees, *Bombax malabaricum* (De Clercq). The tops have been carved and crowned with a twig of decorated bamboo. These are the posts that have been used for buffalo sacrifice. Some of the older posts throw new roots and again become tall, beautiful trees, a living testimony to the prestige of those who planted them. Sometimes, in front of such a house, is an immense, decorated bamboo, which can shoot up to more than sixty feet, thus completing the ritual decor.

The houses' interiors are dark and almost empty except at the back, where a third of the width is occupied by an enormous dais made of planks or woven bamboo, which is about a foot off the ground and runs the entire rear length of the house. Against the wall behind the dais is a row of large jars. Over the large jars hang one or two tiers of little, neckless jars. The number varies with the wealth of the master of the house. Each end of the large room, the *wah* (which we shall refer to as the reception room), is bounded by an immense rice granary, set on four or six strong stilts. These pillars are an extension of the two lines of columns that support the roof parallel to the ridgepole.

Each granary occupies only the middle third of the width of the longhouse. The back third is occupied by the dais, part of which serves as a bed for the master and mistress of the house. This sleeping area of the dais is delineated by a board or a pile of baskets or boxes, which separates this area from the reception room. The front third of the longhouse is, in contrast, kept clear, except for a dish shelf, or, at worst, a neat pile of firewood. This front third thus forms a corridor through which passage from

Horns of sacrificed buffalo are piled near the outskirts of Mnong Gar village of Sar Lang after Great Earth Festival.

one end of the longhouse to the other is unimpeded. Except for each extremity of this large dwelling, the granaries are grouped in pairs with their back partitions touching. It is at this point that the *nal*, or private door, opens in the front wall.

The women do the cooking under the low floor of the granary on a hearth composed of three cylinders made of packed earth from a termite nest. When all of the women in the longhouse are cooking, smoke invades every corner including the reception room.

Each granary belongs to one independent family. If the family consists only of a couple and their young children, the family limits itself to a granary with four pillar supports covering a single hearth. But if the family includes several adults—a newly married daughter or the widowed mother or sister of one of the couple—the granary has six pillars and covers two hearths, one of which is used by the mistress of the house and the other by her protégés.

Thus each family's domicile is determined by its granary. To refer to someone's residence, one says *hih nâm* (house granary), whereas *root* refers to the whole longhouse, which contains several *hih nâm*.

Agricultural system

Like most of the other Proto-Indochinese, the Mnong Gar are semi-nomadic farmers who practice *miir*, a method of shifting cultivation that consists of clearing a section of forest, burning what has been cut, and sowing the paddy (rice grains) over the field fertilized by the ashes. The field is abandoned after one harvest (sometimes, but rarely, two). In this way the crops are moved almost every year, and the same area is replanted only after a fallow period of about ten or twenty years. When arable land is too far away to be convenient, the village site may be moved. But should an epidemic result in the death of several residents, the village is always relocated. Village sites that have been temporarily abandoned can be identified by the presence of fruit trees or edible plants, such as a type of eggplant, and by the rows of false kapok trees—memorials to buffalo sacrifice.

Mnong Gar family, which had stored its harvest in a temporary granary, is now moving the filled baskets indoors.

These shifting cultivators can reckon the passage of time only by a spatial reference point—that part of the forest that has been felled and burned—in short, by the "eaten" forests. In this way, they designate each year by the name of the eaten forest. When the Mnong Gar wish to calculate the exact age of a child, for example, they need only recall the name of the forest eaten at the time of his birth, break one twig for each of the forests eaten since that event, and count the total number of broken twigs. The title of the book on which this article is based, *We Have Eaten the Forest of the Rock Spirit Gôo*—as translated from French—simply stands for the year 1949 at Sar Luk. It was in this village that I lived from September, 1948, to February, 1950, after several months traveling in the region to learn the language.

Even without cultivation, the forest offers important sources of food: wild vegetables and plants, such as leaves of *pai sei* (*Gnetum gnemon*), bamboo shoots, and various tubers, and game, which the Mnong Gar usually trap. (But fishing is by far a more important source of protein than trapping.)

The Mnong Gar raise some smaller animals for food: pigs, chickens, dogs, and sometimes a few ducks. Buffalo are very difficult to raise and are usually bought from other tribes and used as the sacrificial animal of choice.

Commercial activity

The tribe engages in other productive activities. Their basketry is of excellent craftsmanship. This is man's work. Weaving is done by women, and it, too, is extremely beautiful.

Commerce is based on a complex system of barter. Each article is evaluated and paid for by a whole series of barterable items: jars, pigs, skirts, and buffalo. The most valuable items, such as jars and gongs, are not made by the Mnong Gar but, as is the case with other Proto-Indochinese and with Proto-Malays, are obtained by a long bartering circuit from the plains people. To this system must be added a type of European money, the Indochinese piaster, which came into use a few decades ago. The piaster has been replaced by the *dong*, the official currency of the Vietnamese state. Commercial and all other Mnong Gar transactions are always carried out in the presence of at least one go-between (*ndraany*), but more usually two.

Social customs

As will become evident in the course of this article, the jar occupies a special place in Mnong Gar life, as it does for the other Proto-Indochinese. The jars are glazed pottery of Vietnamese or Chinese origin, usually reddish brown. Occasionally the word "alcohol" will be used to describe their contents, but in fact, this term in something of a poetic exaggeration. *Rnööm* is nothing more than a rice beer that cannot really be compared to either our distilled spirits or our wines. The beer mash (*coot*), which is made of rich flour and rice husks, is allowed to ferment for several days (or at most about a month) in a sealed jar (*yang*). If there is to be a sacrifice, a small amount of *coot* is taken for the anointment, and then the jar is prepared in the usual manner. It is stuffed with leaves or sword grass to keep the fermented material on the bottom of the receptacle, and the jar is filled to the brim with water. The quantity of water added varies from about one to ten quarts, depending on the size of the jar. The *rnööm* is now ready, but before it can be drunk it must be consecrated. A drinking straw (*gut*) is stuck into the jar as several verses are recited; care is taken to insure that a few drops of water fall on the ground.

The beverage is drunk by drawing on one end of the *gut*, while the other end touches the bottom of the jar. The drink becomes alcoholic as the water flows through the fermented mass. One drinker may not be replaced at the jar by another until the first has drunk two draughts of *rnööm*. (If a singing contest is in progress, then the number of draughts to be drunk, always even in this case, must be equal to the number drunk by the preceding contestant.) In addition, the next drinker does not take his turn until the assistant sitting at the opposite side of the jar has added twice the contents of a fire-etched bamboo tube, buffalo horn, or plastic glass that has been filled with water from a receptacle by his side. Thus, as each drinker takes his turn, the *rnööm* becomes progressively weaker, and after a few hours it is quite innocuous.

After having finished this article, the reader may come to the conclusion that the Mnong Gar are consummate drunkards. But the majority of the days described here are special occasions. Besides, I am under the impression that the men of the forest are not the only people in the world to douse a marriage or a wake. Not only is their only strong drink less alcoholic than any of our mass-produced commercial spirits, but, in addition, their opportunities to drink are considerably less frequent than ours. The Mnong Gar only uncork a jar when they must pay honor to the spirits or to a visiting foreigner. More is necessary than dissatisfaction with water. To indulge in a drinking party without having a religious motive—merely for the sake of social drinking or solitary tippling—is inconceivable to them.

Before their country was included in the political system of the French colonial regime, the social space of the Mnong Gar did not extend beyond the territorial limits of the village. Today, they are all included in a hierarchy of administrative organization maintained externally, but the village system remains as a substructure. Each village includes three or four "sacred men in the forest and the village," who serve both as arbiters for the collective rituals, such as the agrarian rites and village reconstruction, and for the problems involving land—in particular, the selection and apportioning of forest lots to be eaten.

A man becomes a *kuang*, that is, a man of power, when he has amassed enough possessions to immolate a buffalo. Each additional buffalo sacrifice adds to his prestige, especially when an exchange of sacrifices (*tâm bôh*) is involved. An exchange of sacrifices creates a strong alliance between the two celebrants.

The shaman, too, occupies a special position in Mnong Gar society. The shaman (*njau*) is the intermediary between the patient and the *caak*, the malicious sorcerers, and the *yaang*, the spirits inhabiting nature.

The Mnong Gar family organization is principally based on the *mpôol*, which we translate as "clan": that is, a group of individuals who claim a common maternal ancestor. The clan name and the family possessions are transmitted, not by the father to the children, but by the mother to the children. For example, the members of the clan Rjee belong to the clan because their mother, not their father, belongs to it. Members of the same *mpôol* may neither marry nor have sexual relations with each other. They are, in fact, considered as sisters and brothers if they are of the same generation; as fathers, mothers, and children or uncles, aunts, nephews, and nieces if they belong to two succeeding generations; and finally as grandparents and grandchildren if they belong to two generations separated by a third. No matter how far back the first common female ancestor may be found in the genealogy, two individuals that for us wouldn't even be considered as cousins call each other "mother" and "children" or "brother" and "sister." It is this situation that forms the basis of the tragedy to follow.

THE "INCEST" OF TIENG AND AANG . . . WHO HAD A COMMON ANCESTOR 15 GENERATIONS AGO *This account is taken essentially unedited from the author's diary. It forms part of Chapter III of the book, Nous Avons Mangé la Forêt de la Pierre-Génie Gôo, published in 1957 by Mercure de France, Paris.*

VIETNAM, NOVEMBER 26, 1948

At a quarter to six in the morning they came to take me to Kröng-Jòong's house for the great annual sacrifice, "The Blood Anointment of the Paddy" (*Mhaam Baa*). He is one of the sacred men in the forest and the village at Sar Luk, and he observes and executes the rites most meticulously. Yesterday had been devoted to a preliminary rite, "The Taking of the Straw" (*Sok Rhei*) and, like all the agrarian rites, it had ended with a drinking party. This drinking party will continue, without letup, throughout the next few days devoted to celebrations of the agricultural cycle. The Blood Anointment of the Paddy comes as a brilliant climax to the end of the year.

When I arrived, Kröng was preparing the rice-flour paste that he would use to paint geometric designs on the pillars and beams of the granary, and then on all of his household possessions. He was painting the jars when Kroong-the-Big-Navel burst in shouting: "Aang-the-Widow has been lying with her brother Tieng!" [The Mnong phrase was much more crude.] Baap Can, who had been sitting by the fire smoking, stared at Kroong in bewilderment. He didn't seem to understand. Kroong repeated his sinister news. Then Baap Can turned to me: "Serious *beng* [taboo]," he told me. "Sticking a knife in a pot, *beng*; copulation between sister and brother, *beng*." And he added, "The lightning strikes," and with his hand he made the gesture of cleaving his skull in two. Kroong told us how he and Kraang-the-Bladder had surprised the couple last evening behind Chaar-Rieng's hut. They had recognized Tieng at once by the gleam of his tin comb, and had shouted at him. The man had bolted, dropping a hairpin from his chignon. They had picked it up to use as incriminating evidence. Aang, who was drunk, had not moved. She had just lain there, stretched out on the ground.

"Who was it?"

"I'm drunk. I don't know."

"It was Tieng, your own brother."

"How should I know?"

Tieng had remained in hiding in the bush. Meanwhile, some of the other drinkers joined Kroong and Kraang to question Aang, or to comment on the scandal. No more had been seen of Tieng last night. He waited until all the curious had retired before sneaking back to Chaar-Rieng's hut. Chaar-Rieng was his *kôony* (mother's younger brother), with whom he lived.

Aang-the-Widow could hardly be called beautiful. She had a bad figure, was flat-chested and swarthy. Yet, her expression was witty, and what was rare for a Gar girl, her eyes had an ardent expression. She lived with her brother Tôong-Biing, a calm, stolid fellow who was an excellent basketmaker, but terribly poor. Her eldest brother, Sieng, also widowered, lived at Little Sar Luk, a hamlet of only one hut about two miles from the village.

On the other hand, Tieng was one of the handsomest men in Sar Luk. He was always impeccable. His hair was pulled tightly into a chignon, and it was always decorated with a big comb and a handsome, tin-plated pin. He wore necklaces around his neck, bracelets on his arms. His apron loincloth was tied tightly around his waist. When Tieng's wife died, his uncle Chaar-Rieng went to Phii Srôony to get Tieng and his five-year-old daughter, Jôong, and brought them to Sar Luk to live. Tieng's eldest brother still lived in Phii Srôony, the family's original home.

I had been aware that Aang often hung around Chaar-Rieng's place, especially when his nephew was there. I had only a vague impression that they might be lovers; the Gar are always very discreet. But I had quite forgotten that they were of the same clan. Aang and Tieng were both of the *mpôol* Cil.

A few days earlier, when I was working at my desk, I heard cries from Tôong-Biing's hut. I rushed out and asked someone else who had also been attracted what was happening. "Tôong-Biing is beating his sister," was the reply.

"Why?" I had asked.

No answer.

They told me the reason today. Biing, the wife, had been scolding Aang for flirting with her brother Tieng. Aang not only told her to mind her own business but, when Biing continued to reprimand her, Aang slapped her face. When her husband returned, Biing told him what had happened. Tôong was furious and gave his sister a good beating. So, although people had been aware of the incestuous relation between Tieng and Aang, nobody had yet caught them at it.

Baap Can had recovered from his astonishment. He was now bursting with indignation.

"The lightning strikes," he said, "when sister sleeps with brother. . . . It strikes not the guilty, but the leading men of the forest and village.

The dragon flays . . .
the tiger devours . . .
the elephant impales

the sacred men in the forest and the village. It is a very serious matter. The offenders must *saa ê* [eat excrement] of pig, dog, hen, duck, and man."

I asked him: "You mean really eat?"

"No, only lick with the tip of the tongue. Then the rain will stop. It is *beng* for sister and brother to sleep together. When the couple are of different clans, though, it isn't *beng*."

Baap Can was convinced, as were the others, that once the expiatory sacrifices had been performed, these incestuous relations could not lead to a birth. [But Aang gave birth to a son in July, 1949.] Nevertheless, incest brings the threat of unnatural death to all people of importance: that is, not only to the traditional *kuang*, but to people like Truu, the canton head living at Sar Luk; his deputy; and even to me, because I am closely involved in the life of the village. Incest disturbs the order of nature. The rain will dig deep ravines, cause landslides. Water will gush from the earth.

The celebration of *Mhaam Baa* was not interrupted by the disclosure of the scandal, but the incident of Tieng and Aang was to provide a subject for discussion in every home and, for

Baap Can, an opportunity to display his learning. He would sing the "verses of justice" (*noo ngöi dôih*), blaming the couple for their obstinacy and emphasizing the horror and disgust aroused by their misconduct.

About ten o'clock, Krae, the headman of Bboon Rcae, turned up at Sar Luk completely drunk, bawling and gesticulating, his eyes bloodshot. (Bboon Rcae is an administrative area formed by Sar Luk and nearby Paang Döng.) He was of the *mpôol* Cil and went into a fury when he learned what had happened in his clan. He burst into Chaar-Rieng's house in a drunken rage, shrieking: "We must tie them up! Bring them to trial immediately." Then he ran, staggering to the canton deputy's place, still shrieking, "Tie them up."

Baap Can arrived and tried to calm him down. He declared that the couple could not be tied up, that they couldn't even be judged on the spot. And he improvised these lines:

Drink well, eat well,
Tomorrow we will pass judgment.
Drunk with beer, drunk our body,
Yoo would take no account of it . . .
Tomorrow we'll all question them.
Aang has made love with Tieng.

His song explained that people were busy with *Mhaam Baa* today; they should drink and have a good time. Tomorrow would be time enough to settle the matter. There is a time for everything. (*Yoo* is a Mnong word by which they had named me —fully, Yoo Sar Luk.)

But Krae would not be dissuaded. If no one would listen to him, he would tie them up himself. He would drag them to the lake. He was, after all, a headman and a Cil. I, too, tried to get him to listen to reason, but he continued to argue. Finally, someone solved the problem by sitting him down in front of a jar. After drinking his fill, he fell asleep.

During the morning the sky had darkened. The storm broke at about five in the afternoon. We were to have four days of torrential rain broken only by periods of drizzle; four somber days without a ray of sunshine on a sea of mud and water. Over and over a lamentation was heard: "Rain, terrible *beng*; lovemaking [again, their term was more earthy] between sister and brother. Rain."

NOVEMBER 27

The *Mhaam Baa* sacrifices went on. We were at the venerable Tôong-Mang's house. He was speaking of yesterday's downpour, today's threatening weather, and the drizzle. No doubt there would be a devastating deluge. Such were the consequences of incest.

Taang, eldest brother of the offending Tieng, arrived a short time ago from Phii Srôony. He has gone with Chaar-Rieng to the residence of Taang-Jieng-the-Stoop-Shouldered, richest Cil in the village. The two men seemed weary, depressed by the enormity of Tieng's offense. Nevertheless, Chaar competed with Baap Can in reciting the Cil clan genealogies (Baap Can's father was also a Cil). Sieng-the-Widower and Tôong-Biing, who were too poor to manage even a proper *Mhaam Baa*, were squatting discreetly in a corner. They were crushed by what had happened.

This evening it was the canton chief Truu's turn to perform his *Mhaam Baa*. I was greatly surprised to find Aang serving the company, bringing tubes of rice beer to the various guests. She moved among us, naked to the waist, and wore no ornaments. Her skin seemed a little darker than usual. Was it shame, or the result of having drunk too much last night? Her gestures were clumsy when she attempted to mix with the others, but she didn't seem dejected in the least. Rather, she appeared to be surprised by all the commotion her affair had caused. Moreover, the discussions went on in front of her, as if she were not there. Everyone was scornful of the *mpöol* Cil; even Truu, whose father was a Cil, spat on the ground to show his disgust.

Somewhat later in the evening Tieng appeared. He had not been seen since the night before last. It was his uncle's turn to make the sacrifice, and he had come to invite us to drink at his place. Handsome Tieng, usually so elegant, was completely undone. He was wearing none of his ornaments; his hair was disheveled and his features drawn. His eyes avoided ours. He hadn't dared to raise his voice for the invitation.

NOVEMBER 28

The sacred men shared the gifts among themselves. Each household had given chicken legs and measures of *rnööm* as a payment for their participation in the rituals performed during these two days of sacrifices. All of the men of the village were there because the division of lots in the new *miir* would be discussed. Inevitably, the talk came around to the case of incest, and they speculated on how Aang would manage to get a pig for the sacrifice because her brothers had none. Her brothers have decided to go to work on a plantation. The salary will be meager, but enough to complete the sum necessary to pay for the piglet. In addition, Tôong-Biing, an excellent basketmaker, will weave me some carrying baskets and winnowing baskets for the Musée de l'Homme.

Bbaang-Dlaang, the sector chief, came through Sar Luk to pick up Truu and some of the young villagers. He came to see us, and repeated what he had told the old men yesterday: Although the incestuous couple would have to make the expiatory sacrifices, they would not have to pay the fine. Normally a case of incest is settled in the following way: If the guilty couple is rich, they must offer for sacrifice a buffalo with horns a cubit in length (about half a yard). And they have to provide five *rnööm* between them. In addition they must each give three large, old jars. This entails a heavy expenditure. But if the guilty couple is poor, they must offer a pig with a five-span measurement (the circumference just behind the forelegs; a span is the distance between outstretched extremities of the thumb and middle finger), one jar of rice beer, and two large jars each, as a fine. The jars given in payment of the fine are shared among the sacred men and the other *kuang*, for it is the men of importance who have the most to fear from the consequences of incest.

Finally, around noon, Kroong-Biing (known as Kroong-the-Short) arrived. He was wearing a magnificent coat of long black pile, cut in the European style. Kroong-the-Short is the "brother" (first cousin, for us) of Baap Can and Truu, and like them, his father was a Cil. He is a renowned judge, a "man of great learning," and he had been asked to participate in the trial.

It was decided that since Truu and the young men accompanying him were absent, the group would proceed only with the settlement of the Tieng affair. Aang's sacrifice would be put off until the district chief and his companions returned. In actuality, the affair had already been settled during the discussions around the jars. It now was only a matter of legal and public recognition of the offense and of carrying out the sentence—the sacrifice.

When we arrived at Chaar-Rieng's place, two medium-sized jars (*yang drôh*) were already tied to a stake. One member of the group explained that the two *rnööm* were Tieng's. He had used the two *yang drôh* because he didn't have a large jar; in fact, one of the jars had actually been given by Aang. The pig had been firmly tied to a pillar by the hind legs. It was squealing and struggling violently. One of the men pulled a long straw from the roof, and with another man's help he took the piglet's measurement—two spans and two fingers.

The offending couple was then ordered to summon the whole village. Aang was embarrassed and hesitated. Tieng scolded her a little to work up his own courage. He too seemed afraid to take that step. Little by little the house filled. The women, most of them carrying babies in blankets on their backs, slipped in and squatted under the granary. Some of the men settled themselves on the dais. Others sat on their heels near the door. Newcomers squeezed in where they could. Finally, Bbang-Jieng-the-Pregnant arrived. He is the sacred man who keeps the ritual wood used to kindle the fires in the clearing of the forest. He was completely drunk and bawling vociferously. The theme of his tirade was, of course, "lying together, a sister and brother." He was not alone in his drunken state; the drinking straws have seen steady use these last two days. Aang-of-the-Drooping-Eyelid belched in my face that she was drunk (and she was not to sober up for two days). Bbaang-the-Stag reeled after Bbaang-the-Pregnant, waving his arms wildly in an effort to keep his balance. The air had become unbreathable, with so many pipes and the rekindled hearths producing smoke that was trapped in the house by the rain. To this was added the odor of an alcohol-sodden crowd, which had been drenched in the rain before jamming itself into the house.

Tieng and Aang had returned before everyone in the village had arrived at Chaar-Rieng's place. They finished filling the jars. Nobody paid the slightest attention to them. The least distracted of the audience listened to Kroong-the-Short recite the genealogy of the Cil clan in a quickening tempo. He started with Ting-Mang who had four daughters; Loong; Jieng, ancestor of Choong (ex-chief of the canton of Yön Dlei); Dloong, ancestor of Aang-the-Widow; and Bo', the accused man's grandmother. The speaker rattled off the generations of ancestors:

Dloong married Bbaang, bore
Grieng, Grieng married Kroong,
bore Nguu, bore Ngaa, bore Sraang,
bore Laang.
Laang. . . .

When he got to Sieng, Tôong, and Aang (the accused woman and her brothers), he started over again with Ngaa and recited the genealogy of her father, thus coming to himself, Kroong-Biing.

He recited this double genealogy with an amazing rapidity. By tradition, these recitations have become long poems. The first word of each line is formed by the last word of the preceding line.

Taang from Phii Srôony took his turn in reciting the genealogies. He is Tieng's brother (the same mother and father), and their genealogy is the same as that of Chaar-Rieng, their maternal uncle, in whose house this scene took place.

It is necessary to go back fifteen generations to find the offending couple's common ancestor, Ting-Mang. Actually, I was the only one to have troubled to make this calculation; the sole objective of these genealogical recitations is to provide a formal demonstration of what everyone has been convinced of all along —the couple are brother and sister.

The discussion turned to the procedures to be followed for the sacrifice. It was the drunken Bbaang-the-Stag and Bbaang-the-Pregnant who proved to be the most shrewd. They were the only ones to think of a most important matter, the claiming of the gifts given by the lover to his sister. "Necklaces, bracelets, rings, little bells . . . must all be brought to the watering place," bawled Bbaang-Jieng, guffawing with satisfaction. But Tieng was hardly rich, and the only gift he had given Aang was a small, rectangular box containing a mirror, called *khôop* in Mnong. The *khôop* was added to the hairpin that Tieng had lost when the couple was caught.

Sieng-the-Widower, Aang's eldest brother, tried to give a scoop carved from an internode of giant bamboo to one young man after the other in the group. He wanted them to use it to collect human and animal excrement. They all refused, recoiling. The most outspoken of the young men exclaimed: "*Beng* to pick up dung."

One of them explained: "We are afraid of contagion. We're afraid that lightning will strike us or make us sick."

Another said: "To take the dung of pigs, dogs, man, buffalo, chickens . . . it is sacred [*weer*]. We're afraid of soiling our hands."

So I said to them: "But you collect it to fertilize the vegetable beds." [At the time I was trying to introduce fertilization—without success.]

"For the vegetable beds it is not sacred, but ordinarily it is sacred."

Faced with the refusal of all the young men, Sieng-the-Widower decided to collect small samples of the different excrement himself with a piece of wood. "A little bit of each," Kroong-the-Short told me.

The accused couple did not have a buffalo horn, so instead they filled two bottles with rice beer. Tieng gave his bottle to Tôong-Biing, Aang's second brother, who was carrying a hollowed-out gourd bottom containing beer mash and pieces of charcoal.

When it was time to leave for the ceremony, Aang began to protest: "I was completely drunk. I didn't know what I was doing. . . . I didn't understand what was happening. . . . I didn't know who was covering me."

Her face darkened, and she became more and more obstinate. Tieng was as limp as a rag, but he made a half-hearted show of urging his sister to get on with what had to be done.

It was still drizzling. Early in the afternoon, Tieng carried the piglet down to the watering place, followed by all the villagers, slipping and slithering in the mud. At the junction of the tributary Daak Mei and the river Krong Knô, Tôong-Biing cut a bamboo stalk into three. He took a piece and frayed one end into a tassel, sharpened the other end into a point, and cut a notch in the middle. He prepared another of the bamboo pieces in exactly the same way and stuck both of them into the border of the path that ran above the level of the river. He took the third piece of bamboo, frayed both ends, and set it in the notches of the two upright sticks. He had thus made an H-shaped altar, plumed at the top and crosspoints.

While Tôong-Biing was constructing the altar, the young men immolated the victims. They slit the pig's throat and caught the blood in a large Vietnamese bowl. They poured some of the blood from the bowl over the beer mash and charcoal in the gourd, which Tôong-Biing held. They cut a duck's throat over the same gourd and then allowed the blood to drip into the watering place. Finally, they slit a chicken's throat over the watering place and covered the wound with beer mash. When the mash had become soaked with blood, they put it in the gourd. Thus the gourd contained charcoal plus the elements of each offering: beer mash soaked in the blood of the three victims.

Tôong-Biing set the gourd down at the base of an upright stake and intoned a prayer.

The offending couple came forward. With the thumb and index finger of the right hand they took some of the pig's blood from the large Vietnamese bowl, then the blood of the duck and the chicken by passing these two fingers over the open wounds of each of the victims. Aang and Tieng went into the water together and made an invocation. When it was finished, they dipped their bloodstained fingers into the water, rubbing them together. Meanwhile, Tôong-Biing, still squatting, had gone on praying:

One cannot copulate with his sister;
do not hold it against us, O Spirit.
One cannot exchange sacrifice with his ancestor;
do not hold it against us, O Spirit.
One cannot marry, if maternal uncle and niece;
do not hold it against us, O Spirit.
One cannot fight, if father and son, if termite and termite nest;
do not hold it against us, O Spirit.

He anointed the right *nsôopm* (tassel) and then the ground. From time to time, Baap Can or another old man recited some verses aloud with Tôong, without moving from his place.

Sieng put the gifts given to each other by the lovers into the bamboo scoop containing samples of various excrement, and poured rice beer over the whole thing. Then he placed a chicken feather and a duck feather toward the front of the scoop. Now they were ready to proceed with the *siam ê' sür, siam ê' sau* ("giving the excrement of the pig and dog to be eaten"). As the guilty couple waded into the middle of the river, Tieng pretended to jostle Aang to make her go ahead of him. Kröng-Jôong, the sacred man, went into the water, followed by Sieng carrying the bamboo scoop. Kröng-Jôong placed himself in front of the two offenders, at an equal distance from each. He took a feather and dipped it in the revolting mixture and drew the feather first across Tieng's chin, counting "one," and then across Aang's chin, "one," then back to Tieng, "two," and Aang, "two," and so on, eight times. All the while, Kröng-Jôong intoned a long invocation principally intended for the dragon (water) spirit. From the beginning, the backs of the offenders had been turned to us. Each time the feather touched his chin, Tieng was dou-bled over by violent retching; Aang did not flinch once.

When Kröng had finished his invocation, he threw the feather in the water. Sieng emptied the contents of the scoop in the river, then threw in the scoop. Tieng and Aang washed their chins, legs, and arms. Kröng was on the point of coming out of the water without having purified himself when two or three people in the group shouted to remind him of his oversight. He then went back to the middle of the river and washed his arms and legs.

Tôong-Biing had not stopped praying during the ceremony. Finally, he poured rice beer over the gourd containing the beer mash and charcoal saturated with the victims' blood. He went into the river carrying a bottle of *rnööm* and the gourd, and, keeping the gourd upright on the water, he poured the *rnööm* into it, praying all the while. Then he let it float downstream and begged the charcoal to bring the presents to *Yaang Rmeh* (the dragon spirit). He finished by pouring the entire contents of the bottle into the stream, and returned to the river bank. Everyone went back to the village.

The drizzle, which hadn't let up during the ceremony, became a violent downpour toward the end. But in spite of the rain, the remains of the sacrificed animals would be burned out of doors, because, for this type of sacrifice, it is forbidden to burn the victims indoors, as is normally done with small animals.

The crowd had gathered again at Chaar-Rieng's house. The jars were to be consecrated, and this is the office of "those who have dealt justice." Kroong-the-Short and I were given the first jar. Kröng and Bbaang-the-Pregnant took their places at the second jar. We stuck our drinking straws in the jars, with many invocations referring to the triple sacrifice just performed. I began drinking at the first jar, and Kröng at the second.

Then Bbaang-the-Pregnant took the Mnong bowl contain-ing the blood-saturated beer mash and went to his house, accom-panied by the offending couple (and me as an observer). The ritual wood for setting fire to the forest was to be anointed. But it was in a large winnowing basket that had been wedged between a rafter and the roof, and they weren't able to pull it out. Therefore, they anointed not only the wood that protruded from the basket, but the basket as well. The anointments were reinforced by invocations; the only actors in this scene were the sacred men and the offenders.

Kroong-the-Short had taken my place at the first jar, and he

Receiving the "feeding exchange" in a ceremony of "exchange of buffalo sacrifices" is Baap Can, who is one of the accusers in the Mnong Gar incest case.

Early in the ceremony at riverside to expiate the incest, Aang's brother Tôong-Biing prays before a small altar.

(Opposite) Convicted couple is "fed" with excrement of pig and dog. Tieng is at the left, nearly hiding his "sister" Aang.

was still drinking when we returned from the anointment of the ritual firewood. He tackled Tieng. "You can't live here anymore. You must leave, marry elsewhere. . . . I am your *kôony*; come and live with me. You can gather the forest vegetables and bring the firewood."

Taang from Phii Srôony backed him up, saying to his brother: "Go with Kroong-Biing. Aang will look for another husband here. . . ." But Tieng refused to answer his brother as he had his uncle.

Kroong-Biing wanted to get his nephew to marry Grieng, a pretty girl who had been pledged to him for a debt (no connection with the Grieng in the genealogy). When a free man marries a slave, he does not lose his own freedom, but his children take their mother's station, and a man must be a very hard worker if he is to liberate his wife and children. Tieng is not. But that didn't seem to be what was on his mind now or what made him resist so stubbornly.

The fast-talking Kroong-Biing became more and more persuasive, boasting of his reputation and wealth. He showed Tieng how pleasant life would be with him at Ndut. Taang continued to support Kroong-Biing's proposal, stressing that the offending couple must separate, that a tremendous opportunity was being offered to his brother to be able to live with a man of such reputation. Taang, at that point, considered the problem settled, and even went so far as to advise Kroong-Biing to make sure that Tieng would work hard. Tieng, squatting among the men during the long palavers on his future, had not said a single word. Behind his wall of obstinate silence was refusal.

After half an hour of this, Kroong-the-Short decided to change the subject. He sang and dictated old songs to me. The songs, in which he boasted of his amours, soon degenerated into drinking songs, and even into obscene ditties. There were loud bursts of laughter from everyone; the atmosphere was transformed.

Thanks to Kroong-the-Short and the rice beer, the company had relaxed completely. Even the offenders found the new mood infectious. Tieng, who replaced Aang in pouring in the measures of water, had found his voice again. He informed Chaar-Rieng that this very evening he would perform the sacrifice to lift the taboo that was weighing so heavily on himself and his family because of his offense. And, when Aang came to invite me to the sacrifice around eight o'clock, she had the nerve to appear at my house unaccompanied, and being alone with me, she asked for a cigarette. Not a woman in the village had dared to go so far before.

All of the residents of the longhouse had gathered in Chaar-Rieng's place, but hardly any of the other villagers joined us. The events of the day had satiated the curious, and the thirsty had little more to hope for. All that had been done was to prepare a tiny neckless jar (*yang ke'it*) that was put on the ground near the dais. Near the little jar they placed a chicken, whose legs had been tied together, and an empty *yang dâm* (taller than a *yang ke' it*).

Chaar-Rieng had brought his leather pouch, which contained magic quartz stones. He took them out of the pouch and put them in a Vietnamese bowl, which had been placed at the foot of a little jar of rice beer.

Tieng then slit the chicken's throat over the bowl containing the magic stones. Chaar joined his wife, son, and little Jôong (Tieng's daughter) where they were sitting, just under the granary. After allowing the blood to flow copiously into the receptacle, Tieng got up and anointed the foreheads of the other four members of the household with the bloody wound of the victim. Then he took the *yang dâm* in both hands and made eight circles over the heads of the seated group, pleading:

. . . Let the beams of the granary hold fast,
let the pillars of the granary grow,
let the rice in the big pot cook.
The wild animals follow the night;
the kuang follow the word,
the thunder follows at once.
In future let us seek for buffalo every day,
let us seek for jars every month,
let us have rice and paddy every day.

He set down the little neckless jar behind the group, but they made him put it in front of them, and everyone touched it in turn. Then Tieng spat in his hand, touched the *yang dâm* and then the chest of Rieng (Chaar-Rieng's wife), repeating the gesture for the other three members of the household (when the person being anointed was a man, he touched the forehead instead of the chest).

Tieng then left the group formed by his maternal uncle's

household and went to the one formed by his brother Taang, which included Taang's wife and baby. They were sitting on the dais apart from the other group, because coming from the forest they could not receive "the whirling of the jar above their heads" at the same time as the people from the village. He began the same performance with them. Meanwhile, Chaar put away his blood-anointed, magic stones.

Finally, with the assistance of his brother and uncle, Tieng consecrated the tiny *yang ke' it* next to the dais. The three men coughed slightly and flicked the surface of the water in the *yang ke' it* to sprinkle a few drops of water on the ground. Tieng sucked some *rnööm* into the drinking straw and closed the top end with his index finger. He then went about sprinkling drops of *rnööm* "on the head of the door and on the heads of the hearthstones," repeating his previous prayer. He went back to his two companions, gave the drinking straw to his brother, and took the Vietnamese bowl. With the blood it contained, he anointed the top of the door, the tops of the hearthstones, and the jars. Meanwhile, Taang stuck the drinking straw into the *yang ke' it*. Then he and Chaar repeated the formulas of the vows together.

Now everything was in order. Tieng had cleansed the community, which had been stained by his incest, and purified his uncle's household and that of his brother of the evil he had brought upon them. His offense had been washed away. He had been tense during the performance of the rites. Now his face relaxed. He was a liberated man.

POSTSCRIPT: *Poor Tieng's peace of mind did not last long. The next day he was found hanging by his loincloth from the roof beam of Chaar-Rieng's granary. Perplexed as to how to remake his life, perhaps unable to face separation from Aang, he had committed suicide.*

RICHARD A. GOULD

JOURNEY TO PULYKARA   In November, 1969, I received a report of a small group of Australian Aborigines who had never
seen Europeans. They were said to be living in the heart of the
Gibson Desert, at a place called Pulykara, near Mount Madley,
about 330 miles northwest of the Warburton Ranges Mission.
They were discovered by Bob Verburgt, then a patrol officer for
the Weapons Research Establishment at Woomera. This was four
months after the astronauts had made their first moon landing,
and it seemed to me then, as I am sure it did to many others, that
there was no place left on earth that Western technology had not
penetrated. It was ironic to think that while the rest of the world
fought wars, built and destroyed cities, created art and literature,
the ancestors of these people and the people themselves—as
recent archeological evidence suggests—remained completely
unaware and unaffected by it all.

At the time of their discovery, my wife and I were organizing an archeological field camp at the Warburton Ranges in
Western Australia, and could not visit these Aborigines until our
own project was well under way. Five months later, in April,
1970, we set out from Warburton in search of them.

Although our previous visit to this area in 1966–67 had provided the opportunity for us to live with and study a group of
Aborigines who had formerly been to white settlements and had
subsequently returned to the desert and resumed their nomadic
existence, we had never before encountered anyone so isolated
from, or untouched by, Western culture. The Aborigines living
at Warburton, many of whom came from areas adjacent to the
Mount Madley region, admitted that they, too, did not know
who these people were—a remarkable admission from people
whose network of kin relationships often extends over hundreds
of miles.

During the five-month interval, a Western Australian Native
Welfare patrol had contacted them briefly and brought a young
man named Yutungka into Warburton to be circumcised. He
was accompanied by an elderly man named Tjitjinanya. The
group had been isolated for so long that Yutungka was well
past the age when men normally are circumcised, and he was

anxious to have it done as soon as possible. For many years his group had not met with other groups of Aborigines to form a gathering large enough for the precircumcision ceremonies to take place.

The operation was performed early in April, and we offered to transport the two men back to their country as soon as Yutungka was well enough to go. We also took with us an elderly Aborigine named Minmara, an intelligent man of outstanding good humor, whom we had come to know well during our previous stay in the desert. We had been with him many times in his own country, about 150 miles northwest of Warburton, and by now he was familiar with the nature of our work. We brought him with us in the hope that, in his own way, he would be able to explain to the others what we were doing. With small, unacculturated groups there is always the danger that the anthropologist's presence will disrupt their activities. We wanted to observe as much as possible of their normal daily routine, but we also wanted to record what we saw with photographs, maps of their camp, tape recordings, and ordinary field notes. Minmara, already familiar with our equipment, could reassure the others.

We outfitted two vehicles for the trip, a Land Rover and a two-wheel drive truck. Because of the distance, supplies were a problem and limited us from the start. We had to be completely self-sufficient. The truck was loaded with drums of fuel and water and we intended to drive it as far into the desert as possible. For two days we drove up a deserted rocket range access road, locally called the "Gunbarrel Highway," to a point about 80 miles from where the Aborigines were said to be camped. Then we refueled the Land Rover and left the truck where it would serve as a gas station for us on our return trip.

During the trip out, Minmara did several things that seemed odd and unlike him. On one occasion he asked me for some cigarettes. Because I want to avoid having to feed the people we are with, I always try to be generous with tobacco instead. For anthropologists, feeding the people is a never-ending problem. If we are to observe their normal food-getting behavior, we cannot always feed them. This leaves us open to accusations of stinginess. On this trip, however, I had brought only plugs of chewing tobacco. Minmara had never before asked me for cigarettes and, in truth, I had never seen him smoke them. Neverthe-

GREAT SANDY DESERT

TROPIC OF CAPRICORN

GIBSON DESERT

Alice Springs

Mount Madley

Pulykara

Warburton
Mission

Laverton

GREAT VICTORIA
DESERT

Cundeelee

PERTH

SYDNEY

INDIAN OCEAN

MELBOURNE

AUSTRALIA

less, he seemed disappointed when I offered him some chewing-plugs. Later he came to me again and asked for my rifle and one bullet. Minmara had borrowed my rifle many times before to go kangaroo hunting, but he had always asked for as many bullets as he could get. When I asked him why he wanted only one bullet this time, he seemed genuinely at a loss to explain. After I gave him the gun and the single bullet, he walked to the edge of our camp where the other two men could see him, loaded the rifle, and fired it off into the air. Then he returned the gun to me and in a low voice explained that these were ignorant men who did not know about such things. This really floored me, since I could remember when, not so very long ago, Minmara himself had been a desert Aborigine just like these men. He obviously had meant to smoke the cigarettes in front of them as well, to impress them with his newfound sophistication.

We continued our cross-country trip to the west, skirting several sand hills and wide stretches of burned-over country. Yutungka excitedly pointed out places where he himself had set the fires. As we were traveling in a time of drought, the wind was shifting the sand in many burned-over places. At Warburton, less than an inch of rain had fallen in two years, and conditions looked similar here. I was particularly anxious to observe these Aborigines under drought conditions, since our previous trip to the Gibson Desert had been during a period of exceptionally good rains, with a corresponding abundance of

plant and animal foods. Eventually we saw Mount Madley—two tiny rock knobs standing about 25 feet above the surrounding sand plain, yet appearing highly significant in comparison with the relatively flat terrain. Claypans and salt lakes provide the few landmarks in this region, which on the whole is among the most featureless and unfriendly looking country we have ever seen in the Australian desert. The spinifex, a spiny grass that grows in clumps of varying size and density throughout the Gibson Desert, appeared parched and yellow. There were some signs of recent rain on several claypans we crossed, but rain in

At the claypan of Walaluka, fifty miles from Pulykara, Yutungka tests the water and finds it potable.

this region is notoriously fickle and often falls only in localized patches. The mulga scrub we passed also looked dry and brittle. On our previous trips in the Gibson Desert, we had seen the country at its best; now it seemed we were seeing it at its worst.

Arriving at Pulykara on the morning of April 20, we found that the Aboriginal camp consisted of three small clusters of hearths, each surrounded by cleared patches of sand—the sleeping and sitting areas—and a low brush windbreak. The arrangement was typical of the winter campsites of Gibson Desert Aborigines, which we had observed on previous occasions. Situated on the slope of a sandhill at the edge of a dry lake bed, it was surrounded by a profusion of flies, an inevitable feature of Aboriginal camps. The wind was blowing fairly hard when we arrived, and it was apparent that there was little natural cover here or anywhere nearby. Burned acacia bushes and a few low clumps of ti tree, spinifex, and saltbush gave the whole place a rather cheerless look. The water hole, a so-called native well dug about 15 feet in the lake bed to the water table, lay about 425 feet southwest of the camp. These native wells are, in most cases, nothing more than soakages into which the Aborigines dig for water. Often they get deeper as the water table retreats downward. Pulykara, a classic example of this type of well, had a flow at that time of about a gallon in ten minutes. We had already been told that Pulykara was one of the most dependable water sources in the region and was virtually permanent.

No one was visible when we arrived at the camp, but on top of the sandhill there were several emaciated, howling dingoes, dogs kept by the Aborigines and sometimes found wild. Yutungka set fire to some ti trees as a smoke signal to indicate our presence, while Tjitjinanya and Minmara went on foot over the sandhill to look for the people. A few minutes later they returned with Tjitjinanya's wife, a tiny woman with a greatly distended stomach. She had heard us approaching—the whine of a Land Rover's gears can be heard for miles—and was frightened, so she ran off into the sandhills to hide. The others, she said, had left earlier to look for food.

This timidity was apparently one reason why this group had not been contacted earlier. Later on, Yutungka told us that when he was a small boy, a truck (probably another Land Rover) had passed this way with one man driving it. Everyone had run into the sandhills and watched the white man from behind some bushes. The vehicle missed the camp by about a quarter of a mile, passing on the far side of a sandhill to the north, where the man had stopped and spent the night before continuing his journey in the morning. The Aborigines stayed awake all that night watching him, but they never revealed themselves. This, no doubt, must have happened many times to government patrols sent out to locate desert Aborigines.

After the others arrived, there were nine people, comprising three small families, present: Yutungka's mother and father, Tjitjinanya and his wife, and finally a third couple and their two daughters—a six-year-old named Pannyi and an infant. While talking with them we quickly discovered several words derived from English, and learned that the young couple had previously spent some time at the Carnegie Homestead, a remote sheep station a little more than 100 miles southwest of Mount Madley. Also, Yutungka's father said he had once spent a few days at Jiggalong, a mission and Aboriginal reserve about 200 miles northwest of Mount Madley. Aside from these instances and Yutungka and Tjitjinanya's recent trip to Warburton, these people had lived all their lives in this area of the desert. As Betsy was the first white woman that most of them had seen, the women could not stop touching her arms and hair and discussing her appearance. Some of them had a few scraps of clothing given them by the preceding patrols, and they possessed a steel axhead. The tenth member of the group, a young man named Yiwa, had gone off to the west by himself to look for some spearwood. We missed seeing him, since he still had not returned when we departed for Warburton. These people spoke a dialect, which they called Ngatjara, one of the many mutually intelligible dialects spoken by Aborigines throughout the Gibson Desert.

Yutungka was clearly delighted to see his parents and other relatives again. They greeted him by wailing loudly, while his mother flailed herself on the head with a wooden bowl until the blood ran freely from her scalp. This was out of sorrow for the pain he had undergone while being initiated at Warburton and in recognition of the death-rebirth symbolism of the whole initiation ceremony. Once these formalities were over, the group settled down to discuss their recent activities and, no doubt, us, while we set up our own camp about 100 yards away. Yutungka kept everyone up late that night with his dramatic and highly animated account of his experiences at Warburton.

The Gibson Desert Aborigines live entirely by hunting and gathering wild foods. They do so in what is probably the poorest environment, in terms of food resources, of any in the world where people have lived by foraging directly off the land. In our earlier studies we found that the Aborigines in this area subsist on 38 edible plant species, called *mirka*, and 47 named varieties of meat and fleshy foods, called *kuka*. *Kuka* is always preferred over *mirka*, but our studies indicated that *mirka* is almost always more important in the over-all diet. As there are no large game animals, the kangaroo, which rarely exceeds 100 pounds, is the largest animal hunted, although they are uncommon in the Gibson Desert. Herds of game animals, such as one finds in Africa today, do not exist in this area. Most of the protein obtained by these people comes primarily from two species of goanna lizard found in the sandhill and sand plain country. With the exception of rare occasions when heavy rains have fallen for two or more consecutive seasons in one spot, providing abundant vegetation and therefore attracting game, the diet is almost entirely vegetarian, revolving around at least seven staple plant foods. I have defined a staple here as any plant species that, singly or in combination with another, accounted for at least 50 percent of the total diet by weight during the period it was collected and consumed. Other edible plants act to supplement and vary the diet. Although men hunt regularly for kangaroos, emus, wallabies, and other game, it is the women who are the mainstay of the economy and who provide virtually all of the vegetable foods, as well as much of the small game.

Compared with other hunting-and-gathering societies, the Gibson Desert Aborigines fare poorly even in the best of seasons. For example, the !Kung Bushmen of the Kalahari Desert of Africa, a group recently studied in detail by anthropologist Richard Lee, distinguish 54 edible species of animals (including some, such as giraffes and various antelopes, that are larger than anything found in the Australian desert) and 85 edible plant species, one of which, the mongongo nut, accounts for one-half to two-thirds of the total vegetable diet by weight. The Bushmen, therefore, can afford to pass up such small game as rodents, snakes, lizards, termites and other insects, all of which are eagerly sought by the desert Aborigines.

Any anthropological discussions about the material culture, social organization, and religion of the desert Aborigines must be seen in terms of the basic ecological considerations. Not only is the Gibson Desert generally impoverished in edible plant and animal species; it is also unreliable in terms of the ripening and availability of these species. There are no regular wet and dry seasons, such as one finds in the Kalahari or even in tropical Australia. Rainfall, generally low to begin with, fluctuates tremendously with time and place. . . . The table opposite for vegetable staples for 1966–67 represents a foraging season under optimum conditions of rainfall for this region: a kind of Aboriginal woman's "shopping list" at a time when there was plenty of rain to stimulate plant growth. The table for 1969–70, although complete for only eight months, shows the plants collected by these same people as staples during a drought year.

It was with this general background of information in mind that we began our visit with the desert Aborigines at Pulykara. On the day we arrived, Yutungka's mother appeared carrying a wooden bowl containing ten grubs and a piece of backbone from a feral cat, which she had evidently taken with her as a

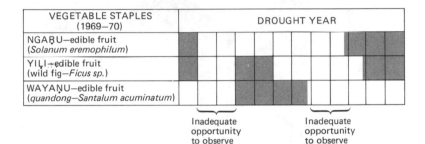

VEGETABLE STAPLES (1966–67)	WET YEAR											
	J	F	M	A	M	J	J	A	S	O	N	D
YAWALYURU—edible berries (*Canthium latifolium*)			▓	▓								
KALPARI—edible seeds (*Chenopodium rhadinostachyum*)				▓	▓							
WANGUNU—edible seeds (*Eragrostis eriopoda*)					▓	▓						
KAMPURARPA (fresh)—edible fruit (native tomato—*Solanum sp.*)							▓	▓	▓			
WAYANU—edible fruit (quandong—*Santalum acuminatum*)								▓	▓			
YILI—edible fruit (wild fig—*Ficus sp.*)										▓		
NGARU—edible fruit (*Solanum eremophilum*)	▓	▓										
KAMPURARPA (dry)—edible fruit (native tomato—*Solanum sp.*)	▓											▓

VEGETABLE STAPLES (1969–70)	DROUGHT YEAR											
NGARU—edible fruit (*Solanum eremophilum*)	▓									▓	▓	
YILI—edible fruit (wild fig—*Ficus sp.*)	▓			▓	▓							▓
WAYANU—edible fruit (quandong—*Santalum acuminatum*)				▓	▓	▓						

Inadequate opportunity to observe   Inadequate opportunity to observe

snack to eat while out looking for grubs. The young woman, named Yatungka, arrived in camp shortly afterward with a wooden bowl filled with about ten pounds of sun-dried quandong, a native fruit with a large kernel, of which only the outer husk is eaten. I was immediately interested, because neither woman had been out collecting for more than a couple of hours that day. Also, the people seemed in good condition. Things might be hard at Pulykara during the drought, but certainly no one was starving or even close to it.

In the days that followed we settled into a routine of steady, low-key observation as the Aborigines went about their daily affairs. On most days I went out hunting with Yutungka and one or more of the other men, while Betsy either stayed in camp or went foraging with the women. Although we traveled as much as ten to fifteen miles a day in search of game, the results of the hunt were poor. At no time did we see any fresh kangaroo or emu tracks and, after four days of effort we had obtained only a feral cat, a falcon, and three rather small goannas. For me these hunting trips were useful, more for the opportunity of learning about the country around Pulykara and getting to know the men better, than for the game we caught.

Foraging, on the other hand, was more successful. There was an extensive area of quandong trees located about two miles from camp on the other side of the dry lake. Here it was possible

Yutungka cleans the feathers from a falcon killed during a hunt. Hunting, however, provides only a small part of the group's food.

to collect almost unlimited amounts of the sun-dried fruit from the ground directly beneath each tree. As long as the weather is dry, this fruit, which the Aborigines call *tjawili*, can lie on the ground for months without spoiling. A woman, working for about an hour, could collect between ten and twenty pounds, depending on the size of her wooden bowl. Not only was the *tjawili* abundant and easy to collect, but on this occasion it was easy to transport, as well, because the walk across the lake bed was fairly short and flat. Grubs, although hardly a staple at this time, were larger and more abundant than we had ever seen in our

After several hours in the bush, Yatungka and her daughter Pannyi return with about ten pounds of sun-dried quandong.

previous travels through the desert. Pried from the roots of small acacia bushes and from the stems of desert poplar trees that were dying from the drought, they are prized for their flavor by the Aborigines and are eaten either raw or lightly roasted. What impressed me most, however, was the ease and relative speed with which the women found enough food for the whole group, even under what seemed, superficially, to be adverse conditions. It was neither gourmet eating nor a balanced diet, but it was enough; and it took only a few man-hours to collect. So much for the commonly held view of hunter-gatherers as people without any leisure time because of their constant need to search for food. Under the conditions at Pulykara, the women spent most of their day in camp sleeping or talking among themselves. Their foraging was so efficient that it gave them abundant time to relax, while at the same time it freed the men for hunting and other activities. It also became obvious that the group could never have survived on the fruits of hunting alone, although no opportunities for getting game were overlooked.

Another glance at the tables will reveal several essential differences between foraging in a relatively wet season and foraging in a drought. While the drought reduced the available species of staple food plants from seven to three, the over-all amounts of food collected and the work required to collect them remained about the same. (Despite the incompleteness of our observations in 1969–70, there is good evidence to suggest that there were no more than three staples that year.) That is, in both wet and dry years large quantities of these staples can be collected by the women without consuming too much time or effort in the process. Of course, our observations at Pulykara were brief, but these were augmented by further studies made with similar groups closer to the Warburton Ranges Mission. It is also important to note that the periods of availability of the same plant species vary greatly from one year to the next. *Ngaru*, for example, appears to ripen earlier and last longer in dry seasons than in wet years, while *yili*, "wild figs," and *tjawili* ripen at almost opposite times in a dry year from one that is wet. In addition, these food resources can vary dramatically from place to place. No wild figs were available in the Pulykara area during our visit in April, but they were abundant at that time in areas closer to Warburton.

Each morning when the men and I set out to hunt, some of

the camp dogs tried to follow us. The men would constantly turn and drive them back toward camp, since they did not want them along on the hunt. Under traditional nomadic conditions, dingoes are a liability on hunts, as they tend to frighten game. These Aborigines hunt mainly from concealment, that is, from behind blinds of brush or rock or, sometimes, by careful stalking when an animal is encountered in the open. In either case, dogs are not wanted. Nevertheless, I noticed that Yutungka's favorite dog, Pitji-pitji, would continue with us, lurking cautiously about a quarter of a mile behind us or off to one side. Its presence was tolerated as long as it did not get too close to us or otherwise interfere with the hunt.

We counted nineteen dingoes in and around the camp, all of whom would join in piercing choruses of howling in the morning or at night. They were often fondled but rarely fed, although the people expressed sympathy for their hunger. Once, after I had given a piece of candy to Tjitjinanya's wife, she covered the eyes of the dog she was carrying. When I asked about this, she said the dog was *ngaltutjara*, "the one to feel sorry for," because it could not have the food, so she was covering its eyes in the hope that it would not see her eating.

Not only were these the skinniest dogs I have ever seen, but they were also compulsive cringers and skulkers. Throughout our stay we had to be on guard against their getting into our belongings, since we found that they will eat almost anything. Despite our efforts, one of them consumed the electric plug and three feet of heavy-duty electric wiring from our portable generator. On past occasions dingoes have devoured boots, entire boxes of detergent, and magazines; occasionally, they have even pierced tin cans with their teeth and extracted the contents with their incredibly prehensile tongues. One glance and a hissing shout of *payi* was always enough to drive them away for a while, but it was a never-ending battle in which the dingoes' perseverance inevitably won out.

Most Aborigines, both men and women, have their favorite dogs, but we noticed from the start that Yutungka's mother behaved very strangely toward her dogs. She carried this behavior to a fanatical extreme, and we christened her the "Dog Lady" because of it. She cared for about a dozen dogs, which formed a seething pack around her whenever she was seated in her camp. She seldom fed them but fussed over them constantly in other ways. When they were asleep she built little shade-shelters of twigs and boughs for them, which she moved periodically as the sun's shadow shifted, being careful all the while not to disturb the sleeping dogs. Like most of the others, she was naked when we met her on the first day, but Tjitjinanya had given her some tattered dresses and other clothing he had acquired during his brief stay at Warburton. Instead of wearing these herself she laid them over the dogs while they slept during the day. At this time the days were warm, about 80 degrees Fahrenheit in the shade, but at night it was close to freezing. On chilly nights the desert Aborigines always sleep next to a fire with their dogs huddled around them to keep warm; Yutungka's mother, of course, had most of the pack wrapped around her. One night I tried taking flash photographs showing how the people sleep with their dogs. No one minded the picture-taking except the dogs: I had not reckoned on their reaction to the flash. After my first photograph, they ran off into the sandhills while the people lay shivering by their little fires, bereft of their doggy "blankets." I apologized, but it was a while before the dogs came back.

The Gibson Desert Aborigines are among the last people anywhere who still make and use stone tools as a regular part of their culture. On our previous trips into the desert we learned that these people possess a limited variety of stone tools used for cutting meat and sinew, as well as for scraping or adzing wooden tools. They classify these tools as *tjimari* and *purpunpa*, respectively. For archeologists in particular this is useful information, since they are concerned much of the time with the ways in which ancient stone artifacts were made and used. Since this activity rapidly declines once the Aborigines obtain metal tools, we were fortunate to see as much of this skill in action as we did. But there were still some unanswered questions; the most important of these was the role of hand axes and hand-held stone scrapers.

All of the groups we had previously observed had already obtained enough steel axes for their needs. Aboriginal stone axes had been seen in use by earlier scholars such as anthropologists Norman Tindale and Donald Thomson, but their classification within the native system remained uncertain, along with other details concerning their manufacture and use. As I had hoped for some time to find a group of desert Aborigines who had not

While carrying a dog around her waist, Tjitjinanya's wife sympathetically covers its eyes so it will not see her eat a piece of candy.

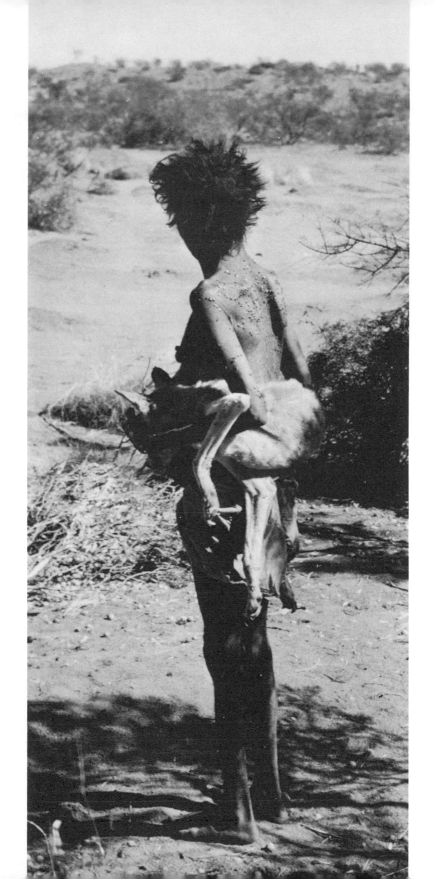

Yutungka's mother huddles with her dogs on an early winter morning at the camp at Pulykara. At right, Yutungka stands halfway down a 15-foot-deep native well.

yet transferred to the use of steel axes, the group at Pulykara proved ideal. The single steel ax they possessed was not sufficient for their needs as its large size made it awkward to handle and limited its usefulness; therefore, they continued to make and use large, hand-held stone tools along with other kinds.

The people at Pulykara classified all hand-held scrapers and hand axes as *purpunpa*, regardless of size. Always trimmed on one edge only, they were used exclusively for cutting and shaping wooden objects. In general, hand axes and large stone scrapers were trimmed by chipping just enough to provide a steep working edge suitable for woodworking. These observations are of particular interest to Australian archeologists, since recently accumulated evidence points to the persistence of a hand-held, stone flake tool tradition in some parts of Australia for over 30,000 years. Although various hafted stone tools, some of them quite delicately made, appeared at least 6,800 years ago in the Gibson Desert, they never displaced the tradition of making large, hand-held tools. Further analysis of the tools will be needed before this pattern can be described in detail, but preliminary studies indicate that we are dealing here with one of the most dramatic and well-documented examples of cultural conservatism in the world.

By our fifth day at Pulykara our supplies were dwindling and it was obvious that we had to leave before we consumed our reserves. In the Australian desert one always keeps enough

extra food and water for a possible breakdown or emergency en route. The evening before we left there was an intense discussion in camp. Tjitjinanya wanted to return to Warburton with us—he craved the excitement of other people. The women countered him, saying they liked the things he had brought for them from the mission but they wanted him to remain at Pulykara with them. The argument went on late into the night, and in the end Tjitjinanya agreed to stay. Betsy and I did not interfere, but we both knew that it was far better at that time for Tjitjinanya and his wife to stay in the desert. For one thing, the two older men at Pulykara address Tjitjinanya as *kamuṟu* and regard him as a mother's brother—an obligatory sharing relationship in which most of the goods and services flow from the sister's son to the mother's brother. Tjitjinanya and his wife have no children of their own, and since they are both getting old and one of them is infirm much of the time, they must consider who will support them in their old age. Even under the harsh conditions of desert existence, the Gibson Desert Aborigines do feed and look after old or sick people—but only if a sharing relationship based on kin ties exists between the people involved. Tjitjinanya and his wife had no close kin at Warburton and might suffer privation there. On the other hand, because of Tjitjinanya's *kamuṟu* relationship to the oldest man in each of the other families at Pulykara, they had, in effect, two families working for them, gathering food, firewood, and other necessities. It was undoubtedly wiser for them to remain at Pulykara, and I was relieved when the ladies finally won out. We left for Warburton the next morning, accompanied by Minmara, while the others remained at Pulykara.

What had we achieved by making this trip? Certainly we made no startling or fantastic discoveries; we found no "vanished tribes." Essentially, these people at Pulykara were like those we had encountered in our earlier work in the Gibson Desert. Although they live in a poor and undependable physical environment, they have survived and developed rich oral traditions and ceremonies along with a social system of amazing subtlety and complexity. Further research must inquire into how these systems are supported by the economy and how, in turn, they serve to maintain the economy. Our trip to Pulykara offered us another glimpse of the day-to-day economy of a nomadic group of Aborigines, and increased our understanding of how these people have adapted to their desert existence. However, there still are things we do not know. For example, how do people like this support themselves in a drought of ten or twelve years duration?

Like many anthropological expeditions, we obtained scientifically useful results without undue hardship or excessive fanfare. And from a personal point of view, there was something esthetically satisfying about this trip. We met these people on their own terms, in their own country. It was indeed a pleasant change from meeting Aborigines, as we have so often, living on the fringes of white settlements where they are increasingly dependent on the white man's culture. The friendliness, independence, and pride of this small community provided a rare and rewarding experience.

WILLIAM IRONS

THE TURKMEN NOMADS Until a century ago, Turkmen nomads migrated seasonally over the Central Asian steppe in search of pasture, their mobility preserving their independence from neighboring sedentary governments. Today they have lost their independence, but in remote areas many still cling to their nomadic way of life.

The Turkmen inhabit a region divided between three countries—Afghanistan, Iran, and the Soviet Union—and their population is a million and a half. Although they have all been brought under the control of these countries, conquest and settlement were accomplished piecemeal, affecting some areas sooner and more drastically than others. Among those who have remained nomadic, tradition is largely intact, and when I began my study of the Turkmen in the winter of 1965, I decided to concentrate on this group.

The devotion of these people to a migratory way of life can be understood only in historic perspective. The Turkmen are by tradition a pastoral people, and for them nomadism is a way of using sparse and seasonably variable pasture for livestock production. But it was, in the past, something more: a means of resisting firm government control. Such resistance was a consciously maintained tradition among the Turkmen, and nomadism was the chief means to this end.

Their eagerness to resist the power of sedentary states grew out of an understanding of what government control meant to settled people. In the harsh social environment of the traditional Middle East and Central Asia, settled people were frequently exploited through the imposition of heavy taxes and rents.

The Turkmen not only avoided such exploitation, but by raiding and collecting tribute from their sedentary neighbors, they went a step further and put themselves in the position of the exploiter. A century ago they were notorious as brigands and especially as slave raiders. Slaving activities were conducted primarily in northeastern Persia (now Iran): Turkmen raiding parties ambushed caravans or attacked villages, retreating quickly with their captives to their own territory.

The portion of the Central Asian steppe inhabited by the

Turkmen stretches east from the Caspian Sea to the Amu Darya, a large river that empties into the Aral Sea. The central part of this area is the Kara Kum, or "black sand," a vast, largely uninhabited and uninhabitable desert. The majority of the Turkmen are concentrated in two somewhat more fertile regions bordering the Kara Kum. One area consists of the banks of the Amu Darya; the other is a long strip of plains and low mountains, lying south of the Kara Kum and separating it from the Iranian Plateau. My study was carried out in a section of the latter area—in the Gorgan Plain of northern Iran.

All nomadic Turkmen are divided into residential groups known as *obas,* and my research was focused on a single *oba* consisting of sixty-one households. This group migrates within the Gokcha Hills, a patch of low hills that protrudes into the Gorgan Plain. An *oba* is associated with a definite territory, and all of its members share common rights over that territory, including the right to use the pastures and any natural source of water there. All have the right to dig wells, but once such wells have been dug they become the private property of the persons who expended their labor in digging them. Similarly, all may plow up virgin land for cultivation, but once someone plows a section it becomes his private property.

Throughout the year these nomads live in yurts, a Central Asian tent, which consists of a hemispherical wooden frame covered with felt. They make their living primarily by raising sheep and goats, and their pattern of migration is largely determined by the needs of their animals and by variations in pasture and water supply. The climate of the Gorgan Plain is characterized by definite wet and dry seasons. The wet season begins in the winter, and during this season the Gokcha Hills and surrounding steppe are covered with a short, but relatively thick, crop of grass giving the appearance of a vast, freshly mowed lawn. Winter temperatures are mild, rarely dipping below the freezing point. The rainwater, as well as occasional melted snow, collects in scattered depressions to form pools from which water is taken for household needs. During this season, the nomads camp where water and suitable pasture can be found. Ample pasture is usually available close to their dry-season location, so that most of their migrations are quite short. In this respect, they differ considerably from many of the pastoral peoples in and around the Iranian Plateau who make long seasonal moves ranging over vastly differing ecological zones.

Among the Turkmen, the seasonal migrations of camps differ from the movements of livestock. The nomad camps of the Gokcha Hills alternately collect at wells and disperse over the surrounding territory, while the livestock move between the Gokcha Hills and the Gorgan River, thirty miles to the south, thus covering a larger area. This means that the Turkmen camp near their herds only during a portion of the year.

The reason for this lies in the needs of their livestock. During the latter part of the winter, the lambing season begins and the Turkmen must be near their herds to assist in cases of difficult birth and to care for the lambs, which are kept inside the yurts at night to protect them from the cold. Because the lambs are too weak to travel far, they must be pastured near the camp. Even after the young animals are weaned, the adult females must be milked daily, and for this reason, the nomads still keep the livestock near their camp.

With the onset of summer, the dry season begins, and the green pastures of spring are gradually transformed to a barren brown. The rainwater pools disappear, and now the nomads must camp near their wells. When the pastures become sparse and desiccated, the animals stop giving milk, and it is no longer necessary to keep them nearby. They are then sent south to the banks of the Gorgan River, where they graze the stubble of harvested fields. The younger men of each household accompany their family's livestock and live separately from the rest of the household, with only a small lean-to-like tent for shelter.

This division of labor is possible because herding, as well as other forms of economic production, is organized by extended families, consisting of an older man and his wife, his married sons with their wives and children, and his unmarried sons and

A woman milks a ewe; milk and mutton are important subsistence products.

daughters. Each family produces only a part of what it consumes: milk and milk products, meat, felts and carpets for their yurts, and a small amount of grain. In hope of a late spring harvest, wheat and barley are planted during the winter in valley bottoms or other depressions where water tends to collect. This is a gamble, however, since often the crop does not develop, but when a crop can be harvested, the yield is generally sufficient to make up for the losses of grain put down as seed in bad years.

The rest of their needs must be purchased. Cash income comes from the sale of wool, felts, carpets, and animals for meat. The basic item in their diet is bread, and they purchase the bulk of the wheat from which the bread is made. Rice, tea, and sugar must all be bought. Clothing, cloth, metal tools, and nowadays, a hand-powered sewing machine and a transistor radio, are other items that a typical nomadic Turkmen family buys. About once a month, two or three men from each *oba* travel to the nearest city to purchase supplies and to sell their products: animals, wool, and carpets. Thus, the pastoral economy of the Turkmen is market-oriented, even though production is organized along family lines.

The organization of the extended family reflects a strong emphasis on descent in the male line, which runs through all Turkmen social institutions. When a man's daughters marry they go to live with their husbands' families, whereas his sons

Turkmen exercise their horses by holding afternoon races.

bring their wives into his household, where they assume the dual role of wife and daughter-in-law. A man's grandchildren in the male line grow up in his household, and he commonly refers to them as his "sons" and "daughters." When, with the passing of generations, his grandsons become old men and the heads of extended families of their own, they will camp together and co-operation between them will be extensive. If any one of them is offended by an outsider, the group will band together to seek redress. Small patrilineages of this sort provide the model in terms of which the larger political units of Turkmen society are organized.

The older men, who make the important decisions, know their genealogies well. Each of them can, on the basis of his genealogy, identify a group of people who share with him a common ancestor in the male line four generations back, and a slightly larger group of people descended from a common ancestor five generations back, and so on, until he has identified himself with descent groups including thousands of families. Ultimately all Turkmen believe they are united by their genealogies as the descendants of a single man, Oghuz Khan. Although the remoter generations of these genealogies are vague and legendary in character, this is of no practical importance since the Turkmen take them seriously as a basis for arranging their social obligations.

Traditionally, the primary function of these descent groups was defense of the individual's rights through violence, or the threat of violence. Defending one's patrilineal kinsmen when their rights were violated was a basic duty in Turkmen social life. This was extremely important, because the absence of state control and of tribal offices with sufficient authority to enforce law and order meant that the strength of a Turkmen's patrilineage was the only guarantee of his rights.

When someone violated a Turkmen's rights by robbing him, injuring him, or killing him, his patrilineal kinsmen were obligated to seek redress by whatever means was necessary, even including violence. In cases of murder, for example, either the murderer or one of his lineage-mates was killed in revenge. Who sought redress for the victim and who defended the culprit were matters determined by genealogy and by the gravity of the affair. Small problems could be handled by the immediate families of the victim and the culprit. As matters increased in seriousness, a wider and wider circle of people who shared common patrilineal descent was called upon for assistance.

Those who were, on the basis of their genealogy, close to neither party also had a prescribed role. It was their obligation to attempt to bring about a peaceful settlement and, if possible, to prevent bloodshed. If the offense was slight, they merely advocated peaceful discussion and suggested compromise. In cases of murder, the neutral party aided the culprit by hiding him from the victim's kinsmen and by helping to arrange his escape to some distant place of refuge. Protecting those who came seeking refuge was part of the obligation of neutral parties to prevent bloodshed. The Iranian government has been attempting to eliminate this traditional system of self-help and to enforce law and order itself; in remoter areas, however, it has not always been successful.

The composition of Turkmen *obas*, like many other aspects of Turkmen social structure, reflects the importance of patrilineal descent. Most of the men of any *oba* are closely related in the male line; in addition, there are usually a number of unrelated families who have come to the *oba* fleeing feuds in their home territory. While these refugees reside there, the *oba* will protect their rights of person and property against outsiders.

The men of an *oba* traditionally selected a headman, who took charge of all dealings with the outside world. Today, in theory, he is appointed by the government, but in practice the local officials usually allow the men of the *oba* to indicate the man they want as their headman. The headman has no authority, but merely acts as a spokesman for the *oba* as a whole. Any important decision must be based on consensus; it must be preceded by discussion by all the men of the *oba*. Usually a headman is selected for his intelligence and integrity and for his ability to speak Persian, the language of the government officials with whom he must deal.

Ordinarily a group of fifteen to thirty *obas*, which belong to the same descent group and occupy contiguous tracts of land, form what the Turkmen call an *il*, a word best translated as tribe. In the days of intertribal warfare, the *obas* of such a tribe were usually on peaceful terms with one another. Tribes that adjoined were usually hostile, and there was much raiding between them.

One of the functions of the Turkmen tribe that has not survived government control is the practice of protecting neighboring sedentary villages. These villages were especially vulnerable to the raids of the Turkmen, and to gain a measure of security and protection each village paid tribute to the Turkmen tribe nearest it. In return, the tribe agreed not to raid the village, and to prevent raids by other Turkmen tribes. They also agreed to compensate the village for losses if they were unsuccessful in preventing raids by other tribes. In effect, the exchange of protection for tribute was a peaceful substitute for raiding.

The Turkmen were able to resist government control, to raid, and to collect tribute because their nomadic way of life made them an effective military force. They were good horsemen and were well supplied with horses. Raids, both of sedentary villages and of other nomads, were frequent events and provided the Turkmen with excellent military conditioning. When clashes with the Persian military forces occurred, normally hostile tribes would unite to turn out a large body of cavalry. This seasoned cavalry could usually hold its ground against the Persian forces, but even when met by superior strength, the Turkmen did not surrender. Instead, they would retreat into the desert north of the Gorgan River, taking their families and live-stock with them.

Thus, mobility preserved the power and independence of the Turkmen; this was why they consistently avoided anything that would compromise it. Much of the territory they inhabited was naturally fertile and was crossed by numerous streams. The construction of irrigation works and the practice of intensive agriculture could have made this land more productive. Perma-nent houses at their dry-season locations could have increased their comfort. The Turkmen, however, would not accept such trends away from nomadic life. They concentrated instead on livestock production, on raiding, and on the collection of tribute.

During the last century, the political independence of the Turkmen has gradually been whittled away. Advances in military technology have shifted the balance of power between the no-madic tribes and settled society and have led to the conquest of the nomads by sedentary powers. Most of the Turkmen were conquered by the Russians during the latter half of the nine-teenth century. Those on Iranian soil were subdued and brought under firm control in 1925.

The objective of conquering governments has been to en-courage a transition to a more sedentary and peaceful way of life. Such a transition, however, could rarely be accomplished at once. The nomads viewed settlement as a consolidation of governmental authority over them, and were not eager to take up sedentary life. For this reason, in the thirties the Iranian government began a policy of forced settlement not only of the Turkmen but of all of the Iranian tribes. The nomads I studied had been forced to build permanent houses at their dry-season locations in 1936. For five years, under the watchful eyes of government authorities, they lived in these houses during the dry season and migrated with their yurts only during the wet season. This form of semi-sedentary life developed naturally out of their pattern of pasturing sheep away from their dry-season camps. That it caused no economic difficulties is revealing. The

A woman lashes together the frame of a yurt. Assembling the yurt is a woman's job, although men help when many hands are needed.

Oxcarts are often used for travel where land is flat.

nomads had maintained a completely mobile existence for political rather than for economic reasons, and a transition to a
semi-sedentary existence could be made without economic
difficulty.

In 1941, Russia occupied northern Iran because it was fearful of Iranian co-operation with the Germans, and the process of
settlement was reversed. The Iranians had been interested in
modernization, but the Russians were interested only in sufficient order to keep their supply lines to their Western allies
open. Many of the Turkmen who had resented forced settlement
reverted to nomadism. The people with whom I recently lived
destroyed the houses they had been forced to build and returned

to living year-round in yurts. Security deteriorated, and banditry became rife in the remoter and more arid regions, such as the Gokcha Hills.

After the Second World War, the authority of the Iranian government was restored in the Gorgan Plain and efforts to modernize the Turkmen were renewed. The government had come to understand the limited value of the type of force measures used in the thirties. Its objective was not to reduce the Turkmen to the traditional position of exploited peasantry, but rather to integrate them into a society that was on the way to becoming a modern nation. This meant the terms would have to be satisfactory to the Turkmen themselves. In line with this policy, persuasion was used rather than force. Great progress was made in the fertile and populous region south of the Gorgan River.

In the Gokcha Hills, things changed more slowly. By 1960, the government had eliminated banditry, clearing the way for further progress. The Turkmen of this region, however, have remained nomadic to the present. Nevertheless, there are indications that they too will eventually be caught up in the trend of modernization.

The Gokcha Hills Turkmen are beginning to realize that their nomadic way of life has no place in the future. In 1967, when I left the *oba* that I had studied, their headman had begun to discuss the need of a school for their children. He is an intelligent man, aware that his own children will have new opportunities if they become literate. He is convinced, however, that they cannot persuade a government school teacher to live in a community that consists only of yurts. He has been telling the men of his *oba* that they need a school, and that in order to have one they will have to build houses as they did in 1936.

The headman will find that winning the men of his *oba* to this view is a difficult task. Eventually, however, they will build houses and a school, and ultimately they will be drawn into the mainstream of Iranian national life.

JOAN MENCHER

NAMBOODIRI BRAHMANS OF KERALA *"His person is holy; his directions are commands; his movements are a procession; his meal is nectar; he is the holiest of human beings; he is the representative of God on earth." This description of a Namboodiri Brahman of Kerala is in an official nineteenth-century document of Travancore.*

The Malayalam-speaking state of Kerala, in the extreme southwest part of India, is covered with foliage so rich and dense that, at least superficially, it looks like a lush South Sea island. From north to south the state falls into three natural divisions: a narrow coastal strip of sandy beaches and beautiful coconut groves, punctuated by many inlets and inland waterways; a middle area of undulating countryside, with long, winding, paddy fields surrounded by hills covered with thick vegetation; an inland region of highlands, formerly the home of tribal groups and now largely given over to the cultivation of tea in the south and coffee in the north. The physical features of the countryside have never encouraged the formation of compact dwelling areas, so the unit of rural settlement is a single dwelling, rather than a village as in the rest of India.

Kerala has also differed from the rest of the country in its traditional social organization. To both specialist and layman, one of the most interesting characteristics of Indian social life is the caste system. The term "caste" refers to a group in which membership is determined by birth, and which is hierarchically graded with respect to other such groups. This places restrictions on eating with members of other castes and on intermarriage (normally a person must marry within his own caste, although in some cases women are allowed to marry into a higher caste), and under certain conditions caste members consider themselves to be "polluted" by direct or indirect contact with members of lower castes.

The system has been more highly structured and more rigidly enforced in Kerala than in any other part of India. The dispersed houses, surrounded by their large compounds, have made it relatively easy for high-caste Malayalees (Malayalam-speaking inhabitants of Kerala) to maintain their rules of pollution. Today the entire society is in a state of transition.

Among the Kerala castes, the Namboodiri Brahmans ranked highest in religious and in economic and political life. The houses of the Namboodiris, known as *illams*, were surrounded by spacious gardens. Most were palatial structures built of laterite and cemented with mud or mortar. Traditionally, the Namboodiri aristocrats were self-sufficient in their *illams*; they were cared for by servants who paid homage to them in every possible way,

Two Namboodiri women, at left, are accompanied on their way to temple by a Nayar maidservant. Palm leaf umbrellas protect against both rain and sun, and they also help in preserving a type of purdah typical of this country.

and their fields were farmed by tenants who provided rice and other necessities of life.

One of the most striking features of the Namboodiris was their relationship with several of the high castes of Kerala, particularly the Nayars. In a Namboodiri family, only the eldest son was allowed to marry in his own caste (although it was permissible for him to take more than one wife). The family property was never divided, and this custom maintained the economic position and social prestige of the family.

The younger sons, according to tradition, had no property of their own and were expected to remain celibate and devote their lives to religion. However, even records from the Middle Ages indicate that it was customary for them to form marital liaisons with women from Nayar subcastes or other, smaller, high non-Brahman castes. (The Nayars constituted about 18 per cent of the population of Kerala, according to the last caste census, made in 1931.) The Nayars, as well as the other small caste groups who took Namboodiri younger sons as mates for their women, were matrilocal: that is, a woman remained in her natal home after marriage and raised her children there, living under the authority of an uncle or an elder brother. Among these castes, it was customary for a man to spend most of his life in his own home and visit his wife only at night. The matrilocal groups were also matrilineal, with inheritance of property through the female line. The Namboodiris, on the other hand, were patrilocal (a married couple and their children lived in the husband's ancestral home) and patrilineal (inheritance passed from father to son).

Traditionally, there were two kinds of marriage among the Nayars, the *tali kettu kalyanam* and the *sambandham*. The *tali kettu kalyanam,* or *tali*-tying ceremony, could be held at any time before a girl reached puberty. The *tali* (a gilded, leaf-shaped pendant on a chain) was tied around a girl's neck either by a member of a family of similar rank or by someone in a higher subcaste.

There have been several interpretations of this rite. Some scholars have suggested that at an earlier period it actually constituted a formal marriage; others, that it represented a kind of coming-of-age ceremony. On the other hand, a French anthropologist, Louis Dumont, has suggested that it was a local adaptation of a customary South Indian rite, because the *tali* is the symbol of marriage in all partrilineal groups in that area.

In any case, following the *tali* ceremony, and after a girl's first menstruation, she formed what is called a *sambandham* union (the customary nuptials of a man and woman) with a man of her own subcaste or a higher one. Since property was inherited through the Nayar female line, there was no need for her *sambandham* mate to care for her or their children.

There has been considerable controversy in the Indian courts as to whether such a union constituted a marriage. However, it is clear that the Nayars—but not the Namboodiris—so

Nayar women leave after worship in a temple that is in Namboodiri household.

viewed them. From the Namboodiri point of view, such unions
with Nayars were convenient, in that they provided semi-perma-
nent or permanent liaisons for the younger sons. From the
Nayar point of view, a Namboodiri younger son was considered
a good partner because of his caste prestige. According to one
Malayalee historian, there was a considerably larger Namboodiri
population in Kerala in the fourteenth century, and if that is
true, such liaisons were more common at that time than in the
early twentieth century.

The history of the Namboodiri community still presents
certain puzzles, not the least of which is the date of their arrival
in Kerala. According to the legendary *Keralolpatty* (an account
of Kerala history, said to have been set down in writing in the
eighteenth century, more than two hundred years after the first
appearance of the Portuguese on the coast), Brahmans were
brought to the southwest coast of India by the godlike sage-
warrior Parasurama. They settled in thirty-two *grammam* in the
north (now the South Kanara District of Mysore State) and
thirty-two in the south of Kerala.

It is hard to define a Namboodiri *grammam* in simple terms.
Each *grammam*, at least each major one, had its own temple
and its own authorities for religious and secular laws and their
enforcement, although some of the smaller or lower-ranking
grammam deferred to the authorities in neighboring major ones.
Most *grammam* were somewhat localized geographically, and
their *illams* were within a radius of ten to twenty-five miles of
the *grammam* temple. But since the territories of two *grammam*
might overlap, these cannot be thought of as communities in the
usual sense.

There does not seem to be any factual basis for the legend
of Parasurama. The majority of modern historians hold that the
Namboodiris came to Kerala sometime between the first century
B.C. and the fourth century A.D. The evidence for their place of
origin is slight, but all authorities agree that they probably did
come from outside of Kerala, bringing with them many new customs and traditions that eventually mingled with those of the
earlier inhabitants of the region.

Even the source of the name Namboodiri has been disputed.
Perhaps the most reasonable suggestion is that its root is *nambu*,
meaning "sacred" or "trustworthy," and *tiri*, which literally
means a "light," but which is often used in Kerala as a high-

caste honorific suffix. Today, the caste name Namboodiri, or Namboodiripad, is often used as a surname. The term *pad* added to the name usually indicates that the man belongs to the highest of the Namboodiri subgroups.

There is also considerable argument among Malayalee historians as to when the Namboodiris became landed aristocrats, if they have always practiced primogeniture, and on many other related questions. Further, the relationship of the Namboodiris with the matrilineal castes has also been a matter of speculation. Some Malayalee historians believe that the Nayars of Kerala were not matrilineal before the tenth century A.D., but that they became so under the pressure of a hundred years of intermittent warfare with the Chola empire on the east coast. Others maintain that Nayar matrilineality has had a far longer history, perhaps deriving from a matrilineal tribal system, perhaps from an earlier bilateral system, in which equal emphasis was given to the mother's and father's sides, and property could be inherited from either or both parents.

Perhaps the only aspect of their history that is known definitely is that the heyday of the Namboodiris lasted from the twelfth century until the end of the seventeenth. During that time, the political structure of Kerala was feudalistic, resembling in some ways the continental system of Europe in the thirteenth and fourteenth centuries. The petty chieftains sometimes exercised the right of taking up arms among themselves, and on occasion even waged war against their own feudal heads. Many important temples had their own *Samketams*—well-defined areas in which Namboodiri temple authorities acted as civilian petty chieftains and had sovereign rights.

Namboodiri *grammam* dealt only with Namboodiri affairs, and had no say in the relationships between individual Namboodiri families and their tenants of the Nayar or lower castes. On the other hand, the Namboodiris had the unique role of being above and beyond territorial concerns. They could move freely from one area to another, even between two at war.

Namboodiris were ranked in several ways on the basis of the privileges they possessed—to some extent by their wealth, and in part by their occupation. According to the Cochin census report of 1901, "special privileges in regard to the performance of religious rites and . . . matters of a purely social nature serve as the best basis for a subdivision of the Nambutiris in the order of social precedence as recognized amongst themselves."

There were ten of these privileges, including the right to teach the Vedas (the four earliest sacred texts written in San-

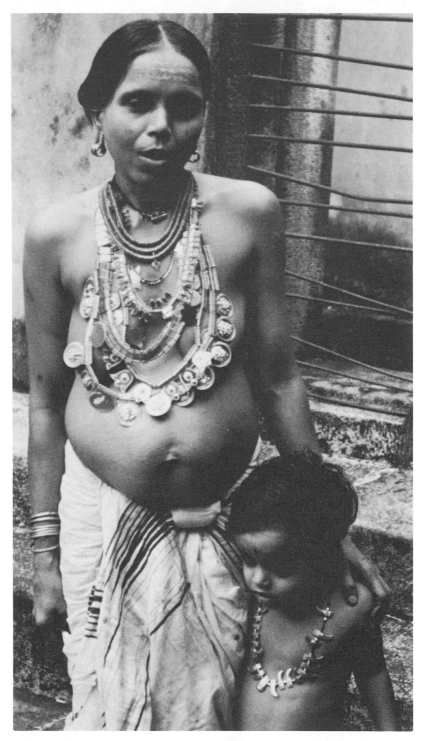

Jewelry, much of it made of solid gold, is worn only for special occasions.

Ritual purification ceremony is being performed with traditional implements.

skrit) or Shastras (books of sacred law composed later than the Vedas); to perform sacrifices; to officiate as family priests; to become a *sanyasi*, or holy man; to study the Vedas; to perform priestly functions in temples; to cook for all classes of Brahmans; to take part in certain semi-humorous "shows"; to bathe in the same place with other Brahmans; and to eat in the same row (*literally* in a row) with other Brahmans. These rights were listed in a traditional order: those possessing the first had the right to the remaining nine, those possessing only the third had the right to three through ten, and so on.

The geographic distribution of the Namboodiris seems always to have been uneven. In certain areas there were thick concentrations, while others contained a few *illams* at most. It is striking but, under the conditions, not surprising, that the largest number, including almost all of the high-ranking ones, are to be found where the greatest amount of land could be given over to rice cultivation. Apart from gifts by local rulers and the like, most of the Namboodiri wealth came from the land. On the other hand, the owners refused to deal directly with that land, preferring to leave agricultural management to tenants. Throughout Kerala, rice, and occasionally coconuts, have been given over to tenant cultivation, whereas the majority of cash crops, such as pepper, have been cultivated by Nayar or Moslem landowners with the help of hired laborers.

Traditionally, as we have said, the property of a Namboodiri *illam* could never be partitioned. One result has been that the Namboodiris survived as a landed aristocracy, in contrast to Brahmans in other parts of India, where the family property was divided every second generation or so.

The Namboodiris were also considered to be the highest spiritual authorities in Kerala, and the repositories of learning. They were well versed in Sanskrit literature and were skilled at composition and teaching in that language. The Namboodiris were also extremely strict about rules of pollution. Indeed, Kerala, because of its dispersed settlement pattern and loose political structure, has been the one place where the concept of "distance pollution" has been most highly developed. Thus, a Nayar was allowed inside a Namboodiri house, but he could not touch anyone or enter the kitchen or the *puja* room (where religious rituals are performed daily). A Namboodiri male with a

Nayar wife would go to her only after his evening meal and would leave in the morning before his purificatory bath.

Members of the lower Nayar castes, such as washermen, were allowed only on the veranda of the house, and members of the various service castes, such as blacksmiths or carpenters, were expected to remain in the compound and not come near the veranda, although an exception was made for a carpenter carrying his tools. In descending order, each caste group had a specified distance to maintain from the Namboodiri house and from individual Namboodiris.

Many traces of the accent on distance pollution still exist. Obviously, they cannot now be enforced on the road or in a public place, but in a Namboodiri's own compound he can require that members of lower castes maintain the requisite distances. On the whole, the younger Namboodiris, both male and female, say that they do not believe in or practice the restrictions and privileges.

Traditional life was simple and austere. At the age of about seven, Namboodiri boys entered upon a period called *Brahmacharyya*, which lasted until they were almost fifteen. During this time they were supposed to study the Vedas and to undergo certain deprivations: for example, they were not allowed to sleep during the daytime, and were expected to abstain from all luxuries, including clothing of all kinds except for a small strip of cotton cloth and an inch-wide leather strap across one shoulder. The teacher (guru) was empowered to punish them severely for the slightest error.

Girls remained at home. Usually they were taught to read and write either by an older member of the family, a teacher who might be of a slightly lower caste or, occasionally, by their mothers. The sole purpose of this education was to enable them to read the sacred epics—that is, the *Mahabharata*, the *Ramayana*, and the *Bharatham*, the last a book devoted to the experiences of Lord Krishna. In the sixth year, there was a ceremony for "removing the hair"; until this time girls were not allowed to let their hair grow long. After the ceremony, in which only a small piece of hair was cut off, the observance of "touch pollution" began. A girl was expected to fast every Monday and to pray to God for the longevity of her husband-to-be, for the death of the husband was usually blamed on the wife.

Traditionally, there was a tendency for a girl to be married to someone who lived within two or, at most, three days' walk from her parents' *illam*, often within the same *grammam*. Today, although many marriages are with nearby *illams*, some girls marry men who live as much as 200 miles away, although this is rare. Among today's educated Namboodiris, considerations of wealth and education play some part in selection of a husband.

Because of the problems involved in getting a girl married, any offer was normally accepted. There was a saying among the elderly Namboodiri women: "Even if it is a monkey of our own caste who asks for a girl, we must give her." Postpubertal marriage was most frequent, but younger girls were also married. Dowries were, and continue to be, extremely high, despite legislation prohibiting them. In 1962, they ranged from $1,000 to almost $5,000, not including the cost of the wedding and the attendant ceremonies. (In rural India, $1,000 buys as much as $4,000–$5,000 in the United States.)

At one time, men often took second and third wives in exchange for getting their daughters married, thus escaping some of the heavy burden of dowries, but this has stopped completely since the enactment in 1956 of a bill prohibiting Hindu polygamous marriages. Today, when a man has difficulty getting his daughter married, he sometimes tries to get one of his unmarried younger brothers to take a wife in exchange. Brother-sister exchange is becoming more common because most of the men now marry Namboodiri women. In marked contrast to the rest of south India, they do not allow marriage between first cousins. Marriage to a more distantly related member of one's mother's natal *illam* or to a relative of one's father's sister's husband is permitted.

The traditional position of the woman was extremely difficult. After marriage a girl had no right in her parents' house. Until her death she lived in her husband's house and could only visit her parents if her mother-in-law and husband gave her permission. As one young girl put it to me: "Whether she was happy or miserable in the husband's house, she had no other choice. Sometimes the man had one or two other wives, and those elder sisters [a term sometimes used for elder co-wives] might have hurt her because they were jealous. Still she was expected to live with all this and think only pious thoughts about God and attend to her household duties."

It was not uncommon for a twelve-year-old girl to be mar-

Young Brahmacharyya boy must dress only in a loincloth and leather strap.

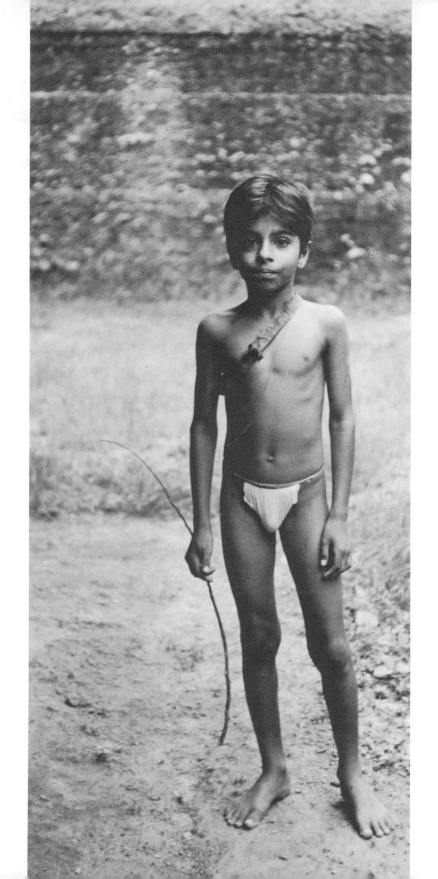

Traditional folk dance, Kaikuttykali, is performed by these Namboodiri women.

ried to a man in his sixties who had several wives. He might have married the younger girl in order to get one of his own daughters married. The young bride was expected to observe *gosha* (a kind of purdah) and not to allow any man other than her own husband, sons, and stepsons to see her. When her husband died, she was not allowed to remarry, but was forced to devote the rest of her life to piety.

At the end of the eighteenth century, the British took over direct political control in Malabar, and came to play a major role as advisors in Cochin and Travancore. At that time, the Namboodiris, deprived of their political role but still maintaining their status as religious authorities, withdrew to their estates. Their attitude at that time is illustrated by the words of an elderly Namboodiri man: "When the British came, we were sitting with hatred in our minds towards these people and towards their education. Our real eminence came in things like the Murajapam [56-day Vedic recitation] in Trivandrum."

While the Nayars took rapidly to modern education, the Namboodiris remained aloof, preferring to reemphasize their spiritual sanctity and purity. About the turn of the century, Namboodiri youth, especially some of the younger sons who were brought into contact with educated Nayar males through their *sambandham* relationships with Nayar women, became aware of the growing gap between the Nayar position in society and that of the Namboodiris. They saw Nayars agitating for partition of their ancestral land, and even Nayar girls being educated and having a freedom denied the Namboodiri women. Above all, during the first quarter of the twentieth century they slowly became aware that if they agitated for change, even if it displeased the more orthodox, they might stand to benefit.

In this climate the Namboodiri reform movements began. In effect, what the reformers asked for meant the end of the traditional Namboodiri family system and the group's position as a landed aristocracy, and it is not surprising that many of the leaders of the reform movement were the "underprivileged" younger sons. It was clear that there would be a total reworking of Namboodiri life if men began to receive a modern education, if each son was allowed to marry within the Namboodiri castes, if permission was granted to partition the family property, and finally, if education for Namboodiri girls became a reality.

While some *illams* resisted reform, others took to it eagerly. The area of most rapid change was near Trichur, where a rebellion against the head of the Vedic school occurred in 1917.

In the majority of *illams* today, younger sons marry within their own community, and most boys are given a modern education. However, there is still a considerable range in orthodoxy. Some of the isolated *illams* might still belong to the early nineteenth century: at the other end of the spectrum are *illams* whose property has been completely divided, where both men and women are educated and hold regular jobs, where all castes interact with complete freedom, and which, as a result, are scarcely recognizable as Namboodiri establishments.

Most of the orthodox or wealthy Namboodiris, plus the majority of elder sons (even in modernized *illams*) and others concerned about the maintenance of their caste purity and their economic and social privileges, have tended since 1947 to align themselves with the Congress Party (the political party of Nehru and Shastri). On the other hand, many of the women and younger sons accept Marxist or Communist ideologies. Some members of the reform movement have, of course, stayed loyal to Congress, at the same time siding consistently with the more socialist-minded members.

Woman has vowed to donate her weight, in this case in coconuts, to her temple.

It is clear that as more and more Namboodiri young people are educated and enter various occupations, they will become less differentiated from other Kerala castes. (It is impossible to know how many Namboodiris there are today. There has not been any census conducted on a caste basis for thirty-five years.) Fewer and fewer are studying the Vedas and learning how to maintain traditional rituals. However, they probably will remain relatively highly placed. Even with land limits currently being introduced all over India, they are well off compared to the lowest castes. In another sense, the Namboodiris are a part of the newly emerging middle classes, for as individuals they are clearly in transition from one social system to another. One might safely predict that the unique Namboodiri culture will slowly disappear.

WILLIAM F. PRATT

THE ANABAPTIST EXPLOSION The survival of the Hutterites
and the Amish, two religious sects whose communities are found
in various parts of the United States and Canada, is a cultural
anachronism. That these Anabaptist societies have persevered over
several hundred years fraught with persecution and rejection is
surprising enough. That they have maintained their medieval
faith and their unsophisticated styles of life in a rapidly changing
urban-industrial environment, is an ecological phenomenon of
considerable moment. But of particular interest is their traditionally high level of fertility, which has persisted while their
mortality rates have approximated that of the surrounding society.
Consequently they have experienced a phenomenal growth from
natural increase, which has created portentous problems for them.

The Hutterites, settled in South Dakota, Montana, and the
prairie provinces of Canada, and the Amish, formerly centered
in Pennsylvania and Ohio, have birthrates of 46 and 33 per 1,000
population, respectively. A century and a half ago, the United
States birthrate was a lofty 55—over three times higher than its
present level: in 1967 it had dropped to an all-time low of 17.9
births per 1,000 population. It is against this shifting background
that the continuing high fertility of the Hutterites and Amish is
so startling.

Comparable fertility rates show that from age 20 Hutterite
women have much higher birthrates than those of American
women in general. Even in their late childbearing years (40 to
44) their birthrate exceeds that of American women in their
peak childbearing years (20 to 24). (The Amish women, in a
somewhat freer society, have birthrates about midway between
those of Hutterites and of American women in general.) It may
be that two centuries of high fertility, combined with the
inbreeding brought about by the social isolation of the Hutterites,
has created a unique strain of the human species—a strain distinct in its fertility from any other people. Indeed, the Hutterites,

Adapted from "Pockets of High Fertility in the United States," *Population
Bulletin*, November, 1968, Population Reference Bureau, Inc. (Robert C.
Cook, Editor).

with an annual natural increase of about 4 per cent, are possibly the fastest growing population on earth. Between 1950 and 1965, their numbers almost doubled, from 8,500 to 15,000. The United States growth rate, by contrast, is only .79. This would double the population in about 90 years, compared with a doubling among Hutterites about every 17 years.

The fertility of the two Anabaptist sects is one reflection of their rigidly theocratic cultures, which have managed to survive in an urban-industrial nation of 200 million that is wholly alien in outlook to the sects' own beliefs. At the same time, their rigid separatism, their being conscientious objectors, and their rapid growth have made these sects a focal point of hostility among their neighbors. The problems of the Amish families with respect to public education are familiar. As for Hutterite colonies, land laws have been proposed several times, and in some cases passed, to restrict their spread. At their present growth rate, Hutterites would number 64,500 by the year 2000, and more than 55 million by 2168. Today, their colonies occupy about 1,000 square miles; by the year 2000, they would occupy an area almost equaling Connecticut.

The difference in birthrates of the two sects is intriguing. It undoubtedly reflects differences in social organization and comparative success in adapting to the secular milieu of modern America. Despite their common origins and life style, they differ significantly in important respects.

Hutterites: a dissident sect

The Anabaptists of the Reformation comprised several quite different sects, from the radical and violent Munsterites to the equally radical but wholly non-violent Hutterites. What they shared was the label "Anabaptist"; it referred to their central belief in adult "rebaptism," baptism upon the confession of faith. All these Protestant sects were religious responses of the socially disinherited of the Holy Roman Empire in the late fifteenth and sixteenth centuries.

Peasants, journeymen, and the landless were the most abject victims of that period's crises. Many turned from a cheerless reality to the comforts of a religion that made a virtue of their poverty and built a brotherhood on their passive suffering. But then, Martin Luther and Huldrich Zwingli alike, having gained their patrimony from the state, turned upon the rabble. In 1527, the Swiss Anabaptists responded by formalizing many of the tenets that still characterize Hutterites and Amish. Among these are adult baptism, separation of church and state by the withdrawal of believers, and an emphatic rejection of violence. From the outset, then, Anabaptism was regarded as a threat to the established religious and secular authorities, both old and new.

Unsafe in Zurich, the Swiss Brethren—the main body of Swiss Anabaptists—found refuge in Nikolsburg, Moravia, where their mounting numbers undoubtedly created severe economic strains. These were soon reflected in doctrinal disputes between a liberal majority and a strict, radical minority. The radicals, proclaiming Christian communism, worshiping separately, holding fast to adult baptism, and rejecting military violence even to defend themselves, were expelled in 1528. At that time they symbolically spread a cloak upon the ground to receive their worldly goods. This formally inaugurated the practice of "community of goods," which made them unique among sects descending from the Swiss Brethren. Under the organizational genius of Jacob Hutter (martyred in 1536) this radical group became known as Hutterites.

Although their communities flourished and increased through the first 100 years, they stood constantly in the shadow of persecution and dispersal. Between 1529 and 1622, an estimated 85 communal households, averaging from 300 to 400 members, had been established. But, by 1625, the sect had almost completely migrated to Hungary. There, the re-establishment of Catholic authority and the rise of the Jesuits overcame the reluctance of the nobility to persecute the Hutterites. Invasion by the Turks added to their troubles. Also, considerable internal discord arose and by the end of the seventeenth century, membership had been greatly reduced by apostasy to Catholicism.

Of the faithful, most migrated to Slovakia, Transylvania, and Walachia, and later to Russia. Here, unable to re-establish communal life, they accepted the individual family culture practiced by the Mennonites, an independent Anabaptist movement that also had set up some communities in Russia. In the 1870's, fearing Czarist persecution, most Hutterites migrated to the United States where, returning to their former, communal order, they established three colonies, comprising about 440 persons.

Thus began a demographic epic. As of January, 1965, there were 162 organized communities, averaging 94 "souls," in the U.S. and Canada. This growth to over 15,000 people is about a 33-fold increase, or over five doublings of population in less than a century.

These figures are the more remarkable because the Hutterites have been a "closed population" since arrival in America. Their growth has come entirely from natural increase, the excess of births over deaths.

Even when adjusted for differences in age distribution, the Hutterite death rate is only 85 per cent of the United States figure. The Hutterite rate for infant mortality in the past was above the national figure, but with improving medical care and health practices this too may now be equal to or less than for the nation as a whole.

Some practices, such as considerable reliance upon mid-wives, remain old-fashioned, but in general the Hutterites have adopted modern medical facilities. Although their anti-intellectualism and separation from the world have deprived them of the outstanding medical personnel they had in an earlier era, Hutterites do not hesitate to send ailing members to the Mayo Clinic and other medical centers. A recent study suggests that they may be spending more per capita on drugs and medical care than do most Americans. If their favorable mortality has been purchased at the cost of greater dependence upon the outside, it is nonetheless consistent with their historical emphasis on health and medical practice.

The exceptionally high fertility of Hutterite women is most sharply seen in their average completed fertility. It totals 10.4 live births, owing partly to the remarkably high rates of child-bearing in the later fertile years. According to sociologists J. W. Eaton and A. J. Mayer, the fertility rate of over 425 per 1,000 for Hutterite women aged 35–39 exceeds that for women in any other culture now on record. Even at ages 40–44, Hutterites have a fertility rate higher than women in France, Sweden and the United States during their years of maximum fertility, ages 20–29.

So striking a deviation suggests that something more than social or theocratic mores are involved. The inbreeding within the Hutterite population must be considerable. Since the 440 original brethren with only 15 patronyms among them (70 per had only five patronyms) came to America a century ago, they have attracted no "new blood." In view of the higher mortality of Hutterite women in the childbearing years and the continued reproduction of those women rugged enough to stay the course, genetic components favoring a superfecund strain in the species must have been added to the Hutterite gene pool. The degree to which inbreeding may have made this population genetically more uniform (homozygous) would depend on birth and marriage patterns within the colonies. Until a detailed genetic analysis of the Hutterite pedigree becomes available, it is impossible to derive accurate inbreeding coefficients and thereby add greatly to our knowledge of what inbreeding does to human populations.

At any rate, Hutterite fertility has few restrictions and strong positive encouragement from the culture. Hutterites take literally the Biblical injunction to "be fruitful and multiply": sex as pleasure is devalued and confined to marriage, the chief end of which is to beget children. Birth control, including the rhythm method, is prohibited. All but a very few Hutterites marry, divorce is unknown, and remarriage after the death of a spouse is frequent. The only major restraint upon fertility is the relatively late age at marriage, combined with prohibition of premarital sexual intercourse. Sociologist John A. Hostetler reports that in 1965 the average age at marriage was 23.5 for men and 22.0 for women, compared with the national averages of 22.8 and 20.6 for men and women, respectively.

These direct factors are supported by the general cultural patterns of community life. Lack of privacy in one's household and possessions would make difficult the use of most mechanical or chemical contraceptive methods; and failure to bear children within a reasonably short time after marriage or the last birth starts gossip and insinuations about one's health and the health of one's marriage. The same lack of privacy makes premarital sexual adventures unlikely, not to mention the severe guilt and ostracism that a premarital pregnancy would bring.

In any case, there is little, if any, motivation for birth control. Unlike outsiders, the Hutterite family does not face the economic uncertainties that attend death and unemployment; it does not have the responsibilities of maintaining its own separate household and facilities; above all, it escapes "keeping up with the Joneses." The simplicity of Hutterite consumer needs, the economies of communal life, the low educational costs, and the early age at which youth enter the colony's productive enterprise all keep the costs of childbearing very low compared to the general population. This would seem to leave the state of the woman's health and the strains of childbearing as the only plausible focus for trying to limit the number of children, and so far, these considerations have had no observable impact on fertility.

In view of its remarkably high fertility and rapid natural increase, the intriguing question is: how has this anti-intellectual, medieval communal order managed to adapt itself to a highly secular, urban-industrial environment and its rapidly changing technology? Other Anabaptist groups have clearly not resisted surrounding secular influences so well.

No longer subject to the whimsies of noble patrons, as in Europe, each Hutterite colony is an independent corporate enterprise integrated with the larger American economy. Hutterite economy is more specialized in agriculture today than when they were in Europe; they have sacrificed many of their former crafts and trades for modern mechanical skills and the economies of wholesale purchasing.

But their assimilation is exclusively at the economic and corporate level. Life within the contemporary colony is a revitalized communal order. Esthetic and individualizing interests are suppressed, as of old, by a common style in all things—a style marked by simplicity and sturdiness of materials. Thus active economic choice does not intrude, and invidious status differences do not arise. Financial matters and control of funds are strictly communal. Although not motivated by profit, Hutterites are shrewd businessmen who must maintain a substantial level of savings for contingencies and for building new colonies every generation or less.

So far as possible labor remains communal, and responsibilities are divided according to age, sex, and "election" as in former times. Cooking is done in a communal kitchen; eating is in a common dining hall. Although each family has one to two rooms in a communal apartment, toilet facilities are shared.

By isolating themselves socially, Hutterites sustain a strong sense of solidarity and a remarkable integrity of their communal life. Their rural location; the restrictions on working for outsiders; their language and quaint clothing: all help to separate them from the world. Information about the outside is primarily through the daily newspaper and farm journals, plus infrequent trips to town; but radios, TV, and movies are forbidden.

Although bilingual and maintaining their level of literacy, they refuse state education beyond the legal required age, and maintain a parochial school in the colony to keep the children at home. The "English" teacher, certified by the state or province, generally lives in the colony, but is as physically and socially isolated as Hutterite courtesy and hospitality will allow.

This social isolation of the Hutterite group itself is reinforced by a psychological turning inward. By constant reflection on their historical persecution and references to it, Hutterites maintain a fearful view of the outside world. The conditioning begins in earliest childhood, when Santa Claus is described as a bogeyman who kidnaps naughty children; consequently the youngster shrinks from strangers. Also, the fundamentalist religious message stresses God's wrath and vengeance upon those who enter the world, or behave in worldly ways (against the community rules), and his forgiving love for those who repent. These teachings begin in the communal kindergarten and continue in the "German" school to age 15, where they are reinforced by the strict teacher. In sum, a somewhat paranoid fear of, and prejudice toward, the larger society is ritually induced from childhood, while the ascetic discipline of the community life comes to be viewed as the comforting, forgiving, God-given haven.

Contemporary Hutterites are keenly aware that colony size is also basically important. By limiting colonies to a maximum of about 150 members, they can preserve close interpersonal relations, with privacy nearly impossible and competing cliques seldom arising. When the colony population becomes too large, however, stresses do occur and feelings polarize along family and kinship lines.

This internal source of disruption is normally muted in several ways that characterize Hutterite communal life: the economic independence of the family is eliminated; family-centered activities are minimized; men and women are separated in labor, dining, and worship; and household privacy is limited.

North American society also fosters their internal solidarity. From time to time their colonies have been harassed by neighbors and by attempted legislative restrictions; these plus the jibes and prejudice of outsiders suffice to keep their fears very much alive, even though their rights have been strongly protected.

Most significant perhaps is that the outside no longer offers a viable living alternative for the individual Hutterite or family. Neither by education, social skills, nor psychology is the Hutterite prepared to compete in the larger society. Since 1918, no more than 2 per cent of all Hutterites have ever forsaken their colonies. The young man who does "try the world" almost invariably feels a keen sense of loneliness and returns in short order, expressing a sense of guilt tòward his parents.

Stresses and strains

To the casual observer, Hutterite society may present the illusion of unchangeability over 400 years of history. A paradox is closer to the truth: they have changed, and in fundamental ways, in order to remain the same. A simple example is the principle of adult baptism. Although it is still observed in form, and plays a crucial part in Hutterite socialization, it has long since lost its original meaning. Today's young Hutterite adult does not "choose" the community life after having experienced and rejected the "world" on its own terms. He has been very successfully conditioned to fear the outside, to feel inadequate in the face of it, to cherish the psychological shelter of the community.

Will the adaptive processes that have so far preserved the Hutterite culture continue to operate in the indefinite future? This will depend on how much the stresses and strains are intensified by the phenomenal population growth.

The communal operation has an ideal or optimal labor demand that implies a population of about 100 persons in all ages. As sociologist Victor Peters observes: "A new colony with a population of about 100 persons will have an adult labor pool . . . of about 30 men and women. Approximately 15 . . . will be male, which means that almost all of them will be in charge of an office or enterprise. . . . As the population increases, there are duplications in the various enterprises (by a system of assistants)."

This is the stage at which invidious distinctions among equals arise and cause tensions; the basis for cliques and divisions along family lines now begins to emerge. The resulting tensions play upon the problem of esthetics and the adoption of consumer conveniences. In short, the intimate, primary relations of colony life begin to give way to more formal regulations and supervision. However, when colony size reaches about 150 members, the more informal, brotherly atmosphere of community life is re-cstablished in Hutterite fashion. The oversize community splits, amebalike, into two communities: one new and one old.

The rapid increase in colonies provides a classic illustration of ecological competition for territory, and of population's role in intersocietal conflict. Hutterite aloofness is a source of prejudice, their economic efficiency is a source of envy, their refusal to bear arms can raise hostility to the boiling point. More direct and basic, the colonies, like corporate farms elsewhere, have reduced the population base that formerly provided support for the economies of local towns. The Hutterite ability to purchase wholesale from more distant centers further depresses the economy of these nearby towns. In some instances, Hutterite refusal to participate in local programs, such as rural electrification, has denied these services to other local farmers.

Against the resulting hostility Hutterite protestations about contributing to the health of state and national economies, about paying school taxes from which they receive little benefit, about not drawing upon outside welfare funds to which they contribute, and about not contributing to problems of crime or mental illness are of little avail.

True, opposition so far has not blunted either their financial security in the general economy or their constitutional protections as citizens. Nonetheless, they have experienced outbreaks of vandalism against some of their colonies, especially in wartime, and there have been numerous proposals to restrict their land buying. A land law in Alberta requires that Hutterites purchase new colonies at least 40 miles away from any other and not exceeding 64,000 acres. To challenge such laws, Hutterites have been obliged to set up something hitherto alien to them—a national church. Though this secondary organization has had little effect on the daily operations of the colonies, it contains the seeds for wielding financial power and regulating communal life in a non-Hutterite way.

Given that this sect will number about 64,500 people in the year 2000, it is reasonable to expect that outside opposition will press harder for changes in Hutterite life. Moreover, given that Hutterites would number 55 million in another 168 years, it is clear that either their growth rate or their way of life, and probably both, must give way to change before that time. A fascinating experimental case study in the social consequences of demographic patterns appears to be rapidly unfolding before our eyes.

Despite various similarities between the two sects, the story of the Amish is far more of a contrast with that of the Hutterites, especially in modern times.

The Amish arose as a branch from the Mennonites, an independent Anabaptist movement centering in the Netherlands. The Mennonites envisaged small, homogeneous, and self-sufficient communities living a scriptural way of life. Unlike Hutterites, they advocated no theocratic communism or any other economic mode of community life. In practice, like the majority of Swiss Brethren, they embraced the doctrine of Christian stewardship of private property and made the family the basic economic unit of their society.

However, the fanatical Mennonite preacher, Jakob Ammann, preached a harsher system of discipline. In 1693, angered by the refusal of a group of ministers to confer on this issue, he censured the lot of them and founded his own sect, the Amish. Thus was Amish life rigorously formalized and made more repressive.

Also for comparison: the migrations of the Amish—unlike those of Hutterites—have always occurred within the sphere of advancing Western culture rather than its backwash.

From communities widely scattered over western Europe, the Amish emigrated to the United States over a long period of time, beginning with the first settlement, in Pennsylvania, in 1727. After the Napoleonic wars, large numbers of Amish fled Alsace and Bavaria, settling in Ontario, Illinois, and Ohio. Shortly, they were followed by others from central Germany, who settled in Ohio, Pennsylvania, and Maryland. By 1900, the Amish had either abandoned Europe or been reabsorbed by the Mennonites.

Through exceptional frugality, industry, and farming skill, the Amish prospered in their earlier years in America, compared with their neighbors. Today the economic situation is reversed. The modern non-Amish farmer, utilizing farm machinery forbidden to the Old Order Amishman, is far more productive and also much less burdened by a large family. (Reference to the "Old Order Amish" reflects the fact that over more recent times, the traditional order of Amish life has eroded and produced several schisms.)

By 1960, there were 258 loosely defined Amish "districts" in 19 states, with a total Amish population of about 43,000. Six years later the population had grown to 49,370, an increase of just under 15 per cent, compared with 9 per cent for the United

States as a whole. The Amish increase would be even greater were it not for their steady loss of members who "emigrate" to the larger secular society.

In any case, the noticeably higher increase in the Amish population results almost exclusively from their higher fertility.

Young Amish join their elders at a Pennsylvania country auction while the young ladies gather around buggies that brought them. Each sex is wearing its typical costume, which is topped by hat or bonnet. In this pacifist sect the fully mature men wear beards but shun mustaches, which are held to be martial. More individualistic than Hutterites, the Old Order Amish are also seeing more of their young men "emigrate" to the even freer secular society around them.

Interestingly, the Amish apparently have a higher rate of twin births compared with the general population, suggesting the presence of a distinct genetic factor. Equally interesting is the lower fertility of the Amish compared with the Hutterites. Any superfecundity among the Hutterites might explain part of this difference. But, since the Amish have lower fertility than many other contemporary populations, a significant portion of the difference with the Hutterites must come from the spread of birth control methods among the Amish.

Their higher fertility compared with that of the United States reflects a continuing influence of their fundamentalist views, but their lower fertility compared with Hutterites reflects the erosion of their large-family ideal. Although Amish couples marry somewhat younger than Hutterites, they produce fewer children per family. The median number of children in an Amish

family is 6.7; it is 10.4 among the Hutterites. Yet Amish doctrine, no less than that of the Hutterites, prohibits contraception and promotes the large-family ideal. Moreover, unlike Hutterites, they reject modern technology. This difference theoretically promotes the need for many farmhands, and these must come from the young. The Amish youth, like his Hutterite counterpart, enters the economic life of his community at about age 15.

In relations with the larger society, the Amish have probably been hurt less by population growth than the Hutterites. They have been less of a competitive threat to their neighbors because their farming methods are less efficient and they do business in the local community rather than through their own communal organization, as Hutterites prefer to do. On the other hand, the simple mode of Amish life undoubtedly restricts the growth of local business, especially in farm equipment and through a wide range of consumer goods.

It is in relation to the internal life of their communities that population growth has undoubtedly been more distressing for the Amish than for the Hutterites. The family basis of Amish economy means that as population increases, the community must spread geographically. This makes it increasingly difficult for each member to be equally well acquainted with all the others; consequently, those who see each other more often tend to form cliques. Moreover, the young people are forced to move away from the family home and seek new land when the family farm can no longer be subdivided. This development breaks down the positive controls with which kinship maintains conformity. In addition high fertility increases the proportion of young dependents.

Actually, a population increase only creates pressure for change, and it is the type of community organization that determines the form of change. The small size of the Amish economic unit—the family—has severely restricted adaptability.

Unable to supply all its needs, either from its own resources or those of the Amish community, each family is compelled to operate directly in the larger market. Moreover, refusal to adopt fully modern farm technology restricts productivity and, therefore, family income. In turn, the income has to be spread among family members who include a higher proportion of non-productive dependents.

Equally significant, the family system involves transmission of property through inheritance. With large numbers of children (an average of three or four sons), the size of an inheritance naturally decreases, providing a smaller income base for the next generation. The average size of an Amish farm has declined from several hundred acres in the eighteenth century to less than 50 acres today.

In turn, smaller home farms compel many unemployed

young Amish to seek labor on other farms or in industry. Recent studies in Middlefield, Ohio, reveal that only 47 per cent of the Amish labor force was engaged in full-time agriculture. Employment outside the community exposes the Amish youth to worldly standards and friendships, and to more lucrative modes of livelihood. Even the young person who returns to farming brings an intense awareness of the advantages of modern methods.

It is the formation of cliques, combined with this exposure to outside influences, that generates considerable pressures for change, not only in farming methods but in all other areas of Amish life. This explains why, today, there are several different degrees of departure from standards of the Old Order Amish. In short, adaptation for the Amish has meant a progressive loss of members who have discarded many of the old ways, though many still call themselves Amish.

Dogma in a changing world

The story of the Hutterites and Amish offers a number of interesting things for contemporary man to think about. Two seem outstanding.

First, the impact of population on human affairs is dramatically demonstrated. Population movements do not enter human affairs only in the simplified Malthusian manner of too little food and too many people. Rather the impact of population on human affairs is pre-eminently determined by social organization. For both the Hutterites and Amish their very high levels of population increase have intensified competition with the larger society they prefer to avoid, and have heightened intergroup conflict. Also for both, population increase has violated the primacy of informal, intimate social contact of each with all. This is most clearly seen among today's Amish; many of their people have spread geographically beyond the possibility of regular, daily interaction among all family members.

A similar process operated upon the Hutterities before their American adventure. Today, of course, Hutterites dull the effect of population growth by regularly dividing colonies when cliques arise and tensions become marked. But their conflict with the outside has sprouted the roots of a truly formalized secondary association: they have had to form a national church, with all its undesirable potential for regulation and control. This dynamic effect of population growth on social change seems everywhere unavoidable.

And this leads naturally to the second observation. Man

does not live by ideology alone. Despite the rigid and unreflective character of their doctrines, these two groups have experienced fundamental changes in their social organization. It is this unreflective certainty in the rightness of their doctrines—and the blinders they place on the next generation—that blinds both sects to the dynamic causes of their tribulations and their successes. The Hutterites, for instance, do not attribute the successful revival of their life in America to the economic efficiency of corporate farming, but to God's pleasure in their devotion. By the same token, they are unlikely to view their uncontrolled fertility as a principal factor in the probable unhappy course of future events. Perhaps they reflect a quite general human failing today: our conventional ways of thinking no longer provide rational solutions for contemporary problems of human ecology, such as that of population pressure so well illustrated by the Hutterites and Amish.

MURIEL SCHEIN

ONLY ON SUNDAYS   The 430 inhabitants of Kriovrisi, a remote village high in the Pindus Mountains of northwestern Greece, belong to an ethnic minority know as Koutsovlachs. They are Greek in religion and other major cultural characteristics, not the least of which is the position of women.

Residing in stone houses clustered on a steep mountain slope, the people of Kriovrisi eke out a living from small, barely arable plots in the shallow valley below the village and from overgrazed pastures and pine forests on the surrounding mountainsides. The majority of the men are shepherds, keeping flocks of sheep and goats; the rest farm or engage in miscellaneous occupations. Their work requires a multiplicity of skills, entrepreneurship, travel, and contacts. In contrast, the lives of the women are similar; all perform the basic tasks of cooking, cleaning, clothes making, and child rearing.

The contrast between the diversity of men's labors and the similarity of the women's was brought home to me when my husband and I spent a year studying the lives of the people of Kriovrisi. Despite my urban American background and my specialized training for ethnographic research, I could immediately empathize with the women and discuss problems of household management with them; whereas my husband found that the men's routine activities were not at all like any work he knew, and he had to learn about them from scratch. In both cultures, all females are taught household skills early in their lives; males, however, may have one of a variety of jobs, choosing a specific occupation and learning the requisite skills much later.

Like many others, I have long been interested in this widespread contrast between the lives of men and women. My own concern with women's liberation led me to observe the lives of women in Kriovrisi and to compare them with our own. In my opinion, the conditions underlying women's lives in villages like Kriovrisi and in cities like New York lead ultimately to feelings of discontent among women. Yet I know that Kriovrisi women are content with their lives, and I recognize the validity and appropriateness of their feelings. Current thought tempts one to say that the position of Kriovrisi women results from male oppression. However, although male chauvinism indeed exists in the daily life of Kriovrisi (and of New York City), it is nowhere the cause of female oppression. Seen from afar, the activities and prestige of each sex form parts of a total system. Here, then, we can examine the lives of women in one small village and perhaps understand one part of this system.

In Kriovrisi, a man's achievements—the type of work he does, the degree of financial success, his largesse toward other men—partly determine his own and his wife's social rank. Nonmanual labor is more prestigious than manual labor. The wife of a shepherd or a farmer will at times have to work in the fields or the pastures. Based on this criterion the wives of the village stock merchant, of the village cheese merchant, and of the village secretary rank highest. Most occupations, however, involve manual labor, so that the rest of the villagers are then judged according to their earnings. The merchants are the wealthiest, and shepherds tend to be wealthier than any others.

A further consideration is independence. It is preferable to work for oneself, but a wealthy hired herder will receive more prestige than a poor independent shepherd. The uses to which a man puts his income also affect his rank and, therefore, that of his wife. These uses include meat once a week, wine and liquor for guests, urban-style clothing, a house in good repair, and a secondary school education for his sons. In addition, he must be generous outside his household, treat other men to coffee or drinks in a cafe, and publicly pay large sums to the bands of musicians who come to Kriovrisi on festival days.

The behavior and demeanor of her children, their progress in school, and their prospects for marriage and work also contribute to a woman's position. It is a great disappointment if a woman is childless, but it is considered foolish and animallike to have more than four children. When children are below school age, they are their mothers' special responsibility. Our landlady, Evanthia, told of a time during the Greek civil war (1947–49) when she was alone in her home with her young son when the enemy arrived. She feared for her son's life not only because she loved him but also because if anything had happened to him, "my husband would have killed me."

If children attend school regularly, learn to read, write, and count, and win prizes on the annual day of promotion in June, both they and their parents receive praise. Passing the examination to attend secondary school located in the county seat brings even more honor to parents, especially to mothers. As they mature, children must behave respectfully toward their elders. A well-behaved child, on entering a room or store where people are sitting, always says, "Good-day to you," and "good-bye" on leaving; to omit this will bring forth comments on the child's upbringing. Thus, the low opinion that the village women had of one woman, who was poor and who, with her husband, had once held unpopular political views, was ameliorated somewhat by the educational achievements and good manners of her three sons.

The marriages parents arrange for their children can also bring prestige. If a mother has raised her daughter to be a skilled housekeeper and if a father has amassed a dowry of $2,000 or more, they can find a suitable husband for her, say, a clerk in a town bank. Such a marriage means upward mobility for the daughter and is a tribute to her parents' farsightedness.

A woman's household skills, the final criterion of prestige, also bear on the other criteria, for her children's behavior and her husband's business success depend to some extent on how well she feeds and clothes them. Her house must always be presentable; indeed, cleaning and decoration are frequently done with the thought that "someone might drop in." This standard requires daily airing of rugs and blankets, sweeping, polishing of the glass shades from the kerosene lamps (Kriovrisi has no electricity), and two or three trips to one of the 13 village springs for water. Women take pride in this hard work.

Daily household work includes food preparation. The housewife provides coffee and bread for breakfast, the main meal at noon or one o'clock, and a supper of leftovers and salad at seven or eight o'clock. Because the midday meal is the most important, providing the most nourishment, it requires planning and creativity. As one woman put it after we had finished the midday meal, "Well, that's another day taken care of." A good housewife can feed unexpected guests, and can offer sweets, coffee, and liqueurs to afternoon and Sunday visitors.

In addition to the daily routine, there are other occasional but essential tasks. Women bake all the bread, which constitutes half the diet, a dozen or so loaves at a time. They are very critical of their own and others' bread, often comparing lightness, texture, and taste. Periodically, clothes, blankets, and rugs must be washed and clothing ironed. The industrious housewife collects brushwood to burn in the oven and chops the firewood that her husband or son has brought from the forest. The most fastidious and admired housewives clean their houses thoroughly once a year, usually in June. This can take two or three weeks and involves not only scrubbing and repairing furnishings but also covering the walls with lime, which makes them white and bright and "kills germs."

When all of these maintenance tasks are done, women devote their time to other, more creative work in which they take a great deal of interest, and which provides a more durable basis for prestige. In May or June they begin to wash and dye wool gathered from their own sheep or purchased from shepherds. They spend all their free time spinning. Once the wool is spun, the women knit underwear, socks, and sweaters, or weave blankets and rugs. The older women sometimes make original patterns while the younger women copy designs of rugs that they see in urban magazines. They discuss and compare each other's rugs, most of which are for household use. Only a few of these are sold at the annual bazaar held in the county seat. Married women work on items for their own houses, while unmarried women make their trousseaux.

In part, then, women derive their identity from their work. Men do certain things, women do others. Women take pride in their ability to do necessary work that men and children cannot do for themselves. When Evanthia's sons were leaving on their winter migration with their flocks, her daughter, Amalia, packed their clothes and set aside food. I suggested that the men could do that themselves. Amalia said, "They're men and they don't know how," then added that men are not inclined to do this work and do not want to learn, for it would be inappropriate for them.

A woman gains her identity and prestige primarily from family and household activities. A woman's personal creations, represented, for example, by woven woolen articles, can be worked on only when the major and most time-consuming treadmill tasks of household maintenance are done. Her only other products are her children. It is not surprising, then, that a woman's prestige derives, not from her own achievements, but from those of other members of her household and family line. Even the name that many people know her by is not her own, but her husband's. She takes not only his last name but also his first; if his name is Takis, she is known to his relatives and friends as (Mrs.) Takina.

In contrast, men engage in various business pursuits, and have personal transactions with men from other households, as well as with merchants and government officials outside of Kriovrisi. Their prestige and rank are not limited to household and family, although these are important.

In Kriovrisi, this situation exists because there is no alternative role for women. Not only would few men and women seriously consider other activities as appropriate for women, but the village's economic and social structure does not permit other possibilities. Females are brought up solely to perform the combined role of wife and mother. When a girl is born, the joy at her birth is tinged with disappointment. Although all children are valued, sons affirm their fathers' masculinity. Furthermore, daughters are an economic burden. Sons bring in money in the form of a wife's dowry, daughters take it away for their dowries.

Young girls are encouraged to perform womanly tasks. By the time they are six, they learn to spin, using a stick and a bit of old wool their mothers have given them. Two or three will stand on a pathway, in perfect imitation of their mothers, spinning and talking. Both boys and girls begin school at age six, but six grades are considered sufficient for girls. They will, after all, marry; secondary education is not necessary for that. In Kriovrisi only 4 girls out of 62 unmarried girls of the appropriate age were attending secondary school or a university in 1967–68. It is a different matter for boys, who are encouraged to go on to the six-year high school if they can. Since not all boys can make a decent living in the village, an education is important for it may lead to economic and social mobility outside the village. Although schooling is free, the student must pay for room and board in the town. While some return on this investment can be expected for males, this expense would be a waste for females who need the money for dowries. In addition, the income an educated boy can earn helps to dower his sister.

So girls finish school at age 12. Having learned to sweep, fetch water, and care for young children, they now begin to weave and knit. They practice by knitting heavy sweaters or weaving saddle blankets and pack bags from coarse wool. After a year or so, they start to use finer wool to weave the rugs, blankets, and pillow covers that will form part of their trousseaux. At 13 or 14, they begin to take over the heavier household tasks, while their mothers do the cooking.

During these years, girls spend most of their time with other girls, a pattern that they will continue for the rest of their lives. In Kriovrisi, the separation of space into male and female worlds is not as sharp as in some Greek villages, where women are forbidden to enter cafes, but it exists. Males, when not working, relax in cafes or near the village office with other males. A female spends any free moment she has with other females in or near the house. This leisure is always busy leisure. On most occasions, a woman's hands are occupied with some useful work. As Evanthia said, "If I sit with my hands empty, I feel I've done nothing; but if I spin, at least I've eked out a few cents." Friends will spin or weave together, they may help each other work, or they may bake a cake together. It is only on Sundays that their hands are free from labor for an hour or two; then after church, they will walk around the village together, dressed in their finest.

Public contacts between young men and women are limited. Again, on Sundays, they may meet, perhaps during their stroll. On festival occasions, when a gypsy band visits the village, boys and girls do traditional dances together.

At this time, the parents are arranging the girls' marriages. Only recently have a few girls begun to choose their mates. Parents look first among the best families of Kriovrisi, thus insuring that their daughters will remain nearby, and that the bride and her in-laws will not be strangers to each other. More and more often, however, because of the population decline in Kriovrisi, they must ask friends and relatives outside the village to find mates. When a suitable mate is found, both sets of parents negotiate the dowry, and the marriage ceremony takes place soon afterward.

After marriage, the male-female separation may continue, depending on the type of household that the bride and groom establish. There are two major kinds of households: the nuclear family, composed of a married couple and their children; and the stem family, composed of a married couple, their son, and his wife and children. Most households begin as stem families, becoming nuclear if the two couples quarrel and separate or if the elders die. In such households the division of labor between males and females tends to have more daily importance than the conjugal ties.

In 1968, Ioannis, a young shepherd from Kriovrisi, married Sophia, a girl from another village. She moved into his household, comprised of his parents and his four sisters. After the wedding, Sophia and Ioannis rarely appeared together. He was either in the pastures with the sheep or in a cafe with other young men. She was always in the company of at least one sister-in-law or other female relative.

The bride begins a second phase of her education when she marries. Sophia's mother-in-law, Anna, and sisters-in-law were, for example, teaching Sophia how to spin, a skill that for some reason she had never acquired. At first Sophia did the heavy work and only such minor cooking tasks as making salad, while Anna did most of the cooking. The bride gradually learns the finer aspects of cooking. This is considered wise and proper, for there is an old story about a woman who wanted her daughter-in-law to do all the cooking. The daughter-in-law did, but because she came from a wealthier household, she used only butter and no oil in her cooking. Soon the woman discovered that there was no butter left, and from then on she did all her own cooking.

In her new household, the bride is subject to the authority of her husband and of her in-laws, both male and female. Among the women, a division of labor and a hierarchy of authority develops. In this particular household, Anna was in charge; of her four daughters, the eldest (20 years old) was second in command and directed the other three, as well as Sophia, in their tasks.

The relationship between mother-in-law and daughter-in-law tends to be fraught with tensions, as attested to by the many jokes that women tell. It seems that daughters-in-law are expected to be lazy. Once when I was standing with my arms folded, our landlady, Evanthia, said to me, "Why are you standing with your arms like that? Do you think you're a new daughter-in-law?" The bride must learn to perform household tasks in a way that pleases her mother-in-law. If she is strong-willed, then fights are likely to ensue.

The newly married woman may also have to deal with the contradictions between her roles as wife and as daughter-in-law. As a wife, her status complements that of her husband; as a daughter-in-law, her status supplements and competes with that of her mother-in-law. This may cause severe conflicts in some households, as when mother-in-law and daughter-in-law disagree on how money should be spent. Women have a great deal of control over economic matters within the household. In Kriovrisi, the mother-in-law can retain this control even after her son has married and, in some cases, even after her own husband, the nominal household head, has relinquished his power or has died.

A few households in Kriovrisi were notorious for fights between mother-in-law and daughter-in-law. In one of them, Argorou, the mother-in-law, who was 78 years old and half-blind, ended the argument by gratuitously proclaiming, "All right, I'll leave. Just give me some bread and cheese and I'll go away. Don't worry about me." Her daughter-in-law, Olga, was put in the position of having asked Argorou to leave, which she had not done. Olga came to tell our landlady the story of the fight. After she left, I asked Evanthia why these fights happened. Smiling slyly, she said, "Her husband likes his mother too much." We talked some more about the problem, and it emerged that Olga had no choice, for village women view a bad husband or mother-in-law as just the luck of the game and feel they can do nothing about it. Evanthia sat silent for a moment, then said, "But, still, it's not right. Olga should be treated better than that. Even a daughter-in-law is human."

In many cases, the women live together amicably and provide company for each other in a way that prevents their work from becoming the alientating experience it can be for women living in nuclear families like our own. The division of labor among females also permits the multitude of tasks to be done efficiently. In addition, within the context of her role, a woman has much to look forward to, for one day her life will be easier; she will have a daughter or daughter-in-law to do the heavy work, she will cook, she will play with her grandchildren, and she will have the right, as a mother-in-law, to sit and do nothing, if she wishes, but talk with old friends for an afternoon hour.

There are many resemblances between this situation and that of other societies, including our own industrialized, urban society. The sexual division of labor, based on the long maturation period of human offspring, is a social adaptation, probably as old as human society, that has enabled human groups to survive. Since females must care for the young, their mobility is restricted. While males can range farther afield, females stay fairly close to the place of residence, caring for it and also engaging in food-getting activities that do not take them far away. A division of labor among females, such as described for Kriovrisi, allows greater efficiency in the pursuit of these activities. Likewise, among males who engage in various means of livelihood, cooperation and specialization between two or more males also renders food-getting more efficient.

Changes are slow to take place in this division of labor, which underlies so many other social patterns. Despite time- and energy-saving devices, such as wood-burning stoves and, more recently, propane gas burners instead of fireplaces, liquid dish detergent (as Evanthia said, "Things are much easier with 'Thrill'"), and ready-made clothes instead of homespun, the role of women seems to have changed little since the nineteenth century, at least as it is portrayed by the old women of Kriovrisi today. A woman's basic tasks are the same, the separation of male and female worlds continues, and the working of wool continues to absorb any excess time or energy.

It is only in cities that change can occur. There are girls, whose parents were born in Kriovrisi and later emigrated to a city, who now go to secondary school and the university. One such girl, the daughter of an Athens cheese merchant, went to a French private school there and attended law school. Another attends the university in Ioannina. The urban environment provides jobs suitable for women, such as teaching positions, secretarial jobs, or sales positions. In Kriovrisi, there is room for only one teacher (a male) and no business concern needs women.

In the city, major technological changes enable women to spend much less time and energy at household tasks. All clothes are ready-made. Running water and electricity, laundromats and prepared foods decrease much of the household labor. These changes permit the nuclear family to predominate, for one woman can do all the necessary tasks with time to spare.

In Greece, as in the United States, women in cities are beginning to be discontent with, and to question, traditional roles. Maria, a 45-year-old woman from Kriovrisi, lived with her husband in Ioannina, a city of some 40,000 people, and had a 15-year-old daughter studying to be a French teacher. Maria felt that "in Greece, women have no value; their work is considered to be worthless, and the work itself is hard." Her husband disagreed, adding that "perhaps village women have to work hard, but it is different in the city." Perhaps the difficulty Maria felt, living in the city, was the loneliness of solitary household work; perhaps it was also her awareness of the increased opportunities that were open to her daughter.

Urban women, however, feel pressure not to work outside the household. Many men feel dishonored if their wives work, and women feel that once they have children they would be neglecting their duties if they went to work. These attitudes reflect both an economy unable to provide adequate work even for its male population and the prevailing ideology of appropriate male and female roles. In 1967 a popular song, "The Girls Who Go Two by Two," dramatized the confined role of Greek women:

Young girls in pairs
passing by,
shy and embarrassed
the young girls hurry by.
Young girls looking in the
mirror, the mirror.
Every night secretly they watch
themselves getting older
with fear in their hearts.
Young girls are so so pretty,
so so unlucky.
You see the ugliness of
their parents.
They'll pay for it very dearly.
One day, dejected, they'll
stand before the altar.
Their mothers will cry,
relatives, in-laws.
The unlucky girls have
nothing more to say.

In Kriovrisi, what little questioning there is does not go far. Zoe, 23 years old, lives with her husband, her mother-in-law, and a year-old daughter. She is much put-upon by both her husband and her mother-in-law. Her husband yells at her at the slightest excuse and continually gives her orders. Her mother-in-law constantly criticizes her work. One winter day after a heavy snowfall, the stove, for some reason, would not work. We were all cold and uncomfortable. Zoe's brother had been married a few days before, and she wanted to visit him and his bride on the other side of the village. But her mother-in-law forbade her to go. Her baby was crying a lot because she had just been weaned. In exasperation, Zoe said to me, "Don't ever become a mother. It's not worth it." Six months later, when the weather was warm, I went to visit her. Zoe's daughter was playing on the floor of a sunny room in a new house. Zoe told me she was pregnant, and although she would have preferred to wait another year, she was very happy about it. "You should have children," she said. "But you told me never to become a mother," I reminded her. "I didn't mean it," she said. "We should marry, have children, and raise them. What else are we put on earth for?"

PART FIVE

RELIGION AND RITUAL

Shamanism

Religious behavior and belief constitute an area of human activity that is often intensely subjective and may involve seemingly bizarre actions. Because of this element of subjectivity, magic and religion are difficult to approach in a scientific manner. At present a rising general interest in hallucinogenic drug taking and the occult both lend themselves to sensationalism and misinterpretation. How can the anthropologist discover and present a balanced picture of emotionally charged subjects such as ritual, sorcery, magic, and witchcraft? Anthropologist John Middleton asserts that:

... beliefs in magic and in witchcraft are integral parts of cultural life and can therefore be understood only in their total social context. They have a coherent logic of their own, given certain premises as to the mystical powers of certain human beings (even though "scientifically" these premises may not be correct). These beliefs provide explanations for coincidence and disaster, they enable individuals to project their hopes, fears and disappointments onto other human beings, and by thus personalizing the forces of what we might call "fate" or "chance" enable those afflicted by them to deal with them by direct social action . . .[1]

In Michael J. Harner's "The Sound of Rushing Water" and in Richard Borshay Lee's "Trance Cure of the !Kung Bushmen" we meet a religious functionary generally referred to by anthropologists as the *shaman*. The term "shaman" derives ultimately from the Tungus-speaking peoples of eastern Siberia and refers there to a part-time magician and curer who acquired his power directly from a supernatural source without the aid of an established church. The practice of shamanism often involves the use of complicated sleight-of-hand and optical illusion, especially in curing activities. Among certain North American Indians, for example, the shaman may be inspired during a trance to "see" the illness inside the patient's body, which he then "extracts" through sucking or other manipulations. Eventually he produces an object— perhaps a small lizard or a feather—in his hand, which he will claim was the sickness that he has now removed. Presumably, then, the patient recovers. Even for anthropologists familiar with the ways of shamans it is impossible to say with certainty whether this behavior is always the crass flummery that it seems to be. French anthropologist Claude Lévi-Strauss suggests that in presenting such a performance the shaman is reliving certain events in the same deeply personal way that a patient undergoing psychoanalysis relives the crucial events that led to his disturbance.[2] Yet there are cases, too, of shamans who carry out these performances in a completely cynical and premeditated manner.

Among the Jívaro Indians described by Harner there can be little doubt of the sincerity and conviction on the part of the shaman, particularly because of the use of the hallucinogenic drug *ayahuasca*. The anthropologist sampled this drug and experienced many of the sensations reported by his shaman informants. So vivid are these sensations that the Jívaro believe the drug-induced state to be the real world, with the conscious world of everyday life only an illusion. Despite the seemingly mystical character of these sensations, the behavior and shared attitudes of Jívaro shamans are highly structured, particularly around the use and misuse of *tsentsak* (mystical darts possessed by a potent shaman). This reliance on drug taking characterizes shamanism in many American Indian societies, but it is not universal. Most shamanism, however, does involve a trancelike state during which the practitioner identifies illnesses and accomplishes other supernatural tasks. The !Kung Bushmen do not use drugs, yet through intense mental concentration and physical exertion they are able to enter a trance (called "half-death"). Shamans achieve this state in order to transmit curative properties to the patient or to achieve a kind of x-ray vision to "see" the sex of unborn children. Bushman trance curing differs from shamanism as is usually understood in that it requires the cooperative efforts of a group of dancers to enable a person to enter the trance; in fact, "true" or typical shamanism may consist only of variations on general themes in different cultures such as the need for a trancelike state or the extraction and removal of illness-inducing substances. In societies such as that of the Jívaro, shamans can practice harmful magic (witchcraft) against certain victims; in others, such as that of the Bushmen, this practice is rare and relatively unimportant. In both Jívaro and Bushman society certain kinds of generally similar behavior are used to achieve personally satisfying physical and emotional states; these kinds of behavior—varying considerably in specific detail within each culture but with certain common elements—are found in many other "churchless" cultures as well. The principal utility of the concept of shamanism lies not so much in whether it is identical in all societies that practice it as in the opportunity a concept such as this offers for understanding social as well as individual bases of religious behavior even in cultures with no established church.

Syncretism

Unlike the Jívaro and the Bushmen, the Zulus of South Africa and the Indian tin miners of Bolivia have a long history of contact and interaction with Europeans. In each case traditional rituals and beliefs have been modified and in some cases blended with introduced elements of Christianity. This process of compromise is usually referred to by students of religion as *syncretism*, although anthropologists have sometimes used the term *stimulus diffusion* to describe this process as it applies to wider areas of cultural activity outside religion. In cases of stimulus diffusion, the general concept of a particular cultural activity is transmitted from one group to another without a transfer of the precise details of that activity.[3] In such cases cultures are highly selective in the traits they choose to adopt, and they usually invent or adapt new content for the new activities. The result is sometimes a completely new set of cultural activities that help people adapt to the changed conditions of their surroundings. New religions, cults, rituals, and systems of belief may evolve in this manner. And this process of evolution has been especially rapid where traditional societies have been contacted (and in most cases, exploited) by industrialized Western societies.

James W. Fernandez ("Zulu Zionism") points out many examples of syncretism in his account of the evangelical movements in South Africa: The use of circles as religious symbols (representing the intimacy of traditional round Zulu houses and cattle kraals), the identification of the Holy Spirit with the traditional Zulu cult of the dead, and immersion in sea water (similar to traditional Zulu purification) are some. The general impression is that these rituals are less Christian than they look. The familiar ingredients of evangelical Christianity are there (white robes, crosses, laying on of hands, baptism, and so forth), but they form an overall pattern that is neither completely Christian nor traditionally Zulu. As Fernandez showed, in 1971 Zionism was a new religion that helped the Zulus to adapt to the impoverishment and disadvantages of life in apartheid South Africa.

The deep Bolivian tin mines provide the setting for an even more dramatic religious adjustment in June Nash's account, "Devils, Witches, and Sudden Death." Bolivian Indians were miners before the arrival of Europeans, but with the machinery of modern technology they dig deeper than ever and experience dangers and circumstances more frightening than ever. Syncretism is present here, too, as in the merger of certain Catholic deities with traditional figures (the Inca maiden, Nusta, for example, is identified with the Virgin of the Mineshaft). The devil is Tio, and Nash's account revolves around the offerings made to Tio by the miners to appease his appetite for human flesh. As Nash points out, "most miners reject the claim that belief in the Tio is pagan sacrilege. They feel that no contradiction exists, since time and place for offerings to the devil are clearly defined and separated from Christian ritual." In fact, the miners see their sacrifices to Tio as a mark of their religious sincerity and true devotion to God. A Catholic priest or theologian might not agree with this sentiment, but the Bolivian mineshafts are a long way from Rome. For the miners joint participation in these rituals of sacrifice offers a chance for peace of mind under conditions of constant stress, and after reading Nash's account one cannot help but wonder if more formalized churchly behavior would accomplish this as effectively.

Both the Zulus of South Africa and the Bolivian tin miners have blended traditional religious elements with those of introduced Christianity to provide new patterns that are personally satisfying under conditions of economic and physical stress. In each case the anthropologist has provided a valid scientific account of religion as an adaptive social process.

Notes

1 John Middleton, *Magic, Witchcraft, and Curing*, New York, Natural History Press, 1967, p. x.
2 Claude Lévi-Strauss, "The Sorcerer and his Magic," in *Structural Anthropology*, New York, Basic Books, 1963, p. 181.
3 A. L. Kroeber, "Stimulus Diffusion," *American Anthropologist*, vol. 42, 1940, pp. 1–20.

MICHAEL J. HARNER

THE SOUND OF RUSHING WATER He had drunk, and now he softly sang. Gradually, faint lines and forms began to appear in the darkness, and the shrill music of the *tsentsak*, the spirit helpers, arose around him. The power of the drink fed them. He called, and they came. First, *pangi*, the anaconda, coiled about his head, transmuted into a crown of gold. Then *wampang*, the giant butterfly, hovered above his shoulder and sang to him with its wings. Snakes, spiders, birds, and bats danced in the air above him. On his arms appeared a thousand eyes as his demon helpers emerged to search the night for enemies.

The sound of rushing water filled his ears, and listening to its roar, he knew he possessed the power of *tsungi*, the first shaman. Now he could see. Now he could find the truth. He stared at the stomach of the sick man. Slowly, it became transparent like a shallow mountain stream, and he saw within it, coiling and uncoiling, *makanchi*, the poisonous serpent, who had been sent by the enemy shaman. The real cause of the illness had been found.

The Jívaro Indians of the Ecuadorian Amazon believe that witchcraft is the cause of the vast majority of illnesses and nonviolent deaths. The normal waking life, for the Jívaro, is simply "a lie," or illusion, while the true forces that determine daily events are supernatural and can only be seen and manipulated with the aid of hallucinogenic drugs. A reality view of this kind creates a particularly strong demand for specialists who can cross over into the supernatural world at will to deal with the forces that influence and even determine the events of the waking life.

These specialists, called "shamans" by anthropologists, are recognized by the Jívaro as being of two types: bewitching shamans or curing shamans. Both kinds take a hallucinogenic drink, whose Jívaro name is *natema*, in order to enter the supernatural world. This brew, commonly called *yagé*, or *yajé*, in Colombia, *ayahuasca* (Inca "vine of the dead") in Ecuador and Peru, and *caapi* in Brazil, is prepared from segments of a species of the vine *Banisteriopsis*, a genus belonging to the Malpighiaceae. The Jívaro boil it with the leaves of a similar vine, which probably is also a species of *Banisteriopsis*, to produce a tea that contains the powerful hallucinogenic alkaloids harmaline, harmine, d-tetrahydroharmine, and quite possibly dimethyltryptamine (DMT). These compounds have chemical structures and effects similar, but not identical, to LSD, mescaline of the peyote cactus, and psilocybin of the psychotropic Mexican mushroom.

When I first undertook research among the Jívaro in 1956–57, I did not fully appreciate the psychological impact of the *Banisteriopsis* drink upon the native view of reality, but in 1961 I had occasion to drink the hallucinogen in the course of field work with another Upper Amazon Basin tribe. For several hours after drinking the brew, I found myself, although awake, in a world literally beyond my wildest dreams. I met bird-headed people, as well as dragon-like creatures who explained that they were the true gods of this world. I enlisted the services of other spirit helpers in attempting to fly through the far reaches of the Galaxy. Transported into a trance where the supernatural seemed natural, I realized that anthropologists, including myself, had profoundly underestimated the importance of the drug in affecting native ideology. Therefore, in 1964 I returned to the Jívaro to give particular attention to the drug's use by the Jívaro shaman.

The use of the hallucinogenic *natema* drink among the Jívaro makes it possible for almost anyone to achieve the trance state essential for the practice of shamanism. Given the presence of the drug and the felt need to contact the "real," or supernatural, world, it is not surprising that approximately one out of every four Jívaro men is a shaman. Any adult, male or female, who desires to become such a practitioner, simply presents a gift to an already practicing shaman, who administers the *Banisteriopsis* drink and gives some of his own supernatural power—in the form of spirit helpers, or *tsentsak*—to the apprentice. These spirit helpers, or "darts," are the main supernatural forces believed to cause illness and death in daily life. To the non-shaman they are normally invisible, and even shamans can perceive them only under the influence of *natema*.

Shamans send these spirit helpers into the victims' bodies to make them ill or to kill them. At other times, they may suck spirits sent by enemy shamans from the bodies of tribesmen suffering from witchcraft-induced illness. The spirit helpers also form shields that protect their shaman masters from attacks. The following account presents the ideology of Jívaro witchcraft from the point of view of the Indians themselves.

To give the novice some *tsentsak*, the practicing shaman regurgitates what appears to be—to those who have taken *natema*—a brilliant substance in which the spirit helpers are contained. He cuts part of it off with a machete and gives it to the novice to swallow. The recipient experiences pain upon taking it into his stomach and stays on his bed for ten days, repeatedly drinking *natema*. The Jívaro believe they can keep magical darts in their stomachs indefinitely and regurgitate them at will. The shaman donating the *tsentsak* periodically blows and rubs all over the body of the novice, apparently to increase the power of the transfer.

The novice must remain inactive and not engage in sexual intercourse for at least three months. If he fails in self-discipline, as some do, he will not become a successful shaman. At the end of the first month, a *tsentsak* emerges from his mouth. With this magical dart at his disposal, the new shaman experiences a tremendous desire to bewitch. If he casts his *tsentsak* to fulfill this desire, he will become a bewitching shaman. If, on the other hand, the novice can control his impulse and reswallow this first *tsentsak*, he will become a curing shaman.

If the shaman who gave the *tsentsak* to the new man was primarily a bewitcher, rather than a curer, the novice likewise will tend to become a bewitcher. This is because a bewitcher's magical darts have such a desire to kill that their new owner will be strongly inclined to adopt their attitude. One informant said that the urge to kill felt by bewitching shamans came to them with a strength and frequency similar to that of hunger.

Only if the novice shaman is able to abstain from sexual intercourse for five months, will he have the power to kill a man (if he is a bewitcher) or cure a victim (if he is a curer). A full year's abstinence is considered necessary to become a really effective bewitcher or curer.

During the period of sexual abstinence, the new shaman collects all kinds of insects, plants, and other objects, which he now has the power to convert into *tsentsak*. Almost any object, including living insects and worms, can become a *tsentsak* if it is small enough to be swallowed by a shaman. Different types of *tsentsak* are used to cause different kinds and degrees of illness. The greater the variety of these objects that a shaman has in his body, the greater is his ability.

According to Jívaro concepts, each *tsentsak* has a natural and supernatural aspect. The magical dart's natural aspect is

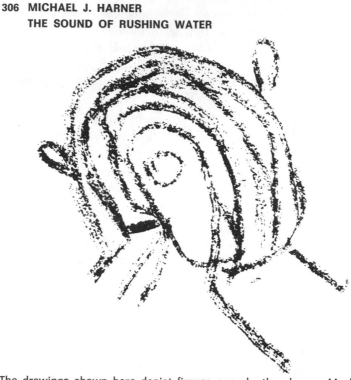

The drawings shown here depict figures seen by the shaman Mashu
while under the power of the powerful *Banisteriopsis* drink, *natema*.
Above is the head of a jaguar that appeared in one of Mashu's visions.
The shaman, who had never drawn before, used pencil and paper
supplied by the author.

Whenever the shaman is curing or bewitching, his head remains
covered by this halo-like crown. The crown can be seen by those
drinking *natema*, but remains hidden from other onlookers.

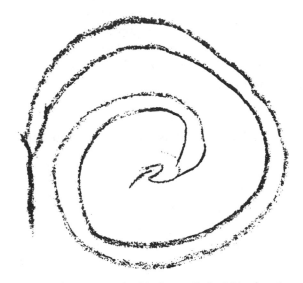

This snake *tsentsak* was seen by Mashu, coiled within the stomach of one of his patients. To work his cure, Mashu then sucked this supernatural essence from the patient's abdomen.

Many times the Christian missionary had told Mashu of the devil feared by white men. But since he had never seen the spirit, Mashu remained skeptical. Some time later, after drinking *natema*, Mashu was confronted by this figure of the "white man's devil." Since that time, Mashu has remained convinced of this spirit's reality.

that of an ordinary material object as seen without drinking the drug *natema*. But the supernatural and "true" aspect of the *tsentsak* is revealed to the shaman by taking *natema*. When he does this, the magical darts appear in new forms as demons and with new names. In their supernatural aspects, the *tsentsak* are not simply objects but spirit helpers in various forms, such as giant butterflies, jaguars, or monkeys, who actively assist the shaman in his tasks.

Bewitching is carried out against a specific, known individual and thus is almost always done to neighbors or, at the most, fellow tribesmen. Normally, as is the case with intratribal assassination, bewitching is done to avenge a particular offense committed against one's family or friends. Both bewitching and individual assassination contrast with the large-scale headhunting raids for which the Jívaro have become famous, and which were conducted against entire neighborhoods of enemy tribes.

To bewitch, the shaman takes *natema* and secretly approaches the house of his victim. Just out of sight in the forest, he drinks green tobacco juice, enabling him to regurgitate a *tsentsak*, which he throws at his victim as he comes out of his house. If the *tsentsak* is strong enough and is thrown with sufficient force, it will pass all the way through the victim's body causing death within a period of a few days to several weeks. More often, however, the magical dart simply lodges in the victim's body. If the shaman, in his hiding place, fails to see the intended victim, he may instead bewitch any member of the intended victim's family who appears, usually a wife or child. When the shaman's mission is accomplished, he returns secretly to his own home.

One of the distinguishing characteristics of the bewitching process among the Jívaro is that, as far as I could learn, the victim is given no specific indication that someone is bewitching him. The bewitcher does not want his victim to be aware that he is being supernaturally attacked, lest he take protective measures by immediately procuring the services of a curing shaman. Nonetheless, shamans and laymen alike with whom I talked noted that illness invariably follows the bewitchment, although the degree of the illness can vary considerably.

A special kind of spirit helper, called a *pasuk*, can aid the bewitching shaman by remaining near the victim in the guise of an insect or animal of the forest after the bewitcher has left.

This spirit helper has his own objects to shoot into the victim should a curing shaman succeed in sucking out the *tsentsak* sent earlier by the bewitcher who is the owner of the *pasuk*.

In addition, the bewitcher can enlist the aid of a *wakani* ("soul" or "spirit") bird. Shamans have the power to call these birds and use them as spirit helpers in bewitching victims. The shaman blows on the *wakani* birds and then sends them to the house of the victim to fly around and around the man, frightening him. This is believed to cause fever and insanity, with death resulting shortly thereafter.

After he returns home from bewitching, the shaman may send a *wakani* bird to perch near the house of the victim. Then if a curing shaman sucks out the intruding object, the bewitching shaman sends the *wakani* bird more *tsentsak* to throw from its beak into the victim. By continually resupplying the *wakani* bird with new *tsentsak*, the sorcerer makes it impossible for the curer to rid his patient permanently of the magical darts.

While the *wakani* birds are supernatural servants available to anyone who wishes to use them, the *pasuk*, chief among the spirit helpers, serves only a single shaman. Likewise a shaman possesses only one *pasuk*. The *pasuk*, being specialized for the service of bewitching, has a protective shield to guard it from counterattack by the curing shaman. The curing shaman, under the influence of *natema*, sees the *pasuk* of the bewitcher in human form and size, but "covered with iron except for its eyes." The curing shaman can kill this *pasuk* only by shooting a *tsentsak* into its eyes, the sole vulnerable area in the *pasuk's* armor. To the person who has not taken the hallucinogenic drink, the *pasuk* usually appears to be simply a tarantula.

Shamans also may kill or injure a person by using magical darts, *anamuk*, to create supernatural animals that attack a victim. If a shaman has a small, pointed armadillo bone *tsentsak*, he can shoot this into a river while the victim is crossing it on a balsa raft or in a canoe. Under the water, this bone manifests itself in its supernatural aspect as an anaconda, which rises up and overturns the craft, causing the victim to drown. The shaman can similarly use a tooth from a killed snake as a *tsentsak*, creating a poisonous serpent to bite his victim. In more or less the same manner, shamans can create jaguars and pumas to kill their victims.

About five years after receiving his *tsentsak*, a bewitching shaman undergoes a test to see if he still retains enough *tsentsak* power to continue to kill successfully. This test involves bewitching a tree. The shaman, under the influence of *natema*, attempts to throw a *tsentsak* through the tree at the point where its two main branches join. If his strength and aim are adequate, the tree appears to split the moment the *tsentsak* is sent into it. The splitting, however, is invisible to an observer who is not under the influence of the hallucinogen. If the shaman fails, he knows that he is incapable of killing a human victim. This means that, as soon as possible, he must go to a strong shaman and purchase a new supply of *tsentsak*. Until he has the goods with which to pay for this new supply, he is in constant danger, in his proved weakened condition, of being seriously bewitched by other shamans. Therefore, each day, he drinks large quantities of *natema*, tobacco juice, and the extract of yet another drug, *pirípiri*. He also rests on his bed at home to conserve his strength, but tries to conceal his weakened condition from his enemies. When he purchases a new supply of *tsentsak*, he can safely cut down on his consumption of these other substances.

The degree of illness produced in a witchcraft victim is a function of both the force with which the *tsentsak* is shot into the body, and also of the character of the magical dart itself. If a *tsentsak* is shot all the way through the body of a victim, then "there is nothing for a curing shaman to suck out," and the patient dies. If the magical dart lodges within the body, however, it is theoretically possible to cure the victim by sucking. But in actual practice, the sucking is not always considered successful.

The work of the curing shaman is complementary to that of a bewitcher. When a curing shaman is called in to treat a patient, his first task is to see if the illness is due to witchcraft. The usual diagnosis and treatment begin with the curing shaman drinking *natema*, tobacco juice, and *pirípiri* in the late afternoon and early evening. These drugs permit him to see into the body of the patient as though it were glass. If the illness is due to sorcery, the curing shaman will see the intruding object within the patient's body clearly enough to determine whether or not he can cure the sickness.

A shaman sucks magical darts from a patient's body only at night, and in a dark area of the house, for it is only in the dark that he can perceive the drug-induced visions that are the supernatural reality. With the setting of the sun, he alerts his *tsentsak* by whistling the tune of the curing song; after about a quarter of an hour, he starts singing. When he is ready to suck, the shaman regurgitates two *tsentsak* into the sides of his throat and mouth. These must be identical to the one he has seen in the patient's body. He holds one of these in the front of the mouth and the other in the rear. They are expected to catch the supernatural aspect of the magical dart that the shaman sucks out of the patient's body. The *tsentsak* nearest the shaman's lips is supposed to incorporate the sucked-out *tsentsak* essence within itself. If, however, this supernatural essence should get past it, the second magical dart in the mouth blocks the throat so that the intruder cannot enter the interior of the shaman's body. If the curer's two *tsentsak* were to fail to catch the supernatural essence of the *tsentsak*, it would pass down into the shaman's stomach and kill him. Trapped thus within the mouth, this essence is shortly caught by, and incorporated into, the material substance of one of the curing shaman's *tsentsak*. He then "vomits" out this object and displays it to the patient and his family saying, "Now I have sucked it out. Here it is."

The non-shamans think that the material object itself is what has been sucked out, and the shaman does not disillusion them. At the same time, he is not lying, because he knows that the only important thing about a *tsentsak* is its supernatural aspect, or essence, which he sincerely believes he has removed from the patient's body. To explain to the layman that he already had these objects in his mouth would serve no fruitful purpose and would prevent him from displaying such an object as proof that he had effected the cure. Without incontrovertible evidence, he would not be able to convince the patient and his family that he had effected the cure and must be paid.

The ability of the shaman to suck depends largely upon the quantity and strength of his own *tsentsak*, of which he may have hundreds. His magical darts assume their supernatural aspect as spirit helpers when he is under the influence of *natema*, and he sees them as a variety of zoomorphic forms hovering over him, perching on his shoulders, and sticking out of his skin. He sees them helping to suck the patient's body. He must drink tobacco juice every few hours to "keep them fed" so that they will not leave him.

The curing shaman must also deal with any *pasuk* that may be in the patient's vicinity for the purpose of casting more darts. He drinks additional amounts of *natema* in order to see them and engages in *tsentsak* duels with them if they are present. While the *pasuk* is enclosed in iron armor, the shaman himself has his own armor composed of his many *tsentsak*. As long as he is under the influence of *natema*, these magical darts cover his body as a protective shield, and are on the lookout for any enemy *tsentsak* headed toward their master. When these *tsentsak* see such a missile coming, they immediately close up together at the point where the enemy dart is attempting to penetrate, and thereby repel it.

If the curer finds *tsentsak* entering the body of his patient after he has killed *pasuk*, he suspects the presence of a *wakani* bird. The shaman drinks *maikua* (*Datura* sp.), a hallucinogen even more powerful than *natema*, as well as tobacco juice, and silently sneaks into the forest to hunt and kill the bird with *tsentsak*. When he succeeds, the curer returns to the patient's home, blows all over the house to get rid of the "atmosphere" created by the numerous *tsentsak* sent by the bird, and completes his sucking of the patient. Even after all the *tsentsak* are extracted, the shaman may remain another night at the house to suck out any "dirtiness" (*pahuri*) still inside. In the cures which I have witnessed, this sucking is a most noisy process, accompanied by deep, but dry, vomiting.

After sucking out a *tsentsak*, the shaman puts it into a little container. He does not swallow it because it is not his own magical dart and would therefore kill him. Later, he throws the *tsentsak* into the air, and it flies back to the shaman who sent it originally into the patient. *Tsentsak* also fly back to a shaman at the death of a former apprentice who had originally received them from him. Besides receiving "old" magical darts unexpectedly in this manner, the shaman may have *tsentsak* thrown at him by a bewitcher. Accordingly, shamans constantly drink tobacco juice at all hours of the day and night. Although the tobacco juice is not truly hallucinogenic, it produces a narcotized state, which is believed necessary to keep one's *tsentsak* ready to repel any other magical darts. A shaman does not even dare go for a walk without taking along the green tobacco leaves with which he prepares the juice that keeps his spirit helpers alert. Less frequently, but regularly, he must drink *natema* for the same purpose and to keep in touch with the supernatural reality.

While curing under the influence of *natema*, the curing shaman "sees" the shaman who bewitched his patient. Generally, he can recognize the person, unless it is a shaman who lives far away or in another tribe. The patient's family knows this, and demands to be told the identity of the bewitcher, particularly if the sick person dies. At one curing session I attended, the shaman could not identify the person he had seen in his vision. The brother of the dead man then accused the shaman himself of being responsible. Under such pressure, there is a strong tendency for the curing shaman to attribute each case to a particular bewitcher.

Shamans gradually become weak and must purchase *tsentsak* again and again. Curers tend to become weak in power, especially after curing a patient bewitched by a shaman who has recently received a new supply of magical darts. Thus, the most powerful shamans are those who can repeatedly purchase new supplies of *tsentsak* from other shamans.

Shamans can take back *tsentsak* from others to whom they have previously given them. To accomplish this, the shaman drinks *natema*, and, using his *tsentsak*, creates a "bridge" in the form of a rainbow between himself and the other shaman. Then he shoots a *tsentsak* along this rainbow. This strikes the ground beside the other shaman with an explosion and flash likened to a lightning bolt. The purpose of this is to surprise the other shaman so that he temporarily forgets to maintain his guard over his magical darts, thus permitting the other shaman to suck them back along the rainbow. A shaman who has had his *tsentsak* taken away in this manner will discover that "nothing happens" when he drinks *natema*. The sudden loss of his *tsentsak* will tend to make him ill, but ordinarily the illness is not fatal unless a bewitcher shoots a magical dart into him while he is in this weakened condition. If he has not become disillusioned by his experience, he can again purchase *tsentsak* from some other shaman and resume his calling. Fortunately for anthropology some of these men have chosen to give up shamanism and therefore can be persuaded to reveal their knowledge, no longer having a vested interest in the profession. This divulgence, however, does not serve as a significant threat to practitioners, for words alone can never adequately convey the realities of shamanism. These can only be approached with the aid of *natema*, the chemical door to the invisible world of the Jívaro shaman.

RICHARD BORSHAY LEE

TRANCE CURE OF THE !KUNG BUSHMEN *"Bushman medicine is put into the body through the backbone. It boils in my belly and boils up to my head like beer. When the women start singing and I start dancing, at first I feel quite all right. Then in the middle, the medicine begins to rise from my stomach. After that I see all the people like very small birds, the whole place will be spinning around and that is why we run around. The trees will be circling also. You feel your blood become very hot just like blood boiling on a fire and then you start healing. When I am like this [telling the story] I am just a person. The thing comes up after a dance, then when I lay hands on a sick person, the medicine in me will go into him and cure him."*

The speaker, whose words I have translated, is a Bushman. The !Kung Bushmen, a non-Bantu, click-speaking (the exclamation point stands for a click sound) people of the Kalahari Desert in Botswana, are one of the last peoples of the world to maintain a hunting and gathering way of life—until 10,000 years ago, the universal mode of human organization. According to the Bushman belief, each tribe and race in the world has a distinctive kind of medicine. The Bantu medicine consists of witchcraft and sorcery. The European medicine is contained in pills and in hypodermic syringes. The Bushman medicine, or *n/um*, is a physical substance that lies in the pit of the stomach of the *n/um kausi*, or "medicine owner." Medicine was given by God to Bushmen in the beginning, but men can transfer medicine from one body to another; this, in fact, is the main reason why Bushman trance dancers cure by laying on of hands on patients or subjects and by rubbing sweat. Normally medicine lies dormant. It is necessary to dance in order to heat it up. In their view, dancing makes the body hot. When the medicine reaches the boiling point, the vapors rise up through the spinal column, and when the vapors reach the brain, the dancer enters trance.

The dance ordinarily begins in the evening when a handful of women light a central fire and begin to sing. The dancing circle has a tight, symbolic organization. In the center is the fire,

314

representing medicine, which must be kept burning throughout the all-night dances. Surrounding the fire and within the circumference of the circle, the women sit shoulder to shoulder facing inward. The women are primarily singers, dancing only occasionally. The men dance in an outer, circular rut, stamping around and around hour after hour, now clockwise, now counterclockwise. Beyond these two tight circles of singers and dancers sit the spectators—the children and those dancers who have paused and are temporarily resting.

The songs are sung without words, in the form of yodeling accompanied by syncopated hand clapping. There is a generally known repertoire of about ten named songs, each commemorating game animals or natural phenomena, such as the giraffe, rain, God, and mongongo nuts. Each has a recognizable tune and associated dance steps. However, they do not attempt in the dance to imitate the behavior or locomotion of animals.

Phase I—working up—Chaxni Chi ("Dance and Song")

Soon after the women begin singing, some of the men enter the circle to dance. They maintain a tightly hunched posture, arms close to the sides and semiflexed, there is a parsimony of movement, and the body is held stiff from the waist up. Short, heavy footfalls describe complex rhythmic figures built on quarter- and eighth-notes and formed into five- and seven-beat phrases. Artifacts of the dance include chains of rattles tied around the ankles, a walking stick to support the torso, and an indispensable fly whisk.

A dance lasts from five to ten minutes, with a short break followed by another dance of equal length. The women determine the beginning and end of each number and the choice of songs. For the first two hours of dancing the atmosphere is casual, even jovial.

Phase II—entering a trance—n/um n/in!uma ("Causing Medicine to Boil")

Several of the dancers appear to be concentrating intently; they look down at their feet or stare ahead without orienting to distractions around them. The body is tense and rigid. The footfalls are heavy and the shock waves can be seen rippling through the body. The chest is heaving, veins are standing out

A dancer begins working into a trance. The dancer, wearing a sardine key in his ear, is guided by a fellow dancer until, near "half death," he collapses. A few moments later, he rises from his comatose state and transmits "medicine" by the laying on of hands.

on the neck and forehead, and there is profuse sweating. This phase lasts for thirty to sixty minutes.

The actual entrance into trance can be gradual or it can come suddenly. In the first instance the trancer staggers and almost loses balance. Then other men, who are not in trances, come to his aid and lead him around in tandem until the trancer shouts and falls down in a comatose state—called "half-death" by the Bushmen. The sudden entrance is characterized by a violent leap or somersault and an instant collapse into the half-death.

Phase III—half-death

Now the trancer is stretched out on the ground outside the dance circle. While the others continue dancing, some men work over the trancer. They rub his body with their hands and with their heads so that the body is kept warm and made to shine with sweat. The trance performer is rigid, arms stiff at the

sides or extended. His body may tremble, and he moans and utters short shrieks.

Phase IV—active curing—n/um ("Medicine")

The culmination of the trance episode occurs when the performer rises up to move among the participants and spectators to "cure." The technique used is laying on of hands. The performer's eyes are half-closed. He rubs the subject with trembling hands and utters moans of rising intensity, punctuated by abrupt, piercing shrieks. The trance performer goes from person to person repeating this action, ensuring that every person present is treated. He may break off curing to dance for a few minutes. This appears to reinforce the tranced state and to forestall a premature return to a normal state. If there is a sick person present at the dance each trance performer will make a special effort, often giving ten or fifteen minutes worth of treatment to this one individual.

Phase V—return to a normal state

The active curing phase lasts about an hour, after which the trance performer usually lies down and falls asleep. It is common for medicine men to have two trance episodes per night, one about midnight and the other just after dawn. The dance continues all night, reaching a peak intensity between midnight and 2:00 A.M. when the maximum number of medicine men are in trance. It slackens off in the predawn hours and then builds up to full strength again at sunrise with a renewed round of trances. The dance continues until midmorning and usually terminates by 10:00 or 11:00 A.M. Some memorable dances, however, continue throughout the day and into the following night, terminating thirty-six hours after they have started. What makes these marathon dances possible is the change-over of personnel. Although there are always ten to thirty people actively participating in the dance, individuals are constantly entering and leaving the circle in four- to six-hour shifts.

Apart from a male initiation ceremony, called *choma*, which takes place every four or five years during the winter, the Bushmen have no ceremony that is tied to the annual cycle, such as the first fruits rituals of the Australian aborigines. The Bushmen dance at all seasons of the year, winter and summer, with no discernible changes in frequency. There are, however, marked differences between separate Bushman camps in the frequency of occurrence of dances. Small camps of fewer than twenty people hold dances about once a month. Large camps with forty to sixty people dance about once a week. At one camp, which had a reputation for fine music, dances occurred as often as four nights a week. There is some indication that the Bushmen prefer to dance at the time of the full moon, but I could discover no reason for this preference beyond the simple fact that the light is better. A dance is a major all-night affair that involves the majority of the adult members of the camp. It is worth noting that the dance is a social and recreational event as well as an opportunity for trance performance. Many of the young men dance for no more profound reason than to show off their fancy footwork. There is a juxtaposition of the sacred and the profane in the dance, with the intense involvement of the trance performers contrasting with a background of casual social chatter, laughter, and flirtation.

Women, as well as men, have power to cure. A medicine woman, behind, leads her subject into trance.

A dance will spring up spontaneously if the informal organizers can talk up enthusiasm for it. Three kinds of circumstances favor its initiation: the presence of meat in a camp, the arrival of visitors, and the presence of sickness in a camp.

The trance phenomenon of the Bushman is a culturally stereotyped set of behaviors that induces an altered state of consciousness by means of autosuggestion, rhythmic dancing, intense concentration, and hyperventilation. These exertions produce symptoms of dizziness, spatial disorientation, hallucinations, and muscular spasms. The Bushmen were never observed to use any drug or other external chemical means of inducing these states. The social functions of the trancers are to cure the sick, influence the supernatural, and provide mystical protection for all members of the group.

The key symbols and metaphors that are found in the Bushman trance complex are the concepts of boiling, fire, heat, and sweat.

Boiling (n!um—to boil) refers not only to the boiling of water on the fire but also to the ripening of plants. Water, like medicine, is dormant when cold, but powerful when hot. Similarly plant foods are dormant when young and unripe but become nutritionally potent when ripe. Thus there is a symbolic association of boiling water, cooked meat, ripened berries, and activated medicine. Sometimes this metaphor is extended, in a joking manner, to nubile maidens who have reached menarche. These young women are now considered "ripe" for intercourse and impregnation.

Fire (da) is the source of heat (khwi) for boiling water, cooking meat, and for activating medicine. The central fire symbolizes medicine, and rubbing of live coals on the body, which is often done, was interpreted by one informant as a means of rapidly incorporating the sources of medicine. Another informant interpreted fire rubbing as a means of heating up internal medicine. These two views are not necessarily contradictory. Trance performers use the same word (da) to describe both the central dance fire and the fire within their own bodies, which heats up the medicine.

Sweat (cho) is the most important of the trance symbols for it is the palpable and visible expression of medicine on the surface of the body. Sweat is symbolically equated with the steam rising from boiling water and with the vapors that rise from the medicine boiling in the pit of the stomach.

The production and transmission of sweat is the key element in the curing ritual. Illness is lodged at sites on the body of the sick person and can be driven out by the implanting of medicine.

There is an important contrast to be made between Bushman sweat symbolism and that of the sweat lodge and sweat house religions of North American Indians. In these rituals sweating is interpreted as a means of purification of the body. The perspiration, therefore, carries the negative or harmful substances out of the body. The Bushman belief specifies the opposite—the sweat is itself the positive and life-giving substance. In the sweat house it is necessary for the patient to perspire in order to be cured. In the Bushman case only the curer must sweat in order for the medicine to be effective.

The act of curing involves the laying on of hands, and the rubbing of medicinal sweat onto and into the body of the sick person. If the patient complains of chest trouble, the curer's attention will be focused there; similarly with other complaints located in specific organs, the curer will work on the afflicted part. In this ritual it is not necessary for the patient to enter trance in order for the cure to be effective. Often three or four curers will work simultaneously or in shifts on the body of a sick person. Thus there is no concept of individual responsibility if the cure is successful or unsuccessful. A demand of payment for the curer's service is not a common feature among the Bushmen, although some curers do receive payment when they are called in to give treatment to neighboring Bantu peoples.

In addition to healing, another class of powers attributed to the trance performer is the ability to see the ghosts of ancestors, to see at a distance, and x-ray vision.

Spirits of the dead may be responsible for causing sickness. The ritual curer in trance is able to see the shade hovering at the edge of the dance circle. These shades are invisible to all but the most experienced curers. Having diagnosed the source of the illness the curer then pleads with the ghost to make it go away. The following chant is used:

Why do you bother this one?
Go away and don't trouble us;
We love this man.
What have we done to you?

Some trance performers claim the ability to see distant scenes. On one occasion a performer stopped curing, walked to the edge of the circle of firelight and facing north described the scene at a Bantu village forty miles away. On another occasion a performer pointed to the horizon and announced that trouble was coming from the west. (As far as I know it never materialized.) This power was commonly attributed to trance performers, although I rarely observed it to be exercised.

X-ray vision takes the form of determining the sex of infants *in utero*. I lack a statistically significant sample of these predictions (only ten births occurred during the study period), so I cannot judge the effectiveness of this technique.

The Bushmen believe that, in the past, a few of the very powerful curers had the ability to transform themselves into lions and to stalk the desert in search of human prey. Lions ordinarily do not attack men, and hunters occasionally drive lions off fresh kills in order to scavenge the meat. On the several occasions when a lion has attacked a man, the Bushmen attributed the attack to a human curer-turned-lion. Since such incidents occur perhaps once or twice in a decade, there is little reinforcement for the belief in the malevolence of trance performers.

It is instructive that, apart from this belief, all of the !Kung folk beliefs about trance performers assign to them a benevolent, positive, and socially constructive role.

This positive evaluation of the trance performer's role is most clearly demonstrated in the offering of mystical protection. It is the performer's duty to lay hands on all who are present at a dance, including men, women, children, and young infants. Thus one sees the curers moving around the dance circle and through the spectators, treating each individual in turn, even though there is no sickness in the camp.

The !Kung Bushman trance complex resembles in some ways the classic shamanism of Siberia and native North America. Both the Bushman and the shaman complexes emphasize individual trance as a means of activating extraordinary healing powers. In addition the trance complex as a system of explanation of misfortune has some correspondence to the institution of witchcraft found in many non-European societies. However, the Bushman case differs from shamanism and witchcraft in critical areas.

The well-known distinction between the shaman, whose powers derive from direct contact with the supernatural, and the priest, who learns a codified body of ritual knowledge from older priests, is blurred in the Bushman context. Unlike the shaman who contracts directly with the spirit world, the Bushman trance performer derives his power from within the social body itself.

The Siberian shaman, to take one example, is a lone figure whose power comes from "spirit possession." This supernatural contract—he has entered into a pact with the supernatural— tends to alienate the shaman from his community, and it is significant that the shamanistic role serves as an outlet for emotionally unstable individuals. In American Indian societies, such as the Pawnee, the shamans as a group are set off from the community in a formal fraternity of medicine men. In a number of African societies the shaman may assume the role of an authoritarian prophet figure and may gather a considerable following around him. In all these cases the medicine men are collectively and individually regarded by the laity as awesome and potentially dangerous.

The Bushman trance performer, by contrast, maintains strong social ties with the community. Indeed, recruitment and training of performers forges bonds of affection between the novice and his mentors, and between the curers as a group and the rest of the community. The Bushman curers do not form an exclusive minority of unusually gifted men, nor are they organized into a secret society with special access to the mysteries. The ability to enter trance and cure is possessed by half of the adult men (and by a number of the women).

This close identification of the trance performer with the community at large becomes evident when we consider the logic underlying the Bushman conception of the sources of healing power and the sources of misfortune. The Bushmen regard the healing power as being derived from other living men. Illness and misfortune, however, are brought mainly by the spirits of the dead and other forces external to the living. In other words they seek within the social body for benevolent powers, but project the blame for malevolence to forces outside of the social body. Such a conception of health and disease serves to bind together the living in a common front against hostile external forces.

Societies in which sorcery, shamanism, and witchcraft are prevalent divide good and evil into a radically different projective system. In these societies, malevolence springs from within the social body as well as from without. Witches, sorcerers, and wizards are all conceived of as living humans who (willfully or not) cause harm. To combat this malevolence, the individual may resort to the services of another sorcerer sympathetic to his cause. It is true that in witch-oriented societies not all evil is defined as coming from the living. However, the logic of the system leads inevitably to such features as good and bad shamans, good and bad sorcerers, and a spiral of magical attack and counterattack.

When misfortune strikes a member of a witch-oriented culture, he is likely to seek its source among the living members of the community. In many cases the prime suspects are the individual's close relatives. The hostility that is an inevitable by-product of interpersonal relations is thus translated from the profane into the realm of the sacred. Nevertheless the hostility must be absorbed largely by the social body. The Bushmen, simply by attributing misfortune to an external source, have evolved a projective system that dissipates, rather than intensifies, interpersonal hostility.

It would be misleading to allow the reader to draw the conclusion that all the problems of social living are resolved by the Bushmen in the trance performance and its associated system of explanation. Although the role of "witch" is not an institution of Bushman society, there is a prevalent belief that a living man can (willfully or unknowingly) cause harm to others by neglecting to propitiate his ancestors.

I cite a case in which two old men, Kumsa and Neysi, had been feuding with each other over a period of years. Once, when Kumsa became ill, he complained that Neysi was indirectly the source of his difficulty. This accusation of witchcraft took the following form.

Neysi has spoken ill of me. His ancestors have overheard these words and now they have come to bother me. Why can't Neysi control his ancestors?

In order to clear himself of the charge, Neysi was required to come to Kumsa's bedside and to plead publicly with his offending ancestors to leave Kumsa in peace. In this ritual of reconciliation Neysi used an incantation that is similar to that used by a trance performer when he sees a ghost hovering at a dance.

This territory here is ours to share. Now the ghosts should just go away and let this man live in peace. . . . Because of my words the ghosts are trying to kill Kumsa. Now I say—Kumsa is my child. Ghosts! Go away!

However, this incident was an isolated occurrence; by far the more common attribution of malevolence was to a ghost who was acting entirely of its own volition—uninfluenced by human manipulation.

In conclusion, the attainment of a trance is a co-operative enterprise involving both women and men. The trance performance itself is characterized by a lack of secrecy and a high degree of mutual aid. The psychological rewards of the trance experience are available to a high percentage of the adult men of the community. All members including women and children enjoy the benefits offered by the mystical protection of the curer. The socially positive evaluation of the trance performer's role in society is congruent with the Bushman belief that misfortune springs largely from the dead, and not from the agency of living men. The !Kung Bushman trance performance can be regarded as a drama in which the stresses and tensions of social life are transformed into a common struggle against the external sources of malevolence.

JAMES W. FERNANDEZ

ZULU ZIONISM   On any Sunday afternoon in any city in South Africa, small groups of people dressed in colorful robes rush to their appointed places of worship in vacant lots or roadside parks. Since these black Africans have neither the permission of the South African government nor the means to build churches of any permanence, the greatest number of them worship in the open air on land that is otherwise unused. Over the years their rituals have worn away the grass, churning and beating the soil into shallow trenches that are nearly perfect in their circularity. On weekdays, I would experience an archeologist's feeling of discovery as I passed by these sites of former, intense activity in the wastelands of the city. But I had only to return the following Sunday to find them alive with chanting worshipers.

The more than three thousand independent sects, cults, and churches, large and small, that flourish among South Africa's blacks represent attempts to combine, in one form or another, traditional views with those of Christianity. These movements present us with novel and often creative styles of life, and they have an exuberance that rewards those who seek to learn more about them.

In South Africa, the blacks, predominantly Bantu peoples like the Zulu, constitute an overwhelming majority of the population (68 percent). Some 10 percent of the country's people are coloreds of mixed European and African descent who are a distinct group, politically and socially. Virtually all governing power and social prerogative is exercised by the 19 percent of the population that is white. The small remaining number of people are Asian.

In recent years the modern world has forcibly exported its culture of science, technology, and material consumption to the countries of the Third World. We may forget that long before we began to export our scientific-technological culture, we were making devoted efforts through missionaries to export a more metaphysical, otherworldly, and ascetic religious one. I have been studying the reactions to that earlier enterprise. Regardless of how Africans will eventually respond to our secular culture, their response to the earlier evangelization has not been one of simple imitation. The deeply ingrained religious beliefs and practices of African peoples have not been abruptly abandoned.

The new religions springing up today are called movements because they are attempts to move away from colonial domination and deprecation toward a more authentic and satisfying African society and culture, which will combine African and European influences without a grievous sense of disparity.

Part of our interest in such syncretic movements arises from our having seen their like before. History presents us with many examples of contact between peoples that resulted in a synthesis of old and introduced elements. Christianity itself, we know, grew out of a mixture of Hebrew and Hellenic cultural elements. The two influences are emphasized in varying degrees in Christianity's many branches and denominations. Similarly, the new African religions differ among themselves, in their adherence to Christianity on the one hand and to traditional beliefs and practices on the other. Some are very traditional, while others are virtually indistinguishable from their Christian mission antecedents. Some are down to earth, and some enthusiastic. Some are large, holding many thousands in the same communion. Others are small in number and ephemeral in time.

The Zulu Zionists are part of a colorful movement that ranges from hundreds of small, transient groups to established churches with thousands of members. The enthusiasm they generate in worship is dramatic to the eye and ear. This movement is instructive even in the smallest groups because the fundamental syncretic and adaptive processes of culture contact, often obscured in larger and more complex movements, are very evident in them.

The name Zionism, to which these groups are attracted, has nothing to do with contemporary politics or the return of the Jews from the Diaspora. In a vague way, some Zionists feel that the name does demonstrate their attachment to the biblical homeland and more specifically to the Old Testament, the part of the Bible they find particularly relevant. But for most Zulu, it is an attractive term, alliterative with their own tribal name and evocative of an ancient place of spiritual authority. "It refers to a mountain on which the Holy Spirit healed man," some say.

The term, surprisingly enough, was brought to South Africa at the turn of the century from Zion City, Illinois, on the shores of Lake Michigan, by missionaries from John Alexander Dowie's Christian Catholic Apostolic Church in Zion. These missionaries, called Zionists in South Africa, believed in the spiritual power of divine healing by the laying on of hands and in baptism and healing by triune immersion. Dowie's own theocratic community in Zion City soon broke up, however, and the mission effort was abandoned by the end of the first decade of the century.

Meanwhile, the South African Zionists, who had also begun to experience division among themselves, were to feel a second influence from American enthusiastic revivalism. This was the influence of Pentecostal or Apostolic Faith missionaries who preached Pentecost, or "baptism in the Holy Spirit." These missionaries, in their turn, ceased to have any important direct effect on Zulu Zionism after World War I.

But indirectly, elements of both evangelizations remain, and Zulu Zionists continue to place central emphasis on healing by faith and the laying on of hands, on repeated immersion, and on the efficacy of the Holy Spirit. Zionist pastors who succeed in building up large congregations still try to establish self-sufficient theocratic communities with crafts and local industries free from external contamination. These communities are not much different from the original Zion City, which under Dowie's direction was aimed at excluding the patent immoralities of Chicago and northern Illinois.

Actually, not many large Zionist congregations are forthcoming. The qualities of charismatic enthusiasm necessary to Zionist prophecy are not usually compatible with the executive talents needed for large-scale organization. It is not unusual to find a pastor ejected from his own community, as was Dowie himself. By the 1920's, not long after the period of the evangelization, there were already dozens of these small Zionist churches. They now number in the hundreds, carrying such resplendent names as the Church of God in Christ Zionist (300 members), Zion Apostolic Gaza Church of Heaven (50 members), and the Circle Zion Church of God (12 members).

On Sunday afternoons, the various parks and empty lots of South African cities are dotted with the brightly clad devotees of these different religious persuasions. The women gather first, coming from the servants' quarters in which they are housed, for Zionism is largely the religion of the servant classes. They may come in their robes or bring them in bags. As they deck themselves out, they chat excitedly with other early arrivals. They sit together in the grass until the *mfundisi* (minister) and his deacons, one or two in number, arrive. The deacons, young men training for the ministry, are often quick to take any disgruntled members off to a circle of their own.

Membership in these circles is volatile, and members, predominantly women, are ready to move on if the service does not meet their requirements or if the minister seems to be a man of inadequate power. On the other hand, the *mfundisi*, trying to extend his influence and his income from the small offerings available to him, may move out to other circles that seem to have weak leaders, sending back a deacon as assistant minister to manage the affairs of his original circle. Sometimes this can be well managed, and an able and ambitious man can become bishop to many circles. But as often, his deacon or an interloping minister without a circle will intervene. Sometimes no leader will appear, and the common members will continue to arrive and wait for several Sundays in a row, finally moving off to worship in other circles. Or, the bishop will one day return to an old circle to find a new *mfundisi* not in his allegiance. When this happens a quiet struggle usually ensues between them. They test each other in strength of preaching, of praying in tongues, of the laying on of hands. Eventually the issue is decided; but if it is not done quickly, the membership, dismayed at this burden on their worship, will abandon the *mfundisi* to their struggle.

The circle formed at a Zionist service is a simple affair, yet it is the center of compact and highly charged religious activity. It is so important to the worship of these small Zionist congregations that it is often painted on the beaten mud or concrete floors of huts or township dwellings where the Zionists meet in inclement weather or at night. To Zionists, the circle has a deep symbolic significance, which is the more surprising because no explanation is ever given of their colorful garments, appliqued with stars, moons, and crosses that simply come in dreams.

The importance of the circle can only be grasped when one considers the round world in which the Zulu traditionally lived: round beehive houses protected by a circle of thorn bushes, the whole surrounding a circular pen—the heart of the kraal—which contains the main object of Zulu devotion and desire, the cattle. Amidst the harsh rectangularity, the gridiron of Western urban life of which the Zulu cannot become a part, their circles recapture this round world: the circle within a circle of traditional Zulu life. Just as they try to return yearly to kraals in the reserve to renew a sense of traditional composure and a special power over their afflictions, so they recapture some of that composure and power within their circles.

When the congregation, usually ten to twenty people, at last

arrives, they gather around in a circle while the *mfundisi* or his
deacon talks about the good results of previous worship and
healing and the plans for future meetings. If he feels the moment
propitious, the *mfundisi* may at this point deliver a homiletic.
He extends a hand over the circle to bless it. The membership

The *mfundisi*, surrounded by the congregation, blesses the circle.

then begins to sing, usually songs from missionary hymnals
accompanied by a drum.

After several minutes of this, someone may burst out speaking in tongues or take up a passionate testimony. Others will
begin to run clockwise around the circle, "heating it up" and
making it congenial to the coming of the Holy Spirit. The songs
and the drum pick up tempo as those afflicted, who have previously identified themselves to the *mfundisi,* are brought into the
center of the circle for the laying on of hands amidst the circling
membership. This is usually done by the *mfundisi* or his assistant, or by a deaconess (*makokeli*). Dancing and weaving in
unison with the songs and drum, they grasp various parts of the

afflicted body, spasmodically, compulsively, transferring the power of the Holy Ghost from within themselves to the afflicted individual.

It is at this time, particularly, that possession by the Holy Spirit may take place. Such a powerful penetration by the supernatural occurs that the recipient seems to lose his senses. He begins to shudder and shake and to exclaim in descending bursts of sound, "Heh! heh! heh! heh! ohh!" His muscles may

"Heating up the circle" creates a propitious atmosphere for the coming of the Holy Spirit.

jerk and shoot him forth uncontrollably in one direction or another. If this happens within the circle, it is a good sign. It shows the effective encounter and conquest by the Holy Spirit of the evil forces within. It is a most satisfactory consequence of the laying on of hands.

But it may occur even before the person enters the circle or has hands laid upon him. If so, it is a sign of his impurity, of his unacceptability to the Holy Spirit. The reaction may become so powerful that an individual is thrown out upon his back, and when this happens, he must examine his inner self. He must confess those cold-spirited intentions within his own power that closed him to assuagement by the Holy Spirit. In every case, when the Holy Spirit acts powerfully upon a man or a woman, either inside or outside the circle, other members come to his aid, physically supporting him against the raging spirit.

Gradually the vertiginous running about in the circle ends. The action of the Holy Spirit within flows away. It is twilight.

The laying on of hands at the water's edge.

The members move to the outside of the circle and return to softer singing. It may now come upon the minister to embark on a long sermon. Finally, a small suitcase may be set in the center of the circle and the members individually step forth to make a contribution. A benediction is pronounced, and the women resume their chatting. Farewells are said, and the grassy circle, now dusty with the, churning of many feet, is abandoned for another week.

The primary mode of spiritual contact in the meeting just described, the laying on of hands, is an art. A *mfundisi* must know the focuses of affliction. He must know the spiritually sensitive zones: the top of the head, the back of the neck, the small of the back, and the breast bone are most likely spots. He must know *when* to lay on hands. Some ministers, overeager to communicate their powers, lay on hands too quickly. Others build up a tension so that the Holy Spirit charges into the member with thunderous, corporeal consequences.

For the Zionists, the laying on of hands is only a technique.

The crucial element is the Holy Spirit, the circumambient ether, inert to most men but which some men may appropriate for greater strength and power over hardship and evil. The Zionists are held in some disdain by the established churches because they seem to pay only lip service to the other two Persons of the Trinity. But the reason is not so hard to find. The Holy Spirit is much more easily identified with their earlier worship of the spirits of the dead. It was the principal object of the Zulu cult of

Having confessed their worldly sins, the Zionists are baptized in the ocean.

the dead to hold effective communication with these spirits and to obtain from them health, freedom from affliction, and the good things of life. One may even speak of the Holy Spirit in some of these cults as a kind of generic ancestral spirit, a generalization or abstraction from the traditional multitude of particular spirits, that evolved out of culture contact and the challenge of monotheism. Devotion to the Holy Spirit is a kind of ancestor worshiper's version of monotheism.

In the old days among the Zulu, one looked for signs of the presence of spirits in certain natural events: small whirlwinds in the dust of the courtyard, the sound of wind sighing through the reed roofs of the huts, the presence of a serpent coiled in a corner or curling across the kraal. There has always been a tendency to find traces of the spirits in natural phenomena, but among Zionists it is often more explicit—the Holy Spirit is identified with the wind itself. The words spirit and wind are the same in Zulu (*umoya*). The Zionists carry large flags to their circles and plant them on the fringes. They are never so content as when the sea breezes of the Indian Ocean whip these back and forth, a good omen, if not an index, of the forceful presence of the Holy Spirit itself.

If the power of the Holy Spirit is suggested in the wind, it is even more convincingly present in the source of the wind, the ocean itself, whose constant movement suggests omnipotence. Zionists not only use sea water for personal ablutions, but they descend periodically to the ocean for purification and rebaptism in the Holy Spirit. The Zulu have traditionally used streams and ponds to purify themselves. At the Zulu New Year festival, the king would descend to midstream and wash himself with the ashes of sacrificed cattle. The ashes floated down and were in turn taken up by his warriors in the waters below to purify themselves. In these ablutions the king and his warriors were not only purified but were at the same time filled with the power of the royal ancestors.

If the Zionist congregation is a large one, this ocean baptism is a truly impressive event. It takes place at first light in the morning. The members first prepare themselves by confessing to each other on the fringes of the beach. Taking unconfessed sins into the water is dangerous. The Zulu are not good swimmers and the Indian Ocean surf pounds in with a strong undertow. The occasional drownings of Zionists undergoing purification baptism are always explained as a consequence of an unconfessed heart punished by the Holy Spirit. Members who feel themselves particularly impure first purge themselves in the traditional manner by vomiting into a hole in the sand. It is covered over and two candles are lit above it.

After confession, the entire congregation gathers at the top of the beach and dances down to the water's edge singing songs from Christian hymnals and the old regimental songs of the Zulu *Impis* (bands of warriors). It is a scene reminiscent of Zulu power in the last century. As the congregation moves down the beach, the men raise their knees high, stamping down in unison into the sand dunes. When this Zionist *Impi* arrives at the water's edge, they halt and form a line out into the shallow surf. With hands outstretched, the leader then goes forth waist deep into the surf, announcing to the Holy Spirit that men have come to be purified. Then, one by one the Zionists go forth to be totally immersed in the element.

When all are baptized, they reassemble on the beach. Now,

full of power, they dance back to the dunes, again singing the regimental songs. The leader cups his hands over his ears, a sign of the presence of the Holy Spirit within him. If there is anyone in the congregation whose illness has long resisted the ordinary laying on of hands, he is now brought forward. The empowered congregation gathers in a circle around him. Their new spiritual power, concentrated through their leader as he lays on hands, cannot fail to cure even the most chronically afflicted. Then the members disperse. They are purified, in composure with spirit, and have a clarity of vision that immersion in roiling water has always obtained for the Zulu.

Thus, the major ceremonial events of the Zulu Zionist religion are formed out of the bare elements of water, wind, and simple circles in the grass. Any material affluence is denied these servants and workers who are aliens in the European cities of southern Africa. Yet, out of the remnants of their own religious tradition and in syncretism with a new one, their desires and their imaginations obtain, if only on days of worship, a buoyant triumph over depressed circumstances.

DEVILS, WITCHES, AND SUDDEN DEATH Tin miners in the high Andean plateau of Bolivia earn less than a dollar a day when, to use their phrase, they "bury themselves alive in the bowels of the earth." The mine shafts—as much as two miles long and half a mile deep—penetrate hills that have been exploited for more than 450 years. The miners descend to the work areas in open hauls; some stand on the roof and cling to the swaying cable as the winch lowers them deep into the mine.

Once they reach their working level, there is always the fear of rockslides as they drill the face of the mine, of landslides when they set off the dynamite, of gas when they enter unfrequented areas. And added to their fear of the accidents that have killed or maimed so many of their workmates is their economic insecurity. Like Wall Street brokers they watch international price quotations on tin, because a difference of a few cents can mean layoffs, loss of bonuses, a cut in contract prices— even a change of government.

Working in the narrow chimneys and corridors of the mine, breathing the dust- and silicate-filled air, their bodies numbed by the vibration of the drilling machines and the din of dynamite blasts, the tin miners have found an ally in the devil, or Tio (uncle), as he is affectionately known. Myths relate the devil to his pre-Christian counterpart Huari, the powerful ogre who owns the treasures of the hills. In Oruro, a 13,800-foot-high mining center in the western Andes of Bolivia, all the miners know the legend of Huari, who persuaded the simple farmers of the Uru Uru tribe to leave their work in the fields and enter the caves to find the riches he had in store. The farmers, supported by their ill-gained wealth from the mines, turned from a virtuous life of tilling the soil and praying to the sun god Inti to a life of drinking and midnight revels. The community would have died, the legend relates, if an Inca maiden, Nusta, had not descended from the sky and taught the people to live in harmony and industry.

Despite four centuries of proselyting, Catholic priests have failed to wipe out belief in the legend, but the principal characters have merged with Catholic deities. Nusta is identified with the Virgin of the Mineshaft, and is represented as the vision that appeared miraculously to an unemployed miner.

The miners believe that Huari lives on in the hills where the mines are located, and they venerate him in the form of the devil, or Tio. They believe he controls the rich veins of ore, revealing them only to those who give him offerings. If they offend the Tio or slight him by failing to give him offerings, he will withhold the rich veins or cause an accident.

Miners make images of the Tio and set them up in the main corridors of each mine level, in niches cut into the walls for the workers to rest. The image of the Tio varies in appearance according to the fancy of the miner who makes him, but his body is always shaped from ore. The hands, face, horns, and legs are sculptured with clay from the mine. Bright pieces of metal or burned-out bulbs from the miners' electric torches are stuck in the eye sockets. Teeth are made of glass or crystal sharpened "like nails," and the mouth is open, gluttonous and ready to receive offerings. Sometimes the plaster of paris masks worn by the devil dancers at Carnival are used for the head. Some Tios wear embroidered vests, flamboyant capes, and miners' boots. The figure of a bull, which helps miners in contract with the devil by digging out the ore with its horns, occasionally accompanies the image, or there may be *chinas*, female temptresses who are the devil's consorts.

The Tio is a figure of power: he has what everyone wants, in excess. Coca remains lie in his greedy mouth. His hands are stretched out, grasping the bottles of alcohol he is offered. His nose is burned black by the cigarettes he smokes down to the nub. If a Tio is knocked out of his niche by an extra charge of dynamite and survives, the miners consider him to be more powerful than others.

Another spirit present in the mines but rarely represented in images is the Awiche, or old woman. Although some miners deny she is the Pachamama, the earth goddess worshiped by farmers, they relate to her in the same way. Many of the miners greet her when they enter the mine, saying, "Good-day, old woman. Don't let anything happen to me today!" They ask her to intercede with the Tio when they feel in danger; when they leave the mine safely, they thank her for their life.

Quite the opposite kind of feminine image, the Viuda, or widow, appears to miners who have been drinking *chicha*, a fermented corn liquor. Miners who have seen the Viuda describe her as a young and beautiful *chola*, or urbanized Indian, who makes men lose their minds—and sometimes their paychecks.

She, too, is a consort of the devil and recruits men to make contracts with him, deluding them with promises of wealth.

When I started working in Oruro during the summer of 1969, the men told me about the *ch'alla*, a ceremonial offering of cigarettes, coca, and alcohol to the Tio. One man described it as follows:

"We make the *ch'alla* in the working areas within the mine. My partner and I do it together every Friday, but on the first Friday of the month we do it with the other workers on our level. We bring in banners, confetti, and paper streamers. First we put a cigarette in the mouth of the Tio and light it. After this we scatter alcohol on the ground for the Pachamama, then give some to the Tio. Next we take out our coca and begin to chew, and we also smoke. We serve liquor from the bottles each of us brings in. We light the Tio's cigarette, saying 'Tio, help us in our work. Don't let any accidents happen.' We do not kneel

Miners gather in the shaft to prepare for the *ch'alla*, a ceremony in which they will ask the Tio to protect them from accidents.

The Tio is draped with streamers and offered gifts during the *ch'alla*.

before him as we would before a saint, because that would be sacrilegious.

"Then everyone begins to get drunk. We begin to talk about our work, about the sacrifices that we make. When this is finished, we wind the streamers around the neck of the Tío. We prepare our *mesas* [tables of offerings that include sugar cakes, llama embryos, colored wool, rice, and candy balls].

"After some time we say, 'Let's go.' Some have to carry out those who are drunk. We go to where we change our clothes, and when we come out we again make the offering of liquor, banners, and we wrap the streamers around each others' necks. From there on, each one does what he pleases."

I thought I would never be able to participate in a *ch'alla* because the mine managers told me the men didn't like to have women inside the mine, let alone join them in their most sacred rites. Finally a friend high in the governmental bureaucracy gave me permission to go into the mine. Once down on the lowest level of San José mine, 340 meters below the ground, I asked my guide if I could stay with one of the work crews rather than tour the galleries as most visitors did. He was relieved to leave me and get back to work. The men let me try their machines so that I could get a sense of what it was like to hold a 160-pound machine vibrating in a yard-wide tunnel, or to use a mechanical shovel in a gallery where the temperature was 100° F.

They told me of some of their frustrations—not getting enough air pumped in to make the machines work at more than 20 percent efficiency and constant breakdowns of machinery, which slowed them up on their contract.

At noon I refused the superintendent's invitation to eat lunch at level O. Each of the men gave me a bit of his soup or some "seconds," solid food consisting of noodles, potatoes, rice, and spicy meat, which their wives prepare and send down in the elevators.

At the end of the shift all the men in the work group gathered at the Tío's niche in the large corridor. It was the first Friday of the month and the gang leader, Lino Pino, pulled out a bottle of fruit juice and liquor, which his wife had prepared, and each of the men brought out his plastic bag with coca. Lino led the men in offering a cigarette to the Tío, lighting it, and

A miner rests briefly next to the Tío, who has been given a cigarette.

Liquor is used in rituals honoring the Tio. Miners toast him, asking
that he "produce" minerals and let them "ripen," as if the ore was
a farm crop.

then shaking the liquor on the ground and calling for life, "Hallalla! Hallalla!"

We sat on lumps of ore along the rail lines and Lino's
helper served us, in order of seating, from a little tin cup. I was

not given any priority, nor was I forgotten in the rounds. One of the men gave me coca from his supply and I received it with two hands, as I had been taught in the rituals above-ground. I chewed enough to make my cheek feel numb, as though I had had an injection of novocaine for dental work. The men told me that coca was their gift from the Pachamama, who took pity on them in their work.

As Lino offered liquor to the Tio, he asked him to "produce" more mineral and make it "ripen," as though it were a crop. These rituals are a continuation of agricultural ceremonies still practiced by the farmers in the area. The miners themselves are the sons or grandsons of the landless farmers who were recruited when the gold and silver mines were reopened for tin production after the turn of the century.

A month after I visited level 340, three miners died in an explosion there when a charge of dynamite fell down a shoot to their work site and exploded. Two of the men died in the mine; the third died a few days later in the hospital. When the accident occurred, all the men rushed to the elevators to help or to stare in fascinated horror as the dead and injured were brought up to level O. They carried the bodies of their dead comrades to the social center where they washed the charred faces, trying to lessen the horror for the women who were coming. When the women came into the social center where the bodies were laid out, they screamed and stamped their feet, the horror of seeing their husbands or neighbors sweeping through their bodies.

The entire community came to sit in at the wake, eating and drinking in the feasting that took place before the coffins of their dead comrades. The meal seemed to confirm the need to go on living as well as the right to live.

Although the accident had not occurred in the same corridor I had been in, it was at the same level. Shortly after that, when a student who worked with me requested permission to visit the mine, the manager told her that the men were hinting that the accident had happened because the gringa (any foreign-born, fair-haired person, in this case myself) had been inside. She was refused permission. I was disturbed by what might happen to my relations with the people of the community, but even more concerned that I had added to their sense of living in a hostile world where anything new was a threat.

The miners were in a state of uneasiness and tension the rest of that month, July. They said the Tio was "eating them" because he hadn't had an offering of food. The dead men were all young, and the Tio prefers the juicy flesh and blood of the young, not the tired blood of the sick older workers. He wanted a *k'araku*, a ceremonial banquet of sacrificed animals.

There had not been any scheduled *k'arakus* since the army put the mines under military control in 1965. During the first half of the century, when the "tin barons"—Patiño, Hochschild, and Arayamao—owned the mines, the administrators and even some of the owners, especially Patiño, who had risen from the ranks, would join with the men in sacrificing animals to the Tio and in the drinking and dancing that followed. After nationalization of the mines in 1952, the rituals continued. In fact, some of the miners complained that they were done in excess of the Tio's needs. One said that going into the mine after the revolution was like walking into a saloon.

Following military control, however, the miners had held the ritual only once in San José, after two men had died while working their shift. Now the Tio had again shown he was hungry by eating the three miners who had died in the accident. The miners were determined to offer him food in a *k'araku*.

At 10:30 P.M. on the eve of the devil's month, I went to the mine with Doris Widerkehr, a student, and Eduardo Ibañez, a Bolivian artist. I was somewhat concerned about how we would be received after what the manager of the mine had said, but all the men seemed glad we had come. As we sat at the entry to the main shaft waiting for the *yatiris*, shamans who had been contracted for the ceremony, the miners offered us *chicha* and cocktails of fruit juice and alcohol.

When I asked one of the men why they had prepared the ritual and what it meant, his answer was:

"We are having the *k'araku* because a man can't die just like that. We invited the administrators, but none of them have come. This is because only the workers feel the death of their comrades.

"We invite the Pachamama, the Tio, and God to eat the llamas that we will sacrifice. With faith we give coca and alcohol to the Tio. We are more believers in God here than in Germany or the United States because there the workers have lost their soul. We do not have earthquakes because of our faith before God. We hold the crucifix to our breast. We have more confidence before God."

After two men died in an explosion, the miners held a *k'araku*, an ancient ceremony involving the sacrifice of two llamas.

DEVILS, WITCHES, AND SUDDEN DEATH

Most miners reject the claim that belief in the Tio is pagan sacrilege. They feel that no contradiction exists, since time and place for offerings to the devil are clearly defined and separated from Christian ritual.

At 11:00 P.M. two white llamas contributed by the administration were brought into level O in a company truck. The miners had already adorned the pair, a male and a female, with colored paper streamers and the bright wool earrings with which farmers decorate their flocks.

The four *yatiris* contracted for did not appear, but two others who happened to be staying at the house of a miner were brought in to perform the ceremony. As soon as they arrived, the miners took the llamas into the elevator. The male was on the right and the female to his left, "just the same as a marriage ceremony," one miner commented. Looking at the couple adorned with bright streamers and confetti, there was the feeling of a wedding.

Two men entered the elevator with the llamas and eight more climbed on top to go down to level 340. They were commissioned to take charge of the ritual. All the workers of 340 entered to participate in the ceremony below and about 50 men gathered at level O to drink.

At level 340 the workers guided the *yatiris* to the spot where the accident had occurred. There they cast liquor from a bottle and called upon the Tio, the Awiche, and God to protect the men from further accidents—naming all the levels in the mine, the various work sites, the different veins of ore, the elevator shaft, and the winch, repeating each name three times and asking the Tio not to eat any more workers and to give them more veins to work. The miners removed their helmets during this ritual. It ended with the plea for life, "Hallalla, hallalla, hallalla." Two bottles of liquor were sprinkled on the face of the rock and in the various work places.

The *yatiris* then instructed the men to approach the llamas with their arms behind their backs so that the animals would not know who held the knife that would kill them. They were also told to beg pardon for the sacrifice and to kiss the llamas farewell. One miner, noting what appeared to be a tear falling from the female's eye, cried and tried to comfort her. As the men moved around the llamas in a circle, the *yatiris* called on the

Malkus (eagle gods), the Awiche, the Pachamama, and finally the Tiyulas (Tios of the mines), asking for their care.

The female llama was the first to be sacrificed. She struggled and had to be held down by two men as they cut her jugular vein. When they disemboweled her, the men discovered that she was pregnant, to which they attributed the strength of her resistance. Her blood was caught in a white basin.

When the heart of the dying llama had pumped out its blood, the *yatiri* made an incision and removed it, using both his hands, a sign of respect when receiving an offering. He put the still palpitating heart in the basin with the blood and covered it with a white cloth on which the miners placed *k'oa*—an offering made up of herbs, coca, wool, and sweets—and small bottles of alcohol and wine.

The man in charge of the ceremony went with five aides to the site of the principal Tio in the main corridor. There they removed a piece of ore from the image's left side, creating a hole into which they put the heart, the blood, and the other offerings. They stood in a circle, their heads bent, and asked for safety and that there be no more accidents. In low voices, they prayed in Quechua.

When this commission returned, the *yatiris* proceeded to sacrifice the male llama. Again they asked the Tio for life and good ore in all the levels of the mine, and that there be no accidents. They took the heart, blood, *k'oa*, and bottles of alcohol and wine to another isolated gallery and buried it for the Tio in a place that would not be disturbed. There they prayed, "filled with faith," as one commented, then returned to the place of the sacrifice. The *yatiris* sprinkled the remaining blood on the veins of ore.

By their absorption and fervid murmuring of prayers, both young and old miners revealed the same faith and devotion. Many of them wept, thinking of the accident and their dead companions. During the ritual drinking was forbidden.

On the following day those men charged with responsibility for the ritual came to prepare the meat. They brought the two carcasses to the baker, who seasoned them and cooked them in large ovens. The men returned at about 1:15 P.M. to distribute the meat. With the meat, they served *chicha*. Some sprinkled *chicha* on the ground for the Pachamama, saying "Hallalla," before drinking.

The bones were burned to ashes, which were then offered to the Tio. The mine entrance was locked shut and left undisturbed for 24 hours. Some remarked that it should be closed for three days, but the company did not want to lose that much time.

During the *k'araku* the miners recognize the Tio as the true owner of the mine. "All the mineral that comes out from the interior of the mine is the 'crop' of the devil and whether one likes it or not, we have to invite the Tio to drink and eat so that the flow of metal will continue," said a young miner who studied evenings at the University of Oruro.

All the workers felt that the failure of the administrators to come to the *k'araku* indicated not only their lack of concern with the lives of the men but also their disregard of the need to raise productivity in the mine.

When the Tio appears uninvited, the miners fear that they have only a short time to live. Miners who have seen apparitions say the Tio looks like a gringo—tall, red-faced, with fair hair and beard, and wearing a cowboy hat. This description hardly resembles the images sculptured by the miners, but it does fit the foreign technicians and administrators who administered the mines in the time of the tin barons. To the Indian workers, drawn from the highland and Cochabamba farming areas, the Tio is a strange and exotic figure, ruthless, gluttonous, powerful, and arbitrary in his use of that power, but nonetheless attractive, someone to get close to in order to share that power. I was beginning to wonder if the reason I was accepted with such good humor by the miners, despite their rule against women in the mines, was because they thought I shared some of these characteristics and was a match for the devil.

Sickness or death in the family can force a man in desperation to make a contract with the devil. If his companions become aware of it, the contract is destroyed and with it his life.

The miners feel that they need the protection of a group when they confront the Tio. In the *ch'alla* and the *k'araku* they convert the power of the Tio into socially useful production. In effect, the rituals are ways of getting the genie back into the bottle after he has done his miracles. Security of the group then depends upon respect toward the sacrificial offering, as shown by the following incident told me by the head of a work gang after the *k'araku*:

"I know of a man who had a vein of ore near where the bones of the sacrificial llama were buried. Without advising me, he made a hole with his drill and put the dynamite in. He knew very well that the bones were there. On the following day, it cost him his life. While he was drilling, a stone fell and cut his head off.

"We had to change the bones with a ceremony. We brought in a good shaman who charged us B$500 [about $40], we hired the best orchestra, and we sang and danced in the new location where we laid the bones. We did not work in that corridor for three days, and we spent all the time in the *ch'alla.*"

Often the miners are frightened nearly to death in the mine. A rock falls on the spot they have just left, a man falls in a shaft and is saved by hitting soft clay at the bottom, a tunnel caves in the moment after a man leaves it—these are incidents in a day's work that I have heard men say can start a *haperk'a,* or fear, that can take their lives.

A shaman may have to be called in to bring back the spirit that the Tio has seized. In one curing, a frightened miner was told to wear the clothing he had on when the Tio seized his spirit and to enter and give a service to the Tio at the same spot where he was frightened. The shaman himself asked the Tio to cure his patient, flattering him, "Now you have shown your power, give back his spirit."

The fear may result in sexual impotency. At one of the mines, Siglo XX, when there is full production, a dynamite blast goes off every five minutes in a procedure called block cave-in. The air is filled with smoke and the miners describe it as an inferno. Working under such tension, a shattering blast may unnerve them. Some react with an erection, followed by sexual debilitation. Mad with rage and fear, some miners have been known to seize a knife, the same knife they use to cut the dynamite leads, and castrate themselves. When I visited this area, I noticed that the Tio on this level had a huge erection, about a foot long on a man-sized figure. The workers said that when they find themselves in a state of impotency they go to the Tio for help. By exemplifying what they want in the Tio, they seek to repair the psychic damage caused by fear.

After feasting on the meat of the llamas and listening to stories of the Tio, I left the mine. The men thanked me for coming. I could not express the gratitude I felt for restoring my confidence in continuing the study.

Shortly thereafter I met Lino Pino returning from a fiesta for a miraculous saint in a nearby village. He asked me if I would be *madrina* at his daughter's forthcoming confirmation, and when I agreed, his wife offered me a tin cup with the delicious cocktail she always prepares for her husband on the days of the *ch'alla*, and we all had a round of drinks.

Later, when I knelt at the altar rail with Lino and his daughter as we received the wafer and the wine, flesh and blood of another sacrifice victim, I sensed the unity in the miners' beliefs. The miraculous Virgin looked down on us from her marbelized, neon-lit niche, her jewelled finger held out in bene-diction. She was adequate for that scene, but in the mine they needed someone who could respond to their needs on the job.

In the rituals of the *ch'alla* and the *k'araku* the power of the Tio to destroy is transformed into the socially useful functions of increasing mineral yield and giving peace of mind to the workers. Confronted alone, the Tio, like Banquo's ghost, makes a man unable to produce or even to go on living. Properly controlled by the group, the Tio promises fertility, potency, and productivity to the miners. Robbed of this faith, they often lose the faith to continue drilling after repeated failure to find a vein, or to continue living when the rewards of work are so meager. Knowing that the devil is on your side makes it possible to continue working in the hell that is the mines.

PART SIX

DEVELOPMENT AND UNDERDEVELOPMENT

Anthropologists and the Third World

During the last few years the term "Third World" has been used increasingly to describe the condition of certain nations and ethnic minorities that have not shared fully in the economic benefits arising from the Industrial Revolution. These people stand in marked contrast to those of the "developed" or industrialized nations, and from colonial times onward people of the Third World have suffered from the dual problems of economic exploitation and cultural domination by industrialized powers. The following articles explore a spectrum of the anthropologists' involvement with the plight of some Third World peoples. Attitudes among anthropologists toward problems of contemporary economic development and culture change vary greatly, and we cannot hope to present all points of view or resolve the differences. Some anthropologists feel a deep moral obligation to use their knowledge to influence and direct the course of change within the societies they study; others adopt a sort of detached point of view in which knowledge sought will not be distorted by overinvolvement in the problems and sufferings of the people being studied. The articles presented here fall between these extremes. Each effectively portrays a situation arising from the encounter between industrialized and Third World societies.

"Vanishing Ainu of North Japan" by Shin'ichiro Takakura presents a situation characterized by culture loss over a long span of time and emphasizes the history of the native Ainu of Hokkaido and the Kurile Islands as a steadily declining minority of the population of Japan. Their decline began long before the Industrial Revolution but was hastened by the rise of industrialism and particularly by strong nationalistic tendencies in Japan during World War II. Today, as Takakura points out, Ainu cannot speak their native language, they live in undistinguished rural villages with none of the character of their ancient settlements, and they no longer live off the land. Anthropologists have tried to salvage information about traditional Ainu life and have encouraged such undertakings as a reconstructed Ainu settlement; but Takakura essentially provides an example of a traditional culture that has not successfully adapted to contact with modern Japanese society. He points out, ". . . the Ainu's daily life is not different from that of the Japanese. Ainu villages have disappeared, and their religion is lost." Ainu culture today is preserved only in an embalmed form, like a museum specimen that is imperfectly understood and will not play an important part in the current life of Japan, one of the world's most highly industrialized nations. Takakura's approach to the Ainu is that of a culture-historian intent on showing the world what it has lost with the decline of this once-vigorous and unique society.

For the Indians described by Norman A. Chance ("The Changing World of the Cree") the contact situation has reached a critical point. It remains to be seen whether the Cree will retain their "Indian-ness" or will choose instead a way of life oriented toward the rapidly expanding Canadian timber and mining industries. At present the upbringing and education of Cree children places them in two worlds—an Indian world as infants and small children and a white man's world as students in boarding schools near the industrial towns. Thus these young Indians face an identity crisis, and so far the issue is in doubt. For example, will a young Cree choose his own marriage partner (as the white man does), or will he let his parents choose (in traditional Cree fashion)? Each summer Cree children return home from the boarding schools to resume life in the surroundings of their Indian background; this no doubt has a profound influence on some. Many youth prefer to go away during the summers to work for mining prospectors and may not return to their home communities for long periods. Many Indians have mastered the skills needed to work effectively in industry, and this could lead inevitably to a loss of their cultural traditions.

Although it is too soon to predict the outcome in the case of the Cree, some successful adaptations are known among other North American Indian societies. Some have adapted by using their income from highly skilled and well-paid jobs to support traditional activities for at least part of each year in their home communities. This is the case with the Mohawk Indians from the Caughnawaga Reservation in Quebec.[1] Since 1886 these Indians have worked as riveters and fitters on high steel structures such as bridges and tall buildings. Since the 1920s Mohawks have worked on New York City skyscrapers. Some work gangs move from city to city on different jobs, while others keep their families in Brooklyn. Many, when they have finished a job, travel back to Caughnawaga to attend longhouse festivals and enjoy the more traditional surroundings. These Indians continue to express satisfaction in their traditional religion, language, cooking, and other cultural pursuits while at the same time performing skilled and useful work in an occupation that epitomizes the industrial society of the First World. Caughnawaga Mohawks have participated in the construction of hundreds of large buildings and bridges including such well-known structures as the Golden Gate Bridge in California and the Empire State Building, the R.C.A. Building, the Triborough Bridge, the Bronx-Whitestone Bridge, the West Side Highway, the Pulaski Skyway, and the George Washington Bridge, all in New York. At the same time they have preserved a greater measure of their traditional culture than was true for the Ainu of Japan.

Earlier notions that the American Indians were a "vanishing race" and that their culture was being assimilated into the great American "melting pot" are not borne out by current observations. Anthropologist Evon Z. Vogt notes:

But what is interesting to the close observer is that, despite all these pressures for change, there are still basically Indian systems of social structure and culture persisting with variable vigor within conservative nuclei of American Indian populations. It would be rash indeed to predict now that these cultural features will completely disappear in the course of acculturation in one, two, or even several generations.[2]

In other words, not all American Indian societies have adapted so successfully as the Mohawk, but many have adapted well enough so that they refuse to disappear. During the last few years many Indians have developed a new awareness of their cultural identity, and today a "Red Power" movement has been gathering momentum throughout the United States and shows signs of revitalizing many traditional and semitraditional Indian institutions.[3] Perhaps the Cree themselves will become involved with this movement, or perhaps they will successfully adapt to the First World entirely on their own. Chance does not attempt to predict the future for the Cree, but he reveals clearly the forces at work in Cree society that could help to determine the outcome.

In "The Great Sisal Scheme" by Daniel R. Gross, we see perhaps the most dramatic case yet of economic and cultural impoverishment in the Third World. Through a close examination of the economic history of the *sertão* region of northeastern Brazil and an analysis of the input and expenditure of calories in workers' households, Gross demonstrates that the introduction of sisal as a cash crop has led to economic disaster in this region. Gross' findings reveal the type of conditions that often cause revolutions. Sisal cultivation has led to a widening of the gulf between a few rich and the many poor of this region. In this case poverty has become so acute that many children show the effects of prolonged malnutrition in the forms of stunted growth and low resistance to disease. These effects were especially noticeable in the countryside, where farmers had become entirely dependent on the sale of sisal while the world sisal market fluctuated up and down (mostly down), but they were also visible in towns such as Vila Nova. Abandoning subsistence agriculture in favor of planting all their fields in sisal, many farmers harvested and processed sisal for the large landowners who owned the all-important decorticating machines needed for this processing. This was hard and poorly paid labor, and the farmer's plight was made worse by the slump in world sisal prices, which sometimes made it uneconomical to harvest small sisal holdings. Thus in a few years the farmer's fields became choked with unusable sisal that rendered these fields virtually unreclaimable. Self-sufficient farmers had been transformed into laborers, and their labor did not earn enough for them to live. With the exception of a few large landowners, the entire population of the *sertão* was in a downward economic spiral.

In hindsight it is clear from Gross' account that the introduction of sisal into this region as a cash crop was a very unfortunate mistake. Proposed development had led, instead, to underdevelopment (unless, of course, one takes the point of view of the few privileged landowners who profited from it all). Gross does not advocate political action as a result of his observations, but neither does he regard the situation in the *sertão* as an acceptable or viable kind of cultural adjustment. This case put the anthropologist's objectivity to a severe test, a kind of test that faces many other anthropologists in the 1970s. One may be tempted in a field study such as this to take sides prematurely out of sympathy for the poor and disadvantaged of the Third World and thus skew the results of the study. Yet, as Gross has shown, the anthropologist can present his evidence in a factual and objective manner and at the same time make it clear where his sympathies lie. By employing the scientific skills of the anthropological observer, Gross has made his case for the poor of the Brazilian *sertão* far more convincingly than if he had engaged in polemic arguments on the subject.

Notes

1   Joseph Mitchell, "Mohawks in High Steel," in *Apologies to the Iroquois* by Edmund Wilson, New York, Farrar, Straus, and Cudahy, 1960, pp. 3–36.
2   Evon Z. Vogt, "The Acculturation of American Indians," *American Academy of Political and Social Sciences*, vol. 311, 1957, p. 138.
3   Stan Steiner, *The New Indians*, New York, Harper & Row, 1968.

VANISHING AINU OF NORTH JAPAN An anthropological tragedy of World War II was the destruction of the last chance to study at firsthand the primitive culture of the Ainu people before it totally disappeared. The remaining Ainu live on Hokkaido, northernmost island of the Japanese archipelago. Perhaps about a hundred "pure" Ainu are left, but only in the sense that each retains pure Ainu blood. Culturally, every Ainu of today is "diluted."

As a race that had its own language, religion, method of house building, and other cultural traits and institutions, the Ainu are a thing of the past. There are what people call "Ainu villages," but this is just a name. Any distinctively traditional way of life is preserved only as a tourist attraction. Today, the Ainu live as the Japanese live—except that many are poorer than ordinary Japanese workers and farmers.

Assimilation and acculturation has been a long and gradual process, going back 500 to 600 years. But it was not until after the turn of the nineteenth century that a decisive change came in the life of Hokkaido. Indeed, in the northeastern part of the island, the Ainu were not assimilated until a few decades ago.

In the sixteenth century the Ainu were distributed more broadly than on Hokkaido alone—throughout all the Kurile Islands, the southern part of Sakhalin, and the northern edge of Honshu, the largest of the Japanese islands. Even then there were only about 40,000 of them. Epidemics from the end of the eighteenth century until the early part of the nineteenth century reduced the population even further. Today, most Ainu people are so mixed with the Japanese race that it is virtually impossible to find statistics for the existing Ainu population, remnants of which still live along the Pacific coast of Hokkaido.

Hokkaido is an island of approximately 34,000 square miles, nearly a fourth of the total area of Japan today. Over 70 per cent of Hokkaido is mountain and forest land, but there is proportionately more plains land that can be cultivated than in Japan in general. The latitude is about the same as the northern half of Italy (41° to 45°), but cold currents in the surrounding seas produce a climate similar to that of northeastern New England or the Maritime Provinces of Canada. Winters are long and severe; then summer brings mean maximum temperatures of about 80° F.

Because of these cold currents, sea mammals may be seen on the coastlines (sea otter, northern fur seal), and there are many varieties of fish in the sea and rivers. On land, there used to be many bear, deer, foxes, and a variety of birds. Their number is considerably lower today as the result of farm settlement —much as in the American West. Before the Japanese began to open the forest, cultivate the land, and exploit the resources, all of which started on a large scale in the 1860's, Hokkaido was mostly covered by forests of birch, poplar, oak, elm, fir, spruce, and pine; there were bushes, shrubs, and an undergrowth of bamboo and other wild grasses.

The inhabitants of this wilderness used the word Ainu when referring to themselves. It meant simply "man." Until the middle of the nineteenth century, the Japanese called them *Yezo*, which originally meant "alien people who live in the north."

In physique, language, customs, manners, and religion, the Ainu differed sharply from the Japanese and other Mongolian people. Physically they were different from other Mongol types in having long heads with broad, flat faces. Eyebrows were high over round, sunken eyes that lacked the typical oblique corners. Their skin was comparatively white, the color of their eyes usually brown (but sometimes blue). These physical characteristics persist in the diluted Ainu today. Some anthropologists believe that the origin of the Ainu was Caucasia, from which they traveled across Siberia, eventually reaching Hokkaido. Probably the Ainu retained the characteristics of prehistoric people of an age before the human race diversified into Mongoloid and Caucasoid, if such a diversification actually occurred.

The Ainu language—as studied and preserved by scholars— borrowed many expressions from neighboring peoples, but it still had distinct characteristics of its own. The language has now been almost completely replaced by Japanese. Although still remembered by a few old people of the Ainu, it is not used in ordinary conversation, but only in prayers and folk songs.

Until the Japanese introduced cultivation to Hokkaido, the Ainu knew nothing of agriculture. In the warm seasons they fished, in the autumn they gathered nuts and the roots of wild grass, and in the winter they hunted. There was no need for agriculture as long as they could get enough food without it. But the migration of Japanese into Hokkaido in the 1860's narrowed the room for wildlife and polluted the streams, so the population had to turn to cultivation for a food supply. Until that time, the Japanese had not encouraged agriculture in Hokkaido, because they profited from trading agricultural products, such as grains and tobacco, for furs from the Ainu.

The Ainu necessarily worked together as a tight community, and goods were distributed according to the needs of the communal society. Small as this society was, however, there were class structures, which included poor and wealthy classes and a limited system of slavery. The slaves were captives of the wars between villages or those who could not maintain themselves in the community—widows, orphans, the mentally retarded, or those who could not pay a "fine" for breaking community rules. The division of labor was very strict. The men hunted and were responsible for ceremonial activities; the women did the housekeeping.

Each village was led by a chief who handled all administrative matters, including war, and was in charge of various ceremonies.

Much tribal administration was based on tradition, and anyone violating the set rules was tried by a special discussion system that the Ainu called *charanke*, which means "to argue." When a violation occurred, nothing happened unless there was a complaint. Ordinarily, someone who suffered damages or felt aggrieved would demand that the accused be punished or that the devil that made the man do wrong be driven away. The two persons (in some cases groups) concerned would discuss the matter between themselves. If they reached a decision satisfactory to both sides—one party to sacrifice something he possessed, or become a slave to the other, or the two to beat each other with clubs, or whatever else might be agreed—this decision was carried out and it was all right with the other villagers. But if the two could not reach a mutually acceptable decision, then a third party intervened—an elder man of the village—and the disputants argued before him. If no satisfactory solution resulted, the two disputants would beat each other with clubs and that ended the affair. The clubs, called *shut*, were two to three feet long and looked like modern baseball bats. The beatings were not perfunctory, but full of force. However, they were not a test of strength; rather, they were meant to drive away the devils and were ceremonial in nature, probably originating in Ainu religion.

After the 1860's, the Japanese government took administrative and judicial power over Ainu villages into its own hands. This process, together with the advance of capitalism and the deterioration of the old ecology, deprived Ainu villages of the unique nature of their community life and destroyed the integrity of their social life. As a result, an Ainu village became just a hamlet where the inhabitants were Ainu, not a community where Ainu lived as they used to live.

A distinctive feature of the Ainu culture was house construction. There were slight regional differences in structure and materials, but the basic techniques were the same for all Ainu. The houses were one-room structures and always faced a fixed direction—usually the east or, if not, the direction from which a river flowed. Facing upstream meant toward the mountains, where the gods were supposed to live. There seem to be two intermixed religious ideas: one, gods come from the east; another, gods come from the mountains. But about this we have no definite information.

The building was a long, rectangular single room. The main windows opened only on one of the narrower ends—the front— and their purpose was to permit gods to enter the house. The entrance for the occupants was on the opposite side, and next to it were the cooking implements. There was no window on the long right wall, but a small window on the left admitted light. Straw mats spread over hay covered the floor. The unthatched ceiling was of attractive shingle construction. On festive occasions, the walls and floors were decorated with mats of patterned designs. Over a large fireplace in the room's center hung pots and pans and a shelf for drying clothes, food, and other things that needed drying. Smoke escaped from triangular windows on the edge of the roof. The fire always burned, for this was the seat of the fire goddess, who protected life.

The left corner farthest from the entrance was the most holy; here the god who was the husband of the fire goddess was enshrined as the protector or guard of the house. A piece of shaved wood that symbolized the god was hung on the wall. Festival ornaments and treasures, such as lacquered woods, swords, and necklaces that were obtained in trade with the Japanese, were also hung or set in this corner of the house.

When a family entertained, the host and hostess sat beside the fire, the rest of the family sat a little farther away toward the entrance to the house, and guests were placed opposite the host and hostess. This seating order was strictly observed.

Storage buildings near the house entrance were oriented in the same direction as the house. The latrine was separately built on the opposite side of a hedge.

The head of the family chose the homesite. He stuck a stick into the proposed location and prayed. If he did not have a bad dream afterward, he constructed his house on that spot, helped by the whole village, and a fete was held when it was completed. In ancient times only the chief's house was big, well furnished, and set apart from the others.

The house was constructed literally from the top down. First, two tripods were erected by tying wooden poles with rope made of vines or bark. Then the beams of the ceiling frame were fastened together in a rectangle on the ground. The tripods were put upon the ceiling beams, a ridgepole placed atop the tripods, and all tied together. This was the ceiling and roof frame. Additional sticks were added from ridge to ceiling, and the roof was covered with grass, bamboo, and bark tied to the framework. Eight or ten posts were sunk in the ground selected for the house. The builders lifted the whole ceiling and roof assembly and placed it on the posts. Walls were made by attaching grass, bamboo, and bark to the posts. Ordinarily the house was about 12 by 18 feet.

Clothes were made of fur or of *attsushi*, cloth made from fibers of elm phloem just inside the bark. Later, as trade was established with the Japanese, cotton became common. Ainu clothes resembled the open-fronted Japanese kimono. Collars, back, sleeves, and hems were embroidered or appliqued with unique Ainu designs, specific to each community. Needlework was the favorite occupation of the Ainu women, who learned the traditional designs in their childhood and did exquisite work with a small knife and a needle. Under the kimono the women wore a one-piece garment to hide their breasts. Usually, both men and women wore a headband, gloves, and socks decorated to match the kimono. From the men's belts hung a small knife scabbard made of wood and decorated with beautiful carving executed by the men. The Ainu wore hoods in winter, and shoes made of salmon or deer skin or sandals made of grapevine bark, but in other seasons they usually went barefoot.

Adults cut their hair at shoulder level and parted it at the center. The men had thick beards; the women were tattooed about the lips and on the backs of their hands and arms. Men's beards and women's tattoos were indications of adulthood. The tattoos were made by rubbing soot into shallow cuts in the skin.

At ceremonies, both men and women wore special decorative kimonos, over which they put foreign clothes, such as the long Japanese coat called *uchikake*. The men wore crowns sculptured of wood and decorated with straw, and long swords strapped across the right shoulder to the left waist. The women put on more decorative headbands and necklaces, and both men and women wore large metal earrings.

When traveling, the Ainu man carried a Y-shaped walking stick. He wrapped his food in a mat, suspended on his back by a rope around his forehead. The mat was useful when he slept, and the walking stick could be used as a spear. A quiver holding wolfsbane-coated arrows and a machete-like knife hung at the waist.

The Ainu were good hunters and skillful trappers who knew the animals' trails. One type of trap was constructed in the following manner: A trigger string was concealed under grass and stretched across a trail. A bow with fully drawn arrow was fastened alongside the path, and the trigger string was connected to it with ropes and sticks. The arrow was aimed at the point where an animal's heart was likely to be when its forepaw touched the trigger string. Another type of trap used a heavy wooden block.

Except for the Ainu in Sakhalin, who utilized dog-drawn sleds, the Ainu had no means of land transportation other than walking. In deep snow they used snowshoes called *teshma*. On the river they took to wooden dugouts. When sailing on the ocean they used the same kind of canoe, attaching a side board and raising a mat for a sail. At night they landed on the beach and made a shelter with the mat. The next day they resumed their travels.

The religion of the Ainu was animistic, and they believed gods existed everywhere. They always worshiped before embarking on any activity, as well as at times of disease and calamity. Pleasant gods were solemnly welcomed with ceremonies and prayers and sent back to heaven. Unpleasant gods were "kicked back to hell" with curses and threats. In both cases, dolls made of wood were considered to operate as intermediators between men and gods. The *ikupasui*, a small stick that was one of the utensils accompanying the sake bowl, was believed by early students of the Ainu to be purely utilitarian—a tool from the sake cup. Later, investigators discovered that, on the contrary, the *ikupasui* was one of the Ainu symbols of a bird; it took sake offerings to the gods.

The Ainu believed that the gods, in their country on the tops of high mountains or in the east, lived the same kinds of lives as human beings, using human foods and offerings. When gods visited the Ainu world, they impersonated animals. For example, the hunting god came as a bear bringing meat and fur to the human world. It could be caught only by a young man whom it had chosen to visit. Therefore, the Ainu had a festival when they caught a bear, and offered many prayers that he would visit again. They would then kill the bear for its meat and fur and send its soul (that is, the god that brought the meat and fur by impersonating a bear) back to the country whence it had come.

When a bear cub or other animal cub was caught, it was kept in a wooden cage specially built for the purpose until matured, because the Ainu believed it could not go back alone when so young. The cage was kept in a fenced-in area outside the god window of the house of the favored youth who caught the cub.

In the autumn, when the cub was about two years old, a festival was held. A special sake was prepared, and messengers were sent to invite the young man's relatives and neighbors. The guests, clad in their best clothes, gathered at the host's house and made rice dumplings and *inau*. *Inau* were sticks of various sizes, small enough to be easily held in one hand, that were decorated with shavings and shreds made by peeling the stick with a knife. Like *ikupasui*, *inau* symbolized birds. (In Ainu religion, birds were intermediaries between men and gods.) In prayer, an Ainu told his wish to the *inau*, who conveyed the message to the gods. Offerings for the gods were also put before the *inau*.

The host, acting as master of ceremonies, approached the bear cage and declared that a farewell ceremony was about to begin. He then designated another young man to draw the bear out of the cage with a rope and to bring it before the *inau* hedge —a fence made of the whittled and shaved wooden sticks. Men drew carved ceremonial arrows that were variations of *inau*, blunted at the ends to prevent their penetrating the bear's skin. The host shot the bear in the heart with a regular, sharp arrow. Then the animal's neck was placed under a log, which the people jumped on to strangle the bear—even if it had been killed by the arrow. At the same time, they shot blunt arrows heavenward to insure the safe return of the bear's soul to the god country.

The dead body was offered to the *inau* hedge and later skinned, except for the head, which was placed in the seat of honor beside the fire. Then a drinking party began. Many sake bowls accompanied by *ikupasui* would be handed among the men, who drank freely after they had offered a drop for the god. The climax of the fete was reached when the women began to sing and drum on the tops of sake vessels and men and women began dancing together. At midnight, the skin was peeled from the bear's head, and the skull was placed on a stick decorated with wood shavings, and offered on the hedge, where it remained indefinitely. The more bear skulls they could exhibit, the more prosperous and happy the family was.

Shamanism—communication with the gods through mediums—was also part of the Ainu religion. While Ainu women could not pray or celebrate the gods directly, the gods could possess them. Thus, Ainu shamans were women who, when possessed, reached a psychological state called *imu*. When in such a state, the shaman babbled, was convulsed, and otherwise acted erratically, uttering what the Ainu believed to be messages from the gods.

The Ainu had an oral literature in the form of long poems called *yukara*. (There were no Ainu letters, and we have no written record.) The poems were recited or, rather, sung to individual melodies by a storyteller of the village. The storyteller (or *yukara* singer, we might say) was, in most cases, an old man or woman. But the storyteller had no monopoly; everybody in the village learned how to recite *yukara*. Some were better than others in recitation and memory, and one of the ablest was selected as the official storyteller of the village. He recited the poems during the evenings of ceremonial days, or, if asked by the villagers, on ordinary evenings.

At one time *yukara* were epics believed to be the voice of the gods describing their ceremonies. In Ainu language, *yukara* originally meant "to imitate" or "to mimic." They were always told in the first person and always ended "So said the god." This indicates *yukara* may have begun as the ceremonial songs or prayers of the shamans.

Later, *yukara* became poetry that, characteristically, told of the acts and loves of a young hero called *Poiyawumpe*, a god's son brought up by human cousins. Just, generous, and brave, he fought for, and finally won, a beautiful girl he had rescued from a disaster, from a "bad guy," or from a devil. These stories, too long to be told in one night, were comparable to the Homeric epic.

Yukara were passed from generation to generation. Just before they vanished from the Ainu culture, the few now known to us were discovered and collected by Dr. Kyōsuke Kindaichi, former professor at the University of Tokyo, Faculty of Letters, who translated them into Japanese.

In addition to the *yukara*, the Ainu had lullabies, love songs, rounds, and simple dances. Among them, the "Dance of Cranes," which imitates the movements of the birds, was particularly popular. The Ainu possessed no musical instruments, but they beat time with their hands for their songs and dances.

Death was a terrifying thought for these people, who believed it to be a punishment of the gods. Epidemics of measles, smallpox, syphilis, and tuberculosis, all brought by the Japanese, killed many Ainu, who believed that the illnesses were spread by a devil. To counter the epidemics, the people set up *inau* on the border of the villages or coasts and spread filthy things over them so the devil could not approach habitations. Devils were supposed to dislike excrement or decaying vegetables, fish, or animals. (Sometimes a child was named "Feces" or "Dung" so the devils would not take him.)

Methods of treating disease were primitive. Those who were ill were beaten with wormwood sticks or forced to creep through fire. Sometimes their faces were smeared with kettle soot, after which they were driven into the woods.

If the victims died, much concern was shown. Relatives and neighbors offered farewell prayers. The bodies were dressed in specially prepared clothes, covered with mats, and buried in a shallow grave over which graveposts were erected. These posts varied according to the sex of the deceased and the region from which he or she came. For example, in the Hidaka area, which supported the densest Ainu population, men had spade-shaped graveposts; those for women were needle-shaped, with holes.

After they buried the dead, the mourners hurried back home and never again visited the grave. The house of the deceased was burned to prevent the return of the devil of death. (In later years, lacking construction materials, the mourners merely changed the position of furniture, and the living members of the family changed clothes so the devil could not recognize them.)

Accidental death was so hated that when it occurred all the neighbors gathered, threatened the devil with swords and screams, and beat the surviving members of the family.

After the Meiji restoration (1868), which followed the opening of Japan to Western influences, the Ainu were integrated with Japanese immigrants in Hokkaido and received the same education as the Japanese. Today, therefore, almost no Ainu can speak his ancient language, which is now preserved only in the names of some cities and villages in Hokkaido. Tattooing is prohibited, and the Ainu's daily life is no different from that of the Japanese. Ainu villages have disappeared, and their religion is lost.

The opportunity to study the old way of life is largely gone. There was in World War II an intensified Japanese ideology that all people in the country were the Emperor's subjects, so that the study of the Ainu as a race distinct from the Japanese was frowned upon by the government. Also, during, and immediately after, the war researchers could not pay much attention to investigation of the Ainu, because of the mobilization of all human and natural resources for the war and because of the confused and unstable social circumstances thereafter. Since 1941 we have had a time of great social change for the Japanese in general, and the pace of social and cultural change among the Ainu has also quickened.

It is regrettable, from an ethnological point of view, that the Ainu people are vanishing, but acculturation has helped to solve some of their problems as a minority group.

NORMAN A. CHANCE

THE CHANGING WORLD OF THE CREE   Three hundred miles
north of Montreal, Canada, halfway between James Bay and Lake
St. John, 1,200 Algonquin-speaking Cree Indians of the Mistassini and Waswanipi bands face a crucial decision. For centuries
the forested land, lakes, and streams of north central Quebec provided these people with the three basic staples of their economic
life: fur, fish, and game. And for centuries the seasonal pursuit
of these staples determined the tenor of Cree life. Each fall, small
groups of related families traveled by canoe to their hunting and
trapping territories, returning in the late spring to the "reserve,"
or reservation settlements, on Mistassini and Waswanipi lakes.
Winter required hard work and considerable social solitude.
Summer, on the other hand, was a time of relative relaxation, of
dances, marriage feasts, trading at the local Hudson's Bay post,
and other social events made possible only by the temporarily
increased population of the reserve community. Until recently,
social change was perceived by the Cree to be a product of this
annual cycle rather than an expression of permanent, non-periodic
changes in their way of life.

   The perception of the world varies with the culture of the
observer. In recent years, more industrialized Euro-Canadians
have come to view the land, lakes, and streams of the Cree in
terms of large stands of marketable pulpwood, valuable minerals, and the potential for developing extensive hydroelectric
power. In 1966, a major Canadian pulp and paper company constructed a multimillion dollar mill and town near the Waswanipi
reserve, and the officials are now actively recruiting a labor force
of over 1,000 woodcutters and 300 millworkers. Copper and
other base metals are being extracted by large mining companies.
New roads have cut through old Indian trapping grounds, and
medium-sized towns like Chibougamau and Chapais have risen
on the site of earlier Indian encampments.

   The impact of these economic developments on Cree Indian
life is profound. Three years ago, the entire population of the
Waswanipi band moved off their isolated reserve in search of
temporary or full-time jobs in nearby lumber camps or with
mining prospectors. Some families have clustered in small

extended kin-groups along a new gravel road that links several frontier towns. Others have migrated to white population centers.

The Mistassini Indians, on the other hand, have been less mobile, although here too, increased numbers of young men and women are moving off the reserve in search of economic and

Many families migrate during the summer to live near places where jobs are available. Eight people live in this tent, which is pitched near a pulp operation.

social opportunities elsewhere. Jobs are fairly abundant in the region, but they often require a knowledge of the French language—a skill held by few Indians. As a result of early Protestant missionizing, the Cree are affiliated with the Anglican church and thus receive their education in Quebec's English-speaking, Protestant school system.

At present, many of the older Indians prefer to bypass the new employment opportunities available to them in favor of more traditional ones. At Mistassini Post, over 50 per cent of the men still engage in trapping as their primary occupation. Fewer of the younger men are spending winters in the bush, however, and those who do often find their earnings are not sufficient to buy the consumer goods and services they now desire.

Here, then, is the crucial decision faced by the Mistassini and Waswanipi Cree: Should they follow the life of the traditional trapper, whose present income is viewed as submarginal, requiring supplementary government welfare "rations" and seasonal labor? Or, should they look for work in non-Indian employment centers?

Many Indians would like to take advantage of a steady cash

Government housing, in some ways like middle-class suburbia, is not particularly practical for subarctic living, but the Indians accept it enthusiastically.

income if they could continue to live on the reserve. As the Cree become more restricted to a limited area, the concept of *their* reserve—as opposed to land owned by non-Indians—serves as a focal point of their identity. Fear of losing one's distinctiveness as an Indian is often expressed by those who migrate to the towns and cities.

Given the natural wealth of the region, one might expect that proper vocational training would enable those Cree wishing to remain on the reserve to exploit their own land. This is not possible, however, since the Indian reserves in this area were allocated as residential settlements only; the amount of land available is too small to exploit profitably. A few jobs are available on or near the reserve in government-sponsored commercial fishing and sawmill operations, but these positions provide adequate incomes for only a relatively small percentage of the expanding Indian labor force.

Under these circumstances, it appears that the economic future of the Cree is of necessity closely tied with that of non-

Lunchtime for a Mistassini family. On the menu are bannock, jam, sugar, and tea. It will be the same tomorrow. It was the same yesterday.

Indian controlled industry. The extent of economic growth will be largely determined by the level of occupational skill attained by Indian workers and by their capacity to adjust to steady wage labor. To assist in this task the Indian Affairs branch of the Canadian government has set up vocational training programs for Indians no longer in school; it has tried to stimulate greater efforts toward community development and local self-government in various Indian residential centers; and it has provided improved family housing for those remaining on the reserve.

The crucial test, however, rests with the young Indians now coming out of school. The first five or six years of the child's life

Although the old people are willing to agree that things must change, they are the ones who maintain and pass on the traditional Indian ways.

are almost wholly Cree in character. He learns the Cree language and family authority patterns, and the traditional Indian norms and expectations appropriate to his age and sex. His contacts with white men are peripheral, perhaps watching summer tourists take pictures at the Post, or visiting the Indian Agent's office with his father.

For the past decade, however, children of parents returning to the bush each fall have been sent to boarding schools located in industrial towns far from home. Just when the child reaches the age where he is prepared to assume a responsible role in Cree family and social life, he is placed in a modern residential school for Indians. Here, instructed by teachers speaking a strange and initially incomprehensible language, living in a large dormitory, and eating different food, the child spends nine months of the year. His teachers know relatively little of his Indian background and see their major task as preparing him for life in a modern industrial society.

Each summer, when the child returns home, the conflict is repeated. Contrasting the two worlds in which he lives he finds that his parents know as little about his school experiences as his teachers know of his home life. The only individuals with whom he can discuss both worlds—the only people who have faced a similar problem—are his age-mates.

This type of discontinued learning, carried through primary and high school, places considerable strain on the young student's personal identity. To choose consciously one way of life over the other, the Indian must either reject those with whom he has had emotional ties since infancy or, conversely, those upon whom he has been dependent for nine months of the year. In either event, by the time the Indian youth is ready to leave school, he faces an identity crisis. In school he has been taught to work hard and to make his own way in the modern world. If he returns home, he will be expected to follow many of the traditions of his Indian past, one of which may involve allowing his parents to choose his future marriage partner.

For the Mistassini and Waswanipi Cree, it is still too early to determine which path the majority of young Indians will take. Whatever the future holds, it will depend partly on their ability to understand better the world of which they are becoming a part. And it will depend on the ability of others to assist the Indian in maintaining a sense of self-respect in situations that often foster self-disparagement through lack of understanding.

DANIEL R. GROSS

THE GREAT SISAL SCHEME   In northeastern Brazil, the lush green coastal vegetation almost hides the endemic human misery of the region. Unless you look closely, the busy streets of Salvador and Recife and the waving palm trees mask the desperation of city slums, the poverty of plantation workers. When you leave the well-traveled coastal highways and go—usually on a dusty, rutted road—toward the interior, the signs of suffering become more and more apparent.

The transition is quick and brutal. Within 50 miles the vegetation changes from palm, tropical fruit, and dark-green broadleafed trees to scrawny brush only slightly greener than the dusty earth. Nearly every plant is armed with spines or thorns. The hills are jagged, with hard faces of rock exposed. This is the *sertão*, the interior of northeastern Brazil.

If the *sertão* were honest desert, it would probably contain only a few inhabitants and a fair share of human misery. But the *sertão* is deceitful and fickle. It will smile for several years in a row, with sufficient rains arriving for the growing seasons. Gardens and crops will flourish. Cattle fatten. Then, without warning, another growing season comes, but the rains don't. The drought may go on, year after dusty year. Crops fail. Cattle grow thin and die. Humans begin to do the same. In bad droughts, the people of the *sertão* migrate to other regions by the thousands.

The bandits, the mystics, the droughts and migrants, the dreams and schemes of the *sertão* hold a special place in Brazilian folklore, literature, and song. Even at its worst, the *sertão* has been a fertile ground for the human imagination.

For two years, I studied the impact of sisal crops—a recent dream and scheme—on the people of the *sertão*. Taking an ecological approach, I found that sisal, which some poetic dreamers call "green gold," has greatly changed northeastern Brazil. But the changes have not been what the economic planners anticipated. And misery has not left the *sertão*.

I lived in Vila Nova, a small village with a population less than 500 about an hour's drive from the town of Victoria in Bahia State. Vila Nova is striking only for its drabness. Weeds grow in the middle of unpaved streets. Facing the plaza is an incomplete series of nondescript row houses. Some have faded pastel façades, others are mud brown because their owners never managed to plaster over the rough adobe walls. The village looks decadent, yet the oldest building is less than 20 years old and most were built after 1963.

Cattle raisers settled the *sertão* 400 years ago when the expanding sugar plantations of the coast demanded large supplies of beef and traction animals. A "civilization of leather" developed, with generations of colorful and intrepid cowboys (*vaqueiros*) clad entirely in rawhide to protect themselves against the thorny scrub vegetation. As the population of the *sertão* grew, many *sertanejos* settled down to subsistence farming. Gradually the entire region became a cul-de-sac, with many small and medium-sized estates occupied by descendants of the *vaqueiros* and others who had drifted into the region.

Life was never easy in this thorny land, for the work was hard and the environment cruel. Yet cooperation and mutual assistance provided assurance of survival even to the poorest. The chief crops were manioc, beans, and corn, and most of what was grown was consumed by the cultivator's family. Most families received some share of meat and milk, and consumed highly nutritious foods like beans and squash, in addition to starchy foods like manioc flour.

When droughts menaced the region all but the wealthiest ranchers migrated temporarily to the coast to work on the sugar plantations. When the rains came again to the *sertão*, they nearly always returned, for the work in the cane fields was brutal and labor relations had not changed greatly from the time when slaves worked the plantations.

Originally from Mexico, sisal was introduced to Brazil early in this century and reached the *sertão* in the 1930's. Farmers found sisal useful for hedgerows because its tough, pointed leaves effectively kept out cattle. The cellulose core of the long sisal leaf contains hard fibers, which can be twisted together into twine and rope. When World War II cut off the supply of Manila hemp to the United States, buyers turned to Brazil for fiber. At first only hedgerow sisal was exploited, but the state of Bahia offered incentives for planting sisal as a cash crop. Since sisal plants require about four years to mature, Brazil did not begin to export the fiber in significant quantities until 1945. The

demand persisted, and by 1951, Brazil was selling actively in the world market as prices rose.

In Vila Nova, a young entrepreneur who owned a mule team, David Castro, heard about the prices being paid for sisal fiber and planted the first acres of sisal in 1951. By 1968, in the county of Victoria where Vila Nova is located, so many people had caught "sisal fever" that half of the total land area was planted in the crop. Sisal is easily transplanted and cultivated, requires little care, and is highly resistant to drought. It has some drawbacks as a cultivated plant, however. At least one annual weeding is necessary or else the field may become choked with thorn bushes, weeds, and suckers (unwanted small sisal plants growing from the base of parent plants). A field abandoned for two years becomes unusable, practically unreclaimable. Despite these difficulties, many landowners planted sisal, especially in 1951 and 1962, years of high prices on the world market.

From the outset, sisal produced differential rewards for those who planted it. Owners of small plots (ten acres or less) planted proportionately more of their land in sisal than did large landowners. Many who owned just a few acres simply planted all their land in sisal in expectation of large profits. This deprived them of whatever subsistence they had managed to scratch out of the ground in the past. But work was easy to find because the need for labor in the sisal fields grew rapidly. When, after four years, the crops were ready to harvest, many small landholders discovered to their dismay that prices had dropped sharply, and that harvest teams did not want to work small crops. They had planted sisal with dreams of new clothes, new homes, even motor vehicles purchased with sisal profits, but found their fields choked with unusable sisal and became permanent field laborers harvesting sisal on large landholdings. In this way, sisal created its own labor force.

The separation of sisal fiber from the leaf is known as decortication. In Brazil, this process requires enormous amounts of manual labor. The decorticating machine is basically a spinning rasp powered by a gasoline or diesel motor. Sisal leaves are fed into it by hand, and the spinning rasp beats out the pulp or residue leaving only the fibers, which the worker pulls out of the whirling blades. Mounted on a trailer, the machine is well adapted to the scattered small-scale plantations of northeastern Brazil.

The decortication process requires constant labor for harvesting the year round. Sisal leaves, once cut, must be defibered quickly before the hot sun renders them useless. Each decorticating machine requires a crew of about seven working in close coordination. The first step is harvesting. Two cutters move from plant to plant, first lopping off the needle-sharp thorns from the leaves, then stooping to sever each leaf at the base. A transporter, working with each cutter, gathers the leaves and loads them on a burro. The leaves are taken to the machine and placed on a low stage for the defiberer to strip, one by one. A residue man removes the pulpy mass stripped from the leaves from under the motor, supplies the defiberer with leaves, and bundles and ties the freshly stripped fiber. Each bundle is weighed and counted in the day's production. Finally, the dryer spreads the wet, greenish fiber in the sun, where it dries and acquires its characteristic blond color.

For the planters and sisal buyers, this method of decortication operates profitably, but for the workers it exacts a terrible cost. The decorticating machine requires a man to stand in front of the whirling rasp for four or five hours at a shift, introducing first the foot and then the point of each leaf. The worker pulls against the powerful motor, which draws the leaf into the mouth of the machine. After half of each leaf is defibered, the defiberer grasps the raw fiber to insert the remaining half of the leaf. There is a constant danger that the fiber will entangle his hand and pull it into the machine. Several defiberers have lost arms this way. The strain and danger would seem to encourage slow and deliberate work; but in fact, defiberers decorticate about 25 leaves per minute. This is because the crew is paid according to the day's production of fiber. Although the defiberer is the highest-paid crew member, many of them must work both morning and afternoon shifts to make ends meet.

A residue man's work is also strenuous. According to measurements I made, this job requires that a man lift and carry about 2,700 pounds of material per hour. The residue man, moreover, does not work in shifts. He works as long as the machinery is running. The remaining jobs on the crew are less demanding and may be held by women or adolescents, but even these jobs are hard, requiring frequent lifting and stooping in the broiling semidesert sun.

With their own fields in sisal, to earn money the villagers had to work at harvesting sisal for large landowners. And because wages were low, more and more people had to work for families to survive. In 1968 two-thirds of all men and women employed in Vila Nova worked full time in the sisal decorticating process. Many of these were youths. Of 33 village boys between the ages of 10 and 14, 24 worked on sisal crews. Most people had completely abandoned subsistence agriculture.

Sisal brought other significant changes in the life of Vila Nova. Because most villagers no longer grew their food, it now had to be imported. Numerous shops, stocking beans, salt pork, and manioc flour, grew up in the village. A few villagers with capital or good contacts among wholesalers in the town of Victoria built small businesses based on this need. Other villagers secured credit from sisal buyers in Victoria to purchase sisal decorticating machinery.

The shopkeepers and sisal machine owners in the village formed a new economic class on whom the other villagers were economically dependent. The wealthier group enjoyed many advantages. Rather than going to work on the sisal machines, most of the children of these entrepreneurs went to school. All of the upper group married in a socially prescribed way: usually a church wedding with civil ceremonies as well. But among the workers, common-law marriages were frequent, reflecting their lack of resources for celebrating this important event.

The only villagers who became truly affluent were David Castro and his cousin. These men each owned extensive sisal plantations and several decorticating units. Most importantly, each became middlemen, collecting sisal in warehouses in the village and trucking the fiber into Victoria. David, moreover, owned the largest store in the village. Since the village was located on David's land, he sold house plots along the streets. He also acted as the representative of the dominant political party in Victoria, serving as a ward boss during elections and as an unofficial but effective police power. There was a difference between David and the large ranch owners of the past. While wealthy men were formerly on close terms with their dependents, helping them out during tough times, David's relations with the villagers were cold, businesslike, and exploitative. Most of the villagers disliked him, both for his alleged stinginess and because he never had time to talk to anyone.

During my stay in Vila Nova I gradually became aware of these changes in the social and economic structure. But I hoped to establish that the introduction of sisal had also resulted in a quantitative, ecological change in the village. At the suggestion of Dr. Barbara A. Underwood of the Institute of Human Nutrition at Columbia University, I undertook an intensive study to determine what influence sisal had on diet and other factors of a few representative households. When I looked at household budgets, I quickly discovered that those households that depended entirely on wages from sisal work spent nearly all their money on food. Families with few or no children or with several able-bodied workers seemed to be holding their own. But families with few workers or several dependents were less fortunate. To understand the condition of these families, I collected information not only on cash budgets but also on household *energy budgets*. Each household expends not only money, but also energy in the form of calories in performing work. "Income" in the latter case is the caloric value of the foods consumed by these households. By carefully measuring the amount and kind of food consumed, I was able to determine the total inflow and outflow of energy in individual households.

Calorie budget of a sisal worker's household

	Average daily caloric intake	Minimum daily caloric requirements	Percent of need met	Percent of standard weight of children
Household	9,392	12,592	75%	
Worker	3,642	3,642	100	
Wife	2,150	2,150	100	
Son (age 8)	1,112	2,100	53	62%
Daughter (6)	900	1,700	53	70
Son (5)	900	1,700	53	85
Son (3)	688	1,300	53	90

For example, Miguel Costa is a residue man who works steadily on a sisal unit belonging to a nearby planter. He lives in Vila Nova in a two-room adobe hut with his wife and four small children, ranging in age from three to eight. During the seven-day test period, Miguel worked at the sisal motor four and a half days, while his wife stayed home with the children. I was able to estimate Miguel's caloric expenditures during the test period. During the same period, I visited his home after every meal where his wife graciously permitted me to weigh the family's meager food supplies to determine food consumption. Each day the supply of beans diminished by less than one-half pound and the weight of the coarse manioc flour eaten with beans dropped by two or three pounds. Manioc flour is almost pure starch, high in calories but low in essential nutrients. At the beginning of the week about half a pound of fatty beef and pork were consumed each day, but this was exhausted by mid-week. The remainder of the family's calories were consumed in the form of sugar, bread, and boiled sweet manioc, all high in calories but low in other nutrients.

Estimating the caloric requirements of the two adults from their activities and the children's by Food and Agriculture Organization minimum requirements, the household had a minimum need of 88,142 calories for the week. The household received only 65,744 calories, or 75 percent of need. Since the two adults did not lose weight while maintaining their regular levels of activity, they were apparently meeting their total calorie requirements. Miguel, for example, had been working steadily at his job for weeks before the test and continued to do so for weeks afterward. Had he not been maintaining himself calorically, he could not have sustained his performance at his demanding job. Despite his small stature (5 feet, 4 inches) Miguel required some 3,642 calories per day to keep going at the job. And

Miguel's wife evidently also maintained herself calorically—pregnant at the time of my visit, she later gave birth to a normal child.

The caloric deficit in Miguel's household, then, was almost certainly being made up by systematically depriving the dependent children of sufficient calories. This was not intentional, nor were the parents aware of it. Nor could Miguel have done anything about it even if he had understood this process. If he were to work harder or longer to earn more money, he would incur greater caloric costs and would have to consume more. If he were to reduce his food intake to leave more food for his children, he would be obliged by his own physiology to work less, thereby earning less. If he were to provide his household with foods higher in caloric content (for example, more manioc), he would almost certainly push his children over the brink into a severe nutritional crisis that they might not survive for lack of protein and essential vitamins. Thus, Miguel, a victim of ecological circumstances, is maintaining his family against terrible odds.

Miguel's children respond to this deprivation in a predictable manner. Nature has provided a mechanism to compensate for caloric deficiencies during critical growth periods: the rate of growth simply slows down. As a result, Miguel's children, and many other children of sisal workers, are much smaller than properly nourished children of the same age. The longer the deprivation goes on the more pronounced the tendency: thus Miguel's youngest boy, who is three, is 90 percent of standard weight for his age. The five-year-old boy is 85 percent; the six-year-old girl, 70 percent; and the oldest boy, at eight, is only 62 percent of standard weight. Caloric deprivation takes its toll in other ways than stunting. Caloric and other nutritional deficiencies are prime causes of such problems as reduced mental capacity and lower resistance to infection. In Vila Nova one-third of all children die by the age of 10.

When I surveyed the nutritional status of the people of Vila Nova, I found a distinct difference between the average body weights of the two economic groups formed since the introduction of sisal (shopkeepers and motor-owners on the one hand, and workers on the other). Since the introduction of sisal the upper economic group exhibited a marked improvement in nutritional status (as measured by body weight) while the lower group showed a decline in nutritional status. The statistics showed that while one group was better off than before, a majority of the population was actually worse off nutritionally.

This conclusion was unexpected in view of the widespread claim that sisal had brought lasting benefits to the people of the *sertão*, that sisal had narrowed the gap between the rich and the poor. Clearly, changes had come about. Towns like Victoria had grown far beyond their presisal size.

But outside the towns, in the villages and rural farmsteads, the picture is different. Having abandoned subsistence agriculture, many workers moved to villages to find work on sisal units. In settlements such as Vila Nova wages and profits depend on the world price for sisal. When I arrived in 1967, the price was at the bottom of a trough that had paralyzed all growth and construction. Wages were so low that outmigration was showing signs of resuming as in the drought years. In spite of local symbols of wealth and "development," my observations revealed a continuation of endemic poverty throughout most of the countryside and even an intensification of the social and economic divisions that have always characterized the *sertão*.

Sisal is not the only example of an economic change that has brought unforeseen, deleterious consequences. The underdeveloped world is replete with examples of development schemes that brought progress only to a privileged few. The example of sisal in northeastern Brazil shows that an ecological approach is needed in all economic planning. Even more important, we must recognize that not all economic growth brings social and economic development in its true sense. As the sisal example shows, a system may be formed (often as part of a worldwide system) that only increases the store of human misery.